A Contemporary
Polish
Cookbook

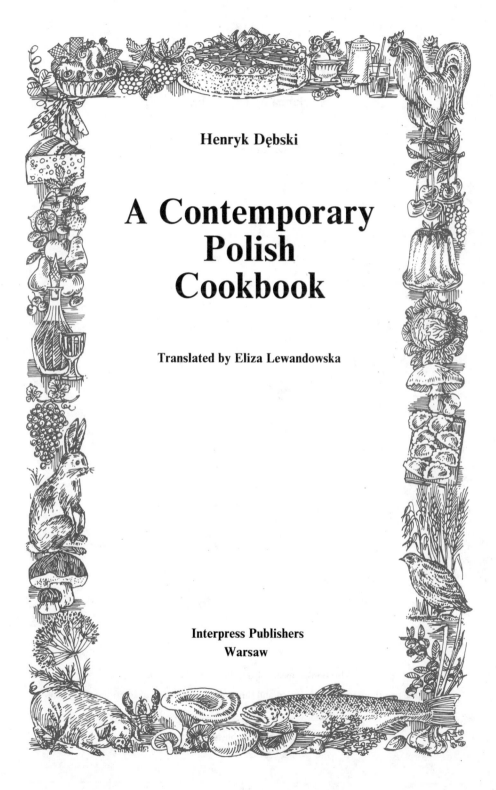

Henryk Dębski

A Contemporary
Polish
Cookbook

Translated by Eliza Lewandowska

Interpress Publishers
Warsaw

Designed by
Hanna Balicka-Fribes

Production editor
Elżbieta Szeszko

This book appears also in Polish and German

This is the two thousand three hundred and thirty third publication of Interpress Publishers

Printed in Poland
ISBN 83-223-2333-6

Table of Contents

A good cook draws on tradition
as well as the present

FROM THE AUTHOR

A Contemporary Polish Cookbook is a kind of guide to the culinary arts in Poland. The traditions of this cuisine go far back, but through the ages they have changed. What the ordinary Pole eats today is not the same as what he ate long ago. More vegetables have been introduced in the kitchen. Dishes that were labour-consuming to prepare have been abandoned in favour of simpler ones. This does not mean that the Poles' all-time favourites have been eliminated. The broths, borschs, żurs, pea soups, cabbage soups, zrazy (meat rashers and rolls), boiled beef, bigos, pierogi, kiełbasas, etc. still reign on our tables as representatives of fine Polish cuisine. In presenting this book the author hopes to add variety to his readers' menus, and to widen the information available about the Polish culinary arts. I have chosen those Polish recipes that are not troublesome in preparation; they are generally designed to serve four persons, but may also be adapted to a household of any size.

This book is dedicated to
France's finest chef,
Paul Bocus

Hors d'Œuvres

Cold Hors d'Oeuvres 11

Ham à la Henry I 11
Ham à la Henry II 11
Ham Rolls 11
General's Smoked Fillet of Beef 12
Rolled Smoked Fillet of Beef 12
Pork Loin in Aspic 13
Admiral's Pork Loin 13
Uhlan's Saddle Bags 14
Pork Hock in Aspic 14
Rolled Bacon in Aspic 15
Tongue in Aspic 15
Pork Liver à la Caviar 16
Meat Pâté 16
Mariner's Steak 16
Beefsteak Tartare 17
Roast Veal 17
Roast Veal Rolled Uhlan Style 18
Marinated Veal 18
Veal à la Salmon 18
Wrocław Veal 19
Captain's Rolled Veal Breast 19
Galantine of Veal 20
Veal Pâté 21
Veal Keels in Aspic 21
Veal Tongue 21
Galantine of Chicken 22
Chicken in Aspic 23
Chicken in Aspic Moulds 23
Chicken in Mayonnaise 24
Cold Chicken Polish Style 24
Chicken Breasts in Mayonnaise Sauce 25
Chicken Balls 25
Marinated Chicken 26
Uhlan's Chicken Pâté 26
Galantine of Duck 27
Duck with Whipped Cream 27
Duck Malaga 28
Duck Pâté 28
Roulade of Goose 29
Royal Goose Liver Pâté 29
Turkey Malaga 29
Pheasant Malaga 30
Admiral's Pheasant 30
Pheasant Pâté 31
Grass Carp Jewish Style 31
Grass Carp in Aspic 32
Admiral's Grass Carp 32

Roulade of Cod, Haddock, Hake or Gilthead 33
Lvov Cod, Haddock, Hake or Gilthead 33
General's Flounder, Flatfish, Turbot or Sole 34
Carp in Aspic 34
Carp Surprise 35
Warsaw Carp 35
Boatswain's Carp 35
Salmon in Aspic 36
Marinated Salmon 36
Trout in Aspic 37
Trout in Mayonnaise 37
Wrocław Lobster I 37
Wrocław Lobster II 38
Pike Perch in Aspic 38
Stuffed Pike Polish Style 39
Herring in Oil I 39
Herring in Oil II 40
Herring in Oil III 40
Herring in Sour Cream 40
Herring Gipsy Style 41
Giżycko Herring 41
Gdańsk Herring 41
Rollmops 42
Fish Salad 42
Lobster Salad 42
Egg Salad 43
White Bean Salad 43
Green Pea Salad 43
Cauliflower Salad 44
Carrot Salad 44
Tomato Salad I 44
Tomato Salad II 45
Celeriac Salad 45
Potato Salad I 45
Potato Salad II 46

Hot Hors d'Oeuvres 46

Wrocław Croutons 46
Brains on Toast 46
Sardines on Toast 47
Frankfurters on Toast 47
Liver on Toast 47
Castellan's Toast 48
Cracow Soaked Pork Loin 48
Pork à la Tripe 48
Admiral's Pork 49
Beefsteak Polish Style 49
Beef à la Robert 50
Hunter's Beef 50

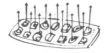

COLD HORS D'ŒUVRES

HAM À LA HENRY I

1/2 lb. cooked smoked ham, 6 3/4 oz. chicken pâté, 5 oz. mushrooms, fat for frying mushrooms, 3 tablespoons whipping cream, 1 cup broth, 3 tablespoons dry white wine, 1/3 oz. tomato paste, egg white, 1/2 oz. gelatin, hard-boiled egg, tomato, lemon and parsley sprigs for garnishing, salt, pepper and lemon juice to taste

Clean the mushrooms, rinse them and slice finely. Fry and allow to cool. Combine with the pâté and whipped cream. Season to taste. Slice the ham, leaving every other slice only partly cut. Place the pâté in the ham pockets, flatten gently, arrange on a platter and garnish. Combine broth with egg white and tomato paste. Keep over low heat, stirring briskly with an egg-whisk. Bring to a boil. Add gelatin soaked in a small amount of cold water and wine. Cook this for a moment. Pour through a cheesecloth and allow to set. When nearly firm, pour over the ham.

HAM À LA HENRY II

1/2 lb. canned ham, 3 1/2 oz. stewed or bottled peaches, 1 1/3 oz. grated horseradish, 2 hard-boiled egg yolks, 1 2/3 oz. ketchup, 5 oz. mayonnaise sauce, 1/3 cup whipping cream, 1 1/3 oz. canned peas, salt, pepper, sugar and lemon juice to taste

Dice the peaches finely. Combine with the horseradish, egg yolks that have been forced through a strainer and ketchup, then season. Cut the ham into slices, leaving every other slice partly uncut. Place stuffing in the ham pockets. Arrange on a platter. Pour mayonnaise sauce blended with whipped cream and peas over this.

HAM ROLLS

4 slices of canned ham, 5 oz. boneless beef, 1 1/3 oz. onions, 1 oz. soured cucumbers, 2/3 oz. marinated mushrooms, egg yolk, 1 oz. sardines,

2/3 cup broth, 3 tablespoons dry white wine, egg white, 1/2 oz. gelatin, 1/3 oz. tomato paste, tomato, plums pickled in wine or vinegar, lemon and lettuce for garnishing, salt, pepper, prepared mustard and lemon juice to taste

Slice finely peeled cucumbers and onions together with mushrooms. Combine with minced meat, crumbled sardines and egg yolk. Add salt, pepper and mustard to taste. Place this on the ham and form into a roll. Arrange on a platter. Garnish and cover with the nearly firm gelatin (prepared as in Ham à la Henry I).

GENERAL'S SMOKED FILLET OF BEEF

5 oz. smoked fillet of beef, 1 2/3 oz. boneless baked chicken, 1 2/3 oz. mayonnaise sauce, 1/2 can sardines, parsley sprigs, 1 2/3 oz. hard cheese, 3 1/2 oz. ketchup, 1 oz. walnut meats, salt, pepper, lemon juice to taste, lettuce, plums pickled in vinegar and hard-boiled egg for garnishing

Chop the chicken meat finely together with parsley sprigs. Add grated cheese, crumbled sardines and mayonnaise. Season to taste. Slice the fillet of beef, leaving every other slice partly uncut. Place the prepared stuffing in the meat pockets. Arrange on a platter and pour ketchup over this. Sprinkle with chopped blanched walnuts and garnish.

ROLLED SMOKED FILLET OF BEEF

5 oz. smoked fillet of beef, 5 oz. mushrooms, 2/3 oz. butter, 3 1/2 oz. lobster tails, 1 2/3 oz. mayonnaise, fresh dill, 2/3 cup whipping cream, 1 1/3 oz. ketchup, salt, sugar and lemon juice to taste, parsley sprigs, capers and canned peas to taste

Clean the mushrooms, rinse them and slice finely. Fry them and allow to cool. Combine with lobster tails, mayonnaise and chopped dill. Season to taste. Cut the fillet of beef into wide slices. Place the stuffing

on the meat and form into a roll. Arrange on a platter. Cover with whipped cream blended with ketchup and seasoning, then garnish.

PORK LOIN IN ASPIC

1 1/4 lb. pork loin, fat for frying, 1/3 oz. flour, 1/3 oz. tomato paste, 2 2/3 oz. onions, 1/2 oz. gelatin, egg white, salt, pepper and lemon juice to taste, hard-boiled egg, plums pickled in vinegar, canned peppers, parsley sprigs, mayonnaise for garnishing

Wash the meat and discard the bones, leaving only small parts of the rib bones. Rub with seasoning and leave in refrigerator for several hours. Dredge the meat with flour, brown in hot fat together with finely diced onion, simmer over low heat, sprinkling with water. Remove the meat when tender. Allow to cool. Cut into slices. Arrange on a platter and garnish. Remove the fat from the sauce. Combine with the tomato paste and egg white. Heat slowly, stirring constantly until boiling point. Add gelatin soaked in a small amount of cold water. Cook this for a moment, then season. Pour through a cheesecloth and allow to set. When nearly firm, pour it over the meat.

ADMIRAL'S PORK LOIN

1 1/4 lb. pork loin, fat for frying, 1/3 oz. flour, 3/4 lb. plums, 1/3 cup dry red wine, 6 3/4 oz. mayonnaise sauce, parsley sprigs, salt, pepper, sugar and lemon juice to taste

Prepare the meat as above. Make openings 1/3—3/4 in. deep and fill with pitted plum halves. Dredge this with flour. Brown in hot fat. Sprinkle with water and bake until tender, basting with the pan drippings. Remove the meat when tender and cut into portions. Arrange on a platter. Cover the remaining plums with water and wine. Bring to a boil. Force the plum mixture through a strainer. Heat until liquid evaporates, cool and combine with mayonnaise, then season (the sauce should be sweet-and-sour). Pour over the meat and garnish.

UHLAN'S SADDLE BAGS

Ca. 1 1/2 lb. pork loin, fat for frying, 1/3 oz. flour, 5 oz. mushrooms, 2/3 oz. butter, 6 3/4 oz. ham, 2 2/3 oz. onions, 1/3 oz. tomato paste, 1 1/3 oz. ketchup, egg white, 1/2 oz. gelatin, salt, pepper, lemon juice to taste, hard-boiled egg, tomato, lettuce, mayonnaise and cucumbers for garnishing

Wash the meat, remove bones, rub with seasoning and leave in refrigerator for 24 hours. Dredge with flour, brown in hot fat together with diced onion and the bones from the pork loin, sprinkle with water and simmer covered over low heat. Remove the meat when tender and cool. Remove the bones from the meat. Mince the meat together with the ham and combine with fried mushrooms and ketchup. Season to taste. Slice the cooled meat across but not to the end. Turn it over and slice in the same way. Place the prepared stuffing in the meat pockets, press by hand and leave in refrigerator until stuffing sets. Slice across the grain into portions. Arrange on a platter and garnish. Remove fat from the sauce. Combine with egg white and tomato paste. Bring to a boil, stirring constantly. Add gelatin soaked in a small amount of cold water. Cook this for a moment, then season. Pour through a cheesecloth and allow to set. When nearly firm, pour it over the prepared meat.

PORK HOCK IN ASPIC

2 1/2 lb. pork hock, 3/4 lb. soup vegetables (carrots, parsley root, celeriac and leek), 2/3 oz. tomato paste, 1—2 egg whites, salt, pepper and lemon juice to taste

Clean the pork hock, singe and cut into portions. Wash the meat and cover with water. Add salt and cook covered over low heat. Towards the end add cleaned and rinsed vegetables. Take out the cooked meat, remove bones and arrange on a platter. Combine the stock (1 cup) with the egg white and tomato paste. Bring to a boil, stirring. Pour through a cheesecloth, then season. Allow to set. Garnish the hock with horseradish, tomatoes, parsley sprigs and plums pickled in vinegar. When nearly firm, pour the aspic over this.

ROLLED BACON IN ASPIC

2 lb. lean bacon, 3 1/2 oz. boneless beef, 1 2/3 oz. hardened French bread, 3 1/2 oz. thin frankfurters, 2 egg yolks, egg for omelet, fat for frying, 2 egg whites, 2/3 oz. gelatin, 1/3 oz. tomato paste, salt, pepper, garlic and lemon juice to taste, hard-boiled egg, tomato and plums pickled in vinegar for garnishing

Wash bacon, remove top layer and even out sides. Pound with a mallet that has been dipped in water. Soak the bread in milk, squeeze out the milk and mince the bread together with the trimmings and beef. Combine with egg yolks and season to taste. Arrange on the prepared bacon. Beat the egg with an egg-whisk. Add salt and pour into hot fat in a frying pan, lifting the sides with a knife to enable the egg to flow to the bottom of the pan. Place the omelet on the bacon, arrange the frankfurters on this and form into a roll. Tie around with a thread, pour fat over this and bake, basting with water, then with the pan drippings. Slice the baked bacon into portions. Arrange on a platter and garnish. Remove fat from the sauce. Combine with the tomato paste and egg whites and bring to a boil. Add gelatin that has been soaked in a small amount of cold water. Cook for a while and season. Pour the sauce through a cheesecloth and allow to set. When nearly firm, pour it over the roll.

TONGUE IN ASPIC

1 1/4 lb. pork tongue, 1/2 lb. soup vegetables (carrots, parsley root, celeriac and leek), 1/3 oz. tomato paste, egg white, 1/3 oz. gelatin, salt, pepper and lemon juice to taste, hard-boiled egg, tomato, plums pickled in vinegar, mayonnaise and parsley sprigs for garnishing

Cook the tongue (as in Pork Tongue Polish Style, q.v.), skin it and slice into portions. Arrange it on a platter and garnish. Combine the tongue stock (1 cup) with the tomato paste and egg white and bring to a boil, strirring with an egg-whisk. Add gelatin that has been soaked in a small amound of water. Cook for a while and pour through a cheesecloth. Season and allow to set. When nearly firm, pour over the garnished tongue and wait until it sets.

PORK LIVER À LA CAVIAR

3/4 lb. pork liver, fat for frying, 5 oz. onions, 4 hard-boiled eggs, 1 2/3 oz. mayonnaise, salt, pepper and seasoning to taste, lettuce, tomato and lemon for garnishing

Wash the liver, remove the outer skin and slice into portions. Fry in very hot fat together with sliced onions. Cool and mince together with the eggs, combine with the mayonnaise and season to taste. Form the meat into balls, flattening them slightly. Arrange on a platter and garnish.

MEAT PÂTÉ

1/2 lb. boneless pork, 1/2 lb. boneless veal, 1/2 lb. fresh bacon, 3 1/2 oz. liver, 2—2 2/3 oz. hardened French bread, 2 dried cèpe mushrooms, 3 1/2 oz. onions, 3 1/2 oz. celeriac, 2—3 eggs, fat for frying, salt, pepper, nutmeg, bay leaf, allspice, marjoram and seasoning to taste

Wash the meat and cut into pieces. Clean, rinse and chop the onions and celeriac. Fry the vegetables and meat slightly, then add the washed mushrooms. Sprinkle with water and simmer covered over low heat. Towards the end add the bay leaf, allspice, crumbled bread and the liver, which has been sliced and scalded with boiling water. Cool this and mince twice, using a pâté insert in the mincer. Combine the meat with the eggs, and season to taste. Place in buttered baking pan and smooth out the surface. Place in another pan with boiling water. Put into the oven and bake for around 50 minutes. Cool the baked pâté, remove from the pan and garnish.

MARINER'S STEAK

1 1/4 lb. boneless steak, fat for frying, 1/3 oz. flour, 1 tablespoon olive oil, 3 1/2 oz. onions, 3 1/2 oz. carrots, 3 1/2 oz. celeriac, 7 oz. mushrooms, 2—2 2/3 oz. ketchup, 1 1/2 tablespoons rum, 2/3 oz. capers, parsley sprigs, salt, pepper and lemon juice to taste

Wash the meat, remove the outer skin, rub with the seasoning and sprinkle with lemon juice. Cover with cleaned and grated vegetables, pour oil over this and leave in refrigerator for 24 hours. Remove the vegetables, pour fat over the meat, dredge with flour and brown on both sides. Sprinkle with water and bake so that the meat remains pink inside. Remove the meat, cool and slice thinly. Arrange on a platter. Clean mushrooms, rinse and slice them. Fry them and combine with ketchup, rum, chopped parsley sprigs and rinsed capers. Season and arrange on the meat, then garnish.

BEEFSTEAK TARTARE

3/4 lb. boneless beef or fillet of beef, 2—2 2/3 oz. onions, 2/3 oz. capers, 4 egg yolks, 1 2/3 oz. dill pickles, 1 1/3 oz. marinated mushrooms, olive oil, prepared mustard, salt, pepper, seasoning and ground paprika to taste

Wash the meat, grind it and combine with oil and seasoning. Rinse onions and dice finely together with a pickled cucumber and mushrooms. Divide the meat into portions on plates or on a platter. Make a hollow in the middle and place the egg yolks in it. Surround the meat with onions, pickles, mushrooms, rinsed capers, mustard and paprika.

ROAST VEAL

1 lb. boneless veal, fat for frying, 1/3 oz. flour, 1/3 cup whipping cream, 1 2/3 oz. mayonnaise, 1 2/3 oz. grated horseradish, 1 oz. raisins, parsley sprigs, salt, pepper, sugar and lemon juice to taste

Wash the meat and remove the outer skin. Rub with the seasoning and dredge with flour. Brown in intensely heated fat and sprinkle with water. Simmer covered over low heat. Remove the meat when tender, slice diagonally into portions and cool. Arrange on a platter. Chill cream, whip it and combine with mayonnaise, horseradish, rinsed raisins, chopped parsley sprigs and seasoning. Correct the seasoning. Pour over the prepared meat. Garnish with tomatoes and stewed peaches.

ROAST VEAL ROLLED UHLAN STYLE

1 1/2 lb. boneless veal, fat for frying, 2/3 oz. dried cèpe mushrooms, 1 oz. capers, 1 1/3 oz. walnut meats, 2 egg yolks, parsley sprigs, 5 oz. mayonnaise sauce, 1 1/3 oz. tomato paste, 2/3 oz. butter, 3 1/2 oz. lobster tails, salt, pepper and lemon juice to taste

Wash the meat and remove the outer skin. Pound until thin with a mallet that has been dipped in water, trimming out the edges evenly. Season and allow to cool for 30 minutes. Wash the mushrooms, soak them and chop finely. Blanch the walnuts, grate them and combine with minced meat trimmings, mushrooms, egg yolks and chopped parsley sprigs. Season to taste and arrange on the prepared meat. Form into a roll, tie with a string and pour the fat over this. Bake, basting with water, then with the pan drippings. Cool when done and cut into slices. Arrange the slices on a platter. Simmer the tomato paste in butter, stirring constantly. Cool and combine with the mayonnaise and lobster tails (optional). Season to taste and pour over the meat, then garnish.

MARINATED VEAL

1 lb. boneless veal, 1/2 cup vinegar, 1/4 cup water, 1 2/3 oz. onion, 1 2/3 oz. celeriac, 1 2/3 oz. parsley root, 1 2/3 oz. carrots, salt, pepper, sugar, bay leaf, allspice, milk

Wash the meat and remove outer skin. Cover with milk and set aside in a cool place for 24 hours. Wash the vegetables, peel and rinse them, then cut into strips. Cover with water. Add the washed meat and seasoning, then cook. Towards the end add vinegar. When done, keep in the marinade for several hours. Remove the meat and cut it diagonally into slices. Arrange on a platter and cover with Tartare Sauce (q.v.). Garnish with tomatoes, pieces of egg and parsley sprigs.

VEAL À LA SALMON

1 lb. boneless veal, 1 1/2 cup dry white wine, 1 1/2 cup water, 1 2/3 oz. celeriac, 1 2/3 oz. parsley root, 1 2/3 oz. carrots, 5 oz. lemons,

1 1/2 tablespoons olive oil, 3 egg yolks, salt, white pepper, sugar, lemon juice, juniper, thyme, cloves and allspice to taste

Wash the vegetables, peel and rinse them, then cut into strips. Wash the lemons, scald, peel and slice them. Cut the slices in half and remove any pits. Wash the meat and remove the outer skin. Cover it with the vegetables and lemons. Place in the refrigerator for 24 hours. Pour the wine and water over this, season and simmer over low heat. Cool the cooked meat in its own stock. Remove the meat and cut into portions diagonally. Arrange on a platter. Strain 1 cup of the stock through a sieve and combine with egg yolks, salt and pepper. Place the dish with this in a larger pan filled with hot water and beat until the sauce thickens, keeping the water hot. Remove the sauce from the heat and add the oil slowly, stirring constantly. Season to taste, pour over the meat and garnish.

WROCŁAW VEAL

1/2 lb. boneless veal roast, 1 cup whipping cream, 1 oz. raisins, 1 oz. almonds, 5—7 oz. stewed peaches, 1 2/3 oz. ketchup, salt, pepper, sugar and lemon juice to taste

Blanch the almonds and chop them finely. Combine with the veal cut into strips, washed raisins and diced peaches. Season to taste and divide into portions. Cover with whipped cream blended with ketchup, then garnish.

CAPTAIN'S ROLLED VEAL BREAST

1 lb. veal brisket, 1 2/3 oz. hardened French bread, 3 1/2 oz. pork fat, 2—2 1/2 oz. thin frankfurters, 2/3 oz. canned peppers, 1 egg, 7 oz. soup vegetables (carrot, parsley root, celeriac, leek), 2/3 oz. gelatin, 2/3 oz. tomato paste, egg white, salt, pepper and lemon juice to taste, hard-boiled egg, plums pickled in vinegar and tomato for garnishing

Wash the meat and separate the rib bones from the brisket, trimming the edges evenly. Cut the pork fat into thin strips and pound lightly

with a mallet that has been dipped in water. Arrange on the frankfurters. Soak the bread in milk, then squeeze it out and mince together with the meat trimmings and peppers. Combine with the egg and season to taste; arrange on the prepared brisket together with the frankfurters. Form the meat into a roll, then wrap in a cloth and tie around with a string. Cover with boiling salted water and simmer covered over low heat. Towards the end add the cleaned vegetables. Remove the cooked brisket and place it on chopping board. Press down with a small board and set aside for cooling. Remove the meat from the cloth and cut diagonally into slices. Arrange on a platter and garnish. Cool 1 cup of the stock and blend with the tomato paste, egg white and lemon juice. Heat until it boils, stirring constantly. Combine with gelatin that has been soaked and dissolved in a small amount of cold water. Bring to a boil and pour through a cheesecloth. Season and allow to set. When nearly firm, pour over the meat.

GALANTINE OF VEAL

1 lb. boneless veal, 2—2 1/2 oz. hardened French bread, 3 1/2 oz. smoked ham, 3 1/2 oz. white mushrooms, 3—4 egg yolks, fat for frying, parsley sprigs, milk, olive oil, 1/2 lb. soup vegetables (carrots, parsley root, celeriac, leek), salt and pepper to taste

Clean the mushrooms, rinse, chop and fry them. Wash the meat and cut off several thin slices. Pound these lightly with a mallet that has been dipped in water. Mince the remaining meat twice, the second time adding bread that has been soaked in milk and squeezed out. Combine with the mushrooms, ham cut into strips, egg yolks and chopped parsley sprigs. Season to taste. Arrange on the prepared meat, wrap in a cloth that has been covered with olive oil and tie around with a string. Cover with boiling salted water and simmer covered over low heat. Towards the end add the cleaned vegetables. Remove the cooked galantine, place on a chopping board, press with a small board and allow to cool. Remove the cloth, cut the meat diagonally into portions and arrange on a platter. Serve with spicy sauces or in aspic.

VEAL PÂTÉ

1 1/4 lb. boneless veal, 7 oz. fresh bacon, 1/2 cup sour cream, 2 2/3 oz. onions, 3 1/2 oz. white mushrooms, 2—2 2/3 oz. hardened French bread, 2 2/3 oz. hard cheese (Gouda), parsley sprigs, 2 eggs, fat for frying, salt, pepper and nutmeg to taste

Clean, rinse and crumble the onions and mushrooms. Wash the meat, dice it and fry together with the onions and mushrooms. Sprinkle with water and simmer covered over low heat. Towards the end add crumbled bread and sour cream. Allow this to cool and mince twice, using a pâté insert in the grinder. Combine with eggs, grated cheese and chopped parsley sprigs. Season to taste. Place in a buttered pan, smooth out the surface and cover with foil. Place in a larger pan with boiling water and cook ca. 60 minutes. Towards the end place the pan in a hot oven. When done allow to cool and remove from the pan. Arrange on a platter and garnish.

VEAL KEELS IN ASPIC

3/4 lb. boneless veal, 2—2 1/2 oz. hardened French bread, milk, 1 2/3 oz. onions for the meat, 5 oz. onions for the stock, 2 egg yolks, 1/2 lb. soup vegetables (carrots, parsley root, celeriac, leek), 1 1/3 oz. raisins, 2/3 oz. gelatin, salt, pepper and sugar to taste

Soak the bread in milk and squeeze out. Peel the onions, rinse them and mince together with the bread and meat. Combine with the egg yolks, season and form into round keels (two to a portion). Cover with boiling salted water. Bring to a boil and remove from the water. Cut the onions and vegetables into strips, cover with boiling salted water and bring to a boil. Towards the end add the keels, seasoning and rinsed raisins. Soak the gelatin in a small amount of cold water. Dissolve it and add to the keels. Bring to a boil and sweeten to taste. Fold into a bowl, pour the sauce over it and allow to set.

VEAL TONGUE

1 1/4 lb. veal tongue, 1/2 lb. soup vegetables (carrots, parsley root, celeriac, leek), 2—2 1/2 oz. ketchup, 1 2/3 oz. walnut meats, 1/3 cup

olive oil, 1/4 cup dry white wine, 1/3 oz. gelatin, 2—3 egg yolks, salt, pepper, sugar and lemon juice to taste

Wash the tongue and remove the roots and gristle. Cover with boiling salted water and cook. Towards the end add the vegetables. When cooked, remove the outer skin from tongue and cut lengthwise in half. Blanch the walnuts and grate them. Brush the tongue with ketchup, sprinkle with the walnuts and arrange on a platter. Soak the gelatin in a small amount of cold water. Dissolve it and combine with olive oil, wine and lemon juice, beating with an egg-whisk. Add the egg yolks gradually and continue beating until the sauce becomes smooth and thick. Season to taste, pour over the tongue and garnish.

GALANTINE OF CHICKEN

Chicken, 1/2 lb. boneless veal or chicken meat, 3 1/2 oz. chicken livers, 2—2 1/2 oz. hardened French bread, 1/2 cup sour cream, parsley sprigs, 3 eggs, 3/4 lb. soup vegetables (carrots, parsley root, celeriac, leek), 2/3 oz. gelatin, 1 1/3 oz. tomatoes, hard-boiled egg, stewed peaches, salt, pepper, nutmeg, tomato paste and vinegar to taste

Wash the chicken and remove the neck and wings. Place it on a chopping board breast down. Cut with a sharp knife along the spine, separating the skin and meat from the bones, beginning with the shoulder and collar bones. Even out the meat slice and cut off the more muscled parts. Mince the chicken and veal three times, using a pâté insert in the mincer. The third time add the bread, which has been soaked in the sour cream and squeezed out lightly, and the rinsed livers. Combine with the chopped parsley sprigs and egg yolks and season to taste. Place the slice of meat with the skin on the chopping board, spread the mixture on it and form into a roll. Wrap this in a cloth that has been covered with olive oil and tie with a string. Clean the vegetables and cover with boiling salted water. Add the chicken bones and cook for 25 minutes. Place the galantine in the water and cook for ca. 50 minutes covered over low heat. If the chicken is an old one, it should be cooked for 60—70 minutes more. When cooked pour out part of the stock, press the galantine down with

a small board and allow to cool. Remove it from the cloth and cut diagonally into portions. Arrange this on a platter and garnish with pieces of tomato, egg and peaches. Pour ca. 2 cups of the stock through a strainer, blend together with the tomato paste and egg whites and beat with an egg-whisk. Heat slowly, beating briskly with the egg-whisk. Bring to a boil and add gelatin that has been soaked in a small amount of cold water. Bring to a boil once more and season. Pour through a cheesecloth and allow to set. When nearly firm, pour over the galantine.

CHICKEN IN ASPIC

Chicken, 3/4 lb. soup vegetables (carrots, parsley root, celeriac, leek), 1/3 cup dry white wine, 1 oz. gelatin, 2—3 egg whites, 5 oz. oranges, 2 2/3 oz. lemons, stewed plums, parsley sprigs, salt, pepper, tomato paste and lemon juice to taste

Wash the chicken and remove the neck and wings. Cut lengthwise into halves. Cover with boiling salted water and cook, covered. Wash the vegetables, peel them, rinse and add to the chicken towards the end of cooking. Take out the chicken when tender and cut into portions, partly removing the bones. Arrange it on a platter and garnish with the oranges, lemon, plums and parsley sprigs. Combine 1 cup of the stock with the wine, egg whites, tomato paste and lemon juice. Bring to a boil, stirring constantly. Add gelatin that has been soaked in a small amount of cold water. Cook for a while and pour through a cheesecloth. Season to taste. When nearly firm, pour it over the chicken and allow to set.

CHICKEN IN ASPIC MOULDS

1/4 chicken, 1/2 lb. soup vegetables (carrots, parsley root, celeriac, leek), 1 oz. gelatin, 2—3 egg whites, 1 2/3 oz. lemons, 2—2 2/3 oz. canned peas, 2—3 hard-boiled eggs, 1 2/3 oz. canned peppers, parsley sprigs, pepper, tomato paste (optional) and lemon juice to taste

Wash the cleaned chicken, cover with boiling salted water and cook, covered. Wash the vegetables, peel and rinse them, then add to chicken

towards the end of cooking. When cooked, take out the chicken, remove skin and bones and dice the meat. Blend 1 1/2 cups of the stock with the tomato paste, egg whites and lemon juice. Bring to a boil, stirring constantly with an egg-whisk. Add gelatin that has been soaked in a small amount of cold water and cook for a while. Pour through a cheesecloth and season. Pour one tablespoon of the gelatin into teacups or moulds and allow to set. Garnish with lemon and peppers and cover this with more gelatin. Allow to set. Add meat, peas, egg halves and parsley sprigs and cover with the remaining gelatin. Place the moulds in the refrigerator for several hours, until the gelatin sets. Just before serving place the molds in hot water for a moment. Take out the moulded gelatin, arrange on a platter and garnish with lettuce.

CHICKEN IN MAYONNAISE

Chicken, 3/4 lb. soup vegetables (carrots, parsley root, celeriac, leek), 1/2 lb. mayonnaise sauce, 2—2 2/3 oz. tomatoes, 1 2/3 oz. plums, 2 2/3 oz. lemons, parsley sprigs, lettuce, hard-boiled egg, salt and pepper to taste

Wash the cleaned chicken, cover with boiling salted water and cook covered over low heat. Wash the vegetables, peel and rinse them and add to the chicken towards the end of cooking. Take out the chicken when tender, cut into portions removing the bones partly and arrange on a platter. When cool cover with the seasoned sauce and garnish. If the chicken is prepared several hours before serving, be sure to add 1 2/3 oz. of nearly firm gelatin to the mayonnaise, which prevents the mayonnaise from becoming yellow.

COLD CHICKEN POLISH STYLE

Chicken, butter, 1 cup whipping cream, 1 2/3 oz. grated horseradish, 1 1/3 oz. raisins, salt, pepper, sugar, lemon and orange juice to taste

Wash the cleaned chicken and rub with seasoning. Set aside in a cool place for several hours. Pour butter over the chicken and bake, basting

with water, then with the pan drippings. Take out the chicken when tender and cut into portions, removing the bones partly. Arrange on a platter and allow to cool. Chill the cream and whip it, adding confectioners' sugar towards the end. Combine with the horseradish, rinsed raisins and season to taste. Pour this over the chicken, garnish and serve at once.

CHICKEN BREASTS IN MAYONNAISE SAUCE

2 chicken breasts, butter, 5 oz. mayonnaise sauce, 5 oz. potatoes, 5 oz. carrots, 5 oz. celeriac, 1 2/3 oz. canned peas, 1 2/3 oz. dill pickles, hard-boiled egg, parsley sprigs, 1 2/3 oz. mayonnaise for salad, salt, pepper, prepared mustard, tomato, cucumber and hard-boiled egg for garnishing

Wash the chicken breasts and rub them with seasoning. Set aside in a cool place for several hours. Pour butter over them and bake, basting with water, then with the pan drippings. Cut the meat into portions when tender, removing the bones partly. Wash, peel and rinse the potatoes, carrots and celeriac. Cook the vegetables, cool them and dice together with the egg and pickles. Combine with the mayonnaise and chopped parsley sprigs and season to taste. Arrange on a platter and cover with the chicken meat. Pour the seasoned mayonnaise sauce over this and garnish.

CHICKEN BALLS

1/4 chicken, butter, 2 oz. rice, 3 1/2 oz. canned peas, 1 2/3 oz. ham, 5 oz. white mushrooms, 3 1/2 oz. mayonnaise sauce, 1/2 cup whipping cream, 1 1/3 oz. radishes, salt, pepper and sugar to taste

Wash the cleaned chicken, rub with seasoning and set aside in a cool place for several hours. Pour butter over it and sprinkle with water. Bake the chicken, basting with the pan drippings. Take out the chicken when tender, remove the bones and dice the meat. Rinse the rice and cover it with a large amount of boiling water. Cook and then strain it. Rinse with hot water and allow to cool. Clean the mushrooms, rinse them and

slice into strips. Fry them and combine with the rice, meat, canned peas, mayonnaise and ham that has been cut into strips. Season to taste and form into round balls. Arrange these on a platter. Clean the radishes, rinse them and grate coarsely, then combine with whipped cream. Season and pour over the balls, then garnish.

MARINATED CHICKEN

Chicken, milk, 1 cup dry white wine, 7 oz. lemons, 7 oz. oranges, 1 2/3 oz. raisins, salt, nutmeg, sugar and lemon juice to taste

Wash the cleaned chicken and cut into 4 portions. Cover it with milk and place in the refrigerator for several hours. Wash the lemons and oranges, then scald with boiling water. Peel and slice them, cutting the slices into halves and removing any pits. Cover with wine and water. Add the pieces of chicken removed from the milk. Cook covered over low heat. Towards the end add rinsed raisins. Season this, place in a large jar and set aside for several hours. Just before serving arrange on a platter and garnish.

UHLAN'S CHICKEN PÂTÉ

Chicken, 5 oz. pork fat, 7 oz. onions, 7 oz. white mushrooms, 1/2 lb. veal or pork brains, 2—2 1/2 oz. hardened French bread, 1/2 lb. soup vegetables (carrots, parsley root, celeriac, leek), 2 eggs, salt, pepper and nutmeg to taste, fat and bread crumbs for baking

Wash the cleaned chicken and remove the bones. Cover them with boiling salted water and cook, adding cleaned vegetables towards the end. Clean, rinse and dice the onions and mushrooms together with the pork fat. Fry this and add to the meat. Simmer until tender, basting with the broth. Remove the outer skin from the brains, rinse and add them to the meat when nearly done together with crumbled bread. When the meat is done allow it to cool and mince it twice, using a pâté insert in the grinder. Combine with the eggs and season to taste. Place in a baking pan that has been buttered and sprinkled with breadcrumbs. Smooth out the

surface and cover with buttered waxpaper. Bake in a medium oven or cook in a double boiler. Cool the pâté, arrange it on a platter and garnish.

GALANTINE OF DUCK

Duck, fat for baking, 1 2/3 oz. hardened French bread, 5 oz. white mushrooms, 5—7 oz. boneless veal, 2 eggs, parsley sprigs, milk, salt, pepper, marjoram and nutmeg to taste

Wash the duck and remove the neck and wings. Place the bird breast down and cut lengthwise along the spine. Separate the meat from the skin and cut slices from the breast. Pound these lightly with a mallet that has been dipped in water and spread out evenly on the skin of the duck, forming a rectangle. Clean the mushrooms, rinse them and slice finely. Soak the bread in milk, squeeze out the milk and mince twice together with the veal and the duck meat. Add the mushrooms, eggs and chopped parsley sprigs. Season to taste. Spread the stuffing out evenly on the meat along the length of the rectangle. Form into a roll and tie it with a string like a ham. Cover with fat, wrap in foil or buttered waxpaper and bake around 80 minutes. Cool, remove the foil and cut diagonally into slices. Arrange on a platter, garnish and pour the nearly firm gelatin over it.

DUCK WITH WHIPPED CREAM

Duck, fat for baking, 1 cup whipping cream, 7 oz. oranges, 1 tablespoon cognac, 1 1/3 oz. raisins, 5 oz. sour cherries, salt, pepper, sugar and marjoram to taste

Wash the cleaned duck. Remove the neck and wings. Rub the bird with the seasoning and set aside in a cool place for an hour. Pour the fat over the duck and bake 60-80 minutes, basting with water, then with the pan drippings. When tender, cut into portions, removing the bones partly. Arrange the bird on a platter. Wash the oranges and scald them. Peel and dice them, removing any pits. Combine with the whipped cream, raisins that have been soaked in cognac and cherries that have been forced through a sieve. Season to taste, pour over the duck and garnish.

DUCK MALAGA

Duck, fat for baking, 2/3 cup Malaga wine, stewed peaches, lemons, tomatoes, parsley sprigs for garnishing, 2/3 oz. gelatin, 1/3 oz. tomato paste, egg white, salt, pepper and lemon juice to taste

Wash the cleaned duck and remove the neck and wings. Rub with the seasoning and set aside in a cool place for an hour. Pour the fat over the duck and bake 60—80 minutes, basting with water, then with the pan drippings. Add wine towards the end. When tender, cut into portions, removing the bones partly. Arrange the bird on a platter and garnish. Skim the fat from the sauce and combine with the tomato paste and egg white. Bring to a boil, stirring with an egg-whisk. Add gelatin that has been soaked in a small amount of water and cook for a while. Season, then pour through a cheesecloth. Allow to cool. When nearly firm, pour the gelatin over the duck and allow to set.

DUCK PÂTÉ

Duck, fat for baking, 5—7 oz. mushrooms, 3 1/2 oz. duck livers, 1 1/3 oz. prunes, 1/3 cup sour cream, 2—2 2/3 oz. hardened French bread, 2 eggs, fat and breadcrumbs for baking pan, salt, pepper and nutmeg to taste

Wash the cleaned duck and remove the neck and wings. Rub with the seasoning and set aside in a cool place for an hour. Pour the fat over the duck and bake, basting with water, then with the pan drippings. Clean the mushrooms, rinse them and add to the duck towards the end together with rinsed livers. Wash the prunes, soak them and remove pits. When the duck is tender, separate the meat from the bones and mince two or three times together with the prunes, mushrooms, livers and bread that has been soaked in sour cream. Combine with the eggs and season to taste. Place in a baking pan that has been buttered and sprinkled with breadcrumbs. Smooth out the surface, cover with foil and bake covered around 40 minutes. Towards the end remove the foil so that a brown crust can form. Cool, place on a platter and garnish.

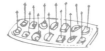

ROULADE OF GOOSE

(Young) goose, 9 1/2 oz. boneless pork, 7 oz. goose livers, 2 2/3—3 1/2 oz. hardened French bread, milk, 1 2/3 oz. pork fat, 2 eggs, 5 oz. mushrooms, fat for baking, salt, pepper and marjoram to taste

Wash the cleaned goose and remove the neck and wings. Place the bird breast down on a chopping board and cut lengthwise along the spine. Separate the skin and meat from the bones and cut slices from the breast. Even out the more muscled parts lightly. Form into a rectangle. Clean the mushrooms, rinse them and slice finely. Fry the mushrooms. Soak the bread in milk and then squeeze out. Mince it twice, together with the meat and livers. Combine with eggs, mushrooms and diced onions that have been scalded. Season to taste. Place the stuffing on the rectangular strip and form into a roll. Tie it with a string like a ham. Pour the fat over it, wrap in foil and bake around 70 minutes. Take out when done and cool. Cut into portions, arrange on a platter and garnish. Pour gelatin when nearly firm over this or serve with an appropriate cold sauce.

ROYAL GOOSE LIVER PÂTÉ

8 1/2 oz. goose livers, milk, goose drippings, 3 1/2 oz. pork fat, 1 2/3 oz. hardened French bread, 1/3 cup sour cream, can of sardines, 5 oz. ham, 3 1/2—5 oz. mayonnaise sauce, salt, pepper and nutmeg to taste

Rinse the livers, cover with milk and set aside in a cool place for an hour. Fry together with finely diced pork fat. Add crumbled bread and sour cream. Simmer for several minutes. Allow to cool, then mince twice, using a pâté insert in the mincer-grinder and adding sardines the second time. Combine with the mayonnaise and ham cut into strips, then season. Place in a pan and set aside to cool. Before serving, dip the pan in hot water for several seconds. Place the pâté on a platter and garnish.

TURKEY MALAGA

(Young) turkey, fat for baking, 1/3 cup Malaga wine, 2/3 oz. tomato paste, 2 egg whites, 2/3 oz. gelatin, oranges, lemons, plums pickled in

wine, tomatoes, parsley sprigs for garnishing, salt, pepper and lemon juice to taste

Wash the turkey and remove the tendons from its legs by cutting the skin near the knee joint. Press the breast by hand until it flattens. Cut off the wings and neck. Rub with seasoning and set aside in a cool place for 2—3 hours. Place the turkey in a roasting pan breast up and pour the fat over it. Bake, basting with water, then with the pan drippings. When done cool the turkey a little. Cut off the thighs, cutting each into two portions. Cut off strips of meat diagonally from the breast, beginning with the shoulder area. Arrange the portioned meat on a platter so that each portion contains a piece of meat from the thigh and breast, then garnish. Skim the fat from the sauce. Add the tomato paste, egg white and wine. Bring to a boil, stirring constantly. Add gelatin that has been soaked in a small amount of water and cook for a while. Pour through a cheesecloth and season to taste. Allow to set. When nearly firm, pour the gelatin over the turkey.

PHEASANT MALAGA

Pheasant, fat for baking, 3 1/2 oz. pork fat, 7 oz. pheasant pâté, 2 egg whites, 2/3 oz. gelatin, 2/3 oz. tomato paste, 1/3 cup Malaga wine, lemon, stewed plums, parsley sprigs for garnishing, salt, pepper, lemon juice and nutmeg to taste

Wash the prepared pheasant, rub with the seasoning and set aside in a cool place for an hour. Tie up the legs and lard the bird with thin strips of pork fat. Tie it up with a string and pour the fat over. Bake, basting with water, then with the pan drippings. When done, cut into portions. partly removing the bones. Place it on a platter, surround with the pâté and garnish. Skim the fat from the sauce and add the wine, egg whites and tomato paste. Bring to a boil, stirring constantly. Add gelatin that has been soaked in a small amount of cold water. Cook for a while and pour through a cheesecloth. Season to taste and allow to set. When nearly firm, pour the gelatin over the pheasant.

ADMIRAL'S PHEASANT

Pheasant, fat for baking, 3 1/2 oz. pork fat, 3 1/2 oz. carrots, 3 1/2 oz. celeriac, 3 1/2 oz. parsley root, 1 2/3 oz. onions, 3 tablespoons olive oil,

1 1/3 oz. tomato paste, 3 1/2 oz. lemons, 1 1/3 oz. raisins, 5 oz. mayonnaise sauce, 3 tablespoons dry white wine, salt, pepper, sugar and lemon juice to taste

Prepare the pheasant and bake as above. Towards the end remove the pork fat and allow a brown crust to form. When done cool and cut into portions. Arrange on a platter. Wash the vegetables, peel them, rinse and cut into strips. Fry them lightly. Sprinkle them with water and simmer until tender. Towards the end add the wine, washed raisins and tomato paste. Cool the vegetables and combine with the mayonnaise and peeled lemons cut into half-slices. Season to taste and pour the sauce over the pheasant, then garnish.

PHEASANT PÂTÉ

Pheasant, fat for baking, 1/2 oz. pork fat, 5 oz. goose livers, 5 oz. mushrooms, 3—4 egg yolks, 3 1/2 oz. hardened French bread, 1/3 cup dry white wine, 2/3 cup whipping cream, 1—1 1/3 oz. almonds, 3 1/2 oz. lemons, milk, 2 2/3 oz. tomatoes, parsley sprigs, salt and pepper to taste

Wash the prepared pheasant and separate the meat from the bones. Cover the bones with water and cook covered over low heat. Fry the meat and fat, sprinkle with the broth and simmer covered. Clean the mushrooms, rinse them and add to the pheasant. Towards the end add the wine. Soak the livers and bread in milk. Squeeze out the bread and mince it together with the prepared meat and livers. Combine with the egg yolks and season. Spread waxpaper in a buttered pan and place the pheasant in this. Smooth out the surface and cover with the waxpaper. Bake, placing the pan with the pâté in a larger dish with boiling water. Bake in a hot oven. When done, allow the pâté to cool in the pan. Place it on a platter and garnish with the whipped cream, blanched almonds, lemons, tomatoes and parsley sprigs.

GRASS CARP JEWISH STYLE

2 lb. grass carp, 1/2 lb. onions, 1 2/3 oz. raisins, 3 egg yolks, 1/3 oz. gelatin, salt, pepper and lemon juice to taste

Wash the cleaned fish and cut into steaks, then add salt. Peel the onions, rinse, dice and cook them. Towards the end add the fish and gelatin that has been soaked in a small amount of cold water. Take out the fish and strain the stock. Beat the egg yolks together with the seasoning. Add the hot stock to this gradually, stirring briskly with an egg-whisk. Place the dish with the egg yolks in a larger dish with hot water and beat until the sauce thickens. Season the sauce to taste and allow to cool. Pour it over the fish and allow to set.

GRASS CARP IN ASPIC

2 lb. grass carp, 1 cup vegetable stock, 1/3 cup dry white wine, 2 egg whites, 1/3—2/3 oz. gelatin, mayonnaise, tomatoes, hard-boiled egg, parsley sprigs for garnishing, salt, pepper and lemon juice to taste

Wash the cleaned fish and cut lengthwise into halves. Remove the spine bones. Cut the fish diagonally into portions. Pour the wine and stock over this. Add salt and cook the fish. Cool it in the stock, then take it out. Arrange on a platter and garnish. Combine the stock with the egg whites and beat with an egg-whisk. Bring to a boil, stirring constantly. Add gelatin that has been soaked in a small amount of cold water. Add the lemon juice and cook for a while. Pour it through a cheesecloth and season to taste. When nearly firm pour it over the fish and allow to set.

ADMIRAL'S GRASS CARP

2 lb. grass carp, 3/4 lb. soup vegetables (carrots, parsley root, celeriac, leek), 5 oz. mayonnaise sauce, 1/3 cup thick sour cream, 1 tablespoon dry white wine, 5 oz. oranges, 5 oz. lemons, 3 1/2 oz. tomatoes, salt, pepper, sugar and lemon juice to taste

Wash the cleaned fish and cut lengthwise into halves. Remove the spine bones. Cut the fish diagonally into portions. Wash, peel and rinse the vegetables and cook them in water. Towards the end add the fish and seasoning. Cool the cooked fish in the stock. Take it out and arrange on a platter. Wash, scald and peel the tomatoes, lemons and oranges. Cut

them into pieces and combine with mayonnaise, wine and sour cream. Season to taste, pour over the fish and garnish.

ROULADE OF COD, HADDOCK, HAKE OR GILTHEAD

1 1/4 lb. frozen fish fillets, 2 2/3 oz. hardened French bread, milk, egg, parsley sprigs, 1 2/3 oz. grated horseradish, 1 oz. powdered milk, 5 oz. celeriac, 1/2 lb. soup vegetables (carrots, parsley root, celeriac, leek), salt, pepper, sugar, nutmeg and lemon juice to taste, olive oil

Put the fillets in a plastic bag and tie it up so that no water can get in. Defrost the fish in a temperature not higher than 68°F. When defrosted sprinkle with lemon juice and set aside for 30 minutes. Soak the bread in the milk, squeeze it out and mince together with the fish. Combine with the horseradish, powdered milk, egg, chopped parsley sprigs and finely grated celeriac. Season to taste. Dampen a linen cloth with water, spread olive oil over it and place the fish mixture in it. Form into a roll 2 in. thick and tie it up with thread. Place in the vegetable stock and cook around 40 minutes over low heat. Take it out when done and cool, pressing down with a small board. Remove the cloth and cut the roulade diagonally into 1/2 in. slices. Arrange on a platter and garnish. Pour the nearly firm gelatin or a cold sauce over the roulade.

LVOV COD, HADDOCK, HAKE OR GILTHEAD

1 1/4 lb. frozen fish fillets, 2 2/3 oz. hardened French bread, milk, 3 1/2 oz. onions, 2/3 oz. butter or margarine, egg, parsley sprigs, 1/2 lb. soup vegetables (carrots, parsley root, celeriac, leek), 3 1/2 oz. prunes, 5 oz. mayonnaise sauce, 3 tablespoons dry white wine, salt, pepper, sugar and lemon juice to taste

Defrost the fillets as above. Soak the bread in the milk and squeeze out. Mince the bread together with the fillets. Combine with the egg, chopped parsley sprigs and onions which have been peeled, rinsed, diced and fried. Season to taste. Form into balls, two to a person. Place in the vege-

table stock and cook around 30 minutes over low heat. When done cool
the balls in the stock and place them on a platter. Wash, soak, and cook
the prunes, then force them through a strainer. Combine with the mayonnaise and wine. Season to taste. Pour the mixture over the fish and
garnish.

GENERAL'S FLOUNDER, FLATFISH, TURBOT OR SOLE

*2 lb. fish, milk, 1 2/3 oz. butter, 3 tablespoons lemon juice, 3 tablespoons
orange juice, 3 tablespoons cognac, 1 2/3 oz. raisins, 3 1/2 oz. mayonnaise
sauce, parsley sprigs, salt, pepper and lemon juice to taste*

Wash the cleaned fish and cut lengthwise into halves. Remove the spine
bones. Remove the skin, starting with the tail end. Cut the fish into portions and cover with milk blended with pepper. Place in the refrigerator
for 2—3 hours. Take out the fish, dry it, add salt and brown on both sides.
Add lemon and orange juices, cognac and rinsed raisins. Simmer around
8 minutes. Cool and arrange on a platter. Combine the mayonnaise with
the fish stock, chopped parsley sprigs and seasoning, then garnish.

CARP IN ASPIC

*2 lb. carp, vegetable stock, 2/3 oz. tomato paste, 2 egg whites, 2/3 oz.
gelatin, hard-boiled egg, mayonnaise, tomato and parsley sprigs for
garnishing, salt, pepper, allspice, bay leaf and lemon juice to taste*

Wash the cleaned fish and cut lengthwise into halves, then into portions.
Rinse it and place in the vegetable stock. Add seasoning and cook over
low heat. When done take it out of the stock and remove the bones. Arrange on a platter and garnish. Cool the stock and blend with the tomato paste and egg whites. Heat slowly, stirring constantly with an egg whisk
until it comes to a boil. Soak the gelatin in a small amount of cold water
and add to the stock. Cook for a while and pour through a cheesecloth.
Season and allow to set. When nearly firm, pour it over the carp.

CARP SURPRISE

2 lb. carp, olive oil for frying, flour, 3/4 cup whipping cream, 3 1/2 oz. prunes, 1 2/3 oz. almonds, salt, sugar and lemon juice to taste

Wash the cleaned fish and cut lengthwise into halves, then into portions. Rinse, then sprinkle with the seasoning and flour. Fry the fish. Wash, soak and cook the prunes, then force them through a strainer. Blanch the almonds and grate them. Combine with whipped cream and the prune paste. Season to taste and arrange the mixture on the carp.

WARSAW CARP

2 lb. carp, 1 2/3 oz. hardened French bread, 5 oz. onions, fat for frying, 2 egg yolks, 3 1/2 oz. almonds, 1/2 lb. soup vegetables (carrots, parsley root, celeriac, leek), parsley sprigs, 5 oz. mayonnaise, 2 tablespoons dry white wine, salt, pepper, sugar and lemon juice to taste, hard-boiled egg, tomato and cucumbers for garnishing

Skin the cleaned carp. Separate the meat from the bones. Soak the bread and squeeze it out. Peel and rinse the onions, then dice them finely. Fry the onions and mince them together with the fish and bread. Combine with egg yolks, chopped parsley sprigs and ground blanched almonds. Season to taste and wrap in the skin, then in a linen cloth that has been covered with fat. Tie it up with a string and place in the vegetable stock. Add salt and cook. Cool the mixture in the stock. Take it out of the stock and remove the cloth. Cut diagonally into portions and arrange on a platter. Combine mayonnaise with wine and lemon juice. Season to taste and pour over the fish, then garnish.

BOATSWAIN'S CARP

2 lb. carp, olive oil, flour, 3/4 cup whipping cream, 1 cup dry white wine, 1 1/3 oz. raisins, 1 2/3 oz. grated horseradish, salt, sugar, pepper and lemon juice to taste

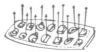

Wash the cleaned fish and cut lengthwise into halves, then into portions. Sprinkle with the seasoning and flour and fry the fish. Remove the bones. cover with wine and place in the refrigerator for 12 hours. Chill the cream, whip it and combine with the horseradish and rinsed raisins. Season to taste and pour over the fish, which has been taken out of the wine. Garnish the fish.

SALMON IN ASPIC

1 3/4 lb. (cleaned) salmon, vegetable stock, 2/3 oz. dry white wine, 1 tablespoon olive oil, 2/3 oz. tomato paste, 2 egg whites, 1/3—2/3 oz. gelatin, mayonnaise, tomato, lemon and parsley sprigs for garnishing, salt, pepper, allspice, bay leaf, nutmeg and lemon juice to taste

Cut the fish lengthwise into halves and remove the spine bones. Skin the fish and cut diagonally into portions. Wash it and place in vegetable stock. Pour in the wine, add seasoning and olive oil and cook over low heat. Take it out when done and arrange on a platter, then garnish. Add egg whites and tomato paste to the stock and bring to a boil, stirring constantly with an egg-whisk. Combine with gelatin that has been soaked in cold water. Cook for a while and pour through a cheesecloth. Season to taste and allow to set. When nearly firm pour over the fish and allow to set.

MARINATED SALMON

1 3/4 lb. (cleaned) salmon, vegetable stock, 2/3 oz. dry white wine, 3 tablespoons olive oil, 1/2 lb. lemons, 2/3 oz. capers, salt, pepper, allspice, bay leaf and lemon juice to taste

Cut the fish lengthwise into halves, removing the spine bones. Skin the fish and cut diagonally into portions. Wash these and cover with vegetable stock, then cook. Wash, scald and peel the lemons. Cut them into half-slices, removing any pits. Add the lemons to the fish towards the end of cooking together with the wine, rinsed capers, seasoning and olive

oil. Season to taste. Allow the fish to cool in the stock and set aside for several hours.

TROUT IN ASPIC

4 trout, fat for frying, 1—1 1/4 cups dry white wine, 1/3 oz. gelatin, 5 oz. lemons, 1 oz. raisins, 5 oz. tomatoes, parsley sprigs, salt, pepper, sugar and lemon juice to taste

Clean the fish and cut along the belly. Gut, taking care not to puncture the gall bladder. Remove the eyes and gills. Wash the fish and sprinkle with seasoning. Place in hot fat to brown, then fry over low heat. When done place on a platter and garnish. Soak the gelatin in a small amount of cold water. Add it to the wine and dissolve, stirring constantly. Bring to a boil together with rinsed raisins. Season to taste and leave to set. When nearly firm, pour it over the fish and allow to set completely.

Note: Trout in aspic may be cooked instead of fried. When done, cool in the stock, arrange on a platter and garnish. Then proceed as above.

TROUT IN MAYONNAISE

4 trout, vegetable stock, mayonnaise, 1 2/3 oz. fish aspic, tomato, lemon, plums pickled in wine, canned peas and parsley sprigs for garnishing, salt, pepper and lemon juice to taste

Clean the fish and cut along the belly. Gut, taking care not to puncture the gall bladder. Remove the eyes and gills. Wash the fish and place in the vegetable stock. Cook and cool them in the stock. Take out the fish and arrange on a platter. Pour mayonnaise blended with nearly firm gelatin over them. Allow to set and garnish.

WROCŁAW LOBSTER I

20 lobsters, 2 hard-boiled eggs, 1 1/3 oz. canned ham, 1 2/3 oz. canned peas, parsley sprigs, 1 1/4 cups broth, 1/3 oz. tomato paste, 2/3 oz. gelatin, egg white, fresh dill, salt, pepper and lemon juice to taste

Scrub the lobsters with a brush under running water holding the trunk. Pull out the middle fin from the tail, together with the black intestine. Place the lobsters in boiling salted water with the dill and cook covered for 15 minutes. When done, remove the meat from the claws and tails. Slice the eggs lengthwise into halves and remove the yolks. Blend the yolks with finely chopped ham and some of the chopped parsley sprigs. Season to taste and stuff the egg whites with this. Arrange in a pan together with the lobsters, peas and parsley sprigs. Blend the broth with the egg white and tomato paste. Bring to a boil, stirring constantly with an egg-whisk. Add gelatin that has been soaked in a small amount of cold water and cook for a while. Pour through a cheesecloth and season to taste. Pour this over the lobsters and allow to set. Before serving, place the mould with the lobsters in hot water for several seconds. Place on a platter and garnish.

WROCŁAW LOBSTER II

20 lobsters, 5 oz. mayonnaise, fresh dill, 1 2/3 oz. tomato, 1 2/3 oz. lemon, 1 2/3 oz. orange, parsley sprigs, 1 2/3 oz. canned peas, 3 table-spoons dry white wine, ketchup, salt, pepper and lemon juice to taste

Cook the lobsters as above. Wash, scald and peel the tomato, orange and lemon, then cut these into pieces. Combine with the lobsters, mayonnaise, peas, chopped parsley and wine. Season to taste. Place in a glass salad bowl and garnish. Sprinkle with ketchup.

PIKE PERCH IN ASPIC

2 lb. pike perch, vegetable stock, 1 1/3 oz. butter, 2 egg yolks, egg white, 1 1/3 oz. raisins, 1 1/3 oz. tomato paste, 1 1/3 oz. yeast babka (q.v.), salt, pepper and lemon juice to taste

Wash the cleaned and drawn pike perch and slice diagonally into 4 parts 1 1/2 in. wide. Separate the meat from the remaining fish. Blend it with the egg yolks, butter and crumbled babka. Combine with rinsed raisins and

season. Fill the fish steaks with the mixture and cover with the stock. Cook this and place on a platter when done. Cool and garnish. Combine the stock with the tomato paste and egg white. Bring to a boil, stirring with an egg-whisk. Add gelatin that has been soaked in a small amount of cold water. Cook for a while and pour through a cheesecloth. Season to taste and allow to set. When nearly firm, pour it over the pike perch.

STUFFED PIKE POLISH STYLE

2 lb. pike, 5 oz. onions, 1 oz. butter or margarine, 2 2/3 oz. hardened French bread, 1 2/3 oz. raisins, 1 2/3 oz. grated horseradish, 2 eggs, milk, 1/3 oz. gelatin, 2 tablespoons olive oil for cloth, 1/2 lb. soup vegetables (carrots, parsley root, celeriac, leek), 2/3 oz. tomato paste, salt, pepper, sugar, allspice, bay leaf and vinegar to taste

Wash the cleaned and drawn pike and separate the flesh from the bones and skin. Peel, rinse and chop the onions finely. Fry them without browning them. Mince together with part of the fish meat and bread that has been soaked in milk and squeezed out. Combine with the remaining fish flesh cut into thin strips, rinsed raisins, horseradish and egg yolks. Season to taste. Wrap this in the fish skin, then in an oiled linen cloth, forming it into a roll. Tie this up with thread and place in the vegetable stock. Add seasoning and cook around 50 minutes over low heat. Take out when done and place on a chopping board. Press down with a small board and allow to cool. Strain the stock (1 1/4 cups) and combine with the tomato paste, soaked and dissolved gelatin and egg whites. Add vinegar and beat with an egg-whisk. Bring to a boil and season to taste. Pour through a loosely woven cheesecloth. When cool, remove the fish from the cloth and slice diagonally into 1/4 in. pieces. Arrange on a platter, garnish and cover with nearly firm gelatin.

HERRING IN OIL I

1 lb. herring (salted), 3 1/2 oz. lemons, 5 oz. apples, 1/3 cup olive oil, allspice, bay leaf and pepper to taste

Rinse the herring. Cut off the heads, fins and a thin strip from the belly. Draw the fish, leaving the milt and roe and discarding the rest. Soak the fish in a large amount of cold water for 12—24 hours, changing the water several times. Cut through the skin along the spine and pull it off carefully. Wash, scald and peel the lemons. Cut them into half-slices, removing any pits. Wash and peel the apples, then cut them in half removing the cores. Cut into pieces. Arrange the fish in a jar in layers together with lemons, apples and seasoning. Pour olive oil over this and set aside in a cool place for several hours.

HERRING IN OIL II

1 lb. herring (salted), 3 tablespoons olive oil, 1 2/3 oz. tomato paste, 1 2/3 oz. raisins, parsley sprigs, nutmeg to taste

Prepare the herring as above. Arrange in a jar in layers together with rinsed raisins and chopped parsley sprigs. Blend the oil with the tomato paste and grated nutmeg. Pour this over the fish. Set aside in a cool place for several hours.

HERRING IN OIL III

1 lb. herring (salted), 1/3 cup olive oil, parsley sprigs, 5 oz. peppers, 5 oz. tomatoes, pepper, thyme and tarragon to taste

Prepare the herring (as for Herring in Oil I). Clean and rinse the peppers and bake them slightly. Peel, grind them and combine with oil, seasoning and chopped parsley sprigs. Wash the tomatoes, scald them and remove skins. Cut tomatoes into pieces. Arrange the herring in a jar in layers together with the tomatoes and cover with oil. Set aside in a cool place for several hours.

HERRING IN SOUR CREAM

1 lb. herring (salted), 2/3 cup sour cream, 1 2/3 oz. grated horseradish, 1 2/3 oz. raisins, parsley sprigs, hard-boiled egg yolk, salt, sugar, pepper and lemon juice to taste

Prepare the herring (as for Herring in Oil I). Combine sour cream with horseradish, rinsed raisins, chopped parsley sprigs and egg yolk that has beeen forced through a strainer. Season to taste. Arrange the herring on a platter and pour the sour cream over them.

HERRING GIPSY STYLE

1 lb. herring (salted), 5 oz. onions, 3 1/2 oz. gherkins, parsley sprigs, 3 1/2 oz. ketchup, 3 tablespoons olive oil, sugar, garlic and prepared mustard to taste

Prepare the herring (as for Herring in Oil I). Peel and rinse the onions. Cut them into half-slices. Cut the gherkins into thin strips and combine with onions, chopped parsley sprigs, ketchup, oil and seasoning. Arrange the herring in a jar and cover with the sauce. Set aside in a cool place for several hours.

GIŻYCKO HERRING

1 lb. herring (salted), 5 oz. apples, 5 oz. cucumbers, 1 2/3 oz. plums, 2/3 cup sour cream, parsley sprigs, salt, pepper, sugar and lemon juice to taste

Prepare the herring (as for Herring in Oil I). Wash and peel the apples and cucumbers and slice them into thin strips together with the plums. Combine with the sour cream and chopped parsley sprigs. Season to taste. Arrange the herring on a platter and pour the sauce over them.

GDAŃSK HERRING

1 lb. herring (salted), 2 cups milk, 5 oz. apples, 2/3 cup dry white wine, 2 egg yolks, salt, sugar and nutmeg to taste

Prepare the herring (as for Herring in Oil I) and soak them in milk. Wash, peel and slice the apples in half, removing the cores. Grate them

coarsely and sprinkle with lemon juice. Bring the wine to a boil and add gradually the egg yolks, which have been blended with the seasoning, stirring quickly with an egg-whisk. Combine with the apples and season to taste. Form the herring into rolls. Arrange on a platter and pour the sauce over them.

ROLLMOPS

1 lb. herring (salted), 3 1/2 oz. onions, 2 2/3 oz. soured cucumbers, 2 2/3 oz. cooked carrots, parsley sprigs, 2/3 cup water, 1/3 cup vinegar, 1 tablespoon olive oil, sugar, prepared mustard and allspice to taste

Prepare the herring (as for Herring in Oil I). Peel and rinse the onions and slice into thin strips together with the carrots and peeled cucumbers. Spread mustard over the herring fillets. Sprinkle with chopped parsley sprigs. Spread the onions, carrots and cucumbers over this and form into a roll. Fasten with a toothpick. Bring the water and vinegar with seasoning to a boil. Allow to cool and pour over the herring in a jar. Sprinkle with the oil and set aside in a cool place for 48 hours.

FISH SALAD

1/2 lb. cooked fish, 5 oz. potatoes (cooked), 3 1/2 oz. dill pickles, 5 oz. apples, 3 1/2 oz. mayonnaise, 3 tablespoons dry white wine, parsley sprigs, salt, pepper and lemon juice to taste

Wash and peel the apples. Cut them into halves and remove the cores. Dice the apples together with potatoes, fish and pickles. Combine with mayonnaise, wine and chopped parsley sprigs. Season to taste. Place in a glass salad bowl and garnish.

LOBSTER SALAD

10—15 lobsters, 7 oz. potatoes (cooked), 2 hard-boiled eggs, parsley sprigs, fresh dill, 3 tablespoons olive oil, salt, pepper, prepared mustard and lemon juice to taste

Cook the lobsters (as in Poached Lobsters, q.v.). Remove meat from the tails and claws. Dice the potatoes and eggs. Combine with the lobsters, oil and chopped parsley sprigs. Season to taste. Place in a glass salad bowl and garnish.

EGG SALAD

4 hard-boiled eggs, 5 oz. potatoes (cooked), 2 2/3 oz. onions, parsley sprigs, 3 tablespoons olive oil, salt and pepper to taste

Peel, rinse and dice the onions together with potatoes and eggs. Combine with chopped parsley sprigs and olive oil. Season to taste. Transfer to a glass salad bowl and garnish.

WHITE BEAN SALAD

1/2 lb. white beans, 5—7 oz. onions (green or shallot), fat for frying, 2—2 2/3 oz. ketchup, parsley sprigs, salt, pepper and sugar to taste

Sort the beans, rinse them and cover with cold water. Bring to a boil and set aside for 2 hours. Cook them in the same water and drain. Peel and rinse the onions. Cut them into pieces and fry them. Combine with the beans, ketchup and chopped parsley sprigs. Season to taste. Place in a glass salad bowl and garnish.

GREEN PEA SALAD

3/4 lb. canned peas, 2 hard-boiled eggs, can of sardines, 3 1/2 oz. mayonnaise, 3 tablespoons sour cream, parsley sprigs, salt and pepper to taste

Dice the eggs and combine with the peas, crumbled sardines, mayonnaise, sour cream and chopped parsley sprigs. Season to taste. Place in a glass salad bowl and garnish.

CAULIFLOWER SALAD

1 1/4 lb. cauliflowers, 2/3 cup whipping cream, 2 hard-boiled eggs, 1 2/3 oz. chives, 1 2/3 oz. grated horseradish, salt, pepper, sugar and lemon juice to taste

Clean the cauliflower and rinse it in slightly salted water. Add sugar to boiling salted water and place the cauliflower in this. Cook it, then allow to cool. Divide into rosettes. Dice the eggs and combine with the cauliflower, finely chopped chives, horseradish and part of the whipped cream. Season to taste and divide into portions. Place the remaining whipped cream on top and garnish.

CARROT SALAD

1 1/4 lb. carrots, milk, 5 oz. apples, 3 1/2 oz. ketchup, 5 oz. lemons, 5 oz. oranges, 1 2/3 oz. mayonnaise, salt, pepper, sugar and lemon juice to taste

Wash, peel and rinse the carrots. Cover with boiling salted water with milk and cook, covered. Wash, peel and rinse the apples. Cut them in half, removing the cores. Wash, scald and peel the lemons and oranges. Dice them together with apples and carrots. Combine with mayonnaise and season to taste. Place in a glass salad bowl. Pour ketchup over the mixture and garnish.

TOMATO SALAD I

3/4 lb. tomatoes, 2/3 cup sour cream, 2 1/2 oz. radishes, 1 2/3 oz. chives, salt and pepper to taste

Wash the tomatoes and cut them into pieces. Clean and rinse the radishes. Cut them into half-slices. Combine with tomatoes, sour cream and chopped chives. Season to taste. Place in a glass salad bowl and garnish.

TOMATO SALAD II

3/4 lb. tomatoes, 3 1/2 oz. mayonnaise, 3 tablespoons dry white wine, 1 2/3 oz. canned peas, 1 2/3 oz. lobster tails, 1 oz. almonds, salt and pepper to taste

Blanch and chop the almonds. Wash and scald the tomatoes, then remove the skins. Cut into pieces and combine with almonds, peas, lobster tails, mayonnaise and wine. Season to taste. Place in a glass salad bowl and garnish.

CELERIAC SALAD

1 lb. celeriac, milk, 3 tablespoons olive oil, 5 oz. mushrooms, 2/3 oz. capers, fresh dill, parsley sprigs, salt, pepper and lemon juice to taste

Scrub the celeriac with a brush under running water. Peel and rinse it. Cover with boiling salted water with milk and cook, covered. When done allow to cool and dice. Clean and rinse the mushrooms, then cut them into thin strips. Fry them and combine with the celeriac, remaining oil, rinsed capers and chopped dill and parsley. Season to taste. Place in a glass salad bowl and garnish.

POTATO SALAD I

3/4 lb. potatoes, 2 hard-boiled eggs, 1 2/3 oz. herring fillets, 3 1/2 oz. mayonnaise, 3 tablespoons sour cream, 1 2/3 oz. chives, parsley sprigs, salt and pepper to taste

Wash, peel and rinse the potatoes. Cover them three quarters with boiling salted water. Cook covered, then drain. Allow remaining water to evaporate and the potatoes to cool. Dice them along with the herring fillets and eggs. Combine with mayonnaise, sour cream and finely chopped chives and parsley. Season to taste. Place in a glass salad bowl and garnish.

POTATO SALAD II

3/4 lb. potatoes, 2—2 2/3 oz. dill pickles, 3 1/2 oz. apples, 1 2/3 oz. radishes, 3 tablespoons olive oil, 1 2/3 oz. chives, salt and pepper to taste

Wash, peel and rinse the potatoes. Cover them three quarters with boiling salted water. Cook covered, then drain. Allow remaining water to evaporate and the potatoes to cool. Wash, peel and cut the apples in half, removing the cores. Dice them along with the potatoes and pickles. Combine with olive oil, chopped chives and cleaned radishes cut into half-slices. Season to taste. Place in a glass salad bowl and garnish.

HOT HORS D'OEUVRES

WROCŁAW CROUTONS

4 small round white rolls, 5 oz. mushrooms, egg yolk, 1 1/3 oz. ketchup, fat for frying, 1 1/3 oz. hard cheese, salt and pepper to taste

Cut off the tops from the rolls and scrape out the inside. Clean and rinse the mushrooms and cut them into thin strips, then fry them. Combine with the egg yolk and ketchup. Season and stuff the rolls with this. Add grated cheese and bake. Serve covered with the tops.

BRAINS ON TOAST

7 oz. long French bread, fat for frying, 1/2 lb. brains, 1 2/3 oz. onions, egg, parsley sprigs, 1 2/3 oz. hard cheese, breadcrumbs, salt and pepper to taste

Cut off the crust from the bread and cut into 1/4 in. slices. Spread butter on one side. Fry the bread, placing the buttered side on the frying pan. Remove the outer membrane from the brains, rinse and chop finely. Peel, rinse and dice the onions, then fry them. Add the brains and continue frying for several minutes, stirring constantly. Add the egg and

continue frying until the mixture is set, then season. Spread this mixture on the toast. Sprinkle with chopped parsley sprigs, grated cheese and browned breadcrumbs mixed with melted butter. Bake the slices of toast.

SARDINES ON TOAST

1/2 lb. long French bread, fat for frying, 1—2 cans of sardines, 2—2 2/3 oz. hard cheese, tomatoes, ketchup, salt and pepper to taste

Cut off the crust from the bread and cut into 1/4 in. slices. Spread butter on one side. Fry the bread, placing the buttered side on the frying pan. Spread sardines and tomato pieces on the toast. Sprinkle with grated cheese and bake.

FRANKFURTERS ON TOAST

1/2 lb. long French bread, fat for frying, thin frankfurters, 2—2 2/3 oz. ketchup, 2—3 egg whites, salt and pepper to taste

Cut off the crust from the bread and cut into 1/4 in. slices. Spread butter on one side. Fry the bread, placing the buttered side on the frying pan. Remove covering, if any, from the frankfurters and cut them into pieces the size of the toast. Place them on the toast. Pour ketchup over this and spread beaten egg whites on top, then bake.

LIVER ON TOAST

1/2 lb. long French bread, fat for frying, 1/2 lb. chicken livers, 1 2/3 oz. onions, hard-boiled egg, 2—2 2/3 oz. hard cheese, 1 oz. almonds, salt and pepper

Cut off the crust from the bread and cut into 1/4 in. slices. Spread butter on one side. Fry the bread, placing the buttered side on the frying pan. Blanch the almonds. Peel, rinse and dice the onions, then fry them. Add the livers and fry the mixture, stirring constantly. Allow to cool and mince

twice along with the egg. Season the mixture and spread it on the toast. Top with almonds and sprinkle with grated cheese, then bake.

CASTELLAN'S TOAST

1/2 lb. long French bread, fat for frying, baked chicken, 1 2/3 oz. ketchup, 1 2/3 oz. walnut meats, salt and pepper to taste

Cut off the crust from the bread and cut into 1/4 in. slices. Spread butter on one side. Fry the bread, placing the buttered side on the frying pan. Blanch and grind the walnuts. Cut the chicken meat into pieces the size of the slices of toast. Place the pieces on the toast. Pour ketchup over this, sprinkle with seasoning and nuts, then bake.

CRACOW SOAKED PORK LOIN

1 lb. pork loin, fat for frying, 1/3 oz. flour, 1/2 lb. onions, 8 diagonal slices of toasted French bread, salt, pepper, caraway seed and ketchup to taste

Wash the meat and separate from the bones. Rub in the seasoning and set aside in a cool place for 24 hours. Sprinkle with flour and brown in hot fat together with the bones. Sprinkle with water and simmer covered over low heat. Take out the meat when tender and cut into thin strips. Remove any bones, slice the meat, add it to the sauce and season. Peel, rinse and slice the onions, cutting the slices in half. Fry them. Dip the toast in the sauce for one minute. Take them out and arrange them on a platter alternately with strips of the pork loin. Sprinkle with the sauce and surround with the onions. Pour the ketchup over this and serve at once.

PORK À LA TRIPE

1—1 1/4 lb. boneless pork, 2/3 oz. fat for frying, 3 1/2 oz. onions, 5 oz. celeriac, 3 1/2 oz. carrots, 5 oz. parsley root, 2/3 oz. flour, 3 1/2 oz.

hard cheese, salt, pepper, marjoram, seasoning and ground pepper to taste

Wash the meat and cut into thin strips. Dredge with part of the flour and brown in hot fat. Sprinkle with water and simmer covered over low heat. Wash, peel and rinse the vegetables and cut them into thin strips. Fry them slightly and add to the meat towards the end of cooking. Heat the fat and blend it with the remaining flour. Brown it lightly and combine with the meat. Cook together with the seasoning and correct if necessary. Place in buttered coquilles and sprinkle with grated cheese, then bake.

ADMIRAL'S PORK

1/2 lb. boneless pork, 1/2 lb. boneless veal, 3 1/2 oz. smoked ham, 5 oz. mushrooms, 2/3 oz. flour, 2/3 cup sour cream, 3 1/2 oz. hard cheese, fat for frying, salt, pepper and seasoning to taste

Clean, rinse the mushrooms and cut them into thin strips together with the pork, veal and ham. Sprinkle with flour and seasoning and brown in hot fat. Sprinkle with water and simmer covered over low heat. Towards the end pour in cream blended with the remaining flour. Bring to a boil and season to taste. Place in buttered coquilles and sprinkle with grated cheese, then bake.

BEEFSTEAK POLISH STYLE

3/4 lb. boneless beef or beef fillet, 5 oz. olive oil, 1 2/3 oz. ketchup, 4 eggs, 3 1/2 oz. hard cheese, fat for frying, salt and pepper to taste

Wash the meat, mince it and combine with the oil and ketchup, then season. Form into round beefsteaks 3/4 in. thick. Place these in very hot fat and fry on both sides, leaving the inside rare. Wash the eggs and break them onto a special egg pan, ready-buttered. Fry the eggs and place them on the beefsteaks. Sprinkle with grated cheese and bake in a hot oven just until the cheese melts. Serve at once.

BEEF À LA ROBERT

1 lb. boneless beef (shoulder, rump, round), fat for frying, 2/3 oz. flour, 1/2 lb. onions (green or shallot), dry red wine, 1 2/3 oz. almonds, parsley sprigs, salt, pepper, bay leaf, allspice, garlic, cloves and thyme to taste

Wash, trim and dice the meat. Sprinkle with seasoning and flour and brown in very hot fat. Sprinkle with water and simmer covered over low heat. Blanch the almonds. Peel, rinse and chop the onions, then fry them. Add them to the meat towards the end of cooking together with the wine, almonds, seasoning and the remaining flour blended with a small amount of cold water. Season to taste.

HUNTER'S BEEF

1 lb. boneless beef (shoulder, rump, round), fat for frying, 2/3 oz. flour, 3 1/2 oz. dill pickles, 5 oz. onions, 1/3 cup sour cream, 2—3 dried cèpe mushrooms, 1/3 cup dry white wine, salt, pepper and ground paprika to taste

Wash, trim and dice the meat. Sprinkle with seasoning and flour and brown in very hot fat. Sprinkle with water and wine. Simmer covered over low heat. Peel, rinse and dice the onions together with the pickles. Fry this lightly and add to the meat towards the end of cooking, together with mushrooms that have been soaked and cut into thin strips. Combine cream with the remaining flour and pour into the meat. Simmer this for a while and season to taste.

Sauces

COLD SAUCES

MAYONNAISE SAUCE

1 cup olive oil, 1—2 egg yolks, salt, pepper, prepared mustard and lemon juice to taste

Have all ingredients at room temperature. Put egg yolks in a bowl, add salt and mustard. Add the oil in a thin drizzle, stirring constantly. When the sauce thickens, add the lemon juice alternately with the oil, stirring constantly. When the sauce is ready, season it to taste.

Note: A teaspoonful of boiled water (cold or hot) may be added while stirring to avoid curdling.

BRISTOL SAUCE

1/2 lb. mayonnaise sauce, 3 tablespoons sour cream, 1 1/3 oz. lobster butter, 1 2/3 oz. soured cucumbers, 1 2/3 oz. tomatoes, 2/3 oz. capers, parsley sprigs, salt, pepper and sugar to taste

Peel and dice the soured cucumbers. Wash, scald and peel the tomatoes. Cut them into pieces and combine with the mayonnaise, sour cream, cucumbers, rinsed capers, chopped parsley sprigs and melted butter. Season to taste. Serve with poultry or game.

POLONIA SAUCE

1/2 lb. mayonnaise sauce, 7 oz. apples, 3 tablespoons dry white wine, 1 2/3 oz. grated horseradish, lemon and orange rind, salt, sugar and lemon juice to taste

Wash and peel the apples. Cut them in half and remove the cores. Grate them coarsely and combine with mayonnaise, wine, horseradish and grated rinds. Season to taste. Serve with poultry and game.

CAVIAR SAUCE

1/2 lb. mayonnaise sauce, 1 1/2 tablespoons dry white wine, 2/3 oz. caviar, 5 oz. grapes, salt, pepper, sugar and lemon juice to taste

Sort the grapes. Rinse and force them through a strainer. Combine with mayonnaise, wine and caviar. Season to taste. Serve with poultry and game.

GENERAL'S SAUCE

1/2 lb. mayonnaise sauce, 1 1/2 tablespoons Tokay wine, 1 1/3 tablespoons cognac, 7 oz. apples, 1 2/3 oz. raisins, 1 1/3 oz. tomato paste, salt, pepper, sugar and lemon juice

Wash and peel the apples. Cut them in half and remove the cores. Grate them coarsely and fry with sugar until translucent, then cool. Combine with mayonnaise, wine, tomato paste and raisins that have been soaked in cognac. Season to taste. Serve with poultry and game.

CHAMBER SAUCE

1/2 lb. mayonnaise sauce, 3 tablespoons sour cream, 1 oz. canned peas, 3 1/2 oz. onions, 5 oz. apples, 1 1/3 oz. canned peppers, 1 2/3 oz. cooked celeriac, parsley sprigs, salt, pepper and lemon juice to taste

Peel, rinse, dice and scald the onions. Strain and drain them. Wash and peel the apples. Cut in half and remove the cores. Grate coarsely together with celeriac. Combine with onions, mayonnaise, sour cream, chopped parsley sprigs, canned peas and thin strips of peppers. Season to taste. Serve with cold meats.

OLD FASHIONED SAUCE

1/2 lb. mayonnaise sauce, 3 tablespoons sour cream, hard-boiled egg, 3 1/2 oz. Roquefort cheese, salt and pepper to taste

Combine mayonnaise with sour cream, grated cheese and chopped egg. Season to taste.

GARLIC SAUCE

1/2 lb. mayonnaise sauce, 2—3 garlic bulbs, 3·1/2 oz. canned peppers, parsley sprigs, butter, salt and pepper to taste

Divide the garlic into cloves. Peel and scald it, then fry in butter. Combine with minced peppers, mayonnaise and chopped parsley sprigs. Season to taste. Serve with vegetables and eggs.

GREEN SAUCE

1/2 lb. mayonnaise sauce, 3 tablespoons sour cream, 5 oz. spinach, 2/3 oz. butter, 2/3 oz. capers, parsley sprigs, salt, pepper and garlic to taste

Sort the spinach. Rinse and scald it, then strain and drain it. Mash it and fry in butter. Cool and combine with mayonnaise, sour cream and chopped parsley sprigs. Season to taste. Serve with meat dishes.

DOMINICAN SAUCE

1/2 lb. mayonnaise sauce, 3 tablespoons sour cream, 1 oz. tomato paste, 1 2/3 oz. canned sardines, 1 2/3 oz. canned peas, parsley sprigs, salt, pepper, sugar, seasoning and lemon juice to taste

Combine mayonnaise with sour cream, tomato paste, crumbled sardines, peas and chopped parsley sprigs. Season to taste. Serve with meat.

TARTARE SAUCE

1/2 lb. mayonnaise sauce, 3 tablespoons sour cream, 2—2 2/3 oz. soured cucumbers, 1 1/3 oz. marinated mushrooms, 2/3 oz. capers, parsley sprigs, salt, pepper, seasoning, sugar and prepared mustard to taste

Peel the soured cucumbers and dice them finely together with the mushrooms. Combine with mayonnaise, sour cream, rinsed capers and chopped parsley sprigs. Season to taste. Serve with meat dishes, vegetables, fish and eggs.

KASHUBIAN SAUCE

1/2 lb. mayonnaise sauce, 3 tablespoons sour cream, 1 2/3 oz. herring fillets, hard-boiled egg, 1 1/3 oz. radishes, chives, salt, pepper and seasoning to taste

Clean, rinse and grate the radishes coarsely. Combine with mayonnaise, sour cream, chopped egg, and finely crumbled fillets. Season to taste. Serve with tomatoes or stuffed cucumbers.

RÉMOULADE

1/2 lb. mayonnaise sauce, 3 tablespoons sour cream, chives, hard-boiled egg, salt, pepper, prepared mustard and seasoning to taste

Chop the chives and egg finely. Combine with mayonnaise and sour cream. Season to taste. Serve with vegetables.

HERRING SAUCE

1/2 lb. mayonnaise sauce, 3 tablespoons sour cream, 5 oz. apples, 2 2/3 oz. herring fillets, parsley sprigs, salt, pepper and lemon juice to taste

Wash and peel the apples. Cut them in half, removing the cores. Grate them coarsely and combine with finely chopped fillets, chopped parsley sprigs, sour cream and mayonnaise. Season to taste. Serve with eggs.

SARDINE SAUCE

1/2 lb. mayonnaise sauce, 3 tablespoons sour cream, can of sardines, 1 1/3 oz. almonds, 1 oz. walnut meats, salt, pepper and lemon juice to taste

Blanch the almonds and walnuts, then chop them. Combine with mayonnaise, sour cream and crumbled sardines. Season this. Serve with fish and eggs.

ZENITH SAUCE

1/2 lb. mayonnaise sauce, 2 tablespoons sour cream, 1 1/3 oz. marinated mushrooms, 3 1/2 oz. canned tuna, 2/3 oz. capers, 2/3 oz. pitted olives, salt, pepper and lemon juice to taste

Chop the mushrooms and combine them with crumbled tuna, rinsed capers, olives, mayonnaise and sour cream, then season. Serve with eggs.

POLISH SAUCE

1/2 cup concentrated orange juice, 1/2 cup concentrated lemon juice, 1 2/3 oz. grated horseradish, salt, pepper, sugar and prepared mustard to taste

Combine orange juice with lemon juice and horseradish, then season. Serve with poultry and game.

GREAT POLAND SAUCE

9 1/2 oz. prunes, 3 1/2 oz. ketchup, honey, salt, pepper and lemon juice to taste

Wash the prunes, soak and cook them. Force them through a strainer and combine with ketchup. Season to taste. Serve with poultry and game.

SEYM SAUCE

1 cup whipping cream, 3 1/2 oz. cranberry preserves, 1 2/3 oz. grated horseradish, 5 oz. apples, 3 tablespoons dry white wine, lemon juice to taste

Wash, peel and cut the apples in half, removing the cores. Grate them coarsely and combine with cranberries and wine. Simmer for several minutes. Allow to cool and blend with whipped cream and horseradish. Season to taste. Serve with poultry and game.

GIPSY SAUCE

7 oz. ketchup, 1 2/3 oz. herring fillets, 1 1/2 tablespoons olive oil, 2 2/3 oz. onions, 1 2/3 oz. dill pickles, salt, pepper and prepared mustard to taste

Peel, rinse and chop the onions finely, together with the pickles and fillets. Combine with olive oil and ketchup. Season to taste. Serve with eggs.

CAPTAIN'S SAUCE

3/4 lb. canned peppers, 3 tablespoons dry red wine, parsley sprigs, salt, pepper, sugar and prepared mustard to taste

Mash the peppers and combine with wine, chopped parsley sprigs and seasoning. Serve with meat, fish, vegetables and eggs.

RATHAUS SAUCE

5 oz. ketchup, 5 oz. onions, 1 1/3 tablespoons olive oil, parsley sprigs, salt and pepper to taste

Peel, rinse and dice the onions finely. Combine with ketchup, olive oil and chopped parsley sprigs, then season. Serve with fish and eggs.

MARSHAL'S SAUCE

1/2 lb. canned peppers, 5 oz. ketchup, salt, pepper, sugar, garlic and olive oil

Combine the ketchup with mashed peppers, garlic and olive oil, then season. Serve with meat, fish and eggs.

RASCAL'S SAUCE

5 oz. ketchup, 3 1/2 oz. canned tuna, 1 2/3 oz. canned peas, parsley sprigs, salt, pepper and lemon juice to taste

Combine ketchup with crumbled tuna, peas and chopped parsley sprigs. Season to taste. Serve with eggs, sauted fish.

HOT SAUCES

WROCŁAW SAUCE

1 1/2 cups poultry stock, 3 tablespoons cream, 2—2 2/3 oz. cucumbers, 2—2 2/3 oz. cooked scooped out carrot balls, 1 oz. flour, 1 oz. fat for frying, fresh dill, salt, pepper, sugar and lemon juice to taste

Peel and rinse the cucumber, then cut it in half lengthwise. Remove the seeds and grate it coarsely. Melt the fat and combine with the flour. Fry it without browning and blend with a little of the cold broth, stirring briskly with an egg-whisk. Bring to a boil, add the cucumber and cook around 10 minutes over low heat, stirring often. Towards the end add sour cream and carrots. Combine the sauce with chopped dill. Season to taste. Serve with poultry and game.

AGA SAUCE

1 1/4 cups poultry stock, 3 tablespoons dry white wine, 3 tablespoons pan drippings from poultry roast, 1 oz. whole-wheat bread, fat for the bread, 1 1/3 oz. ham, 1 oz. fat for frying, 1 oz. flour, parsley sprigs, salt, pepper, ground paprika and seasoning to taste

Dice the bread and fry it in the fat, adding paprika towards the end. Heat fat and blend with flour. Fry without browning and blend with a little of the cold broth, stirring briskly with an egg-whisk. Bring to a boil and add the pan drippings. Cook for around 10 minutes over low heat, stirring constantly. Combine the sauce with wine, thin strips of ham and bread. Bring to a boil and add chopped parsley sprigs. Season to taste. Serve with poultry and game.

MANAGER'S SAUCE

1 1/2 cups poultry stock, 3 1/2 oz. cucumbers, 3 tablespoons sour cream, 1 2/3 oz. tomatoes, 1 1/3 oz. canned peppers, 2/3 oz. capers, 1 oz. butter, 1 oz. flour, fresh dill, salt, pepper, sugar and curry powder to taste

Wash and peel the cucumbers. Wash, scald and peel the tomatoes. Dice them together with the peppers and seeded cucumbers. Heat the fat and blend with the flour. Fry it without browning and blend with a little of the cold broth, stirring quickly with an egg-whisk. Bring to a boil and cook for around 10 minutes over low heat, stirring often. Towards the end add tomatoes, cucumbers, peppers, rinsed capers and sour cream. Combine the sauce with chopped dill. Season to taste. Serve with poultry and game.

SAUCE À LA SOBIESKI

1 1/2 cups poultry stock, 3 tablespoons sour cream, 2—2 2/3 oz. mushrooms, fat for mushrooms, 1 2/3 oz. cooked cauliflower, 1 oz.

canned peas, 1 oz. fat for frying, 1 oz. flour, fresh dill, salt, pepper, nut-meg and seasoning to taste

Clean, rinse and chop the mushrooms finely, then fry them. Heat the fat and blend it with the flour. Fry it without browning and blend with a little of the cold broth, stirring briskly with an egg-whisk. Add the mush-rooms and cook for around 10 minutes over low heat, stirring often. To-wards the end add peas, crumbled cauliflower and sour cream. Combine the sauce with chopped dill and season to taste. Serve with poultry and game.

OLD POLISH SAUCE

1 1/2 cups poultry stock, 3 tablespoons sour cream, 3 1/2 oz. tomatoes, 1 2/3 oz. grated horseradish, 1 oz. fat for frying, 1 oz. flour, parsley sprigs, salt, pepper, sugar, lemon juice and lemon rind to taste

Wash, scald and peel the tomatoes, then dice them. Heat the fat and blend with the flour. Fry it without browning and blend with a little of the cold broth, stirring briskly with an egg-whisk. Bring to a boil and cook for around 10 minutes over low heat, stirring often. Towards the end add tomatoes, horseradish and sour cream. Blend the sauce with chopped parsley sprigs. Season to taste. Serve with poultry and game.

ROYAL SAUCE

1 1/4 cups poultry stock, 1/3 cup dry white wine, 2—2 2/3 oz. mush-rooms, 1 2/3 oz. lobster tails, 1 2/3 oz. dill pickles, fat for mushrooms, 1 oz. fat, 1 oz. flour, fresh dill, salt, pepper and nutmeg to taste

Clean, rinse and dice the mushrooms finely, then fry them. Heat the fat and blend it with the flour. Fry it without browning and blend with a little of the cold broth, stirring briskly with an egg-whisk. Bring to a boil and cook for around 10 minutes over low heat, stirring often. Cut the pickles into thin strips. Add them to the sauce towards the end of cooking together with the lobster tails, mushrooms and wine. Combine the sauce with chopped dill. Season to taste. Serve with poultry and game.

SOUR CREAM SAUCE

1 cup poultry stock, 2/3 cup sour cream, 1 oz. fat for frying, 1 oz. flour, salt, pepper and ginger to taste

Heat the fat and blend it with the flour. Fry it without browning and blend with a little of the cold stock, stirring briskly with an egg-whisk. Bring to a boil and cook for around 10 minutes over low heat, stirring often. Towards the end add sour cream. Season to taste. Serve with poultry and game.

MUSHROOM SAUCE

1 1/4 cups poultry stock, 1/3 cup sour cream, 5—7 oz. mushrooms, fat for mushrooms, egg yolk, 1 oz. fat for frying, 1 oz. flour, parsley sprigs, salt, pepper and seasoning to taste

Clean, rinse and chop the mushrooms finely, then fry them. Heat the fat and blend it with the flour. Fry this without browning and blend with a little of the cold stock, stirring briskly with an egg-whisk. Bring to a boil and cook for around 10 minutes, stirring often. Towards the end add mushrooms. Blend sour cream with egg yolk and pour it slowly into the slightly cooled sauce, stirring briskly with an egg-whisk. Combine with chopped parsley sprigs. Season to taste. Serve with poultry and game.

GHERKIN SAUCE

1 1/2 cups poultry stock, 3 tablespoons dry white wine, 3 1/2 oz. gherkins, 2/3 oz. capers, 1 1/3 oz. walnut meats, 1 oz. fat for frying, 1 oz. flour, parsley sprigs, salt, sugar and tarragon to taste

Heat the fat and blend it with the flour. Fry without browning and blend with a little of the cold stock, stirring briskly with an egg-whisk. Bring to a boil. Add rinsed capers and cook for around 10 minutes over low heat, stirring often. Blanch the walnuts, chop them and add to the sauce towards the end of cooking together with thin strips of gherkins and the wine. Combine the sauce with chopped parsley sprigs. Season to taste. Serve with poultry and game.

SPICY SAUCE

1 1/4 cups poultry stock, 1/3 cup sour cream, 3 1/2 oz. soured cucumbers, 1 2/3 oz. marinated mushrooms, 2/3 oz. capers, fat for cucumbers, 1 oz. fat for frying, 1 oz. flour, parsley sprigs, salt, sugar, pepper, nutmeg and curry powder to taste

Peel the cucumbers, remove the seeds and cut into strips. Add the fat and sprinkle with water, then simmer over low heat. Heat the fat and blend it with flour. Fry without browning and blend with a little of the cold stock, stirring briskly with an egg-whisk. Bring to a boil and cook for around 10 minutes over low heat, stirring often. Towards the end add the cucumbers, rinsed capers, sliced mushrooms and the sour cream. Combine the sauce with chopped parsley sprigs. Season to taste. Serve with poultry and game.

POLISH GREY SAUCE

1 1/2 cups poultry stock, 3 tablespoons dry red wine, 1 2/3 oz. prunes, 1 oz. gingerbread, 1 1/3 oz. raisins, 1 oz. almonds, 1 oz. fat for frying, 1 oz. flour, caramel, syrup, salt, pepper, honey, allspice, cloves and lemon juice to taste

Wash the prunes, soak them, cook and force through a strainer. Blanch the almonds. Heat the fat and blend it with the flour. Fry without browning and blend with a little of the cold stock, stirring briskly with an egg-whisk. Bring to a boil and add the rinsed raisins. Cook over low heat for around 10 minutes, stirring often. Towards the end add the wine, prune purée, chopped alomnds, grated gingerbread, honey and caramel syrup. Season to taste. Serve with poultry and game.

HETMAN'S SAUCE

1 1/2 cups poultry stock, 3 tablespoons dry white wine, 2—2 2/3 oz. thin frankfurters, 1 2/3 oz. smoked ham, 1 2/3 oz. onions, 1 1/3 fat for frying, 1 oz. flour, parsley sprigs, salt, pepper, nutmeg and seasoning to taste

Peel, rinse and chop the onions, then fry them. Combine with the flour. Brown it and blend with a little of the cold stock, stirring briskly with an egg-whisk. Bring to a boil and cook for around 10 minutes over low heat. Remove the skins, if any, from the franfkurters. Cut into half-slices. Add these to the sauce towards the end of cooking together with thin strips of ham. Combine the sauce with chopped parsley sprigs. Season to taste. Serve with poultry and game.

DILL SAUCE

1 1/4 cups stock from bones or meat, 1/3 cup sour cream, egg yolk, fresh dill, 1 oz. fat for frying, 1 oz. flour, salt, pepper and seasoning to taste

Heat the fat and blend with the flour. Fry without browning and blend with a little of the cold stock, stirring briskly with an egg-whisk. Bring to a boil and cook for around 10 minutes over low heat, stirring often. Towards the end add sour cream. Combine the sauce with egg yolk and chopped dill. Season to taste. Serve with meat dishes.

PEPPER SAUCE

1 1/4 cups stock from bones or meat, 1/3 cup dry red wine, 2 2/3 oz. onions, 1 1/3 oz. fat for frying, 1 oz. flour, 1 2/3 oz. walnut meats, salt and pepper to taste

Peel, rinse and dice the onions finely. Fry them, then add the flour. Fry without browning and blend with a little of the cold stock, stirring briskly with an egg-whisk. Bring to a boil and cook for around 10 minutes over low heat, stirring often. Towards the end add the wine. Blanch the nuts and grind them. Force the sauce through a strainer and combine with the nuts. Season to taste. Serve with meat dishes.

CHIVE SAUCE

1 1/4 cups stock from bones or meat, 1/3 cup sour cream, hard-boiled egg, chives, 1 oz. fat for frying, 1 oz. flour, salt to taste

Heat the fat and blend it with the flour. Fry it without browning and blend with a little of the cold stock, stirring briskly with an egg-whisk. Bring to a boil and cook for around 10 minutes over low heat, stirring often. Combine the sauce with sour cream and bring to a boil. Combine with ground egg and chopped chives, then season. Serve with meat dishes.

HORSERADISH SAUCE

1 1/4 cups stock from bones or meat, 1/3 cup sour cream, 3 1/2 oz. stewed peaches, 1 oz. walnut meats, 2—2 2/3 oz. grated horseradish, 1 oz. fat for frying, 1 oz. flour, salt, sugar, lemon juice and lemon rind to taste

Blanch the nuts and grind them. Heat the fat and blend it with the flour. Fry it without browning and blend with a little of the cold stock, stirring briskly with an egg-whisk. Bring to a boil and cook for around 10 minutes over low heat, stirring often. Towards the end add the horseradish, peach purée, grated lemon rind and nuts. Season to taste. Serve with meat dishes.

MUSTARD SAUCE

1 1/3 cups stock from bones or meat, 3 tablespoons sour cream, 2 2/3 oz. onions, 1 1/3 oz. fat for frying, 1 2/3 oz. flour, 1 2/3 oz. prepared mustard, salt and sugar to taste

Peel, rinse and chop the onions finely. Fry them and add the flour. Brown this lightly and blend with a little of the cold stock, stirring briskly with an egg-whisk. Bring to a boil and cook for around 10 minutes over low heat, stirring often. Force the sauce through a strainer and combine with sour cream and mustard. Season to taste. Serve with meat dishes.

SAUCE À LA RADZIWIŁŁ

1 1/3 cups stock from bones or meat, 3 tablespoons dry red wine, 3 1/2 oz. prunes, 1 2/3 oz. almonds, 2—2 2/3 oz. smoked bacon, 2 2/3 oz. onions, 1 oz. flour, salt, pepper, sugar and lemon juice to taste

Blanch the almonds. Wash the prunes, soak them, cook and force through a strainer. Peel, rinse and chop the onions finely. Dice the bacon and partly render down the fat. Add the onions and fry this. Combine with the flour and fry, browning lightly. Blend with a little of the cold stock, stirring briskly with an egg-whisk. Bring to a boil and cook for around 10 minutes over low heat. Towards the end add wine, almonds and prune purée. Season to taste. Serve with meat dishes.

TOMATO SAUCE

1 1/4 cups stock from bones or meat, 1/3 cup sour cream, 1 1/3 oz. tomato paste, fat for the paste, 1 oz. fat for frying, 1 oz. flour, parsley sprigs, salt, pepper and ground paprika to taste

Simmer the tomato paste, stirring constantly. Heat the fat and blend it with the flour. Fry this without browning and blend with a little of the cold stock, stirring briskly with an egg-whisk. Bring to a boil and cook for around 10 minutes, stirring often. Towards the end add tomato paste and sour cream. Combine the sauce with chopped parsley sprigs. Season to taste. Serve with meat dishes.

HUNTER'S SAUCE

1 1/3 cups stock from bones or meat, 3 tablespoons dry red wine, 1/3— 2/3 oz. dried cèpe mushrooms, 1 1/3 oz. smoked ham, 2/3 oz. dry sau-

*sage, 2 2/3 oz. onions (green or shallot), fat for onions, 1 2/3 oz. dill
pickles, 1 oz. tomato paste, 1 oz. fat for frying, 1 oz. flour, salt, pepper,
ground paprika, juniper, allspice, bay leaf, marjoram and seasoning to
taste*

Wash, cook and chop the mushrooms. Cut the pickles and ham into
strips. Wash, rinse and fry the onions. Add the tomato paste and simmer for several minutes. Heat the fat and blend it with the flour. Fry this
without browning and blend with a little of the cold stock, stirring briskly
with and egg-whisk. Bring to a boil and cook for around 10 minutes
over low heat. Towards the middle add the wine, onions with tomato
paste and the pickles, ham, mushrooms, mushroom stock and ground
seasoning. Season to taste. Serve with meat dishes.

POTATO SAUCE

*1 1/3 cups stock from bones or meat, 3 tablespoons sour cream, 5—7
oz. scooped out potato balls, 2 2/3 oz. onions, 1 1/3 oz. fat for frying,
1 oz. flour, parsley sprigs, salt, pepper and seasoning to taste*

Peel, rinse and chop the onions finely. Fry them and combine with the
flour. Fry this without browning and blend with a little of the cold stock,
stirring briskly with an egg-whisk. Bring to a boil. Add potatoes and
cook. Towards the end add sour cream. Combine the sauce with chopped parsley sprigs. Season to taste. Serve with meat dishes.

SOUR CUCUMBER SAUCE

*1 1/4 cups stock from bones and vegetables, 1/3 cup sour cream, 5 oz.
soured cucumbers, butter for cucumbers, 1 1/3 oz. ham, 2/3 oz.
capers, 1 oz. fat for frying, 1 oz. flour, parsley sprigs, salt, white pepper
and sugar to taste*

Peel the cucumbers and cut them into slices, removing seeds. Add the
butter, sprinkle with water and simmer until tender. Heat the fat and
blend with the flour. Fry this without browning and blend with a little

of the cold stock, stirring briskly with an egg-whisk. Bring to a boil and add the cucumbers. Cook for around 10 minutes over low heat, stirring often. Towards the end add the rinsed capers and diced ham, then season. Serve with meat zrazy (q.v.).

ONION SAUCE

1 2/3 cups stock from bones or meat, 3 1/2—7 oz. onions, fat for onions, 1 oz. fat for frying, 1 oz. flour, salt, pepper, sugar, lemon juice, bay leaf, allspice and caramel syrup

Peel, rinse and chop the onions finely, then fry them. Heat the fat and blend with the flour. Fry this without browning and blend with a little of the cold stock, stirring briskly with an egg-whisk. Bring to a boil and cook for around 10 minutes over low heat. Towards the end add the onions, seasoning and caramel syrup. Force the sauce through a strainer and bring to a boil. Season to taste. Serve with meat dishes.

DRIED MUSHROOM SAUCE

1 1/4 cups stock from bones or meat and vegetables, 3 tablespoons sour cream, 1—1 1/3 oz. dried cèpe mushrooms, 1 oz. onions, 1 oz. fat for frying, 1 oz. flour, parsley sprigs, salt, pepper and seasoning to taste

Wash, soak and cook the mushrooms together with chopped onions. Heat the fat and blend with the flour. Fry this without browning and blend with a little of the cold stock, stirring briskly with an egg-whisk. Add strained mushroom stock and cook for around 10 minutes over low heat, stirring often. Towards the end add finely chopped mushrooms and sour cream. Combine the sauce with chopped parsley sprigs. Season to taste. Serve with noodles, macaroni and vegetables.

FRESH MUSHROOM SAUCE

1 1/4 cups stock from bones or vegetables, 1/3 cup sour cream, 9 1/2 oz. fresh mushrooms (cèpes), 2—2 2/3 oz. onions, fat for mushrooms,

1 oz. fat for frying, 1 oz. flour, parsley sprigs, salt, pepper and season-ing to taste

Clean, rinse and chop the mushrooms finely. Peel, rinse and dice the onions, then fry them. Add the mushrooms and simmer until tender, stirring often. Heat the fat and blend with the flour. Fry this without browning and blend with a little of the cold stock, stirring briskly with an egg-whisk. Bring to a boil, add the mushrooms and cook for around 10 minutes over low heat. Towards the end add sour cream. Combine the sauce with chopped parsley sprigs. Season to taste. Serve with vegetables, noodles and meat zrazy (q.v.).

MEAT SAUCE

1 2/3 cups vegetable stock, 5 oz. boneless pork, 2 2/3 oz. onions, fat for the meat, 1 oz. fat for frying, 1 oz. flour, salt, pepper, coriander, caraway seed and seasoning to taste

Peel, rinse and chop the onions finely. Wash and dice the meat, then fry it. Add the onions and brown lightly. Sprinkle with water and sim-mer until tender. Heat the fat and blend it with the flour. Fry this without browning and blend with a little of the cold stock, stirring briskly with an egg-whisk. Bring to a boil and cook for around 10 minutes over low heat, stirring often. Towards the end add the meat and season to taste. Serve with vegetables, noodles and rice.

HUSSAR'S SAUCE

1 1/3 cups stock from bones or meat, 3 tablespoons dry red wine, 2 oz. parsley root, 2 2/3 oz. celeriac, 2 oz. carrots, 1 2/3 oz. onions, fat for vegetables, 1 2/3 oz. grated horseradish, 1 oz. smoked ham, 1 2/3 oz. tomatoes, 1 oz. fat for frying, 1 oz. flour, salt, pepper, sugar, allspice and lemon juice to taste

Scald and peel the tomatoes, then cut into pieces. Wash, peel and rinse the vegetables, then cut them into thin strips. Fry them a little, then

sprinkle with water and simmer over low heat until tender. Heat the fat and blend with the flour. Fry this without browning and blend with a little of the cold stock, stirring briskly with an egg-whisk. Bring to a boil and cook for around 10 minutes over low heat. Towards the end add the horseradish, vegetables, tomatoes and ham cut into thin strips, then the seasoning to taste. Serve with macaroni, noodles, rice and meat.

HAM SAUCE

1 1/4 cups stock from bones or meat, 1/3 cup dry white wine, 2 2/3 oz. ham, 1 2/3 oz. onions, 3 1/2 oz. mushrooms, fat for onions and mushrooms, 1 oz. fat for frying, 1 oz. flour, salt, pepper, juniper and seasoning

Clean, rinse and chop the onions and mushrooms finely. Heat the fat and blend it with the flour. Fry this without browning and blend with a little of the cold stock, stirring briskly with an egg-whisk. Bring to a boil, add mushrooms and onions and cook for around 10 minutes over low heat, stirring often. Towards the end add strips of ham, ground seasoning and the wine. Serve with vegetarian and meat dishes, and eggs.

GENERAL'S SAUCE

3/4 cup pan drippings form pork loin roast, 3/4 cup dry red wine, 1 1/3 oz. tomato paste, 2 2/3 oz. onions, fat for onions, 1 oz. fat for frying, 1 oz. flour, salt, pepper, garlic and seasoning to taste

Blend wine with the pan drippings. Peel, rinse and chop the onions finely, then fry them. Add tomato paste and simmer for a while. Heat the fat and blend it with the flour. Fry it without browning and blend with a little of the cold stock, stirring briskly with an egg-whisk. Bring to a boil and cook for around 10 minutes over low heat, stirring often. Season to taste. Serve with meat dishes.

TOURNAMENT SAUCE

1 cup dry white wine, 1 oz. butter, 1/2 lb. apples, 1 2/3 oz. ketchup, salt, white pepper, sugar and lemon juice to taste

Wash, peel and cut the apples in half, removing the cores. Grate them coarsely. Fry with butter and sugar until translucent. Add wine and continue cooking until thick enough. Combine the sauce with ketchup. Season to taste. Serve with poultry and grilled meat.

FISH SAUCE

1 1/4 cups fish stock, 1/3 cup sour cream, 1 oz. fat for frying, 1 oz. flour, salt and pepper to taste

Heat the fat and blend it with the flour. Fry this without browning and blend with a little of the cold stock, stirring briskly with an egg-whisk. Bring to a boil and cook for around 10 minutes over low heat, stirring often. Towards the end add sour cream. Season to taste. Serve with fish.

MARINER'S SAUCE

1 1/3 cups fish stock, 3 tablespoons sour cream, 3 1/2 oz. mushrooms, fat for mushrooms, 2/3 oz. capers, 1 2/3 oz. anchovy fillets, 1 oz. fat for frying, 1 oz. flour, salt, pepper and lemon juice to taste

Clean, rinse and chop the mushrooms finely, then fry them. Heat the fat and blend it with the flour. Fry this without browning and blend with a little of the cold stock, stirring briskly with an egg-whisk. Bring to a boil, add the mushrooms and rinsed capers and cook for around 10 minutes over low heat, stirring often. Towards the end add sour cream. Combine the sauce with finely chopped fillets. Season to taste. Serve with fish.

LOBSTER SAUCE

1 1/3 cups fish stock, 3 tablespoons sour cream, 1 1/3 oz. almonds, 2 2/3 oz. lobster tails, 1 2/3 oz. canned peppers, 1 oz. lobster butter, 1 oz. flour, salt and pepper to taste

Blanch the almonds. Heat the fat and blend it with the flour. Fry this without browning and blend with a little of the cold stock, stirring briskly with an egg-whisk. Bring to a boil and cook for around 10 minutes over low heat. Towards the end add sour cream, chopped almonds, lobster tails and finely chopped peppers. Season to taste. Serve with fish.

BARRISTER'S SAUCE

1 1/4 cups fish stock, 3 tablespoons sour cream, 3 tablespoons dry white wine, 3 1/2 oz. prunes, 1 2/3 oz. grated horseradish, 1 oz. fat for frying, 1 oz. flour, salt, pepper, sugar and lemon juice to taste

Wash and soak the prunes, cook and force them through a strainer. Heat the fat and blend it with the flour. Fry this without browning and blend with a little of the cold stock, stirring briskly with an egg-whisk. Bring to a boil and cook for around 10 minutes, stirring often. Towards the end add the prune paste, horseradish and sour cream. Combine the sauce with wine. Season to taste. Serve with fish.

SWEET SAUCES

RAISIN SAUCE

1 cup dry white wine, 1 1/3 oz. butter, 1/3 oz. potato starch, 2—2 2/3 oz. raisins, 1 2/3 oz. walnut meats, lemon juice and sugar to taste

Blanch the walnuts and grind them. Combine with boiling milk, butter and rinsed raisins. Gradually add potato starch blended with a small amount of cold water. Cook for a while, then add the remaining ingredients.

VANILLA SAUCE

3/4 cup milk, 3—4 egg yolks, 2—2 2/3 oz. confectioners' sugar, 1 2/3 oz. butter, vanilla bean to taste

Bring the milk to a boil together with finely chopped vanilla bean, then strain. Blend egg yolks with sugar. Gradually pour in the milk in a thin drizzle, stirring briskly with an egg-whisk. Place the dish or pot with the egg yolks in a larger pot with hot water and heat, stirring constantly, until the sauce thickens. Keep the water in the pot near boiling point, but do not allow it to boil. When the sauce thickens, add butter piece by piece. Allow to cool, stirring.

CHOCOLATE SAUCE

3/4 cup milk, 1—1 1/3 oz. cocoa, 2 egg yolks, 1 1/3—1 2/3 oz. confectioners' sugar, 1/3 oz. potato starch, 1 1/3 oz. butter, vanilla bean to taste

Bring the milk to a boil. Blend the cocoa, potato starch and grated vanilla together with a small amount of cold water. Add this slowly to the hot milk, stirring briskly with and egg-whisk. Place the dish or pot with the sauce in a larger dish with cold water. Stir with an egg-whisk until cool, adding the butter piece by piece.

ALMOND SAUCE

3/4 cup cream, 3 1/2 oz. almonds, 1 2/3 oz. confectioners' sugar, 3 tablespoons milk, 1/3 oz. potato starch, 2 egg yolks

Blanch the almonds and grind them. Bring the cream to a boil. Blend the potato starch with milk. Gradually add this to the hot cream, stirring briskly with an egg-whisk. Bring to a boil. Blend egg yolks with the sugar and almonds. Bring the cream to a boil and add to the egg yolk mixture, stirring constantly.

RED WINE SAUCE

1 cup dry red wine, lemon rind, cinnamon and cloves to taste, 1 2/3 oz. sugar, 1/3 oz. potato starch, 1 2/3 oz. raisins

Bring the wine with sugar and spices to a boil, then strain. Blend the potato starch with a small amount of cold water. Pour this in a thin drizzle into the hot wine, stirring briskly with an egg-whisk. Bring to a boil. Add the rinsed raisins and cook for a while over low heat.

ORANGE SAUCE

2/3 cup orange juice, 1/3 cup dry white wine, 1/3 oz. potato starch, lemon juice and orange rind to taste

Bring the wine to a boil together with the orange juice and grated orange rind. Pour this through a strainer, then add the lemon juice. Blend the potato starch with a small amount of cold water. Pour this in a thin drizzle into the hot juice, stirring briskly with an egg-whisk. Bring to a boil.

COFFEE SAUCE

1 cup strong coffee, 1 oz. butter, 1 2/3 oz. confectioners' sugar, 1/3 oz. potato starch

Blend the potato starch with a small amount of cold water. Gradually add this to the hot coffee, stirring briskly with an egg-whisk. Bring to a boil. Add the sugar and butter.

CINNAMON SAUCE

3/4 cup dry white wine, 3 tablespoons water, 3 tablespoons orange juice, 1/3 oz. potato starch, orange rind, cinnamon and cloves, sugar to taste

Bring the wine to a boil together with the water, orange juice, grated rind and ground spices. Pour this through a strainer. Blend the potato starch with a small amount of cold water. Gradually add this to the hot wine, stirring briskly with an egg-whisk. Bring this to boiling point and add the spices.

RASPBERRY SAUCE

2/3 cup dry red wine, 1/3 cup Maraschino liqueur, 9 1/2 oz. raspberries, 1/3 oz. potato starch, sugar

Sort the raspberries. Rinse them and force through a strainer. Add them to the wine and bring to a boil. Blend the potato starch with a small amount of cold water. Gradually add to the hot wine, stirring briskly with an egg-whisk. Bring to a boil and blend with the liqueur. Add sugar to taste.

PLUM JAM SAUCE

1 cup milk, 2—2 2/3 oz. plum jam, 2 egg yolks, 1/3 oz. potato starch, cinnamon, lemon rind and sugar to taste

Bring the milk to a boil together with the cinnamon and grated lemon rind. Pour this through a strainer. Blend the potato starch with a small amount of cold water. Gradually add this to the hot milk, stirring briskly with an egg-whisk. Bring to a boil and cook for several minutes. Blend the egg yolks with the plum jam. Gradually add the milk to the egg yolk mixture, stirring briskly with an egg-whisk. Heat in a double-boiler for 3—4 minutes.

CHERRY OR PLUM SAUCE

3/4 cup water, 3 tablespoons dry red wine, 1/2 lb fruit, 1 1/3 oz. sugar, 1/3 oz. potato starch, cinnamon to taste

Sort the fruit. Wash it and cover with water and wine. Add the cinnamon. Cook this and force through a strainer. Blend the potato starch with a small amount of cold water. Gradually add this to the hot fruit paste, stirring briskly with an egg-whisk. Cook for a while and add sugar to taste.

APRICOT SAUCE

2/3 cup water, 2 2/3 oz. dried apricots, 2/3 cup cream, 1 2/3 oz. sugar, 1/3 oz. potato starch

Wash the apricots and soak them. Cook them, force through a strainer and combine with the cream. Blend the potato starch with a small amount of cold water. Gradually add this to the hot fruit paste, stirring briskly with an egg-whisk. Cook for a while and add sugar to taste.

CARDINAL'S SAUCE

2/3 cup water, 2 2/3 oz. dried apricots, 3 tablespoons dry white wine, 7 oz. rum, 1/3 cup whipping cream, confectioners' sugar, 1/3 oz. potato starch, lemon juice to taste

Wash the apricots and soak them. Cook them, force through a strainer and combine with the wine and rum. Blend the potato starch with a small amount of cold water. Pour in a thin drizzle into the hot fruit paste, stirring briskly with an egg-whisk. Bring to a boil and allow to cool. Chill the cream and whip it. Combine with the sauce and add lemon juice to taste.

MILK SAUCE

1 cup milk, 2 egg yolks, 1 2/3 oz. confectioners' sugar, 2/3 oz. butter, 2/3 oz. flour, 1/2 vanilla bean

Bring the milk to a boil together with finely chopped vanilla bean. Pour this through a strainer. Heat the butter and blend it with the flour. Fry this without browning and blend with a little of the cold milk, stirring briskly with an egg-whisk. Bring to a boil and cook for 6—8 minutes over low heat. Blend egg yolks with the sugar. Combine the milk together with the egg yolk mixture.

Soups

BROWNED STOCK

8 cups water, 1 3/4 lb. bones, 3/4 lb. soup vegetables (carrots, parsley root, celeriac, leek), 3 1/2 oz. onions, 1 2/3 oz. fat for frying, 1 oz. flour, 1 oz. tomato paste, salt, allspice, bay leaf, tarragon, thyme and seasoning to taste

Wash the bones and chop them into pieces. Peel and rinse the vegetables and onions, then cut them into thin strips. Brown them in the fat together with the bones, stirring occasionally. Sprinkle with flour and brown them. Cover with water and cook 2—3 hours over low heat. Towards the end add the tomato paste and ground seasoning. Trimmings from poultry, venison, veal or pork may be added to the stock to make it more concentrated. Pour the stock through a strainer and use for soups.

MEAT STOCK

8 cups water, 1 lb. meat, 3/4 lb. soup vegetables (carrots, parsley root, celeriac, leek, piece of savoy cabbage), 1 2/3 oz. onions, bay leaf, allspice and salt to taste

Wash the meat, cover with cold water and cook for around 60 minutes. Add the cleaned vegetables, onions and seasoning and cook until tender. Towards the end add salt. Pour the stock through a strainer. Use the meat when making stuffing for pierogi (q.v.), patties etc.

BASIC STOCK

8 cups water, 1 lb. bones, 3/4 lb. soup vegetables (carrots, parsley root, celeriac, leek, piece of savoy cabbage), salt

Wash the bones and chop them into pieces. Cover with cold water and cook for around 60 minutes. Add the cleaned vegetables, salt and cook until tender. Pour the stock through a strainer. Remove the bones from the meat and put it in the soup.

POULTRY STOCK

8 cups water, 1 lb. necks and wings, 3/4 soup vegetables (carrots, parsley root, celeriac, leek, piece of savoy cabbage), salt

Prepare the poultry stock as above.

VEGETABLE STOCK

8 cups water, 1 lb. soup vegetables (carrot, parsley root, celeriac, leek, piece of savoy cabbage), salt

Wash, peel and rinse the vegetables, then chop them. Cover with boiling water and cook for around 35 minutes over low heat. Add salt towards the end.

MUSHROOM STOCK

8 cups water, 2/3 oz. dried cèpe mushrooms, 3/4 lb. soup vegetables (carrots, parsley root, celeriac, leek, piece of savoy cabbage), 2 2/3 oz. onions, bay leaf, allspice and salt to taste

Wash the mushrooms and soak them. Cover with water and add the cleaned and rinsed vegetables and onions. Cook covered until tender. Towards the end add the seasoning. Pour the stock through a strainer. Use the mushrooms for pierogi (q.v.), uszka (q.v.) or soups.

FISH STOCK

8 cups water, 3/4 lb. soup vegetables (carrots, parsley root, celeriac, leek), 2 lb. fish, 3 tablespoons dry white wine, 1/6 oz. dried cèpe mushrooms, bay leaf, allspice and salt to taste

Wash, peel and rinse the vegetables. Cover with boiling water and add washed, soaked mushrooms and the seasoning. Cook covered for 15 minutes. Rinse the cleaned fish and cut into steaks. Put them in the stock and add salt. Cook over low heat. Remove the fish when tender. Pour the stock through a strainer and combine with the wine. Use the stock for soups. Serve the fish as an entrée or an hors-d'œuvre.

SOURED BEET JUICE

2 lb. beets, 2—2 2/3 oz. whole-wheat bread, 10 cups water, garlic to taste

Wash, peel and rinse the beets, then slice them. Arrange them in a stoneware pot or a glass jar. Cover with warm boiled water and add crumbled bread and chopped garlic. Cover the pot or jar with gauze or a linen cloth. Tie it up and set aside in a warm place for several days. Pour through a strainer, then into bottles. Close the bottles tightly with corks. Store in a cool, dark place. Use for borsch or other dishes.

ZHUR (SOURED RYE-FLOUR JUICE)

3 1/2 oz. rye, whole-wheat or oatmeal flour, 2 cups water, garlic

Cover the flour with warm boiled water. Blend thoroughly and pour into a stoneware dish. Add garlic. Set aside in a warm place for several days. With its sour flavour and characteristic pleasant aroma it can be used for various soups.

BEEF BROTH

10 cups water, 1 1/4 lb. beef (sirloin, shoulder, shank), 5 oz. soup vegetables (carrot, parsley root, celeriac, leek, savoy cabbage), 2 oz. onions, 9 1/2 oz. brittle beef bones, parsley sprigs, salt, pepper, bay leaf, allspice and seasoning to taste

Wash and chop the bones. Cover with cold water. Add the washed meat and salt. Cook covered for around 2 and a half hours over low heat.

Towards the end add cleaned and rinsed vegetables along with browned onions and the seasoning. Correct the seasoning and sprinkle with chopped parsley sprigs before serving. Serve with macaroni, rice, soft egg noodles or patties. Use the meat for pierogi (q.v.), and patties or serve with vegetables from the broth and cooked potatoes as an entrée.

CHICKEN BROTH

8 cups water, 2 lb. chicken, 3/4 lb. soup vegetables (carrots, parsley root, celeriac, leek, savoy cabbage), 2 oz. onions, parsley sprigs, salt, pepper and allspice to taste

Wash the cleaned chicken and cover with cold water. Add salt and cook covered over low heat. Towards the end add the cleaned and rinsed vegetables, browned onions and seasoning. Remove the chicken when tender. Pour the broth through a strainer. Season to taste. Serve with macaroni, rice, patties and noodles. Serve the chicken together with the broth or as an entrée with an appropriate sauce and vegetables. Before serving sprinkle the broth with chopped parsley sprigs.

ROYAL BROTH

10 cups water, 1 lb. boneless beef, 5 oz. chicken, 3/4 lb. soup vegetables (carrots, parsley root, celeriac, leek), 3 1/2 oz. mushrooms, 3 1/2 oz. chicken livers, parsley sprigs, salt, pepper and seasoning to taste

Wash the meat and cover with cold water. Add salt and cook covered over low heat. Towards the end add the chicken meat and the cleaned and rinsed vegetables. Clean and rinse the mushrooms and cut them into thin strips. Wash and scald the livers, then dice them. Remove the meat when tender. Pour the broth through a strainer. Combine with the livers and mushrooms. Cook for a while and add the diced chicken meat and chopped parsley sprigs. Season to taste. Serve with noodles. Use the meat for a entrée.

CLEAR BORSCH I

8 cups stock from bones and vegetables, 1 3/4 lb. beets, 2 dried cèpe mushrooms, 7 oz. apples (sour), salt, sugar, marjoram, soured beet juice or lemon juice to taste

Wash, peel and rinse the beets. Cut them into thin strips. Cover with the stock. Add the seasoning and washed mushrooms which have been soaked. Cook for a while. Add the soured beet juice and finely diced apples. Set aside for several hours. Pour through a strainer. Season to taste. Serve with uszka (q.v.), patties or bread sticks.

CLEAR BORSCH II

8 cups stock from bones and vegetables, 1 3/4 lb. beets, 2—2 2/3 oz. prunes, 1 2/3 oz. grated horseradish, 1 1/3 oz. tomato paste, 2—3 egg whites, salt, sugar, marjoram and lemon juice to taste

Wash and clean the beets. Bake them in an oven and allow to cool. Peel and grate them coarsely. Wash and soak the prunes. Cook them, then force through a strainer. Combine with the stock, tomato paste, horseradish, lemon juice and egg whites. Beat with an egg-whisk. Bring to a boil, then pour through a linen cloth. Add the beets and seasoning. Bring to a boil, then set aside for several hours.

CHRISTMAS EVE BORSCH

6 cups vegetable stock, 1 cup fish stock (optional), 1 lb. beets, 2 oz. onions, 2/3 oz. dried cèpe mushrooms, 2/3—1 oz. butter, fresh dill, salt, sugar, garlic and soured beet juice to taste

Wash and soak the mushrooms, then cook them. Wash, clean and rinse the beets. Cover with boiling water and cook them. Remove when cooked and peel them, then grate coarsely. Combine the vegetable stock with the fish and mushroom stock. Add the beets and cook for a while. Peel, rinse and dice the onions. Fry them, then add to the strained borsch together with the chopped mushrooms. Season to taste. Serve with mushroom uszka (q.v.).

WHITE BORSCH

8 cups stock from meat and vegetables, 1 lb. beets, 2/3 cup sour cream, 2/3 oz. flour, 2 dried cèpe mushrooms, fresh dill, salt, sugar, bay leaf, allspice and soured beet juice (q.v.) to taste

Clean and rinse the beets, then peel them. Slice them and add to the hot stock. Bring to a boil and set aside for an hour. Wash and soak the mushrooms, then cook them. Pour the borsch through a strainer. Combine with mushroom stock, sour cream blended with flour and seasoning. Cook for a while and season to taste. Just before serving combine with chopped mushrooms and chopped dill. Serve with cooked potatoes sprinkled with pork fat cracklings or hard-boiled eggs.

OLD POLISH BORSCH

8 cups stock from meat and vegetables, 2/3 cup sour cream, 13 1/2 oz. beets, 7 oz. kiełbasa (Polish sausage), 3 1/2 oz. carrots, 3 1/2 oz. celeriac, 3 1/2 oz. parsley root, 2 2/3 oz. onions, fat for frying, 2/3 oz. flour, fresh dill, salt, pepper, sugar, marjoram, seasoning and soured beet juice to taste

Wash and clean the beets, then bake them in an oven. When done allow to cool. Peel them and grate coarsley. Wash, peel and rinse the vegetables, then cut into thin strips. Fry them a little in the fat. Sprinkle with the stock and simmer until tender. Remove the skin from the kiełbasa. Cut it in half, then slice it. Combine with the vegetables, beets, the remaining stock, chopped dill and sour cream blended with the flour. Cook for a while. Season to taste.

LITTLE POLAND BORSCH

8 cups stock from bones and vegetables, 7 oz. boneless beef, 13 1/2 oz. beets, 2/3 cup sour cream, 7 oz. white cabbage, 2/3 oz. dried cèpe mushrooms, 2/3 oz. flour, 1 2/3 white beans, 1 1/3 oz. tomato paste, salt, pepper, sugar, bay leaf, allspice, seasoning and soured beet juice to taste

Wash, clean and rinse the beets. Cover with water and cook them. Allow to cool. Peel and grate them coarsely. Wash and soak the mushrooms, then cook them. Sort the beans and rinse them. Cover with cold water and bring to a boil. Set aside for 2 hours. Cook them in the same water. Wash and mince the meat. Cover with the stock and cook it. Towards the end add the diced cabbage and seasoning. When tender, combine the cabbage with the beets, strips of mushrooms, tomato paste, beans and sour cream blended with the flour. Cook for a while. Add the soured beet juice. Season to taste.

FARMER'S BORSCH

8 cups stock from meat and vegetables, 2/3 cup sour cream, 1 lb. beets, 1 2/3 oz. white beans, 7 oz. peeled potatoes, 3 1/2 oz. onions, 5 oz. apples, 5 oz. tomatoes, 5 oz. cucumbers, 1 1/3 oz. butter, parsley sprigs, salt, pepper, sugar and soured beet juice (q.v.) to taste

Wash and clean the beets, then bake them in the oven. Allow to cool and peel them. Grate coarsely together with rinsed and pitted apples. Cover with the stock and add the soured beet juice. Cook for several minutes over low heat. Set aside for 3—4 hours to bring out the flavour. Sort the beans and rinse them. Cover with cold water and bring to a boil. Set aside for 2 hours. Cook them in the same water. Wash and dice the potatoes. Cover with water and cook them. Wash, scald and peel the tomatoes. Peel and rinse the onions and cucumbers. Cut them into pieces together with the tomatoes. Fry them in butter. Add them together with the beans to the potatoes when the latter are nearly done. Combine with the strained borsch, sour cream and chopped parsley sprigs. Bring to a boil. Season to taste.

VEGETABLE SOUP I

6 cups meat stock, 2/3 cup sour cream, 5 oz. potatoes, 5 oz. savoy cabbage, 3 1/2 oz. carrots, 5 oz. celeriac, 5 oz. cauliflower, 1 2/3 oz. canned peas, 1 2/3 oz. canned beans, 1—1 2/3 oz. tomato paste, 2/3 oz. flour, parsley sprigs, celery leaves, salt to taste

Wash, peel and rinse the vegetables. Cut the carrots and celeriac into strips. Dice the cabbage and potatoes. Cover with the stock and cook this. Somewhere in the middle add the crumbled cauliflower. Towards the end add the tomato paste. When tender, combine the vegetables with the peas, beans and sour cream blended with the flour. Bring to a boil. Season to taste. Before serving combine with the chopped parsley and celery leaves.

VEGETABLE SOUP II

6 cups poultry stock, 2/3 cup sour cream, 5 oz. mushrooms, 1/2 lb. tomatoes, 5 oz. celeriac, 3 1/2 oz. onions, 5 oz. carrots, 3 1/2 oz. hard cheese, parsley sprigs, salt and nutmeg to taste

Clean and rinse the carrots and celeriac. Cut into thin strips. Cover with the stock and cook this. Wash, scald and peel the tomatoes. Dice them and add to the vegetables somewhere in the middle of cooking. Towards the end add strips of mushrooms. Combine the soup with the sour cream, grated cheese and chopped parsley sprigs. Bring to a boil. Season to taste.

STRING BEAN SOUP

6 cups stock from bones and vegetables, 2/3 cup sour cream, 1 lb. string beans, 5—7 oz. tomatoes, 1/3 oz. flour, parsley sprigs, salt and sugar to taste

Wash, scald and peel the tomatoes. Cut them into pieces. Remove the strings from the beans. Cut them diagonally into 1/2 in. pieces. Rinse them, cover with the stock and cook. Towards the end add tomato pieces. Combine the soup with the sour cream blended with the flour. Bring to a boil. Season to taste. Combine with chopped parsley sprigs before serving.

CAULIFLOWER SOUP

6 cups vegetable stock, 2/3 cup sour cream, 1 1/4—1 3/4 lb. cauliflower, 2/3 oz. flour, fresh dill, parsley sprigs, salt and sugar to taste

Rinse the cleaned cauliflower and divide into small rosettes. Cover with the stock. Add the seasoning and cook. Blend the flour with the sour cream. Add to the soup. Bring to a boil. Combine with the chopped dill and parsley sprigs. Season to taste. Serve with toast, soft egg noodles or puffs.

CAULIFLOWER SOUP BELVEDERE STYLE

4 cups vegetable stock, 2 cups milk, 1 1/4 lb. cauliflower, 7 oz. mushrooms, 2 egg yolks, 2/3 oz. flour, parsley sprigs, salt, pepper and lemon juice to taste

Clean and rinse the cauliflower. Divide into small rosettes. Cover with the stock and cook. Clean and rinse the mushrooms. Cut them into strips. Fry them and add to the cauliflower together with boiling milk. Cook this for a while. Heat the fat and blend it with the flour, without browning the latter. Combine with the soup. Bring to a boil. Combine with the chopped parsley sprigs and egg yolks. Season to taste.

GREEN PEA SOUP I

6 cups stock from bones and vegetables, 2/3 cup sour cream, 1 lb. green peas, 2/3 oz. butter, 2/3 oz. flour, parsley sprigs, salt, pepper and sugar to taste

Sort the peas and rinse them. Cover with the stock and cook. Heat the fat and blend with the flour. Fry this without browning. Combine with the peas, sour cream and seasoning. Cook for a while and combine with the chopped parsley. Season to taste. Serve with lasagne and other noodles or with puffs.

GREEN PEA SOUP II

6 cups stock from meat and vegetables, 2/3 cup sour cream, 13 1/2 oz. fresh peas, 9 1/2 oz. carrots, 3/4 cup milk, 2 egg yolks, salt, pepper, sugar, garlic, basil and tarragon to taste

Wash, peel and rinse the carrots. Cut them up and cover with boiling milk. Force through a strainer. Sort the peas, rinse them and cover with the stock, then cook. Combine with the carrots and sour cream. Bring to a boil and combine with the egg yolks and seasoning.

SORREL SOUP

6 cups stock from bones and vegetables, 2/3 cup sour cream, 1/2 lb. fresh sorrel, 1 oz. butter, 1 oz. flour, salt and seasoning to taste

Sort the sorrel and cut off the leaf stalks. Rinse, chop and simmer it in butter. Combine with the stock and sour cream blended with the flour. Cook for a while. Season to taste. Serve with rice, hard-boiled eggs or cooked potatoes sprinkled with pork fat cracklings.

ASPARAGUS SOUP

6 cups stock from bones and vegetables, 2/3 cup sour cream, 1 1/4—1 3/4 lb. asparagus, 2/3 oz. butter, 2/3 oz. flour, parsley sprigs, salt and sugar to taste

Remove the strings from the asparagus and cut off the tops. Rinse the stalks and cut into 3/4 in. pieces. Cover with the stock, leaving out the tops. Cook the asparagus. Towards the end add the tops. Heat the fat and blend with the flour. Fry this without browning. Combine with the soup and sour cream. Cook for a while and combine with chopped parsley sprigs. Season to taste. Serve with toast, almonds or egg dumplings.

SPINACH SOUP

6 cups stock from bones and vegetables, 2/3 cup sour cream, 1 1/4— 1 3/4 lb. spinach, 1 2/3 oz. butter, 2/3 oz. flour, salt and garlic to taste

Sort and rinse the spinach. Strain, drain and mash it. Fry it in butter and cover with the stock. Add the sour cream blended with the flour and cook for a while. Season to taste. Serve with hard-boiled eggs or toast.

DILL SOUP WITH NOODLES

6 cups stock from meat and vegetables, 2/3 cup sour cream, fresh dill, 2/3 oz. flour, 3 1/2—5 oz. brains, 1 2/3 oz. hardened French bread, 2 2/3 oz. onions, 2/3 oz. fat for frying, 2/3 oz. farina, 2/3 oz. flour for noodles, parsley sprigs, 1 egg, salt and nutmeg to taste

Rinse and chop the dill. Cover it with the stock. Combine with the sour cream blended with the flour. Bring to a boil. Season to taste. Peel and rinse the onions. Chop them finely and fry them. Remove the skin from the brains. Rinse them and place in boiling salted water. Cook them, remove from the water and allow to cool. Force through a strainer.

Combine with the onions, farina, flour, egg and chopped parsley sprigs. Correct the seasoning. Shape into long noodles with a spoon. Drop these into the boiling soup. Stir and cook them. Serve at once.

CUCUMBER SOUP

6 cups stock from bones and vegetables, 2/3 cup sour cream, 1 1/4 lb. cucumbers, 1 2/3 oz. tomato paste, butter, 2/3 oz. flour, fresh dill, salt, pepper and sugar to taste

Wash, peel and rinse the cucumbers. Cut into strips, removing the seeds. Combine with the tomato paste and butter. Simmer for around 10 minutes over low heat, stirring constantly. Combine with the stock and sour cream blended with the flour. Cook for a while. Add the chopped dill. Season to taste. Serve with toast.

KOHLRABI SOUP

6 cups stock from bones and vegetables, 1 lb. kohlrabi, 9 1/2 oz. potatoes, 1 oz. fat for frying, 1 oz. flour, fresh dill, salt, pepper and sugar to taste

Wash, peel and rinse the kohlrabi and potatoes. Grate them coarsely. Cover with the stock and cook them. Heat the fat and blend it with the flour. Fry this without browning. Combine with the soup. Bring to a boil. Combine with the chopped dill. Season to taste.

LEEK SOUP

6 cups stock from bones and vegetables, 2/3 cup sour cream, 1 lb. leeks, 13 oz. potatoes, 3 1/2 oz. thin frankfurters, 2/3 oz. flour, salt to taste

Clean and rinse the leeks. Cut them finely. Cover with part of the stock and cook them. Wash, peel and rinse the potatoes. Dice them and cover with the remaining stock. Cook them in this. Combine with the leeks,

sour cream blended with the flour and sliced frankfurters. Bring to a boil.
Season to taste.

CELERIAC SOUP

*6 cups stock from bones and vegetables, 2/3 cup sour cream, 13 oz.
celeriac, 9 1/2 oz. apples, 2/3 oz. flour, parsley sprigs, 1 2/3 oz. butter,
salt, nutmeg and lemon juice to taste*

Wash and peel the apples. Cut them in half and remove the cores. Grate
coarsely together with the peeled celeriac. Fry them lightly in butter.
Combine with the stock and sour cream blended with the flour. Cook for
a while. Combine with chopped parsley sprigs. Season to taste.

CABBAGE SOUP

*6 cups stock from bones and vegetables, 1 lb. white cabbage, 5—7 oz.
tomatoes, 5—7 oz. apples, 2/3 oz. butter, 2/3 oz. flour, 2/3 cup sour
cream, parsley sprigs, salt, pepper, sugar and lemon juice to taste*

Rinse and dice the cabbage. Cover with the stock and cook it. Wash, scald
and peel the tomatoes. Wash and peel the apples. Cut them in half and
remove the cores. Cut them into pieces together with the tomatoes. Heat
the butter and blend it with the flour. Fry this without browning. Combine with the cabbage, tomatoes and apples. Cook for a while. Add the
chopped parsley sprigs. Season to taste. Serve with potatoes.

CAPTAIN'S CABBAGE SOUP

*6 cups stock from bones and vegetables, 1 lb. white cabbage, 1/2 lb.
peppers, 5 oz. smoked bacon, 2 2/3 oz. onions, 2/3 oz. flour, 2/3 oz.
capers, 2/3 cup sour cream, salt, pepper and seasoning to taste*

Rinse and dice the cabbage. Cover it with the stock and cook it. Clean,
rinse and dice the onions and peppers together with the bacon. Partly
render down the bacon. Add the onions and peppers. Fry them lightly.

Sprinkle with water and simmer until tender. Combine with the cabbage, rinsed capers and sour cream blended with the flour. Bring to a boil. Season to taste.

SAVOY CABBAGE SOUP

6 cups stock from meat and vegetables, 2/3 cup sour cream, 1 1/4— 1 3/4 lb. savoy cabbage, 9 1/2 oz. potatoes, 2 2/3 oz. onions, fat for frying, 2/3 oz. flour, salt, pepper, garlic, dill and seasoning to taste

Rinse and dice the cabbage. Cover with the stock and cook it. Wash, peel and rinse the potatoes. Dice them and add to the cabbage towards the end of cooking together with the seasoning. Peel, rinse and chop the onions finely. Fry them lightly. Add the flour and brown it lightly. Combine with the cabbage and sour cream. Bring to a boil. Season to taste.

RED CABBAGE SOUP

6 cups stock from bones and vegetables, 2/3 cup dry red wine, 3 1/2 oz. prunes, 5 oz. lemons, 1 lb. red cabbage, 9 1/2 oz. peeled potatoes, 2 2/3 oz. onions, 1 1/3 oz. fat for frying, 2/3 oz. flour, salt, pepper, sugar and lemon juice to taste

Wash, soak and cook the prunes. Remove the pits and force through a strainer. Wash and scald the lemons. Peel them and cut into half-slices. Rinse and dice the cabbage, removing the core and thick stems. Cover with part of the stock and cook. When done sprinkle with lemon juice. Dice the potatoes and cover with the remaining stock. Cook them and combine with the prunes, cabbage and wine. Rinse and dice the onions. Fry them and add the flour. Brown it lightly. Combine with the soup and bring to a boil. Add the lemons. Season to taste.

SAUERKRAUT SOUP

6 cups water, 1/2 lb. pork ribs or beef, 2 2/3 oz. onions, 1 1/3 oz. fat for frying, 2/3 oz. flour, 1 lb. sauerkraut, 1/2 lb. soup vegetables (carrots, parsley root, celeriac, leek, piece of savoy cabbage), 2/3 oz. dried mushrooms, salt, pepper, seasoning, caraway seed, bay leaf and allspice

Slice the cabbage. Cover it with part of the water and cook. Wash the ribs and cover them with the remaining water. Add salt and cook. Wash, peel and rinse the vegetables. Cut them into thin strips and add to the ribs towards the end of cooking. Remove the cooked ribs. Separate the meat from the bones and dice it. Place in the stock together with the cabbage. Wash, soak and cook the mushrooms. Peel, rinse and chop the onions finely. Fry them lightly and add the flour. Brown lightly and combine with the soup, chopped mushrooms and stock from the mushrooms and seasoning. Cook for a while. Season to taste.

HUNTER'S SAUERKRAUT SOUP

6 cups stock from meat and vegetables, 13 oz. sauerkraut, 7 oz. smoked kiełbasa, 3 1/2 oz. onions, 1 1/3 oz. fat for frying, 2/3 oz. flour, 2—2 2/3 oz. hard cheese, salt, pepper, seasoning and juniper to taste

Shred the cabbage, cover with the stock and cook it. Peel, rinse and chop the onions finely. Fry them lightly and add the flour. Brown it lightly. Combine with the sauerkraut, sliced kiełbasa and ground seasoning. Cook for a while. Place in individual one-serving dishes. Sprinkle with grated cheese and bake. Serve with cooked potatoes sprinkled with pork fat cracklings.

BRUSSELS SPROUT SOUP

6 cups stock from meat and vegetables, 2/3 cup sour cream, 1 lb. Brussels sprouts, parsley sprigs, 2 egg yolks, 2/3 oz. flour, salt and sugar to taste

Clean and rinse the Brussels sprouts. Cover them with the stock and cook them. Force them through a strainer. Add sour cream blended with the flour. Cook for a while. Combine with the egg yolks and chopped parsley sprigs. Season to taste.

BEAN SOUP

6 cups stock from bones and vegetables, 7—8 1/2 oz. white beans, 3 1/2 oz. pork fat, 2—2 2/3 oz. onions, 2/3 oz. flour, parsley sprigs, salt, seasoning and marjoram to taste

Sort and rinse the beans. Cover them with the cold stock. Bring to a boil and set aside for 2 hours. Cook them in the same water. Peel, rinse and chop the onions finely. Dice the pork fat and partly render it down. Add the onions and fry them. Combine with the flour and brown this lightly. Combine with the beans and seasoning. Cook for a while. Season to taste. Serve with lasagne or other noodles.

UHLAN'S BEAN SOUP

6 cups stock from bones and vegetables, 2/3 cup sour cream, 3 1/2—5 oz. white beans, 3 1/2 oz. frankfurters, 3 1/2 oz. smoked bacon, 2 2/3 oz. onions, 2/3 oz. flour, 1 2/3 oz. macaroni, salt, garlic and ground paprika to taste

Sort and rinse the beans. Cover with part of the cold stock. Bring to a boil and set aside for 2 hours. Cook this. Peel, rinse and chop the onions finely. Dice the bacon and partly render it down. Add the onions and fry them. Combine with the remaining stock. Add the macaroni and cook it. Add the sour cream blended with the flour, the beans and sliced frankfurters. Cook this for a while. Season to taste.

CAPTAIN'S BEAN SOUP

6 cups stock from meat and vegetables, 2/3 cup sour cream, 7 oz. white beans, 2/3 oz. dried cèpe mushrooms, parsley sprigs, 3 1/2 oz. lasagne noodles, salt, pepper, seasoning and marjoram to taste

Sort and rinse the beans. Cover with the cold stock. Bring to a boil and set aside for 2 hours. Cook this. Wash, soak and cook the mushrooms.

Cut them into thin slices. Combine with the beans, sour cream and lasagne noodles. Cook for around 5 minutes over low heat. Season to taste. Just before serving combine with chopped parsley sprigs.

POTATO SOUP

6 cups stock from bones and vegetables, 1 1/4 lb. potatoes, 5 oz. kiełbasa, 3 1/2 oz. smoked bacon, 2—2 2/3 oz. onions, 2/3 oz. flour, parsley sprigs, salt, ground paprika and garlic to taste

Wash, peel and rinse the potatoes. Dice them, then cover with the stock and cook them. Peel, rinse and chop the onions finely. Dice the bacon and partly render it down. Add the onions and fry them. Combine with the flour and brown lightly. Remove the skin from the kiełbasa and cut it into half-slices. Add the onions together with the kiełbasa to the soup towards the end of cooking. Combine with the chopped parsley sprigs. Season to taste.

POTATO SOUP WITH CREAM

6 cups stock from bones and vegetables, 2/3 cup sour cream, 3 1/2 oz. walnut meats, 2 egg yolks, 1 1/4 lb. potatoes, parsley sprigs, salt, pepper, seasoning and curry powder to taste

Wash, peel and rinse the potatoes. Dice them and cover with the stock, then cook them. Blanch the walnuts and grind them. Combine with the potatoes, sour cream blended with the egg yolks and chopped parsley sprigs. Season to taste.

POTATO SOUP WITH MEAT

6 cups vegetable stock, 9 1/2 oz. boneless pork, 3 1/2 oz. onions, 1 oz. fat for frying, 1 lb. potatoes, 1 oz. tomato paste, 2/3 oz. fat for roux, 2/3 oz. flour, parsley sprigs, salt, pepper, seasoning, bay leaf and allspice to taste

Wash and dice the meat together with the peeled onions. Fry the meat lightly. Add the onions and brown them lightly. Cover with the stock and cook. Wash, peel and rinse the potatoes. Dice them and add to the meat towards the end of cooking together with the seasoning. Heat the fat and blend with the flour. Fry this and combine with the soup and tomato paste. Cook for a while. Add the chopped parsley sprigs. Season to taste.

MUSHROOM SOUP WITH CREAM

6 cups stock from bones and vegetables, 2/3 cup sour cream, 1 2/3 oz. dried cèpe mushrooms, 1—1 1/3 oz. onions, 1 oz. fat for frying, 1 oz. flour, parsley sprigs, salt and seasoning to taste

Wash, soak and cook the mushrooms covered over low heat together with chopped onions. When done, pour the stock through a strainer. Cut the mushrooms into thin strips. Heat the fat and blend it with the flour. Fry this without browning and combine with the stock, stirring briskly with an egg-whisk. Cook this for a while. Add the sour cream and bring to a boil. Season to taste. Just before serving sprinkle with chopped parsley sprigs. Serve with buckwheat pierogi (q.v.), macaroni or lasagne noodles.

MUSHROOM SOUP WITH PEARL BARLEY

6 cups stock from meat and vegetables, 1/2 lb. potatoes, 1 2/3 oz. dried cèpe mushrooms, 2—2 2/3 oz. pearl barley, 3 1/2 oz. onions, fat for frying, parsley sprigs, salt, pepper and seasoning to taste

Rinse the pearl barley. Cover it with the stock and cook it. Wash, soak and cook the mushrooms. Remove them from the stock and cut into thin strips. Wash, peel and rinse the potatoes. Dice them and add to the pearl barley towards the end of cooking. Combine with finely chopped and fried onions, mushroom stock, mushrooms and chopped parsley sprigs. Season to taste.

FRESH MUSHROOM SOUP

6 cups stock from bones and vegetables, 2/3 cup sour cream, 1 lb. fresh cèpe mushrooms, 10—13 oz. potatoes, 3 1/2 oz. onions, fat for frying, 2/3—1 oz. flour, parsley sprigs, salt and pepper to taste

Clean and rinse the mushrooms, then cut them into thin strips. Peel, rinse and dice the onions. Fry them. Add the mushrooms and simmer over low heat, stirring often. Wash, peel and rinse the potatoes. Dice them and cover with the stock. Cook them. Combine with the mushrooms and sour cream blended with the flour. Bring to a boil. Season to taste. Just before serving sprinkle with chopped parsley sprigs.

WHITE MUSHROOM SOUP WITH CREAM

6 cups stock from bones and vegetables, 2/3 cup sour cream, 13 1/2 white mushrooms, 1 oz. flour, fat for frying, parsley sprigs, salt, pepper and seasoning to taste

Clean, rinse and cut the mushrooms into thin strips. Fry them and cover with the stock. Cook for 6—8 minutes. Heat the fat and combine with the flour. Fry without browning. Combine with the stock and sour cream. Bring to a boil. Add chopped parsley sprigs and season to taste. Serve with macaroni or lasagne noodles.

MUSHROOM SOUP WITH WINE

6 cups poultry stock, 2/3 cup dry white wine, 9 1/2 oz. mushroms, 3 1/2 oz. ketchup, fat for frying, 2/3 oz. flour, parsley sprigs, salt, pepper and thyme to taste

Clean and rinse the mushrooms and cut them into thin strips. Fry them. Heat the fat and blend with the flour. Brown this lightly and combine with the stock, mushrooms, wine and ketchup. Cook for several minutes. Add the chopped parsley sprigs. Season to taste. Serve with lasagne noodles or toasted sponge-cake slices.

ONION SOUP À LA PRZYPKOWSKI

6 cups meat stock, 13 1/2 oz. onions, 2—2 2/3 oz. butter, 7 oz. whole-wheat bread, 2/3—1 oz. butter for the bread, salt, pepper, ginger, cloves and nutmeg to taste

Peel, rinse and dice the onions. Fry them without browning. Cut the bread into cubes. Fry it in the butter. Cover with the stock. Add the onions and cook. Towards the end add the seasoning. Force the soup through a strainer. Bring to a boil. Season to taste. Serve with salted bread sticks.

PEA SOUP WITH POTATOES

6 cups stock from bones and vegetables, 7—8 1/2 oz. peas, 9 1/2 oz. potatoes, 3 1/2 oz. kiełbasa, 3 1/2 oz. smoked bacon, 2 2/3 oz. onions, 2/3 oz. flour, salt, pepper, garlic, marjoram and seasoning to taste

Sort and rinse the peas. Cover them with the stock. Bring to a boil and set aside for 2 hours. Cook this. Wash, peel and rinse the potatoes. Dice them and add to the peas towards the end of cooking. Peel, rinse and chop the onions finely. Dice the bacon and partly render it down. Add the onions and fry them. Add the flour and brown it lightly. Cut the kiełbasa into half-slices. Combine the onions, kiełbasa and seasoning with the soup. Cook for a while. Season to taste.

UHLAN'S PEA SOUP

6 cups stock from bones, 7 oz. peas, 7 oz. boneless pork, 2 2/3 oz. onions, 3 1/2 oz. smoked bacon, 5—7 oz. lasagne noodles, salt, pepper, marjoram and seasoning to taste

Sort and rinse the peas. Cover them with cold stock. Bring to a boil and set aside for 2 hours. Cook this. Peel, rinse and dice the onions together with the meat and bacon. Render down the bacon partly. Add the meat and fry it lightly. Add the onions and fry them. Sprinkle with water and simmer covered over low heat. When tender add the meat to the peas together with the cooked lasagne noodles and seasoning. Cook for several minutes. Season to taste.

TOMATO SOUP WITH CREAM

6 cups stock from bones and vegetables, 2/3 cup sour cream, 1 1/4 lb. tomatoes, 2 2/3 oz. onions, 2/3 oz. flour, parsley sprigs, fat for frying, salt, sugar and seasoning to taste

Wash the tomatoes and chop them finely together with the peeled onions. Simmer this in the fat, stirring often. Force through a strainer and combine with the stock and sour cream blended with the flour. Bring to a boil. Season to taste. Before serving combine with chopped parsley sprigs. Serve with rice or macaroni.

GENERAL'S TOMATO SOUP

6 cups stock from bones and vegetables, 2 lb. tomatoes, 3 1/2 oz. onions, 3 tablespoons olive oil, 2 egg yolks, 1 2/3 oz. walnut meats, parsley sprigs, salt, pepper, garlic and thyme to taste

Peel, rinse and chop the onions finely. Fry them in the oil. Add the washed and cut up tomatoes, Simmer until tender, stirring often. Force them through a strainer. Combine with the stock and cook for a while. Blanch the walnuts and grind them. Combine with the soup, egg yolks and chopped parsley sprigs. Season to taste. Serve with noodles.

UHLAN'S SOURED CUCUMBER SOUP

6 cups broth, 9 1/2 oz. soured cucumbers, 5 oz. onions, 1 1/3 oz. butter, 9 1/2 oz. white kiełbasa, salt, pepper and marjoram to taste

Peel, rinse and chop the onions finely, then fry them. Add peeled and diced soured cucumbers. Simmer until tender, sprinkling with the broth.

Place the kiełbasa in the broth and keep the temperature at 140°F for 10 minutes. Take the kiełbasa out of the broth, remove the skin, and cut it into half-slices. Place it in the broth together with the soured cucumbers and seasoning. Bring to a boil. Season to taste.

ROYAL ZHUREK (WHITE BORSCH)

4 3/4 cups stock from meat and vegetables, 2 cups sour cream, 7 oz. smoked ham, 1 2/3 oz. kiełbasa, 17 oz. scooped out potato balls, 3 1/2 oz. onions, fat for frying, 2/3 oz. flour, parsley sprigs, salt, pepper, seasoning, marjoram and soured rye-flour juice to taste (q.v.)

Wash the potatoes. Cover them with the stock and cook them. Peel, rinse and dice the onions, then fry them. Add thin strips of the ham. Add the onions and ham to the potatoes towards the end of cooking together with sliced kiełbasa. Combine with the soured rye-flour juice and the sour cream blended with the flour. Bring to a boil. Add the marjoram and chopped parsley sprigs. Season to taste.

NAMYSŁOWSKI ZHUREK

6 cups stock from bones and vegetables, 2/3 cup sour cream, 7 oz. kiełbasa, 3 1/2 oz. onions, fat for frying, 1 2/3 oz. grated horseradish, 1 oz. flour, 2 hard-boiled egg yolks, salt, pepper, garlic, sugar and soured rye-flour juice to taste (q.v.)

Peel, rinse and dice the onions, then fry them. Remove the skin from the kiełbasa and cut it into half-slices. Add it to the onions and simmer for a while. Cover with the stock and cook for around 5 minutes over low heat. Combine with the sour cream blended with the flour and soured rye-flour juice. Bring to a boil. Add the horseradish and egg yolks that have been forced through a strainer. Season to taste.

CHRISTMAS EVE ZHUREK

6 cups water, 1—1 1/3 oz. dried cèpe mushrooms, 5 oz. onions, 1 tablespoon olive oil, 5 oz. whole-wheat bread, 2 hard-boiled eggs, salt, pepper, bay leaf, allspice and soured rye-flour juice to taste (q.v.)

Wash, soak and cook the mushrooms. Peel, rinse and dice the onions, then fry them, browning lightly. Cover with the water. Add the seasoning and cook for 6—8 minutes over low heat. Combine with diced bread, mushroom stock, mushroom strips, and soured rye-flour juice. Bring to a boil. Season to taste. Add the eggs cut up into pieces. Serve at once.

POLISH KRUPNIK (PEARL BARLEY SOUP)

6 cups stock from bones and vegetables, 3 1/2 oz. pearl barley, 13 1/2 oz. potatoes, 2/3—1 oz. dried cèpe mushrooms, 2 2/3 oz. onions, fat for frying, parsley sprigs, salt, pepper and seasoning to taste

Wash, soak and cook the mushrooms. Rinse the pearl barley and cover it with the stock. Cook it covered over low heat. Wash, peel and dice the potatoes. Add to the barley towards the end of cooking. Peel, rinse and dice the onions, then fry them. Combine with the soup, strips of mushrooms and mushroom stock. Cook for a while. Add chopped parsley sprigs. Season to taste.

UHLAN'S SOUP

6 cups broth, 1 1/3 oz. dried cèpe mushrooms, 2 hard-boiled eggs, 5 oz. whole-wheat bread, 2/3 oz. raisins, 2 2/3 oz. onions, 1 oz. butter, parsley sprigs, salt and nutmeg to taste

Wash and soak the mushrooms. Cook them and cut into strips. Peel, rinse and chop the onions finely, then fry them. Add bread cubes and brown lightly. Cover with broth. Add mushrooms and rinsed raisins, then cook for a while. Combine with chopped parsley sprigs and season to taste. Serve at once.

HUNTER'S SOUP WITH LOBSTER

6 cups broth, 7 oz. boneless venison roast, 5 oz. lobster tails, 1 1/2 oz. almonds, 2/3 cup sour cream, 3 1/2 oz. whole-wheat bread, 2/3 oz. butter, parsley sprigs, salt and pepper to taste

Blanch the almonds. Cut the bread into cubes and fry it in the butter. Add to the broth together with strips of the meat, lobster tails and almonds. Cook for a while. Add the sour cream and chopped parsley sprigs. Season to taste.

BEER SOUP

4 cups lager beer, 5 oz. whole-wheat bread without crust, 1 2/3 oz. butter, salt, caraway seed and sugar to taste, 2 cups water

Combine the beer with the water, crumbled bread, butter and seasoning. Cook for a while and force through a strainer. Bring to a boil. Season to taste. Serve with crackers.

WINE SOUP

Bottle of dry white wine, 2 cups water, 3 1/2 oz. raisins, 3 1/2 oz. almonds, 3—4 egg yolks, 3 1/2 oz. confectioners' sugar

Blanch the almonds and grind them. Combine the wine with the water. Bring to a boil. Gradually add to the egg yolks beaten with the sugar, stirring briskly with an egg-whisk. Add rinsed raisins and almonds. Serve with ladyfingers.

FARINA SOUP

6 cups stock from poultry and vegetables, 5 oz. smoked ham, 2—3 egg yolks, 1 2/3 oz. farina, parsley sprigs, salt, pepper and seasoning to taste

Bring the stock to a boil. Gradually add the farina, stirring briskly with an egg-whisk. Cook this. Combine with minced ham, egg yolks and chopped parsley sprigs. Season to taste.

CHEESE SOUP

6 cups vegetable stock, 9 1/2 oz. boneless veal, 3 1/2 oz. hard cheese, 2—3 egg yolks, parsley sprigs, salt, pepper and nutmeg to taste

Wash and mince the meat. Cover it with the stock and cook over low heat. Combine with grated cheese, egg yolks and chopped parsley sprigs. Season to taste. Serve with puffs.

COUNT TYSZKIEWICZ SOUP

6 cups stock from poultry and vegetables, 2/3 cup sour cream, 1 lb. cauliflower, 3 1/2 oz. boneless roast chicken, 5—7 oz. tomato royale, 2 egg yolks, parsley sprigs, salt, pepper and seasoning to taste

Clean the cauliflower and rinse in lightly salted water. Divide into pieces and cook in the stock. Combine with the chicken meat and tomatoes cut into strips. Add the sour cream. Bring to a boil. Combine with the egg yolks and chopped parsley sprigs. Season to taste.

CHEF'S SOUP

6 cups stock from bones and vegetables, 2/3 cup sour cream, 1/2 lb. boneless veal, 7 oz. canned peas, 3 1/2 oz. onions, fat for frying, 2/3 oz. flour, parsley sprigs, 2—2 2/3 oz. hard cheese, salt, pepper, marjoram, thyme and seasoning to taste

Peel, rinse and chop the onions finely. Wash, mince and fry the meat lightly. Add the onions and brown them lightly. Cover with the stock and cook the meat. Combine with the peas, sour cream blended with the flour and seasoning. Cook for a while. Combine with grated cheese and chopped parsley sprigs. Season to taste.

GIPSY SOUP

6 cups stock from bones and vegetables, 2/3 cup sour cream, 1/2 lb. peppers, 1/2 lb. potatoes, 3 1/2—5 oz. kiełbasa, 1 1/3 oz. tomato paste, 3 1/2 oz. onions, fat for frying, parsley sprigs, 2/3 oz. flour, salt, pepper, marjoram and seasoning to taste

Clean, rinse and dice the onions and peppers, then fry them lightly. Sprinkle with the stock and simmer until tender. Towards the end add the tomato paste and strips of kiełbasa. Wash, peel and rinse the potatoes. Dice them and cover with the remaining stock. Bring to a boil. Combine with the sour cream blended with the flour, chopped parsley sprigs, seasoning and remaining ingredients. Cook for a while. Season to taste.

HUNTER'S SOUP

6 cups stock from bones and vegetables, 2/3 sour cream, 1 lb. hare meat (front), 3 1/2 oz. onions, fat for frying, 3 tablespoons Madeira wine, parsley sprigs, 2/3 oz. flour, salt, pepper, juniper and seasoning to taste

Peel, rinse and chop the onions finely. Wash the meat and fry it lightly. Add the onions and brown them lightly. Cover with the stock and cook covered over low heat. Remove the meat when tender and discard the bones. Dice the meat and combine with strained stock, sour cream blended with the flour and wine. Bring to a boil. Combine with chopped parsley sprigs. Season to taste. Serve with liver meat balls.

GDAŃSK SOUP

6 cups water, 9 1/2 oz. chicken meat, 9 1/2 oz. soup vegetables (carrots, parsley root, celeriac, leek), 1 cup milk, 1 2/3 oz. macaroni, 1 2/3 oz.

canned peas, 1 2/3 oz. canned string beans, fresh dill, salt, pepper, bay leaf, allspice and seasoning to taste

Wash the chicken meat. Cover it with the water. Add salt and cook the meat. Wash, peel and rinse the vegetables. Cut them into thin strips. Add to the chicken towards the end of cooking together with the seasoning. Remove the meat when tender and discard the bones. Cut the meat into strips. Combine the stock with the macaroni, peas, milk, string beans and meat. Cook until done. Combine with chopped dill. Season to taste.

ŁĘCZYCA SOUP

6 cups stock from bones and vegetables, 2/3 cup sour cream, 3 1/2 oz. white beans, 1 1/3 oz. macaroni, 3 1/2 oz. garlic kiełbasa, 2 2/3 oz. pork fat, 2—2 2/3 oz. onions, 2/3—1 1/3 oz. flour, salt, pepper, marjoram, garlic, ground paprika and seasoning to taste

Sort and rinse the beans. Cover with the cold stock. Bring to a boil and set aside for 2 hours. Cook the beans. Towards the end add the macaroni and kiełbasa cut into half-slices. Peel, rinse and chop the onions finely. Dice the pork fat and partly render it down. Add the onions and fry them lightly. Combine with the flour and brown lightly. Combine with the soup, sour cream and seasoning. Bring to a boil. Season to taste.

LOBSTER SOUP

15 lobsters, 6 cups poultry stock, 3 1/2 oz. canned peas, 7 oz. mushrooms, 2/3 cup sour cream, parsley sprigs, fresh dill, salt and pepper to taste

Scrub the lobsters with a brush under running water, holding the body in your hand. Pull out the center fin from the tail together with the black intestinal vein. Place the lobsters in boiling salted water. Add the dill. Cook covered for around 15 minutes. When done, separate the meat from the claws and tails. Clean, rinse and cut the mushrooms into strips.

Cook them in the stock. Add the lobster meat, peas and sour cream. Bring to a boil. Combine with chopped parsley sprigs. Season to taste. Serve with lasagne noodles.

HUSSAR'S FISH SOUP

6 cups vegetable stock, 1/3 cup sour cream, 1 lb. cleaned fish, 2 hard-boiled eggs, 1 2/3 oz. macaroni, fresh dill, parsley sprigs, 2/3 oz. dried cèpe mushrooms, salt and pepper to taste

Wash the fish and separate the meat from the bones. Cut into cubes together with soaked mushrooms. Cover with the stock and cook over low heat for around 30 minutes. Towards the end add the macaroni. Combine the soup with the sour cream. Bring to a boil. Add eggs cut into pieces and chopped greens. Season to taste.

CHRISTMAS EVE FISH SOUP

6 cups vegetable stock, 1 lb. cleaned fish (carp, pike, pike perch), 1 1/3 oz. dried cèpe mushrooms, 1 oz. butter or margarine, salt, pepper and nutmeg to taste

Wash, soak and cook the mushrooms. Wash the fish and separate the meat from the bones. Cut into samll pieces. Cover with the vegetable and mushroom stock and cook for 30—40 minutes over low heat. Heat the fat and blend with the flour. Fry this without browning. Dilute with a little of the stock, stirring with an egg-whisk. Bring to a boil. Add mushroom strips. Season to taste. Serve with lasagne noodles.

GENERAL'S FISH SOUP

6 cups vegetable stock, 1 lb. cleaned carp, 2/3 cup sour cream, 2/3 oz. flour, 1 2/3 oz. grated horseradish, 1 1/3 oz. raisins, salt, pepper and curry powder to taste

Wash the fish and separate the meat from the bones. Cut it into cubes. Place in the stock and cook for around 30 minutes over low heat. Blend the sour cream with the flour. Combine with the fish. Bring to a boil. Add the horseradish and rinsed raisins. Season to taste.

ROYAL FISH SOUP

6 cups water, 1 lb. cleaned carp, 1/3 cup dry red wine, 2—2 2/3 oz. prunes, 1 oz. almonds, 2/3 oz. raisins, salt, pepper, sugar and lemon juice to taste

Blanch the almonds. Wash, soak and cook the prunes. Force them through a strainer. Wash the fish and separate the meat from the bones. Cut into strips. Cover with the water. Add the seasoning. Cook over low heat for around 30 minutes. Towards the end add the prune paste, rinsed raisins, almonds and wine. Season to taste. Serve with sweet rolls.

GENERAL'S COLD BORSCH

4 cups soured milk, 1 cup sour cream, 1 lb. beets, 5 oz. lobster meat, 3 1/2 oz. almonds, 1 2/3 oz. ham, fresh dill, parsley sprigs, salt and sugar to taste

Wash, peel and rinse the beets. Blanch the almonds, chop them and arrange over the beets. Wrap in foil and bake. Allow to cool and grate the beets. Combine the milk with the sour cream. Beat with an egg-whisk. Add the beets, lobsters, ham strips and chopped greens. Season to taste.

LITHUANIAN COLD BORSCH

6 cups soured milk, 1 cup sour cream, 9 1/2—13 1/2 oz. young beets with leaves, 3 1/2 oz. lobster tails, chives, fresh dill, hard-boiled egg, 3 1/2 oz. boneless veal or chicken roast, 3 1/2 oz. cucumbers, 1 2/3 oz. radishes, salt, sugar and soured beet juice to taste

Rinse, clean and chop the young beets along with the leaves. Cook in a small amount of lightly salted water. Clean and rinse the radishes. Cut them into half-slices. Wash and peel the cucumbers. Cut them into strips, discarding the seeds. Combine the milk with the sour cream. Beat with an egg-whisk. Add the cooled beets, radishes, cucumbers, lobster tails, chopped chives, chopped dill, veal strips, egg cut into pieces and soured beet juice. Season to taste. Set aside in a cool place for several hours.

COLD SORREL SOUP

2 cups broth, 4 cups soured milk, 1 cup sour cream, 5 oz. sorrel, 3 1/2 oz. spinach, 2 hard-boiled eggs, 1 2/3 oz. walnut meats, fresh dill, chives, salt and sugar to taste

Blanch the almonds and chop together with the eggs. Sort the sorrel and spinach. Discard the leaf stems. Rinse throughly. Cover with the broth and cook this, then force through a strainer. Combine the milk with the sour cream and sorrel and spinach paste. Beat with an egg-whisk. Combine with the eggs, walnuts and chopped greens. Season to taste. Serve with cooked potatoes sprinkled with pork fat cracklings.

BUTTERMILK SOUP

6 cups buttermilk, 1 cup sour cream, 7 oz. farmer's cheese, radishes, 2 hard-boiled eggs, 2 2/3 oz. onions, 1 oz. butter, salt and sugar to taste

Peel, rinse and chop the onions finely. Fry them, then allow to cool. Clean, rinse and grate the radishes coarsely. Blend the buttermilk with the sour cream. Beat with an egg-whisk. Add the onions, radishes, eggs cut into pieces and cheese cut into cubes. Season to taste. Serve with cooked potatoes sprinkled with pork fat cracklings.

COLD TOMATO SOUP

2 cups tomato juice, 2 cups sour cream, 2 hard-boiled eggs, chives, fresh dill, salt, pepper and sugar to taste

Blend the sour cream with the tomato juice. Beat with an egg-whisk. Combine with ground eggs and chopped greens. Season to taste.

APPLE SOUP WITH RAISINS

2 cups water, 2 cups milk, 2/3 cup dry white wine, 1 1/4—1 3/4 lb. apples, 2—2 2/3 oz. sugar, 1 2/3 oz. raisins, 2/3 oz. flour, cinnamon and lemon juice to taste

Wash, peel and cut the apples in half, removing the cores. Cut them into pieces. Add the sugar and ground cinnamon. Bring to a boil. Blend the flour with the milk. Add to the apples. Bring to a boil. Add rinsed raisins. Allow to cool. Combine with the wine. Season to taste. Keep the soup in the refrigerator for several hours. Serve with ladyfingers or crackers.

CHERRY SOUP

4 cups water, 2 cups red wine, 1/2 lb. sugar, 2 lb. sour cherries, cinnamon and cloves to taste

Bring the water and sugar to a boil. Allow to cool. Crush the cherries together with the pits. Add the cinnamon and cloves. Set aside in a cool place for 12 hours. Force through a strainer. Add the syrup. Bring to a boil and allow to cool. Combine with the wine. Season to taste. Serve with ladyfingers.

STRAWBERRY SOUP

2 cups dry white wine, 1 cup sour cream, 1 3/4 lb. strawberries, 5 oz. sugar, 1/3 cup Maraschino liqueur, lemon and orange juice to taste

Sort and rinse the strawberries, discarding the stems. Mix in a blender together with the sugar and sour cream. Combine with the liqueur, lemon, orange juice and wine. Serve with ladyfingers.

CHOCOLATE SOUP

2 cups milk, 2 cups cream, 5—6 egg yolks, 1 2/3 oz. powdered chocolate,
3 1/2 oz. raisins, 3 1/2 oz. confectioners' sugar

Blend the milk with the sour cream. Bring to a boil. Beat the egg yolks
with the sugar and chocolate in top of a double boiler. Gradually add the
hot liquid, stirring briskly with an egg-whisk. Add hot water to the bottom
of double boiler. Heat, stirring constantly, until the soup thickens. Keep
the water near boiling point, but do not allow it to boil. Combine with
rinsed raisins. Season to taste. Serve with ladyfingers.

APPLE SOUP

6 cups water, 13 1/2 oz. apples, 1/2 lb. cranberries, 3 1/2—5 oz. sugar,
1/3—2/3 oz. potato starch, 2/3 cup dry white wine, lemon juice to taste

Wash, peel and cut the apples in half, removing the cores. Cut into pieces.
Cover with boiling water. Add the lemon juice and bring to a boil. Set
aside on a plate. Blend the potato starch with a small amount of cold
water. Gradually add to the syrup, stirring briskly with an egg-whisk.
Cook for a while. Sort the cranberries and rinse them. Force them
through a strainer and add to the syrup. Add the apples and the wine.
Add sugar and lemon juice to taste. Serve with macaroni, rice or sweet
toast.

BLUEBERRY SOUP

6 cups water, 2/3 cup sour cream, 1 1/4 lb. blueberries, 3 1/2—5 oz.
sugar, 1/3—2/3 oz. potato starch, cinnamon and cloves to taste

Sort and rinse the blueberries. Cover with boiling water. Add the seasoning. Cook this and force through a strainer. Combine with the sour
cream blended with the flour, stirring briskly with an egg-whisk. Bring
to a boil. Add sugar. Allow to cool. Serve with macaroni.

FRUIT SOUP

*4 cups water, 2/3 cup sour cream, 2/3 cup dry white wine, 1 1/4—1 3/4
lb. fruit (raspberries, strawberries, plums, peaches), 5 oz. sugar, 2/3 oz.
potato starch, lemon rind and vanilla to taste*

Wash and separate the fruit. Cover with water. Add the seasoning. Cook
this and force through a strainer. Gradually add the sour cream blended
with the flour, stirring briskly with an egg-whisk. Cook for a while.
Allow to cool. Combine with the wine and sugar. Serve with sweet toast.

MILK SOUP OLD POLISH STYLE

*6 cups milk, 5—7 oz. bread, 1—1 1/3 oz. butter, 2—2 2/3 oz. almonds,
2—2 2/3 oz. confectioners' sugar, 2 egg yolks, salt to taste*

Blanch the almonds and grind them. Cut the bread into small cubes.
Pour butter over this. Dry in the oven, stirring often. Bring the milk to
a boil and gradually add to egg yolks beaten with sugar, stirring briskly
with an egg-whisk. Pour over the toast. Add the almonds. Season to
taste. Serve at once.

WROCŁAW MILK SOUP

*6 cups milk, 2—3 egg yolks, 3 1/2 oz. poppyseed, 1 2/3 oz. walnut
meats, 2—2 2/3 oz. farmer's cheese, sugar, salt, cloves and cinnamon
to taste*

Blanch the walnuts and chop them. Rinse the poppyseed. Cover with
water and set aside in a cool place for 24 hours. Drain it and grind 3 times.
Bring the milk to a boil together with the seasoning and poppyseed.
Gradually pour into the egg yolks beaten with the sugar, stirring briskly
with an egg-whisk. Combine with the almonds. Season to taste. Divide
into portions and sprinkle with farmer's cheese forced through a strainer.

MILK SOUP WITH ALMONDS

6 cups milk, 3 1/2 oz. almonds, 1 2/3 oz. cocoa, 1/3 cup rum, 2 2/3 oz. confectioners' sugar, 3—4 egg yolks, vanilla bean to taste

Blanch the almonds and grind them. Bring the milk to a boil together with the chopped vanilla bean. Pour through a strainer. Combine the cocoa with a small amount of cold water until all lumps disappear. Add to the milk. Bring to a boil. Combine with the egg yolks beaten with the sugar, rum and almonds. Serve with puffs.

Fish

GRASS CARP SAUTÉ

2 lb. grass carp, 1 1/3 oz. flour, olive oil for frying, salt, pepper and lemon juice to taste

Wash the cleaned and drawn fish and cut lengthwise into halves, removing the spine bones. Cut diagonally into portions. Sprinkle with pepper and with lemon juice. Set aside in a cool place for 30 minutes. Sprinkle with salt and flour and fry.

BAKED GRASS CARP

2 lb. grass carp, fat for baking, 2/3 cup sour cream, salt, pepper and lemon juice to taste

Prepare the grass carp as above. Cut the fish diagonally on both sides, making 1/2 in. thick slits 1 1/4 in. apart. Sprinkle with pepper and lemon juice. Set aside in a cool place for 30 minutes. Add salt and arrange the fish in a greased pan. Bake in the oven, basting with the fat. Towards the end sprinkle with seasoned sour cream.

GRASS CARP BAKED IN FOIL

2 lb. grass carp, fat for baking, 3 1/2 oz. onions, 5 oz. mushrooms, parsley sprigs, salt, pepper, thyme and lemon juice to taste

Prepare the grass carp (as in Grass Carp Sauté). Clean and rinse the onions and mushrooms. Cut them into thin strips. Combine with chopped parsley sprigs and seasoning. Grease the aluminium foil. Arrange the fish on it alternately with the mushrooms and onions. Wrap carefully and bake in a hot oven.

GRASS CARP LITHUANIAN STYLE

2 lb. grass carp, fat for baking, 2 2/3 oz. ketchup, 1 1/3 oz. almonds, 1 oz. butter or margarine for roux, 2/3 oz. flour, 1 cup milk, 1 1/3 oz. caviar, 2 2/3 oz. hard cheese, salt and nutmeg to taste

Prepare the grass carp (as in Grass Carp Sauté). Sprinkle with seasoning and fat, then bake in an oven. Blanch and grind the almonds. Heat the fat and blend it with the flour. Fry without browning. Add cold milk slowly, stirring briskly with an egg-whisk. Bring to a boil. Combine with the caviar and almonds. Season to taste. Cover the fish with this. Sprinkle with grated cheese and bake.

FISHERMAN'S GRASS CARP

2 lb. grass carp, fat for frying, 1 1/3 oz. flour, 2 eggs, 2/3 cup cream, 3 1/2 oz. lobster tails, fresh dill, salt, pepper and ketchup to taste

Prepare the grass carp (as in Grass Carp Sauté). Cut diagonally into portions. Sprinkle with seasoning and set aside in a cool place for 30 minutes. Add salt, sprinkle with flour and fry on both sides. Wash the eggs and break them into the cream. Beat with an egg-whisk. Add the lobster tails and chopped dill. Season to taste. Pour over the fish and bake.

COD, HADDOCK, HAKE OR GILTHEAD SAUTÉ

1 1/4 lb. frozen fish fillets, olive oil, 1—1 1/3 oz. flour, salt, pepper and lemon juice to taste

Place the fillets in a plastic bag. Tie up the bag to keep out the water. Defrost the fillets in water kept at 68°F. Cut the defrosted fillets into portions. Rinse and dry them. Sprinkle with lemon juice and seasoning. Set aside in a cool place for 30 minutes. Sprinkle with flour and place in very hot fat. Brown on both sides. Continue frying over low heat for several minutes.

FRIED COD, HADDOCK, HAKE OR GILTHEAD

1 1/4 lb. fish fillets, olive oil, 1—1 1/3 oz. flour, 2 eggs, breadcrumbs, pepper and lemon juice to taste

Prepare the fillets as above. Dredge with flour, dip in beaten eggs, then coat with breadcrumbs, pressing lightly with your hand. Place the fillets in very hot fat. Brown on both sides. Continue frying over low heat for several minutes.

COD, HADDOCK, HAKE OR GILTHEAD IN PASTRY

1 lb. fish fillets, 3 1/2 oz. flour, olive oil, 1/3 cup milk, 2 eggs, salt, pepper and lemon juice to taste

Prepare the fillets (as in Cod, Haddock, Hake or Gilthead Sauté). Wash the eggs and break them into a blender. Add milk, sifted flour and seasoning. Turn on the blender for 30 seconds. Dip the fillets in the batter and place in very hot fat. Brown on both sides. Continue frying over low heat for several minutes.

COD, HADDOCK, HAKE OR GILTHEAD BAKED IN FOIL

1 1/4 lb. fish fillets, 1 2/3 oz. butter, 2—2 2/3 oz. ketchup, salt, pepper and lemon juice to taste

Prepare the fillets (as in Cod, Haddock, Hake or Gilthead Sauté). Butter the foil and arrange the fish on it. Pour ketchup over the fish. Wrap up and bake in a hot oven.

COD, HADDOCK, HAKE OR GILTHEAD POLISH STYLE

1 1/4 lb. fish fillets, 1/2 lb. soup vegetables (carrots, parsley root, celeriac, leek), 2—2 2/3 oz. onions, 1 1/3 oz. butter, 2 hard-boiled eggs, parsley sprigs, salt, pepper, bay leaf, allspice and lemon juice to taste

Prepare the fillets (as in Cod, Haddock, Hake or Gilthead Sauté). Wash, peel and rinse the vegetables, then cut them into thin strips. Cover with water and cook. Towards the end add the seasoning and fish. Take them

out when done and arrange on a platter. Surround with the vegetables. Pour over melted butter blended with chopped eggs and parsley sprigs.

COD, HADDOCK, HAKE OR GILTHEAD IN SOUR CREAM

1 1/4 lb. fish fillets, olive oil, 1—1 1/3 oz. flour, 2/3 cup sour cream, 1 1/3 oz. raisins, 2—2 2/3 oz. hard cheese, parsley sprigs, salt, pepper and lemon juice to taste

Prepare the fillets (as in Cod, Haddock, Hake or Gilthead Sauté). Dredge with flour and brown on both sides. Pour over seasoned sour cream blended with rinsed raisins and chopped parsley sprigs. Sprinkle with grated cheese and bake.

WROCŁAW COD, HADDOCK, HAKE OR GILTHEAD

1 1/4 lb. fish fillets, olive oil, 1—1 1/3 oz. flour, 1/3 cup dry white wine, 1/2 lb. tomatoes, 1/2 lb. apples, 1 1/3 oz. raisins, pepper and lemon juice to taste

Prepare the fillets (as in Cod, Haddock, Hake or Gilthead Sauté). Dredge with flour and fry on both sides. Wash and scald the tomatoes, then remove the skins. Wash, peel and cut the apples in half removing the cores. Cut into pieces together with the tomatoes. Surround the fish with this. Sprinkle with rinsed raisins. Add wine and simmer over low heat for several minutes. Season to taste.

WARSAW COD, HADDOCK, HAKE OR GILTHEAD

1 1/4 lb. frozen fish fillets, olive oil, 1—1 1/3 oz. flour, 1/3 cup ketchup, 3 tablespoons sour cream, 1 2/3 oz. grated horseradish, 2—2 2/3 oz. hard cheese, parsley sprigs, salt, pepper, sugar and lemon juice to taste

Prepare the fillets (as in Cod, Haddock, Hake or Gilthead Sauté). Dredge with flour and fry on both sides. Combine ketchup with sour cream, hor-

seradish and chopped parsley sprigs. Season to taste and pour over fish. Sprinkle with grated cheese and bake.

COD, HADDOCK, HAKE OR GILTHEAD MASURIAN STYLE

1 1/4 lb. frozen fish fillets, olive oil, 1—1 1/3 oz. flour, 3/4 lb. apples, 1 1/4—1 3/4 lb. sour cream, 1 1/3 oz. tomato paste, egg yolk, 1 1/3 oz. raisins, salt, pepper, sugar and lemon juice to taste

Prepare the fillets (as in Cod, Haddock, Hake or Gilthead Sauté). Dredge with flour and fry on both sides. Wash, peel and cut the apples in half, removing the cores. Grate them coarsely and combine with the sour cream, tomato paste, egg yolk and rinsed raisins. Season to taste. Pour over the fish and bake.

CARP SAUTÉ

2 lb. carp, fat for frying, 5—7 oz. soup vegetables (carrots, parsley root, celeriac, leek), 1—1 1/3 oz. flour, 2 2/3 oz. onions, salt and pepper to taste

Wash, clean, rinse and grate the vegetables coarsely. Dice the onions. Wash the cleaned and drawn carp. Cut it lengthwise into halves, removing the spine bones. Cut diagonally into portions. Rub with the seasoning. Surround with the vegetables and onions. Set aside in a cool place for several hours. Remove the vegetables and dredge with flour. Place in very hot fat and brown on both sides. Continue frying over low heat for several minutes.

BUTTERED POACHED CARP

2 lb. carp, 3/4 lb. soup vegetables (carrots, parsley root, celeriac, leek), 1 1/3 oz. butter, parsley sprigs, salt, pepper, bay leaf and allspice to taste

Wash, peel and rinse the vegetables. Cut them into thin strips. Cover with boiling water, add salt and cook. Wash the cleaned and drawn carp. Cut across into steaks. Place in the stock towards the end of cooking together with the seasoning. Take out the fish when tender and arrange on a platter. Surround with the vegetables. Dot with butter and serve at once.

CARP IN BLACK SAUCE

2 lb. carp, 7 oz. soup vegetables (carrots, parsley root, celeriac, leek), 2 2/3 oz. onions, 1 cup water, 1 cup dark beer, 1/3 cup dry red wine, 1 2/3 oz. walnut meats, 1 oz. butter, 1 oz. flour, pepper, salt, sugar, ginger, marjoram, allspice, bay leaf and lemon juice to taste

Wash, peel and rinse the vegetables. Chop them finely and cover with water, then cook them. Force them through a strainer. Combine with the beer, wine and seasoning. Wash the cleaned and drawn carp. Cut across into steaks. Place in the stock and cook over low heat for around 30 minutes. Take out when done and sprinkle with the stock. Blanch the walnuts and chop them. Heat the fat and blend it with the flour. Fry without browning. Blend with cold stock, stirring briskly with an egg-whisk. Bring to a boil and cook for several minutes. Add seasoning and colour the sauce with caramel. Pour over the carp in an oven-proof dish. Sprinkle with the walnuts and bake.

CASTELLAN'S CARP

2 lb. carp, 2/3 cup dry white wine, 5 oz. prunes, 5 oz. lemons, 1 1/3 oz. grated horseradish, parsley sprigs, butter, salt, pepper, cloves and cinnamon to taste

Wash, soak and cook the prunes. Force them through a strainer. Wash and scald the lemons, then peel them. Cut into half-slices, removing any pits. Prepare the carp (as in Carp Sauté). Cut into portions. Sprinkle with the seasoning and fry lightly. Cover with wine combined with the lemons, prune paste, horseradish, chopped parsley sprigs and seasoning, then bake.

CARP POLISH STYLE I

2 lb. carp, 7 oz. soup vegetables (carrots, parsley root, celeriac, leek), 1 cup water, 1 cup lager beer, 1 oz. butter, 1 oz. flour, 1 1/3 oz. raisins, 1 1/3 oz. almonds, 1 2/3 oz. plum jam, 2—2 2/3 oz. gingerbread, salt, sugar, ginger, allspice, bay leaf and lemon juice to taste

Wash, peel and rinse the vegetables. Cut them into small pieces, cover with water and cook. Wash the cleaned and drawn carp. Cut across into steaks. Place in the stock. Add the beer and seasoning, then cook over low heat. Take out the fish when tender. Pour the stock through a strainer. Blanch the almonds. Heat the butter and blend it with the flour. Fry this without browning. Blend with the stock, stirring briskly with an egg-whisk. Bring to a boil. Add the plum jam, rinsed raisins, almonds and fish. Sprinkle with the gingerbread. Cook over low heat for several minutes. Season to taste.

CARP POLISH STYLE II

2 lb. carp, 7 oz. soup vegetables (carrots, parsley root, celeriac, leek), 1 cup lager beer, 1 cup dry white wine, 2/3 oz. capers, 1 2/3 oz. olives, 1 1/3 oz. grated whole-wheat bread, salt, sugar, ginger, allspice, lemon juice and lemon rind to taste

Wash, peel and rinse the vegetables. Cut them into small pieces. Cover with the wine and cook. Wash the cleaned and drawn carp. Cut across into steaks. Place in the stock. Add the beer and seasoning, then cook. Take out the fish. Pour the stock through a strainer. Place the fish in the stock once more. Add rinsed capers, pitted olives, bread and grated lemon rind. Simmer for several minutes. Season to taste.

NOBLEMAN'S CARP

2 lb. carp, olive oil, 1—1 1/3 oz. flour, 1/3 cup dry red wine, 1/2 lb. Damsons, salt, sugar, cinnamon, cloves, ginger and lemon juice to taste

Prepare the carp (as in Carp Sautè). Sprinkle with the seasoning and flour. Brown on both sides. Wash and pit the plums. Place them in a blender. Add the wine and seasoning. Turn on the blender for 30 seconds. Season to taste. Pour over the carp and bake.

CARP À LA RADZIWIŁŁ

2 lb. carp, 7 oz. soup vegetables (carrots, parsley root, celeriac, leek), 2/3 cup dry red wine, 5 oz. onions, 1 2/3 oz. hardened French bread, butter, 2 egg yolks, 1 2/3 oz. raisins, 1 oz. butter for roux, 1 oz. flour, parsley sprigs, salt, pepper, honey, cloves and lemon juice to taste

Cut the cleaned and drawn carp across the spine into 4 pieces 1 1/4— 1 1/2 in. thick, removing the inedible parts (fins, tail). Wash it thoroughly under running water. Peel, rinse and dice the onions. Fry them without browning. Allow to cool and grind together with the remaining cleaned and boned fish and bread that has been soaked in milk, then squeezed out. Combine with chopped parsley sprigs and egg yolks. Season to taste with salt, sugar and pepper. Fill the fish steaks with the prepared stuffing. Place in the vegetable stock. Add salt and cook over low heat. Take out the fish when tender. Pour the stock through a strainer and combine with the wine. Heat the fat and blend with the flour. Fry without browning. Slowly add the cold stock, stirring briskly with an egg-whisk. Bring to a boil. Add rinsed raisins, ground seasoning and fish. Cook for a while and season to taste.

CRACOW CARP

2 lb. carp, 2—2 2/3 oz. buckwheat kasha, 2/3 oz. fat for kasha, 1 2/3 oz. dried cèpe mushrooms, 2 2/3 oz. onions, 2 egg yolks, fat for fish and onions, 3/4 cup sour cream, salt and pepper to taste

Prepare the carp as above. Rinse the kasha, place in top of a double boiler and cover with boiling salted water (1 cup) with the fat. Add hot water to bottom of double boilder. Cover kasha and cook slowly. Wash, soak and

cook the mushrooms, then cut into thin strips. Peel, rinse and chop the onions finely. Fry them and combine with the cooked kasha, mushrooms, egg yolks and remaining boned, finely diced fish, then season. Fill the fish steaks, pour fat over this and bake. Towards the end pour the seasoned sour cream over the fish.

BUTTERED POACHED BREAM

2 lb. bream, 3/4 lb. soup vegetables (carrots, parsley root, celeriac, leek), 2 2/3 oz. butter, parsley sprigs, salt to taste

Wash the cleaned and drawn fish and cut into portions. Wash, peel and rinse the vegetables, then cut into thin strips. Bring to a boil. Add the fish and salt. Cook over low heat. When done transfer to a platter and surround with the vegetables. Dot with butter and sprinkle with chopped parsley sprigs. Serve at once.

FRIED BREAM

2 lb. bream, fat for frying, 1 1/3 oz. flour, 2 eggs, 2 2/3 oz. breadcrumbs, salt and pepper to taste

Wash the cleaned and drawn fish and cut into portions. Sprinkle with the seasoning. Set aside in a cool place for 30 minutes. Sprinkle with flour. Dip in beaten eggs, coat with breadcrumbs and fry the fish.

WARSAW BREAM

2 lb. bream, fat for frying, 1 1/3 oz. flour, 5 oz. onions, 5 oz. apples, 2/3 cup tomato juice, 2 2/3 oz. grated hard cheese, salt and pepper to taste

Prepare the bream as above. Dredge with flour, fry and transfer to a plate. Peel, rinse and chop the onions finely, then fry them. Wash, peel and

cut the apples in half, removing the cores. Grate coarsely and combine with the onions and tomato juice. Season to taste. Cover the fish in an oven-proof dish. Sprinkle with grated cheese and bake.

BREAM POLISH STYLE

2 lb. bream, 1/2 lb. soup vegetables (carrots, parsley root, celeriac, leek), 1/3 cup dry red wine, 1 oz. butter or margarine, 2/3 oz. flour, 1 2/3 oz. almonds, 1 2/3 oz. raisins, 1 1/3 oz. gingerbread, salt, pepper, sugar, cloves and lemon juice to taste

Wash the cleaned and drawn fish. Cut into portions. Place in the vegetable stock, add salt and cook. Take out the fish and pour the stock through a strainer. Heat the butter and blend it with the flour. Fry this without browning. Gradually add cold stock (3/4 cup) blended with the wine, stirring briskly with an egg-whisk. Bring to a boil. Blanch the almonds. Add to the sauce together with the fish, rinsed raisins, grated gingerbread and seasoning. Add caramel for colour. Simmer over low heat for 6—8 minutes.

WROCŁAW BREAM

2 lb. bream, fat for frying, 1 1/3 oz. flour, 3/4 lb. soup vegetables (carrots, parsley root, celeriac, leek), 3 1/2 oz. canned peppers, 3 1/2 oz. plums, 1/3 cup cream, 1 2/3 oz. hard cheese, salt, pepper and lemon juice to taste

Wash the cleaned and drawn bream. Cut into portions. Sprinkle with pepper and lemon juice. Set aside in a cool place for 30 minutes. Add salt and flour. Fry and transfer to a plate. Wash, peel and rinse the vegetables. Cut into thin strips. Fry lightly, sprinkle with water and simmer until tender. Wash and pit the plums. Cut into thin strips together with the peppers. Arrange the fish in an oven-proof dish. Surround with the vegetables, plums and peppers, sprinkling with the seasoning. Add the sour cream. Sprinkle with grated cheese and bake.

CAPTAIN'S BREAM

2 lb. bream, fat for frying, 5 oz. onions, 1 2/3 oz. dried cèpe mushrooms, 2/3 oz. capers, 1 cup sour cream, 1 1/3 oz. tomato paste, parsley sprigs, salt, pepper and seasoning to taste

Wash, soak and cook the mushrooms. Cut them into thin strips. Wash the cleaned and drawn fish. Cut into thin strips and fry lightly. Add finely chopped onions and brown lightly. Add the mushrooms, rinsed capers, tomato paste and sour cream. Combine with the seasoning and simmer until tender, stirring often. Combine with chopped parsley sprigs. Season to taste.

FRIED TENCH

2 lb. tench, 1 1/3 oz. flour, fat for frying, salt and pepper to taste

Wash the cleaned and drawn tench. Cut lengthwise into halves, removing the spine bones, fins and tail. Cut into portions. Sprinkle with pepper and set aside in a cool place for 30 minutes. Sprinkle with salt and flour, then fry.

FRIED TENCH WITH TOAST

2 lb. tench, 1 1/3 oz. flour, fat for frying, 2 eggs, 2 loaves French bread, salt and pepper to taste

Prepare the tench as above. Cut the bread into thin slices, then into strips. Sprinkle the fish with salt and flour. Dip in beaten eggs and toast, then fry.

POACHED TENCH

2 lb. tench, 3/4 lb. soup vegetables (carrots, parsley root, celeriac, leek), 2 hard-boiled eggs, parsley sprigs, 1 1/3 oz. butter, salt to taste

Wash the cleaned and drawn tench. Cut into portions. Wash and peel the vegetables. Cut them into thin strips. Cover with boiling salted water and cook. Towards the end add the fish. Arrange the cooked fish on a platter. Surround with the vegetables. Sprinkle with chopped eggs and parsley sprigs. Pour butter over this and serve at once.

MARINER'S TENCH

2 lb. tench, vegetable stock, 1 oz. butter, 2/3 oz. flour, 1 cup milk, 7 oz. tomatoes, 3 1/2 oz. lobster tails, parsley sprigs, fat for dish, salt and nutmeg to taste

Wash the cleaned and drawn tench. Cut into portions. Cover with stock and cook. Allow to cool in the stock. Heat the fat and blend with the flour. Fry without browning. Add cold milk, stirring briskly with an egg-whisk. Bring to a boil and season. Wash, scald and peel the tomatoes. Cut them into pieces. Take the fish out of the stock. Arrange in an oven-proof greased dish. Surround with the tomatoes and lobster tails. Sprinkle with seasoning and chopped parsley sprigs. Add the sauce and bake.

TENCH WITH RAISINS

2 lb. tench, vegetable stock, 1/3 cup dry red wine, 1 1/3 oz. butter or margarine, 2/3 oz. flour, 3 1/2 oz. raisins, salt, sugar, cinnamon, cloves, pimento, bay leaf and lemon juice to taste

Wash the cleaned and drawn tench. Cut into portions. Place in the stock. Add the wine and seasoning. Cook over low heat. When done transfer to a plate and sprinkle with the stock. Heat the fat and blend with the flour. Fry without browning. Slowly add the cold strained stock, stirring briskly with an egg-whisk. Bring to a boil. Add the fish and rinsed raisins. Cook for a while and season to taste.

TENCH JEWISH STYLE

2 lb. tench, 1 2/3 oz. almonds, 3/4 lb. onions, 5 oz. bacon, 3 1/2 oz. ketchup, salt, pepper, tarragon and marjoram to taste

Prepare the tench (as in Fried Tench). Blanch and grind the almonds. Peel, rinse and dice the onions. Cut the bacon into slices. Arrange in a dish. Add the fish alternately with the onions, sprinkling with the seasoning and almonds. Add ketchup and cover with the remaining bacon. Bake in a hot oven.

TENCH WITH RED CABBAGE

2 lb. tench, fat for frying, 1 1/3 oz. flour, 1 3/4 lb. red cabbage, 3 1/2 oz. onions, 3 1/2 oz. lemons, 2/3 oz. flour for roux, 1 2/3 oz. raisins, 2/3 cup dry red wine, salt, pepper, sugar and lemon juice to taste

Prepare and fry the tench (as in Fried Tench). Clean, rinse and dice the cabbage. Cover with a small amount of boiling salted water and cook. Wash, scald and peel the lemons. Cut them into slices, removing any pits. Peel, rinse and chop the onions finely, then fry them. Combine with the flour and fry lightly. Combine with the cabbage, wine, rinsed raisins and lemons. Season to taste. Arrange in a dish alternately with the fish. Simmer over low heat for 8—10 minutes.

TENCH WITH SAUERKRAUT

2 lb. tench, 1 1/3 oz. flour, fat for frying, 1 2/3 oz. dried cèpe mushrooms, 1 1/2 lb. sauerkraut, 3 1/2 oz. onions, 2/3 oz. flour for frying, 1 2/3 oz. hard cheese, 2/3 cup sour cream, salt, pepper, caraway seed and seasoning to taste

Prepare and fry the tench (as in Fried Tench). Wash, soak and cook the mushrooms. Slice the cabbage. Cover with a small amount of water and mushroom stock, then cook. Peel, rinse and chop the onions finely, then fry them. Combine with the flour and brown lightly. Combine with

the cabbage, strips of mushrooms and seasoning. Place in an oven-proof dish. Cover with the fish. Add seasoned sour cream. Sprinkle with grated cheese and bake.

TENCH À LA TRIPE

2 lb. tench, fat for frying, 3/4 lb. soup vegetables (carrots, parsley root, celeriac, leek), 3 1/2 oz. onions, 2/3 oz. flour, 1 cup sour cream, parsley sprigs, salt, pepper, nutmeg, seasoning, marjoram, ginger and ground paprika to taste

Wash the cleaned and drawn tench. Cut lengthwise into halves, removing the spine and other bones, fins and tail. Cut into strips. Sprinkle with seasoning and flour, then fry lightly. Transfer to a plate. Wash, peel and rinse the vegetables. Cut them into thin strips and fry lightly. Sprinkle with water and simmer until tender. Combine the vegetables with the fish and sour cream, seasoning and chopped parsley sprigs. Cook for a while and season to taste.

SALMON SAUTÉ

1 3/4 lb. drawn salmon, fat for frying, 1 1/3 oz. butter, 3 1/2 oz. lemon, salt, pepper and lemon juice to taste

Cut the salmon lengthwise into halves, removing the spine bones. Remove the skin and scales. Cut diagonally into portions. Wash, dry and sprinkle with lemon juice and seasoning. Set aside in a cool place for 30 minutes. Place in heated fat and fry on both sides. Skim the fat into a dish and add butter to the fish. Fry for a while and transfer to a platter. Garnish with lemon slices and parsley sprigs.

GRILLED SALMON

1 3/4 lb. drawn salmon, 2 2/3 tablespoons olive oil, 1 1/3 oz. butter, 1 2/3 oz. ketchup, 3 1/2 oz. lemons, salt, pepper and lemon juice to taste

Prepare the salmon as above. Rub it with the oil and arrange on the grill. Bake on both sides. Towards the end pour with butter blended with the ketchup. Serve with lemon pieces.

BAKED SALMON

1 3/4 lb. drawn salmon, 3 tablespoons olive oil, 3 1/2 oz. ketchup, salt and pepper to taste

Cut the salmon lengthwise into halves, removing the spine bones. Remove the skin and scales. Cut diagonally into portions. Wash, dry and sprinkle with seasoning and olive oil. Place in an oven and bake. Towards the end add ketchup.

FRIED SALMON

1 3/4 lb. drawn salmon, fat for frying, 1 1/3 oz. flour, 2 eggs, 3 1/2 oz. breadcrumbs, salt and pepper to taste

Prepare the salmon (as in Salmon Sauté). Sprinkle with seasoning and flour. Dip in beaten egg and coat with breadcrumbs. Place in heated fat and fry on both sides. Continue frying over low heat for several minutes.

SALMON LITHUANIAN STYLE

1 3/4 lb. drawn salmon, 1 1/3 oz. butter or margarine, 1 2/3 oz. olives, 1/3 cup dry white wine, parsley sprigs, salt, pepper, sugar, cloves and lemon juice to taste

Prepare the salmon (as in Salmon Sauté). Rub with seasoning. Sprinkle with lemon juice. Pour the butter over. Add pitted olives and seasoning. Add the wine and simmer until tender.

BUTTERED POACHED SALMON

1 3/4 lb. drawn salmon, 1 1/3 oz. butter, 3/4 lb. soup vegetables (carrots, parsley root, celeriac, leek), 2/3 cup dry white wine, 2 2/3 oz. lemons, salt, bay leaf and pimento to taste

Prepare the salmon (as in Salmon Sauté). Wash, peel and rinse the vegetables. Cut them into thin strips. Cover with boiling salted water and cook. Towards the end add the fish, seasoning and wine. Take out the fish when tender and arrange on a platter. Surround with the vegetables. Dot with butter. Garnish with the lemon pieces. Serve at once.

SALMON POLISH STYLE I

1 3/4 lb. drawn salmon, 1 2/3 oz. butter, 1 cup sour cream, 2 2/3 oz. lobster tails, 2 hard-boiled eggs, parsley sprigs, salt and pepper to taste

Prepare the salmon (as in Salmon Sauté). Add the butter and sour cream, then bake. Towards the end add the lobster tails, chopped parsley sprigs and eggs cut into pieces. Season to taste.

SALMON POLISH STYLE II

1 3/4 lb. drawn salmon, fat for frying, 1 cup dry white wine, 4 egg yolks, 3 1/2 oz. almonds, salt and pepper to taste

Prepare the salmon (as in Salmon Sauté). Cover with the wine. Add the seasoning and cook over low heat. Allow to cool in the wine. Take it out and dry it. Brush with egg yolks. Sprinkle with blanched and ground almonds. Fry on both sides.

TROUT SAUTÉ

4 trout, fat for frying, 2 2/3 oz. lemons, salt and pepper to taste

Clean the trout and draw it, slicing along the belly. Remove the guts, taking care not to puncture the gall bladder. Cut out the eyes and gills. Wash the fish thoroughly in water and dry them. Sprinkle with the seasoning. Set aside in a cool place for 30 minutes. Fry them and arrange on a platter. Garnish with lemon slices.

TROUT BAKED EN PAPILLOTE

4 trout, 7 oz. mushrooms, 2 egg yolks, 1 tablespoon cognac, parsley sprigs, salt, pepper and lemon juice to taste

Prepare the trout as above. Sprinkle with lemon juice and pepper. Set aside in a cool place for 30 minutes. Clean, rinse and slice the mushrooms. Fry them and allow to cool. Combine with chopped parsley sprigs, egg yolks, cognac and seasoning. Surround the trout. Wrap in greased paper, tie up the ends with thread and bake in a hot oven. When done remove the paper and arrange on a platter. Surround with the mushrooms. Garnish with lemon wedges and parlsey sprigs.

FRIED TROUT

4 trout, fat for frying, 1 1/3 oz. flour, 2—3 eggs, 3 1/2 oz. breadcrumbs, 1 1/3 oz. butter, salt and pepper to taste

Prepare the trout (as in Trout Sauté). Dredge with flour. Dip in beaten eggs and coat with breadcrumbs. Brown on both sides. Add butter and fry over low heat for several minutes. Serve with peeled lemon slices.

POACHED TROUT

4 trout, 3/4 lb. soup vegetables (carrots, parsley root, celeriac, leek), 1 1/3 oz. butter, 3 1/2 oz. lemons, parsley sprigs and salt to taste

Prepare the trout (as in Trout Sauté). Wash, peel and rinse the vegetables. Cut them into thin strips and cook. Wash, scald and peel the lemons.

Cut into half-slices. Place in the stock together with the fish. Add salt and cook over low heat. Take out the fish when tender. Arrange on a platter. Surround with vegetables. Sprinkle with chopped parsley sprigs. Dot with butter and serve at once.

TROUT IN SOUR CREAM

4 trout, fat for frying, 1 1/3 oz. flour, 2/3 cup sour cream, 1/3 cup dry white wine, salt and pepper to taste

Prepare the trout (as in Trout Sauté). Sprinkle with pepper and set aside in a cool place for 30 minutes. Dredge with salt and flour. Brown on both sides. Pour over sour cream blended with wine and seasoning, then bake. When done transfer to a platter. Pour the seasoned sauce over this. Garnish with parsley sprigs.

TROUT WITH NUTS

4 trout, fat for frying, 3 1/2 oz. walnut meats, 3 tablespoons dry white wine, 1 2/3 oz. ketchup, salt, curry powder and lemon juice

Prepare the trout (as in Trout Sauté). Sprinkle with seasoning. Set aside in a cool place for 30 minutes. Blanch the walnuts and grind them. Blend with the wine and ketchup. Heat the fat. Add the trout sprinkled with salt. Brown on both sides. Surround with nuts and bake in a hot oven.

TROUT À LA CHAMBERLAIN

4 trout, fat for frying, 1 2/3 oz. almonds, 3 1/2 oz. canned pineapple, 5 oz. strawberries, 3 tablespoons cognac, salt, pepper, sugar and lemon juice to taste

Prepare the trout (as in Trout Sauté). Sprinkle with the seasoning. Brown on both sides. Blanch the almonds and grind them. Place in a blender

together with the pineapple, rinsed strawberries without stems, cognac and seasoning. Turn on the blender for 30 seconds. Pour over the trout and bake in a hot oven.

TROUT POLISH STYLE I

4 trout, 1 2/3 oz. butter, 3 1/2 oz. candied sour cherries, 3 tablespoons cherry brandy, 3 tablespoons vermouth, 3 tablespoons vodka, salt, pepper, sugar and lemon juice to taste

Prepare the trout (as in Trout Sauté). Sprinkle with seasoning. Set aside in a cool place for 30 minutes. Pour the butter over and bake. Towards the end add the cherries, cherry brandy, vermouth and vodka. Take out the trout and arrange on a platter. Pour the seasoned sauce over.

TROUT POLISH STYLE II

4 trout, 1 2/3 oz. butter, 1 2/3 oz. almonds, 1 2/3 oz. walnut meats, 3 tablespoons orange juice, 3 tablespoons dry white wine, salt, pepper, sugar and lemon juice to taste

Prepare the trout (as in Trout Sauté). Sprinkle with seasoning. Set aside in a cool place for 30 minutes. Pour the butter over and bake. Blanch the almonds and walnuts. Grind them and add to the fish towards the end of baking together with the orange juice and wine. Season to taste.

PIKE PERCH SAUTÉ

2 lb. pike perch, 1 1/3 oz. flour, fat for frying, salt and pepper to taste

Wash the cleaned and drawn pike perch. Cut lengthwise into halves, removing the spine bone. Cut diagonally into portions. Sprinkle with pepper and set aside in a cool place for 30 minutes. Sprinkle with salt and flour. Place in very hot fat and fry on both sides. Contniue frying over low heat for several minutes.

134

PIKE PERCH-BAKED LITHUANIAN STYLE

2 lb. pike perch, 1/2 lb. pork fat, 1 2/3 oz. grated horseradish, 2 egg yolks, parsley sprigs, salt, pepper and lemon juice to taste

Prepare the pike perch as above. Sprinkle with lemon juice and seasoning. Spread horseradish blended with egg yolks and chopped parsley sprigs over the fish. Bring the halves together and surround with thin strips of pork fat. Tie with a thread. Arrange in a dish and bake in a hot oven. When done remove the pork fat and arrange on a platter. Garnish with lemons and tomatoes.

PIKE PERCH POLISH STYLE

2 lb. pike perch, fat for frying, 2/3 cup sour cream, 1 2/3 oz. grated horseradish, 2 hard-boiled eggs, parsley sprigs, salt, sugar and lemon juice to taste

Prepare the pike perch (as in Pike Perch Sauté). Sprinkle with salt and pour fat over it. Bake in a hot oven. Blend the sour cream with the horseradish, chopped eggs and chopped parsley sprigs. Season to taste. Pour over the pike perch towards the end of baking.

PIKE PERCH À LA RADECKI

2 lb. pike perch, vegetable stock, 2/3 cup dry red wine, 7 oz. red currants, 1 oz. butter or margarine, 1 oz. flour, salt, pepper and sugar to taste

Prepare the pike perch (as in Pike Perch Sauté). Cut into portions. Cover with stock and cook. Transfer to a plate. Strain the stock and combine with the wine and currants that have been forced through a strainer. Heat the fat and blend with the flour. Fry without browning. Gradually add the cold stock, stirring briskly with an egg-whisk. Bring to a boil. Put in the fish and simmer for a while. Season to taste.

BAKED CATFISH OR BURBOT I

2 lb. fish, 1 2/3 oz. butter or margarine, 2/3 cup sour cream, salt and lemon juice to taste

Make fillets from the cleaned fish. Remove the skin. Wash the fish and cut into portions. Sprinkle with salt and lemon juice. Set aside in a cool place for 30 minutes. Arrange in a dish or pan. Pour butter over the fish and bake. Towards the end of baking pour sour cream over. Season to taste.

BAKED CATFISH OR BURBOT II

2 lb. fish, 1 2/3 oz. butter or margarine, 5 oz. lemons, salt and nutmeg to taste

Make fillets from the cleaned fish. Remove the skin. Wash the fish and cut into portions. Sprinkle with seasoning. Surround with slices of peeled lemon. Wrap in waxpaper or aluminium foil and bake.

CATFISH OR BURBOT CAPUCHIN STYLE I

2 lb. fish, fat for frying, 1 1/3 oz. flour, 1 1/4 lb. sauerkraut, 1 1/3 oz. dried cèpe mushrooms, 5 oz. onions, 1/3 cup sour cream, 2 2/3 oz. hard cheese, salt, pepper, caraway seed, seasoning and lemon juice to taste

Prepare the fish (as in Baked Catfish or Burbot I). Wash, soak and cook the mushrooms. Chop the sauerkraut. Cover with the mushroom stock and cook it. Dredge the fish with flour. Fry it and transfer to a plate. Peel, rinse and chop the onions finely. Fry them and combine with the cabbage and strips of mushrooms. Add seasoning and arrange on a dish. Cover with the fish. Pour sour cream over this. Sprinkle with grated cheese and seasoning, then bake.

CATFISH OR BURBOT CAPUCHIN STYLE II

2 lb. fish, fat for frying, 1 1/3 oz. flour, 3/4 lb. tomatoes, 1 2/3 oz. almonds, 1 2/3 oz. raisins, 2/3 cup sour cream, salt, pepper and lemon juice to taste

Prepare the fish (as in Baked Catfish or Burbot I). Dredge with flour and fry. Wash, scald and peel the tomatoes. Cut into slices. Blanch the almonds and grind them. Arrange the fish in an oven-proof dish. Cover with tomatoes. Sprinkle with seasoning, almonds and rinsed raisins. Cover with sour cream and bake.

CATFISH OR BURBOT JEWISH STYLE

2 lb. fish, fat for frying, 7 oz. onions, 2 egg yolks, 2 tablespoons dry white wine, 1 1/3 oz. raisins, salt, pepper, sugar and lemon juice to taste

Prepare the fish (as in Baked Catfish or Burbot I). Dredge with flour and fry. Peel, rinse and chop the onions finely. Combine with the egg yolks, wine and rinsed raisins. Season to taste. Pour over the fish and bake.

PIKE SAUTÉ

2 lb. pike, 1 1/3 oz. flour, fat for frying, salt and pepper to taste

Wash the cleaned and drawn pike. Cut lengthwise into halves, removing the spine bone. Cut diagonally into portions. Sprinkle with seasoning and set aside in a cool place for 30 minutes. Dredge with flour and brown on both sides. Continue frying over low heat for several minutes.

FRIED EAGLE PIKE

2 lb. pike, 1 1/3 oz. flour, fat for frying, 2—3 eggs, 2—3 oz. bread-crumbs, salt and pepper to taste

Prepare the pike as above. Cut into strips and dredge with flour. Dip in beaten eggs and coat with breadcrumbs. Fry until golden brown.

EAGLE PIKE IN PASTRY

2 lb. pike, fat for frying, 5 oz. flour, 2 eggs, 1/3 cup sour cream, milk, salt and pepper to taste

Prepare the pike (as in Pike Sauté). Sift the flour into a dish. Mix with an egg-whisk with the eggs, sour cream and milk. Mix the batter well to the consistency of sour cream. Add salt. Cut the fish into strips. Dip them in the batter and fry in heated fat. Continue frying over low heat for several minutes.

PIKE GIPSY STYLE

2 lb. pike, 5 oz. onions, 5 oz. dill pickles, fat for frying, 1/3 cup ketchup, parsley sprigs, chives, salt, pepper, sugar, garlic and prepared mustard to taste

Prepare the pike (as in Pike Sauté). Peel and rinse the onions. Cut into strips together with the pickles. Add to the fish together with the chopped parsley sprigs and chives. Add olive oil and ketchup. Bake in a hot oven. Add seasoning.

PIKE PRELATIC STYLE

2 lb. pike, 3/4 lb. soup vegetables (carrots, parsley root, celeriac, leek), 3 1/2 oz. onions, fat, 1/3 cup ketchup, 1 2/3 oz. raisins, 2 tablespoons rum, salt, pepper, sugar, lemon juice and prepared mustard to taste

Prepare the pike (as in Pike Sauté). Wash, peel and rinse the vegetables. Cut them into thin strips and fry them lightly. Sprinkle with water and simmer until tender. Towards the end add the fish, rinsed raisins, ketchup and seasoning. When the fish is tender add the rum. Season to taste.

WROCŁAW PIKE

2 lb. pike, vegetable stock, 1 2/3 oz. almonds, 1 oz. butter or margarine,
2/3 oz. flour, 2/3 cup sour cream, 1 2/3 oz. raisins, 1 2/3 oz. grated
horseradish, 2 egg yolks, salt, sugar and lemon juice to taste

Wash the cleaned and drawn pike. Cut diagonally into portions. Cover
with the stock and cook. Blanch the almonds and grind them. Heat the
fat and blend with the flour. Fry without browning. Gradually add the
cold strained stock blended with the sour cream, stirring briskly with an
egg-whisk. Bring to a boil. Combine with the almonds, rinsed raisins,
horseradish and egg yolks. Season to taste. Pour over the fish and bake.

PIKE OLD POLISH STYLE I

2 lb. pike, 1/2 lb. soup vegetables (carrots, parsley root, celeriac, leek),
1 2/3 oz. almonds, 1 cup dry white wine, fat, 1 2/3 oz. raisins, 1 oz. butter
or margarine for roux, 2/3 oz. flour, salt, pepper, sugar, allspice, bay
leaf and lemon juice to taste

Prepare the pike (as in Pike Sauté). Wash, peel and rinse the vegetables.
Cut them into thin strips and fry them lightly. Cover with water and cook
until tender. Blanch the almonds and grind them. When the vegetables
are nearly cooked add the fish, wine and ground seasoning. Heat the fat
and blend with the flour. Fry without browning. Combine with the fish,
rinsed raisins and almonds. Colour with caramel. Cook for a while and
season to taste.

PIKE OLD POLISH STYLE II

2 lb. pike, vegetable stock, 1 cup dry white wine, 2 2/3 oz. lemons, 5 oz.
apples, 1 oz. whole-wheat bread without crust, 1 2/3 oz. raisins, salt,
pepper, sugar, cinnamon, cloves and lemon juice to taste

Prepare the pike (as in Pike Sauté). Cut diagonally into portions. Cover
with the stock and wine. Cook over low heat. Wash and scald the lemon.

Peel it and cut into half-slices, removing any pits. Wash and peel the apples. Cut them into halves, removing the cores. Cut into pieces. Add to the fish towards the end of cooking together with the lemon, bread, seasoning and rinsed raisins. Season to taste.

PIKE MASURIAN STYLE

2 lb. pike, fat for frying, 1 1/3 oz. dried cèpe mushrooms, 3 1/2 oz. onions, 5 oz. soured cucumbers, 2/3 cup sour cream, 1 2/3 oz. hard cheese, salt, pepper and seasoning to taste

Prepare the pike (as in Pike Sauté), then fry it. Wash, soak and cook the mushrooms. Cut them into thin strips. Peel and rinse the onions, then cut into pieces together with peeled soured cucumbers. Fry the onions lightly. Add to the fish together with the mushrooms and pickles. Cover with seasoned sour cream. Sprinkle with grated cheese and bake.

FRIED EEL

2 lb. eel, fat for frying, 1/2 lb. soup vegetables (carrots, parsley root, celeriac, leek), 1 1/3 oz. flour, 2—3 eggs, 2 2/3—3 1/2 oz. breadcrumbs, salt and pepper to taste

Put the eel to sleep by submerging its head in water with salt and vinegar. Cut the skin around the head and peel it by pulling it down to the tail. Draw the fish and wash thoroughly under running water. Cut into 2 1/2—3 in. pieces. Wash, peel and rinse the vegetables. Cut them into small pieces, cover with boiling water and cook. Towards the end put in the fish and add salt. Allow to cool in the stock. Take out when cool and dry it. Sprinkle with pepper and flour. Cover with beaten eggs and coat with breadcrumbs. Fry in very hot fat, then continue frying over low heat for several minutes. When done arrange on a platter. Garnish the eel with tomato and lemon wedges and lettuce.

BAKED EEL I

2 lb. eel, 1/2 lb. soup vegetables (carrots, parsley root, celeriac, leek), butter, 2—2 2/3 oz. ketchup, 2—2 2/3 oz. hard cheese, salt and pepper

Cook the eel as above and arrange in a buttered dish or pan. Pour over this. Sprinkle with seasoning and grated cheese, then bake.

BAKED EEL II

2 lb. eel, 1/2 soup vegetables (carrots, parsley root, celeriac, leek), butter, 1 2/3 oz. almonds, 3 egg yolks, fresh dill, salt and pepper to taste

Cook the eel (as in Fried Eel). Blanch the almonds and grind them. Arrange the eel in a dish or pan. Spread the egg yolks over it. Sprinkle with seasoning, pour butter over and bake.

WROCŁAW EEL

2 lb. eel, 1 1/4—1 3/4 lb. sour cream, fat, 7 oz. celeriac, 2/3 oz. butter, 2/3 oz. flour, 1 cup broth, 7 oz. mushrooms, parsley sprigs, egg yolk, salt, pepper and lemon juice to taste

Prepare the eel (as in Fried Eel). Wash and peel the celeriac. Grate finely and surround the eel with it. Set aside in the refrigerator for several hours. Remove the celeriac and fry the eel on all sides. Heat the butter and blend with the flour. Fry this without browning. Blend with cold broth, stirring briskly with an egg-whisk. Bring to a boil. Clean and rinse the mushrooms. Cut them into thin strips and fry them. Surround the eel with them. Pour the sauce over this. Add the sour cream and simmer until tender. Take out the fish when tender. Combine the sauce with the egg yolk and chopped parsley sprigs. Add seasoning. Pour over the eel again.

EEL POLISH STYLE I

2 lb. eel, 1/2 lb. soup vegetables (carrots, parsley root, celeriac, leek), 2/3 cup sour cream, 2/3 oz. butter, 2/3 oz. flour, 2 egg yolks, fresh dill, fat, salt, pepper, bay leaf and allspice to taste

Cook the eel (as in Fried Eel). Heat the butter and blend with the flour. Fry without browning. Blend with cold stock (2/3 cup) combined with the sour cream. Bring to a boil. Combine with the egg yolks and chopped dill. Add seasoning. Pour over the eel and bake.

EEL POLISH STYLE II

2 lb. eel, 1/2 lb. soup vegetables (carrots, parsley root, celeriac, leek), 1 cup sour cream, 2/3 oz. lobster butter, 2/3 oz. flour, 2—2 2/3 oz. lobster tails, 1 2/3 oz. almonds, fresh dill, salt and seasoning to taste

Cook the eel (as in Fried Eel). Blanch the almonds. Heat the butter and blend with the flour. Fry without browning and blend with cold cream. Bring to a boil. Pour over the eel. Add the lobster tails, almonds, chopped dill and seasoning. Simmer for several minutes and season.

EEL GOULASH

2 lb. eel, fat, 3 1/2 oz. onions, 2/3 cup sour cream, 1/3—2/3 oz. flour, fresh dill, 5—7 oz. mushrooms, salt, pepper and lemon juice to taste

Prepare the eel (as in Fried Eel). Cut into 1—1 1/3 in. pieces. Clean and rinse the onions and mushrooms. Chop them finely and fry lightly. Add the eel and simmer over low heat, sprinkling with water. Towards the end add the sour cream blended with the flour and chopped dill, then season.

POACHED LOBSTER

25—30 lobsters, fresh dill, parsley sprigs, salt to taste

Scrub the lobsters with a brush under running water, holding the trunk with your hand. Pull out the middle fin and black intestine from the tail. Place the lobsters in boiling salted water with the dill and parsley. Cook covered for around 15 minutes. Take out the lobsters when done and arrange on a platter. Garnish with lettuce leaves.

LOBSTER À LA RADZIWIŁŁ

25—30 lobsters, 3/4 cup thick sour cream, 1 2/3 oz. almonds, 2 2/3 oz. hard cheese, fresh dill, 1 1/3 oz. butter, salt and pepper to taste

Prepare the lobsters as above. When done, take out the meat from the claws and tails. Blanch the almonds and grind them. Butter oven-proof one-serving dishes. Place the lobsters in these. Cover with sour cream blended with seasoning. Sprinkle with grated cheese and almonds. Bake in a hot oven.

LOBSTER LITHUANIAN STYLE

25—30 lobsters, 3/4 cup sour cream, 1 oz. butter or margarine, 2 egg yolks, 1 2/3 oz. grated horseradish, 1 2/3 oz. walnut meats, parsley sprigs, fresh dill, salt and pepper to taste

Prepare and cook the lobsters (as in Poached Lobster). When done take out the meat from the claws and tails. Blanch the walnuts and grind them. Butter oven-proof one-serving dishes. Place the lobsters in these together with the walnuts and horseradish. Cover with sour cream blended with the egg yolks, chopped parsley sprigs and seasoning then bake.

Meat and Game

Captain's Beef Steak **187**
General's Beef Steak **187**
Fillet of Beef with Mushrooms **187**
Tournedos Polish Style **188**
Fillet of Beef Shashlik **188**
Steak with Caviar **189**
Steak Polish Style **189**
Rumpsteak **190**
Beef Entrecôte **190**
Beef Ragout with Mushrooms **190**
Cooked Beef Tongue **191**
Beef Tongue Polish Style **191**
Warsaw Beef Tripe **192**
Lvov Beef Tripe **192**
Lamb Ragout with Tomatoes **192**
Roast Lamb with Sour Cream **193**
Roast Lamb with Vegetables **193**
Lamb Fricassee **194**
Chef's Lamb **194**
Lamb Cutlet Sauté **195**
Lamb Cutlet Polish Style **195**
Manager's Lamb Steak **196**
General's Lamb Fillet **196**
Wrocław Lamb Zrazy **196**
Minced Lamb Zrazy Polish Style **197**
Lamb Shashlik **197**
Roast Wild Boar **198**
Roast Wild Boar with Almonds **198**

Wild Boar Steak **199**
Wild Boar Fillets **199**
Wild Boar Zrazy **199**
Wild Boar Goulash **200**
Roast Venison **200**
Royal Roast Venison **201**
Venison Goulash **201**
Venison Steak **202**
Rolled Venison Zrazy **202**
Hare or Rabbit with Sour Cream **203**
Wrocław Hare or Rabbit **203**
Hare or Rabbit with Cherries **203**
Barrister's Hare or Rabbit **204**
Roast Pheasant **204**
Royal Pheasant **205**
Pheasant Prelatic Style **205**
Pheasant Stew **206**
Pheasant Goulash **206**
Roast Black or Wood Grouse **206**
Black or Wood Grouse Old Polish Style **207**
Roast Wild Goose or Duck **207**
Hetman's Wild Goose or Duck **208**
Roast Quail or Partridge **208**
Hunter's Quail or Partridge **209**
Bachelor's Quail or Partridge **209**
Roast Hazel Grouse **210**
Roast Wood-Pigeon **210**
Roast Coot **210**

ROAST PORK WITH CARAWAY

1 lb. boneless pork (shoulder, neck), 1 1/3 oz. fat for frying, 1/3 oz. flour, 3 1/2 oz. onions, salt, pepper, caraway seed and marjoram to taste

Wash the meat, rub with seasoning and set aside in a cool place (refrigerator) for 24 hours. Dredge with flour and brown in hot fat. Bake the meat, basting with water, then with the pan drippings. Peel, rinse and chop the onions finely. Add to the roast towards the end of baking. Take out the meat when tender. Cut diagonally into portions. Arrange on a platter. Force the sauce through a strainer, then season it. Pour it over the meat. Serve with potatoes, Sautéed Cabbage (q. v.) and salads.

ROAST PORK WITH APPLES

1 lb. boneless pork (shoulder, neck), 1 1/3 oz. fat for frying, 1/3 oz. flour, 3/4 lb. apples, 3 1/2 oz. onions, salt, pepper, sugar and marjoram to taste

Wash the meat, rub with seasoning and set aside in a cool place (refrigerator) for 24 hours. Dredge with flour and brown in hot fat, together with finely chopped onions. Bake the meat, basting with water, then with the pan drippings. Wash, peel and cut the apples in half, removing the cores. Cut into pieces. Take out the meat when tender. Cut diagonally into portions. Arrange on a platter and surround with apples. Force the sauce through a strainer, then season it. Pour it over the meat. Bake for around 5 minutes. Serve with potatoes and Stewed Red Cabbage (q.v.).

ROAST PORK WITH TOMATOES

1 lb. boneless pork (shoulder, neck), 1 1/3 oz. fat for frying, 1/3 oz. flour, 3/4 lb. tomatoes, 2/3 cup sour cream, 1 2/3 oz. walnut meats, 1/3—2/3 oz. flour for cream, parsley sprigs, salt, pepper, sugar and lemon juice to taste

Wash the meat, rub with seasoning and set aside in a cool place (refrigerator) for 24 hours. Dredge with flour and brown in hot fat. Bake the meat, basting with water, then with the pan drippings. Wash, scald and peel the tomatoes. Cut them into pieces. Add to the meat towards the end of baking together with the sour cream blended with the flour. Blanch and grind the walnuts. Take out the meat when done. Cut diagonally into portions. Arrange on a platter. Pour over the seasoned sauce blended with chopped parsley sprigs. Sprinkle with nuts and bake. Serve with potatoes, string beans and salads.

SPICY ROAST PORK

1 lb. boneless pork (shoulder, neck), 1 1/3 oz. fat for frying, 1/3 oz. flour, 2/3 cup sour cream, 3 1/2 oz. onions, 1 2/3 oz. grated horseradish, 5 oz. soured cucumbers, 2/3 oz. butter for cucumbers, 2/3 oz. flour, parsley sprigs, salt, pepper, sugar and curry powder to taste

Wash the meat, rub with seasoning and set aside in a cool place (refrigerator) for 24 hours. Dredge with flour and brown in hot fat together with finely chopped onions. Sprinkle with water and simmer covered over low heat. Peel the soured cucumbers and cut into thin strips. Fry them in the butter. Sprinkle with water and simmer until tender. Take out the meat when tender. Cut diagonally into portions. Arrange on a platter. Blend the sour cream with the flour. Add to the sauce together with the soured cucumbers, horseradish and chopped parsley sprigs. Cook for a while and season. Pour over the roast and heat. Serve with potatoes and tomatoes.

VILNA ROAST PORK

1 lb. boneless pork (shoulder, neck), 1 1/3 oz. fat for frying, 1/3 oz. flour, 1 cup dry white wine, 5 oz. lemons, 5 oz. prunes, salt, pepper, sugar and lemon juice to taste

Wash the meat and rub with seasoning. Surround with peeled lemon slices and pour wine over it. Set aside in a cool place (refrigerator) for 24 hours. Take the meat out of the wine and dry it. Dredge with flour

and brown in hot fat. Bake the meat, basting with wine, then with the pan drippings. Wash the prunes, soak them and add to the roast towards the end of baking. Take out the meat when tender. Cut diagonally into portions. Arrange on a platter. Force the sauce through a strainer, then season it. Pour it over the meat. Serve with rice and lettuce.

COOKED CORNED PORK HAM

7—9 lb. pork ham, 8 cups water, 7 oz. salt, 1/3 oz. saltpetre, 1/3 oz. sugar, 1/3 oz. coriander, 1/3 oz. juniper, 2 garlic cloves, 10 grains allspice, 3 cloves, 1 lb. soup vegetables (carrots, parsley root, celeriac, leek)

For corning buy a medium lean ham from a young pig. Rub the ham with part of the ground seasoning (do not add sugar in the summer). Arrange in a stoneware or enamel dish, cover with a wooden disk and weigh down. Keep at room temperature for 24 hours. Bring the water to a boil and allow to cool. Blend with the remaining seasoning. Pour over the meat and set aside in a cool place (40°—48° F) for two weeks, turning it over every 24 hours. Take it out of the brine, place in a dish with water and set aside for an hour. Take the ham out of the water and tie it up tightly with a string. Cover with boiling water and cook covered over low heat until tender. Add more water as it evaporates. Wash, peel, rinse and dice the vegetables. Add to the meat towards the end of cooking. Take out the ham when done and discard the string. Arrange on a platter and cut into slices. Serve with potatoes, pea purée, Stewed Sauerkraut (q.v.), horseradish or ćwikła (q.v.).

SMOKED OR CORNED HAM BAKED IN FOIL

4 1/2 lb. smoked or corned ham, 1 2/3 oz. almonds, 2 2/3 oz. ketchup

Soak the ham in water for 12 to 24 hours, changing the water several times, depending on the degree of salinity. Take it out of the water and dry with a cloth. Blanch and grind the almonds. Spread ketchup over the ham and sprinkle it with the almonds. Wrap in foil and bake. Serve with prepared mustard, ćwikła (q.v.) or horseradish.

SMOKED OR CORNED HAM IN RED WINE

4 1/2 lb. smoked or corned ham, 3/4 lb. soup vegetables (carrots, parsley root, celeriac, leek), 1 cup dry red wine, 5 oz. onions, 1 2/3 oz. butter, pepper and nutmeg to taste

Soak the ham in water for 12 to 24 hours, changing the water several times, depending on the degree of salinity. Wash, peel and rinse the vegetables. Cut them into strips and fry in butter. Add the ham. Sprinkle it with stock or water and simmer covered over low heat. Towards the end add the wine. Take out the ham when tender and discard the string. Cut into thick slices. Arrange on a platter. Force the sauce through a strainer, then season it. Pour it over the ham. Serve the remaining sauce in a sauce-boat. Serve with scooped out potato balls, croquettes and salads.

ROAST PORK LOIN

1 1/4 lb. pork loin, 1 1/3 oz. fat for frying, 5 oz. onions, 1/3 oz. flour, salt, pepper and caraway seed to taste

Wash the meat and remove the bones, leaving only small fragments of the rib bones. Rub the meat with the seasoning and set aside in a cool place (refrigerator) for 24 hours. Dredge with flour and brown in hot fat. Bake in a hot oven, basting with water, then with the pan drippings. Peel, rinse and dice the onions. Add to the meat towards the end of baking together with the caraway. Take out the meat when tender and cut into portions. Arrange on a platter. Skim the fat off the sauce and season it, then pour it over the meat. Serve with potatoes, Sautéed Cabbage (q.v.), ćwikła (q.v.) or other vegetables.

EDITOR'S ROAST PORK LOIN

1 1/4 lb. pork loin, 1 1/3 oz. fat for frying, 2—2 2/3 oz. walnut meats, egg yolk, 1 1/3 oz. ketchup, 2/3 oz. flour, parsley sprigs, salt, pepper and marjoram to taste

Wash the meat and remove the bones, leaving only small fragments of the rib bones. Cut 3—4 slits in the meat 3/4 in. deep. Rub with seasoning and set aside in a cool place for 24 hours. Blanch the walnuts and grind them. Combine with the egg yolk, ketchup and chopped parsley sprigs, then season. Place in the slits. Tie the meat up with a string. Dredge with flour and brown on all sides. Wrap in foil and bake. Serve with savoy cabbage and salads.

ROAST PORK LOIN WITH PRUNES

1 1/4 lb. pork loin, 1 1/3 oz. fat for frying, 5 oz. prunes, 1 oz. honey, 1/3 oz. flour, salt, pepper and lemon juice to taste

Wash the meat and remove the bones, leaving only small fragments of the rib bones. Rub the meat with seasoning and set to brown in a hot oven. Bake, basting with water, then with the pan drippings. Towards the end add soaked and rinsed prunes. Take out the meat when tender and cut into portions. Arrange on a platter. Force the sauce through a strainer, then season it. Pour it over the meat. Serve with potatoes or Stewed Red Cabbage (q.v.).

WARSAW ROAST PORK LOIN

1 1/4—1 3/4 lb. pork loin, 1 1/3 oz. fat for frying, 2/3 oz. flour, 5 oz. mushrooms, 2/3 oz. butter for mushrooms, 1 oz. walnut meats, 1 oz. horseradish (grated), egg yolk, salt, pepper and nutmeg to taste

Clean, rinse and chop the mushrooms finely, then fry them. Blanch the walnuts and grind them. Wash the meat and separate from the bones. Mince the meat trimmings and combine with the mushrooms, walnuts, horseradish and egg yolk, then season. Cut a slit down the entire length of the meat and place the stuffing in this. Dredge with flour and brown in hot fat. Bake, basting with water, then with the pan drippings. Take out when done and cut into portions. Pour the seasoned sauce over. Serve with potatoes, cauliflower and salads.

PORK RAGOUT WITH SOURED CUCUMBERS

1—1 1/4 lb. boneless pork, fat for frying, 2/3 cup sour cream, 2/3 oz. flour, 3 1/2 oz. carrots, 5—7 oz. soured cucumbers, 2/3 oz. butter, 3 1/2 oz. onions, parsley sprigs, salt, pepper, sugar and seasoning to taste

Wash the meat and cut into pieces, 5—6 per serving. Brown in hot fat. Add peeled, rinsed and diced onions and fry them. Sprinkle with water and add salt. Simmer covered over low heat. Wash, peel and rinse the carrots, then grate them coarsely. Add to the meat towards the end of cooking. Peel the soured cucumbers and cut into strips. Sprinkle with water, add butter and simmer for 10 minutes. Add to the meat when tender together with the sour cream blended with the flour. Cook for a while. Combine with chopped parsley sprigs and season. Serve with potatoes and salads.

PORK RAGOUT SLAVONIC STYLE

1/2 lb. boneless pork, 1/2 lb. boneless chicken meat, 3 1/2 oz. onions, 1 cup sour cream, 5 oz. mushrooms, 5 oz. tomatoes, 2/3 oz. flour, fat for frying, salt, pepper, prepared mustard and seasoning to taste

Wash the pork and chicken meat and cut into strips. Brown in separate pans together with peeled, rinsed and finely chopped onions. Sprinkle with water and simmer covered over low heat. Clean, rinse and cut the mushrooms into strips, then fry them. Wash and scald the tomatoes. Peel them and cut into pieces. When tender, combine the pork and chicken meat with sour cream blended with the flour, mushrooms, tomatoes and seasoning. Simmer for several minutes and season. Serve with potatoes and salads.

SPARERIBS WITH CARAWAY

1—1 1/4 lb. spareribs, fat for frying, 3 1/2 oz. onions, 1 oz. flour, salt, pepper, caraway seed

Wash and drain the spareribs, then cut into portions. Sprinkle with the seasoning and part of the flour. Brown in hot fat and place in another dish. Peel, rinse and dice the onions and fry them in the remaining fat. Add to the meat. Sprinkle with water and simmer covered over low heat. Add water to the sauce as it evaporates. Towards the end of simmering combine with remaining flour blended with a small amount of cold water. Take out the spareribs when tender. Force the sauce through a strainer, then season it. Pour it over the meat and heat. Serve with potatoes, Sautéed Cabbage (q.v.) and salads.

CAPTAIN'S SPARERIBS

1—1 1/4 lb. spareribs, 3 1/2 oz. smoked pork fat, 7 oz. peppers, 3 1/2 oz. onions, 5 oz. tomatoes, 3 1/2 oz. thin frankfurters, 2/3 oz. flour, salt, pepper and ground paprika to taste

Wash and drain the spareribs, then cut into portions. Sprinkle with the seasoning and part of the flour. Dice the pork fat and render it down partly. Add the spareribs and brown them. Add cleaned and diced onions and peppers. Sprinkle with water and simmer over low heat. Add water to the sauce as it evaporates. Remove the covering, if any, from the frankfurters and cut into half-slices. Wash and scald the tomatoes. Remove the skins and cut into pieces. Add to the spareribs towards the end of cooking together with the frankfurters and remaining flour blended with a small amount of cold water, then season. Serve with potatoes.

PORK HOCK OLD POLISH STYLE

2 1/2 lb. pork hock, 2—2 2/3 oz. fat for frying, 5 oz. onions, 5 oz. carrots, 7 oz. parsley sprigs, 7 oz. celeriac, 1 2/3 oz. tomato paste, salt, pepper, garlic

Clean, singe and rinse the pork hock. Cut into portions and wash it. Rub with the seasoning and set aside in the refrigerator for 24 hours. Brown it in very hot fat. Pour out the fat, sprinkle with water and simmer

covered over low heat. Wash, peel and rinse the vegetables. Cut them into strips and fry in the remaining fat. Add to the pork hock towards the end of cooking together with the seasoning. Towards the end of cooking add the tomato paste and cook for several minutes more. When tender, place the pork hock on a platter and surround with seasoned vegetables. Serve with potatoes.

BACON BAKED IN FOIL

1 lb. lean bacon, 1 2/3 oz. ketchup, 2/3 oz. prepared mustard, salt and pepper to taste

Wash the bacon and with a sharp knife cut out a chequered pattern on it, each square measuring 1/5 in. Rub with the seasoning, ketchup and mustard. Arrange on buttered foil and set aside in a cool place for 30 minutes. Close tightly and bake in a hot oven for around 50 minutes. Take out when done and cut into slices. Arrange on a platter and surround with scooped out potato balls. Serve with Sautéed Cabbage (q.v.).

BACON ROLL

2 lb. lean bacon, 3 1/2 oz. boneless beef, 1 1/3 oz. hardened French bread, milk, 2 egg yolks, 1 2/3 oz. hard cheese, 1 2/3 oz. ketchup, parsley sprigs, 1 1/3 oz. almonds, salt, pepper, garlic, marjoram and fat for basting

Wash the bacon and cut off the top layer. Trim the sides even and pound with a mallet that has been dipped in water. Soak the bread in milk, then squeeze it out. Mince together with the bacon trimmings and washed beef. Combine with the egg yolks, chopped parsley sprigs and grated cheese, then season. Arrange evenly on the bacon and shape into a roll. Tie up with a string (like a ham). Pour the fat and ketchup over. Sprinkle with blanched and ground almonds. Wrap this up in the foil tightly and bake. When done take it out of the foil. Cut diagonally into portions and arrange on a platter. Serve with potatoes and Sautéed Cabbage (q.v.).

GENERAL'S PORK CHOPS

1—1 1/4 lb. pork chops, fat for frying, 2/3 oz. flour, 2/3 oz. dried cèpe mushrooms, 7 oz. sauerkraut, 1 2/3 oz. onions, 1 oz. fat, 1/3—2/3 oz. flour, 4 fried crêpes, 2 eggs, breadcrumbs, salt, pepper and caraway seed to taste

Wash the meat and cut off the bones, leaving only small fragments of the rib bones. Remove excess fat from the meat. Cut the meat into chops. Pound lightly with a mallet that has been dipped in water. Shape into oval chops. Dredge with seasoning and flour and fry on both sides. Wash, soak and cook the mushrooms. Take them out and chop them. Dice the cabbage and cover with stock made from the mushrooms and meat. Cook this. Peel, rinse and chop the onions finely. Fry them and blend with the flour. Brown them lightly and combine with the cabbage and mushrooms. Cook for a while and season. Spread on the chops and roll these up in the crêpes. Dip in beaten eggs, then coat with breadcrumbs. Heat in very hot fat on both sides until golden in colour. Serve with potatoes and salads.

WROCŁAW PORK CHOPS

1—1 1/4 lb. pork loin, fat for frying, 2/3 oz. flour, 3 1/2 oz. ham, 1 2/3 oz. hard cheese, 2 egg yolks, 3 tablespoons sour cream, breadcrumbs, salt and pepper to taste

Prepare the chops as above. Mince the ham and combine with grated cheese, egg yolks and sour cream. Dredge the chops with seasoning and flour. Cover with the prepared mixture, coat with the breadcrumbs. Even out the surface, pressing down with your hand. Place in very hot fat and brown. Continue frying over low heat. Serve with French fries, cauliflower and salads.

HUNTER'S PORK ZRAZY

1 lb. boneless pork ham, fat for frying, 2/3 oz. flour for zrazy, 2/3 oz. butter or margarine, 2/3 oz. flour, 3 1/2 oz. onions, 3 1/2 oz. soured

cucumbers, 2/3 oz. dried cèpe mushrooms, 1 oz. smoked· ham, 1 cup broth, 3 tablespoons dry red wine, 1 oz. tomato paste, salt, pepper, allspice and bay leaf to taste

Wash the meat and trim off excess fat. Cut diagonally into 8 pieces. Pound with a mallet that has been dipped in water. Shape into 1/2 in. thick circles with your hand and a knife. Dredge with seasoning and flour and brown on both sides. Wash, soak and cook the mushrooms. Take them out and chop them. Peel and rinse the onions. Cut them up together with peeled soured cucumbers and fry this lightly. Heat the butter and blend with the flour. Fry without browning. Dilute with the cold stock, stirring briskly with an egg-whisk. Bring to a boil. Add the wine, mushrooms, cucumbers, onions, strips of ham and seasoning. Cook for several minutes and season. Pour over the zrazy and simmer for 3—4 minutes, then season. Serve with potatoes and salads.

CHEF'S PORK STEAK

1 lb. pork ham (leg), fat for frying, 2/3 oz. flour, 5 oz. mushrooms, 5 oz. canned peppers, 1/3 cup dry white wine, 3 tablespoons sour cream, 1 2/3 oz. hard cheese, salt, pepper and nutmeg

Wash the meat and trim off excess fat. Cut diagonally into portions. Pound with a mallet that has been dipped in water. Shape into 5/8 in. thick ovals with your hand and a knife. Dredge with the seasoning and flour and fry in very hot fat on both sides. Arrange on a plate. Clean and rinse the mushrooms, then cut into thin strips. Fry in the fat remaining from the steaks. Add sour cream, peppers, cut into thin strips. Simmer for a while. Add the steaks and wine and season. Sprinkle with grated cheese and bake. Serve with French fires, cauliflower and salads.

PORK STEAK À LA RADZIWIŁŁ

1 lb. pork ham (leg), fat for frying, 2/3 oz. flour, 1 2/3 oz. ketchup, 1 2/3 oz. raisins, 2 2/3 oz. ham, 9 1/2 oz. tomatoes, 1/3 cup dry white wine, salt and pepper to taste

Prepare the steaks and fry as above. Wash and scald the tomatoes, then peel the skins. Cut into pieces and surround the steaks. Add rinsed raisins, ketchup and strips of ham. Sprinkle with wine and simmer for several minutes, then season. Serve with French fries, cauliflower and salads.

PORK MEDALLIONS ON TOAST

1 lb. boneless pork (leg), fat for frying, 2/3 oz. flour, 2/3 oz. butter, 2 2/3 oz. bread for toast, 2/3 oz. breadcrumbs, 2 eggs, salt, pepper

Wash the meat and trim off excess fat. Cut diagonally into portions. Pound with a mallet that has been dipped in water. Shape into 5/8 in. thick circles with your hand and a knife. Dredge with seasoning and flour. Cut the bread into thin slices, then into 3/4 in. long strips. Combine with the breadcrumbs. Dip the meat in beaten eggs with toasts, pressing down with your hand. Fry in hot fat on both sides until golden brown. Pour off the fat, add butter and melt it, turning the medallion over to the other side. Serve with French fries, cauliflower, green peas and salads.

PORK CUTLET

1 lb. boneless pork ham (leg), fat for frying, 2/3 oz. flour, 2/3 oz. butter, salt and pepper to taste

Wash the meat and trim off excess fat. Cut diagonally into portions. Pound with a mallet that has been dipped in water. Shape into 1/2—3/4 in. thick cirlces with your hand and a knife. Dredge with seasoning and flour. Fry in very hot fat lightly on both sides, then continue frying over low heat. When done pour off the fat. Add butter and melt it, turning over the cutlet to the other side. Serve with French fries, cauliflower, green peas and salads.

HIGHLANDER PORK CUTLETS

1 lb. boneless pork ham (leg), fat for frying, 2/3 oz. flour, 2/3 oz. butter, 2—2 2/3 oz. breadcrumbs, 2 eggs, salt and pepper to taste

Wash the meat and trim off excess fat. Cut diagonally into portions. Pound with a mallet that has been dipped in water. Shape into 1/2 in. thick circles with your hand and a knife. Dredge with seasoning and flour. Dip in beaten eggs and coat with breadcrumbs, pressing down with your hand. Even out the edges. Fry in very hot fat, reducing the temperature towards the end of frying. When done, pour off the fat and add butter. Melt it, turning the cutlets over to the other side. Serve surrounded with soured cucumbers, cut into cubes and salad made of cooked potatoes, soured cucumbers, fresh chives, olive oil and seasoning.

PORK FILLETS

1 or 2 pork fillets, fat for frying, 2—2 2/3 oz. pork fat, 2/3 oz. flour, 1/2 lb. mushrooms, 1/3 cup dry white wine, 4 slices of toast, fat for toast, 2 2/3 oz. pâté, salt and pepper to taste

Wash the meat and cut into 4 pieces. Pound lightly with a mallet that has been dipped in water. Lard with thin strips of pork fat and dredge with seasoning and flour. Brown on both sides and place on a plate. Clean and rinse the mushrooms and cut them into thin strips, then fry them. Add the fillets and wine, then simmer for several minutes. Fry the toast on both sides. Cover with the pâté and fillets and sprinkle with the mushrooms. Serve with French fires, cauliflower, scooped out carrot balls and salads.

GENERAL'S PORK SHASHLIK

1 1/4 lb. boneless pork (ham), 3 1/2 oz. onions, 3 1/2 oz. smoked bacon, 2/3—1 oz. almonds, 3 1/2—5 oz. prunes, 1 1/4—1 3/4 lb. wine vinegar, 1 tablespoon olive oil, 2/3 oz. flour, fat for frying, salt, pepper, sage, tarragon and cloves to taste

Wash the meat and cut into 1 1/4 x 1 1/4 in. slices 1/4 in. thick. Arrange in a dish and pour vinegar blended with oil and ground seasoning over. Set aside in the refrigerator for 48 hours. Blanch the almonds. Wash the prunes and remove the pits, without cutting the prune in half. Place an

almond in each prune in place of the pit. Peel and rinse the onions, then cut into slices. Place the meat on skewers alternately with pieces of bacon, prunes and onions. Dredge with flour and press down with your hand. Fry on both sides. Serve with cooked rice mixed with finely chopped and fried onions and tomato salad.

MEAT PATTIES

9 1/2 oz. boneless pork, 3 1/2 oz. boneless beef, 2—2 2/3 oz. hardened French bread, 2—2 2/3 oz. onions, 1 egg, breadcrumbs, fat for frying, salt and pepper to taste

Soak the bread and squeeze it out. Mince together with the meat and peeled onions. Combine with the egg and season. Divide into portions. Shape into oval patties coated with breadcrumbs. Place in very hot fat and brown on both sides, then continue frying over low heat for several minutes longer. Serve with potatoes, cauliflower, salads and cabbage.

WROCŁAW GROUND ZRAZY

9 1/2 oz. boneless pork, 3 1/2 oz. boneless beef, 1 2/3 oz. hardened French bread, milk, 1 egg, 2 oz. onions, 2/3 oz. flour, 2/3 cup sour cream, 1 1/3 oz. tomato paste, parsley sprigs, salt, pepper and seasoning to taste

Soak bread in milk, then squeeze out. Peel and rinse the onions, then mince them together with the bread and washed meat. Combine with the egg and season. Make zrazy (two per serving), dredge with flour and fry on both sides. Cover with sour cream blended with tomato paste and seasoning. Simmer over low heat for around 10 minutes, stirring from time to time. Towards the end add chopped parsley and season.

PORK TONGUE POLISH STYLE

1 1/4 lb. pork tongue, 1/2 lb. soup vegetables (carrots, parsley root, celeriac, leek), 2/3 cup sour cream, 1 2/3 oz. grated horseradish, 1 2/3

raisins, parsley sprigs, fat for frying, salt, pepper, sugar and lemon juice to taste

Wash the tongue, cover with water and set aside for two hours. Scrub with a brush and cut off the salivary glands, which are located on both sides at the base of the tongue. Rinse and cover with boiling salted water. Cook for 60—70 minutes. Wash, peel and rinse the vegetables. Add to the tongue in the middle of cooking together with the seasoning. Take out the tongue when done and place in cold water. Cool slightly and remove the skin. Cut lengthwise into portions and arrange in a greased dish. Blend the sour cream with the horseradish, rinsed raisins and chopped parsley sprigs, then season. Pour over the tongue and bake. Serve with rice and salads.

PORK GOULASH

1 lb. boneless pork, fat for frying, 3 1/2 oz. onions, 2/3 oz. flour, salt, pepper, bay leaf, allspice and vegetable bouillon cubes

Wash the meat and cut into cubes. Sprinkle with salt and flour. Brown in very hot fat and place on a dish. Peel, rinse and fry the onions lightly. Combine with the meat. Sprinkle with water and simmer covered over low heat. Towards the end add the seasoning and the remaining flour blended with a small amount of cold water, then season. Serve with potatoes, kasha, macaroni and salads.

GENERAL'S PORK LIVER

3/4 lb. pork liver, fat, 1 oz. pork fat, 1 oz. almonds, 1 2/3 oz. ketchup, 1 2/3 oz. hard cheese, salt and pepper to taste

Blanch the almonds. Rinse and drain the liver and remove the outer skin. Lard with thin strips of pork fat and almonds. Sprinkle with pepper. Pour the fat over and bake in a hot oven. Towards the end pour ketchup over and sprinkle with grated cheese. When done, cut into slices and sprinkle with salt. Arrange on a platter and pour seasoned sauce over. Serve with potatoes and salads.

PORK BRAINS POLISH STYLE

1 lb. pork brains, fat, 3 1/2 oz. onions, 2 eggs, salt and pepper to taste

Remove the outer skin from the brains. Rinse and chop them. Peel, rinse and chop the onions finely. Fry them lightly, add the brains and fry over low heat for several minutes, stirring constantly. Wash the eggs and break them. Combine with the brains and continue frying for several minutes more until the eggs set, then season. Serve with potatoes and fried eggs.

SOUR PORK LIGHTS

1 3/4 lb. pork lights, 5 1/2 lb. soup vegetables (carrots, parsley root, celeriac, leek), 3 1/2 oz. onions, 1 1/3 oz. fat, 2/3 oz. flour, salt, pepper, marjoram, seasoning, nutmeg and lemon juice to taste

Rinse the lights and cut off the windpipe. Cover with boiling water and cook. Drain, rinse and cover with water again. Cook covered over low heat. Wash, peel and rinse the vegetables. Add to the lights in the middle of cooking. Take out the lights when done and cut into cubes. Combine with strained stock. Peel, rinse and dice the onions, then fry them. Add the flour and brown it lightly. Combine with the lights. Cook for a while with the seasoning. Serve with potatoes and salads.

PORK KIDNEYS

1 1/4 lb. pork kidneys, fat, 2 2/3 oz. onions, 2/3 oz. flour, 1 cup broth or stock from bones, salt, pepper, seasoning and marjoram to taste

Wash the kidneys and cut them lengthwise into halves. Cover with water and set aside for 30 minutes. Cover with boiling water and cook, then drain. Rinse, cover with water again and cook. Take them out of the stock and allow to cool. Cut into slices. Peel, rinse and dice the onions, then fry them. Add the flour and brown it lightly. Blend it with the cold

stock, stirring briskly with an egg-whisk. Bring to a boil. Add the kidneys and seasoning. Simmer for several minutes over low heat, then season. Serve with potatoes, kasha and salads.

CASTELLAN'S PORK HEARTS

1 lb. pork hearts, 1/2 lb. soup vegetables (carrots, parsley root, celeriac, leek), 5 oz. white beans, 5 oz. onions, 1 oz. fat, 2/3 cup sour cream, 1 1/3 oz. tomato paste, 2/3 oz. flour, salt, pepper, marjoram, seasoning and ground paprika to taste

Cut the hearts lengthwise and cut out the thick veins. Wash thoroughly, removing any blood clots. Cover with boiling water and bring to a boil. Drain and rinse. Cover with water again. Add salt and cook covered over low heat. Wash, peel and rinse the vegetables. Add to the hearts towards the end of cooking. Take out the hearts when tender and allow to cool. Cut into thin strips. Sort the beans, rinse them and cover with water. Bring to a boil and set aside for two hours. Cook in the same water. Peel, rinse and dice the onions, then fry them lightly. Add the flour and fry, browning lightly. Blend with cold stock from the hearts (ca. 2/3 cup) combined with the sour cream. Bring to a boil. Combine with the beans, tomato paste and hearts. Simmer for a while and season. Serve with potatoes and salads.

PIGS' FEET IN PASTRY

4 pigs' feet, 1/2 lb. soup vegetables (carrots, parsley root, celeriac, leek), 7 oz. flour, 1—2 eggs, ca. 3 tablespoons milk, ca. 3 tablespoons water, 1 1/2 tablespoons olive oil, fat for frying, salt, pepper, allspice and bay leaf to taste

Clean and singe the pigs' feet. Cut lengthwise into halves. Wash, cover with boiling water and bring to a boil. Drain, rinse and cover with water again. Add salt and cook covered over low heat. Wash, peel and rinse the vegetables. Add to the feet towards the end of cooking together with

the seasoning. Take out the feet when tender and discard the bones. Arrange the meat on a chopping board, press down with a small board and allow to set. Sift the flour and combine with the milk, water, oil, egg yolks and stiffly beaten egg white. Add salt. Dip the meat in this batter and place in very hot fat. Brown on both sides. Serve with potatoes and salads.

MANAGER'S FRANKFURTERS

3/4 lb. thin frankfurters, 5 oz. onions, 7 oz. mushrooms, 5 oz. tomatoes, 2/3 cup sour cream, 1 1/3 oz. fat, salt, pepper, ground paprika and marjoram to taste

Wash the frankfurters and remove any covering. Cut into 1—1 1/2 in. long pieces. Wash and scald the tomatoes. Remove the skins and cut into pieces. Clean, rinse and dice the onions and mushrooms. Fry them and combine with the tomatoes, frankfurters and seasoning. Pour sour cream over and bake.

COATED FRANKFURTERS

3/4 lb. thin frankfurters, 3 eggs, 1 2/3—2 oz. flour, salt, pepper and nutmeg to taste, fat for frying

Wash the frankfurters and remove covering, if any. Cut into 2 2/2—3 in. long pieces. Wash the eggs and break them. Separate the yolks from the whites. Beat the whites until stiff and combine with the yolks, sifted flour and seasoning. Dip the frankfurters in this batter and place in very hot fat. Fry on all sides until brown.

ROAST VEAL WITH CAVIAR

1 lb. boneless veal, 2/3 oz. flour, 2/3 cup sour cream, fat, 2/3—1 oz. caviar, 3 1/2 oz. lemon, salt and pepper to taste

Wash the meat and remove the outer skin. Rub with seasoning and dredge with flour. Brown in very hot fat. Sprinkle with water and simmer over low heat, basting with the pan drippings. Towards the end add cream. Take out the meat when tender and cut into slices, leaving every other slice uncut to the end. Place the caviar in the meat pockets. Wash and scald the lemon. Peel it, cut in half, then into slices, removing any pits. Surround the meat which has been placed on an oven-proof platter. Pour over the strained and seasoned sauce. Place in a hot oven for several minutes so that the meat becomes saturated with the caviar. Serve with rice, scooped out potato balls, lettuce and canned peas.

BELVEDERE ROAST VEAL

1 lb. boneless veal, fat, 2/3 oz. flour, 3 tablespoons rum, 2 egg yolks, 1—1 1/3 oz. chocolate pieces, salt, pepper and ginger to taste

Wash the meat and remove the outer skin. Rub with the seasoning and dredge with flour. Brown in very hot fat. Sprinkle with water and simmer over low heat, basting with the pan drippings. Take out the meat when tender and cut diagonally into portions. Arrange on an oven-proof platter. Strain the sauce and combine with the rum and egg yolks. Season to taste. Pour over the roast. Sprinkle with grated chocolate and bake. Serve with rice, lettuce and compote.

AMATEUR ROAST VEAL

1 lb. boneless veal, fat, 2/3 oz. flour, 3 1/2 oz. farmer's cheese, 1 1/2 tablespoons sour cream for the cheese, 1 oz. raisins, 2/3 cup sour cream, parsley sprigs, salt and pepper to taste

Wash the meat and remove the outer skin. Rub with the seasoning and dredge with flour. Brown in very hot fat. Sprinkle with water and bake until tender, basting with the pan drippings. Towards the end add the sour cream. Take out the meat when tender and cut diagonally into slices, leaving every other slice uncut to the end. In the formed pockets place

seasoned farmer's cheese combined with the sour cream, rinsed raisins and chopped parsley sprigs. Arrange on an oven-proof platter. Pour the strained and seasoned sauce over and simmer for several minutes. Serve with rice and lettuce.

VEAL RAGOUT

1 1/4 lb. veal with bones (breast, rib, shoulder), 3/4 lb. soup vegetables (carrots, parsley root, celeriac, leek), 1/3 cup sour cream, egg yolk, 1 oz. butter, 1 oz. flour, parsley sprigs, salt, nutmeg and curry powder to taste

Wash the meat and cover with boiling salted water. Bring to a boil and cook covered over low heat. Wash, peel and rinse the vegetables. Add to the meat towards the end of cooking. Take out the meat when tender and cut into portions. Arrange on a platter. Heat the butter with the flour and fry without browning. Dilute with cold strained stock (1 cup). Bring to a boil, stirring briskly with an egg-whisk and cook for around 10 minutes. Towards the end add the sour cream. Beat the egg yolk. Add some of the sauce, stirring briskly, then combine with the sauce, stirring constantly. Add chopped parsley sprigs and season. Pour over the meat. Serve with rice, carrots with peas, string beans and salads.

VEAL RAGOUT OLD POLISH STYLE

1 1/4 lb. veal with bones (breast, rib, shoulder), 3/4 lb. soup vegetables (carrots, parsley root, celeriac, leek), 1 oz. butter or margarine, 1 oz. flour, 1/3 cup dry white wine, 1 oz. raisins, 1 oz. walnut meats, 1 2/3 oz. prunes, salt, honey, lemon juice and cloves to taste

Wash the meat and cover with boiling salted water. Bring to a boil and cook covered over low heat until tender. Wash, peel and rinse the vegetables and add to the meat towards the end of cooking. Take out the meat when tender and cut into portions. Arrange on a platter. Wash, soak and cook the prunes, then force them through a strainer. Blanch and chop

the walnuts. Heat the fat and blend with the flour. Fry without browning. Blend with the cold strained stock (1 1/3 cups), stirring briskly with an egg-whisk. Bring to a boil and cook over low heat for around 10 minutes, stirring often. Towards the end add wine, the prune paste, rinsed raisins, walnuts and honey. Season to taste. Pour over the meat and bake. Serve with scooped out potato balls and lettuce.

FRIED VEAL BREAST

1 1/4 lb. veal with bones, 7 oz. soup vegetables (carrots, parsley root, celeriac, leek), 2/3 oz. flour, breadcrumbs, fat for frying, salt and pepper to taste

Wash the meat and cover with boiling salted water. Bring to a boil and cook covered over low heat until tender. Wash, peel and rinse the vegetables. Add to the meat towards the end of cooking. Take out the meat when tender and discard the bones and thicker gristle. Arrange on a board, press down and allow to set. Cut diagonally into portions. Dredge with pepper and flour. Dip in beaten eggs and coat with breadcrumbs. pressing down with your hand. Place in intensely heated fat and brown on both sides, then continue frying over low heat for several minutes longer. Serve with potatoes, cauliflower, carrots with peas and salads.

VEAL BREAST WITH FARCE POLISH STYLE

2 lb. veal breast, 3 1/2 oz. hardened French bread, milk, 2—2 2/3 oz. onions, 1—2 eggs, fat for onions, 2/3—1 oz. breadcrumbs, parsley sprigs, fresh dill, fat, salt, pepper and nutmeg to taste

Wash the meat and separate the rib bones from the breast. Make an opening for the farce, slicing with a knife, then with your hand continue opening the meat along the line where it divides naturally into two sections. Peel, rinse and chop the onions finely, then fry them. Soak the bread in milk, squeeze out the milk and mince the bread. Combine with the onions, egg yolks, finely chopped greens, beaten egg whites and bread-

crumbs. Season with nutmeg, salt and pepper. Sprinkle the meat with seasoning on the inside and outside. Stuff loosely with the farce. Pour the fat over and bake, basting with water, then with the pan drippings. Cut the meat into portions when done and pour the seasoned sauce over. Serve with potatoes in all forms, carrots with peas and salads.

ROLLED VEAL BREAST

2 lb. veal breast, 1 2/3 oz. hardened French bread, 5 oz. onions, fat, 1 oz. raisins, 1 1/3 oz. tomato paste, 1 egg, parsley sprigs, salt, pepper and garlic to taste

Wash the meat and slice with a knife, separating the rib bones from the breast. Soak the bread in water or milk and squeeze out the liquid. Mince together with the meat trimmings. Combine with rinsed raisins, tomato paste, chopped parsley sprigs, egg and peeled, rinsed, chopped and fried onions, then season. Spread this evenly on the prepared breast and shape into a roll. Tie it up with thread and rub with fat. Wrap it in foil and bake in a hot oven. Towards the end open up the foil and brown the meat. Take out the meat when tender and cut diagonally into portions. Arrange on a platter. Serve with potatoes, peas, lettuce and salads.

VEAL CUTLET SAUTÉ

1 1/4—1 1/2 lb. veal with bones (rib), 2/3 oz. flour, fat, salt and pepper to taste

Wash the meat and remove the spine bones. Remove membranes and veins. Cut along the ribs into cutlets, leaving a 1 in. rib bone with each cutlet. Scrape off the membrane and any remaining meat from each bone. Pound each cutlet with a mallet that has been dipped in water into 1/2 in. thick ovals. Make incisions along the rims in several places in order to avoid shrinking when frying the cutlets and to retain their original shape when done. Dredge with seasoning and flour and brown on both sides. Continue frying over low heat for several minutes. Serve with French fries, cauliflower, carrots and salads.

VEAL CUTLET WITH MUSHROOMS

1 1/4—1 1/2 lb. veal with bones (rib), 2/3 oz. flour, fat, 1/2 lb. mushrooms, 3 1/2 oz. ketchup, parsley sprigs, salt and pepper to taste

Prepare the cutlets (as in Veal Cutlet Sauté), then fry them. Clean the mushrooms, rinse them and cut into thin strips. Fry them and surround the cutlets with them. Pour ketchup with chopped parsley sprigs over and simmer for several minutes, then season. Serve with French fries, asparagus, peas and salads.

POZNAŃ VEAL CUTLET

1 1/4—1 1/2 lb. veal with bones (rib), 2/3 oz. flour, fat, 5 oz. pork brains, 1 2/3 oz. onions, egg yolk, 2 eggs, breadcrumbs, 4 crêpes, salt and pepper to taste

Prepare and fry the cutlets (as in Veal Cutlet Sauté). Remove the outer skin from the brains, rinse and chop them. Peel, rinse and chop the onions finely, then fry them. Add the brains and fry for a while, stirring constantly. Towards the end of frying add the egg yolk and season. Arrange this on the cutlets and roll into crêpes. Dip in beaten eggs and coat with breadcrumbs. Fry on both sides in very hot fat, then continue frying over low heat for several minutes. Serve with French fries, carrots with peas, cauliflower and salads.

VEAL SCHNITZEL SAUTÉ

1 lb. boneless veal (leg), 2/3 oz. flour, fat, salt and pepper to taste

Wash the meat and remove the outer skin. Cut diagonally into portions. Pound with a mallet that has been dipped in water. Shape into 1/2 in. thick rectangular schnitzels with a meat chopper and your hand. Sprinkle with seasoning and flour. Fry on both sides, then continue frying over low heat for several minutes. Serve with French fries, cauliflower, carrots, lettuce and tomato salad.

VEAL SCHNITZEL À LA AMBASSADOR

1 lb. boneless veal (leg), 2/3 oz. flour, fat, 3 1/2 oz. ham, 5 oz. mushrooms, 2/3 oz. butter, 2/3 oz. flour for roux, 1 cup milk, 3 tablespoons sour cream, 1 2/3 oz. hard cheese, salt and pepper to taste

Prepare schnitzels as above and fry on both sides. Clean, rinse and cut the mushrooms into thin strips together with the ham. Surround the schnitzels with the mushrooms. Heat the butter and blend with the flour. Fry without browning and blend with cold milk, stirring briskly with an egg-whisk. Bring to a boil and cook over low heat for 6—8 minutes. Towards the end add the sour cream and season. Pour over the schnitzels. Sprinkle with grated cheese and bake. Serve with scooped out potato balls, cauliflower and salads.

MINISTER'S VEAL SCHNITZEL

3/4 lb. boneless veal, 1 2/3 oz. hardened French bread, milk, 2—2 2/3 oz. bread for toast, 2 egg yolks, fat, salt and pepper to taste

Soak the bread in milk and squeeze out the milk. Mince together with the meat. Combine with egg yolks and season. Cut the bread into thin slices. Divide the meat into portions. Place on toast slices, shaping into rectangular schnitzels. Fry in very hot fat on both sides. Continue frying over low heat for several minutes. Serve with potatoes, cauliflower, green peas and salads.

VEAL STEAK

1 lb. boneless veal (leg), 3 1/2—5 oz. veal kidney, 2—2 2/3 oz. smoked bacon, 2/3 oz. flour, fat, salt and pepper to taste

Prepare the steaks (as in Chef's Pork Steak). Remove excess fat from the kidney and cut into 4 slices together with the bacon. Pound lightly

with a mallet that has been dipped in water. Fry on both sides. Arrange on the fried steaks and fasten with metal skewers. Serve with French fries, cauliflower, string beans and salads.

VEAL FILLET

1 lb. boneless veal (leg), 2/3 oz. flour, fat, 1/3 loaf of French bread, 5 oz. pâté, 2 eggs, 1 oz. canned peas, 1 oz. ham, parsley sprigs, salt and pepper to taste

Wash the meat and remove the outer skin. Cut against the grain into 8 pieces. Pound with a mallet that has been dipped in water. Shape into elongated leaves with your hand and a knife. Dredge with seasoning and flour. Fry in very hot fat on both sides. Continue frying over low heat for several minutes. Cut off the crust from the bread and cut into slices (8). Fry lightly on both sides. Spread pâté on the bread, then place it on the fillets. Heat in the oven. Wash the eggs and break them into a dish. Beat with an egg-whisk together with a tablespoon of milk. Add salt. Pour into hot fat and fry over low heat. When the omelet sets on the bottom sprinkle with canned peas, and strips of ham and chopped parsley sprigs, then fry this. Place the omelet on a board and cut into 8 triangles the size of the fillets. Arrange on the prepared fillets. Serve at once with French fries, cauliflower, carrots, asparagus and salads.

MARSHAL'S VEAL FILLET

1 lb. boneless veal (leg), 2/3 oz. flour, fat, 1/3 cup dry white wine, 1 1/2 tablespoons rum, 7 oz. stewed or bottled peaches, 1 oz. walnut meats, salt, pepper and lemon juice to taste

Prepare and fry the fillets as above. Blanch the walnuts and grind them. Add to the fillets together with mashed peaches, the wine and rum. Simmer over low heat for ca. 5 minutes, then season. Serve with rice and lettuce.

ROYAL VEAL FILLET

1 lb. boneless veal (leg), 2/3 oz. flour, fat, 1/2 lb. apples, 3 1/2 oz. ketch-up, salt, pepper, sugar and lemon juice to taste

Prepare fillets (as in Veal Fillet), then fry them. Wash, peel and cut the apples in half, removing the cores. Grate them coarsely and add to the fillets together with the ketchup. Simmer over low heat for arround 5 minutes. Serve with rice and lettuce.

VEAL ZRAZY WITH SOUR CREAM

1 lb. boneless veal (leg), 2/3 oz. flour, fat, 1 cup sour cream, 3 1/2 oz. hard cheese, salt and pepper to taste

Prepare the meat (as in Veal Fillet), shaping the slices into circles. Dredge with seasoning and flour, then fry. Cover with seasoned sour cream, sprinkle with grated cheese and bake. Serve with potatoes, cauliflower, asparagus, carrots with peas and salads.

HETMAN'S VEAL ZRAZY

1 lb. boneless veal (leg), 2/3 oz. flour, fat, 2/3 cup dry red wine, 1—1 1/3 oz. dried cèpe mushrooms, 1 1/3 oz. tomato paste, parsley sprigs, salt and pepper to taste

Prepare the zrazy (as in Veal Fillet), shaping them into circles, then fry them. Wash, soak and cook the mushrooms. Chop them and add to the zrazy together with the tomato paste, chopped parsley sprigs and wine. Simmer over low heat for 6—8 minutes, then season. Serve with soft noodles and salads.

ROLLED VEAL ZRAZY POLISH STYLE

1 lb. boneless veal (leg), 2/3 oz. flour, fat, 2/3 cup sour cream, 1 2/3 oz. hardened French bread, 2 2/3 oz. onions, 1 tablespoon breadcrumbs,

2/3 oz. raisins, parsley sprigs, egg yolk, salt, pepper and seasoning to taste

Wash the meat and remove the outer skin. Cut diagonally into 4 portions. Pound into thin slices with a mallet that has been dipped in water. Peel, rinse and chop the onions finely, then fry them. Soak the bread in water or milk, then squeeze out the liquid. Mince it and combine with the onions, breadcrumbs, egg yolks, rinsed raisins and chopped parsley sprigs. Season to taste. Arrange this on the meat slices and shape into rolls. Tie them up with a thread and sprinkle with seasoning and flour. Brown in intensely heated fat. Sprinkle with water and simmer over low heat. Towards the end add the sour cream. Serve with rice and salads.

VEAL BALLS

3/4 lb. boneless veal, milk, 2—2 2/3 oz. hardened French bread, 1 cup sour cream, 2/3—1 oz. flour, 1/3 oz. flour for sour cream, 3 1/2 oz. mushrooms, 3 1/2 oz. tomatoes, 1 1/3 oz. canned peas, fresh dill, fat, salt and pepper to taste

Soak the bread in the milk and squeeze out the liquid. Wash the meat and mince together with the bread. Combine with the egg and season. Shape this mixture into small balls the size of walnuts. Roll them in flour and fry them. Clean, rinse and chop the mushrooms finely, then fry them. Wash and scald the tomatoes. Remove the skins and cut into pieces. Add to the meat together with the mushrooms, peas and chopped parsley sprigs. Add the sour cream blended with the flour and simmer for a while, then season. Serve with boiled potatoes and salads.

VEAL PATTIES WITH VEGETABLES

3/4 lb. boneless veal, milk, 2—2 2/3 oz. hardened French bread, egg, 1 1/3 oz. butter, 3 1/2 oz. carrots, 3 1/2 oz. celeriac, 3 1/2 oz. parsley root, 1 2/3 oz. onions, parsley sprigs, salt and pepper to taste

Wash, peel and rinse the vegetables. Cut into thin strips and cover with boiling salted water, then cook them. Soak the bread in milk and squeeze

out the liquid. Mince together with the meat. Combine with the egg and season. Shape this mixture into patties (two per serving). Place in the vegetable stock towards the end of cooking. Take out when cooked and surround the vegetables. Sprinkle with chopped parsley sprigs. Place a piece of butter on each. Serve with potatoes.

VEAL LIVER WITH SOUR CREAM

3/4 lb. veal liver, milk, 2/3 oz. flour, 2/3 cup sour cream, 7 oz. onions (green or shallot), parsley sprigs, salt, pepper and sugar to taste, fat for frying

Wash and drain the liver. Remove the outer skin. Cover with milk and set aside in the refrigerator for several hours. Take it out, drain it and cut diagonally into 1/2 in. thick slices. Dredge with pepper and flour. Brown on both sides in very hot fat. Peel, rinse and fry the onions, sprinkling them with sugar. Brown them and add to the liver together with the sour cream and chopped parsley sprigs. Simmer for several minutes and season. Serve with potatoes and salads.

VEAL LIVER À LA RADZIWIŁŁ

3/4 lb. veal liver, olive oil, 1 2/3 oz. ketchup, 3 1/2 oz. lemons, 2 2/3 oz. pork fat, parsley sprigs, 3 tablespoons dry white wine, 3 1/2 oz. hard cheese, salt, pepper and tarragon to taste, fat for frying

Rinse and drain the liver. Remove the outer skin. Cover with wine blended with ketchup, olive oil, pepper and tarragon. Set aside in the refrigerator for several hours. Take out the liver from the marinade and lard with thin strips of pork fat. Brown in very hot fat on both sides. Pour the marinade over and bake for several minutes. Wash and scald the lemons. Peel them and cut into slices, removing any pits. Surround the liver with lemon slices and sprinkle with chopped parsley sprigs and grated cheese, then bake. Before serving cut into slices and pour the seasoned sauce over. Serve with potatoes and salads.

GENERAL'S VEAL KIDNEYS

3/4 lb. veal kidneys, fat, 2/3 oz. flour, 5 oz. onions, 3 1/3 oz. ketchup, 1 oz. almonds, salt, pepper and garlic to taste, milk

Wash the kidneys and remove any excess fat. Cut lengthwise into halves. Cover with milk and set aside in the refrigerator for several hours. Take them out and cut into thin slices. Dredge with seasoning and flour, then fry them. Blanch the almonds and chop them. Peel, rinse and dice the onions, then fry them. Add to the kidneys together with the almonds and ketchup. Simmer for a while and season. Serve with scooped out potato balls and salads.

VEAL KIDNEYS WITH TOAST

3/4 lb. veal kidneys, milk, fat, 2/3 oz. flour, French bread for toast, 2 eggs, 1 oz. ham, 1 1/3 oz. canned peas, 1/2 lb. goose liver pâté, parsley sprigs, 2 egg whites, salt and pepper to taste

Wash the kidneys and remove excess fat. Cut into thin slices. Cover with milk and set aside in a cool place for 40 minutes. Take them out and drain them. Dredge with pepper and flour and fry on both sides. Cut off the crust from the bread and cut into slices. Fry on both sides, spread the pâté on them and cover with the kidneys. Wash the eggs and break them into a dish. Combine with ground ham. Pour into hot fat in a frying pan and fry. Add the peas and chopped parsley sprigs. Sprinkle with seasoning and fry. Cut into pieces the size of the kidneys. Arrange on the prepared kidneys and surround decoratively with beaten egg whites, then bake. Serve with scooped out potato balls, cauliflower and lettuce.

VEAL BRAINS WITH MUSHROOMS

1 lb. veal brains, fat, 5 oz. mushrooms, 1 cup sour cream, 1/3 oz. flour, egg yolk, parsley sprigs, salt and pepper to taste

174

Remove the outer skin from the brains and wash them. Scald with boiling water and drain them. Divide into smaller pieces. Clean, rinse and cut the mushrooms into thin strips, then fry them. Dredge with flour. Add the sour cream and bring to a boil. Combine with the egg yolks and chopped parsley sprigs, then season. Cover the brains and bake. Serve with potatoes and salads.

UHLAN'S VEAL GOULASH

1 lb. boneless veal, 3 1/2 oz. onions, fat, 3 1/2 oz. ketchup, 7 oz. apples (sour), 2/3 oz. flour, salt, pepper and curry powder to taste

Wash the meat and cut into cubes. Dredge with flour and brown in very hot fat. Peel, rinse and chop the onions finely, then fry them. Add to the meat. Sprinkle with water and simmer over low heat, stirring often. Wash, peel and cut the apples in half, removing the cores. Cut into pieces and add to the meat towards the end of cooking together with the ketchup and seasoning. Serve with noodles in all forms and lettuce.

GENERAL'S VEAL GOULASH

1 lb. boneless veal, fat, 2 2/3 oz. onions, 3 1/2 oz. mushrooms, 1 2/3 oz. canned peas, 5 oz. tomatoes, 2/3 cup sour cream, 2/3 oz. flour, 1/3 oz. flour for sour cream, parsley sprigs, salt, seasoning, pepper and prepared mustard to taste

Wash the meat and cut into cubes. Dredge with flour and brown in very hot fat. Clean, rinse and dice the onions and mushrooms, then fry them. Add to the meat. Sprinkle with water and simmer over low heat, stirring often. Wash and scald the tomatoes. Peel them, cut into pieces and add to the meat together with the peas, chopped parsley sprigs and sour cream blended with flour. Cook for a while and season. Serve with noodles in all forms and lettuce.

VEAL SHANK BAKED IN FOIL

*2 veal shanks, fat, 1 1/3 oz. walnut meats, 1 2/3 oz. ketchup, 1 2/3 oz.
pork fat, salt and pepper to taste*

Wash the shanks and remove the bones. Lard with thin strips of pork fat.
Blanch the walnuts and chop them. Combine with the ketchup. Place in
the openings where the bones have been cut out. Tie up with a thread
and spread with fat. Wrap in foil and bake in a moderate oven. When
done remove the foil and cut into portions. Serve with potatoes, peas,
lettuce and salads.

GOOD HOUSEKEEPER'S VEAL SHANK

*2 veal shanks, 2/3 oz. flour, 3 1/2 oz. mushrooms, 3 1/2 oz. onions,
3 1/2 oz. celeriac, 3 1/2 oz. canned peas, 2/3 cup sour cream, 1 1/3
oz. almonds, parsley sprigs, salt and pepper to taste*

Wash the shanks and dredge with the seasoning and flour. Brown in
very hot fat. Sprinkle with water and simmer covered over low heat.
Clean and rinse the vegetables and mushrooms. Cut them into thin
strips and add to the meat towards the end of cooking. Blanch and chop
the almonds. Take out the meat when tender and remove the bones. Place
in the sauce again, together with the almonds, peas and chopped parsley
sprigs. Add the sour cream, simmer for a while and season. Serve with
boiled potatoes and salads.

COOKED CALF'S FEET

*4 calf's feet, 1/2 lb. soup vegetables (carrot, parsley root, celeriac, leek),
1/3 cup sour cream (thick), 1 1/3 oz. grated horseradish, 1 2/3 oz.
ketchup, fat, salt and pepper to taste*

Clean and wash the feet, then scald them. Cover with boiling water and
cook. Wash, peel and rinse the vegetables. Add to the feet towards the
end of cooking and add salt. Take out the meat when tender and remove

the bones. Place in a dish and pour seasoned sour cream blended with the horseradish over the meat. Sprinkle with ketchup and fat, then bake. Serve with potatoes and salads.

VEAL TONGUE IN FOIL

1 1/4 lb. veal tongues, 1/2 lb. soup vegetables (carrots, parsley root, celeriac, leek) 3 1/2 oz. ketchup, 1 1/3 oz. raisins, salt, pepper, allspice and curry powder to taste, fat

Wash the tongues and cover with water. Set aside in a cool place for 2 hours. Scrub with a brush and cut out the salivary glands, which are located on both sides at the base of the tongue. Rinse and cover with boiling salted water. Cook covered over low heat for around 60 minutes. Wash, peel and rinse the vegetables. Add to the tongues together with the seasoning in the middle of cooking. Take the tongues out when done, place in cold water and cool slightly. Skin and cut lengthwise. Arrange in greased foil. Sprinkle with rinsed raisins, pepper and curry powder, then ketchup and bake. Serve with rice and lettuce.

VEAL TONGUE À LA AMBASSADOR

1 1/4 lb. veal tongues, 1/2 lb. soup vegetables (carrots, parsley root, celeriac, leek), 1/3 cup sour cream, 5 oz. dried apricots, 1 oz. tomato paste, salt, pepper, sugar and lemon juice to taste

Cook the tongues as above. Remove the skins and cut lengthwise. Wash, soak and cook the apricots, then force them through a strainer. Combine with the sour cream and tomato paste. Season to taste. Pour over the tongues and simmer for several minutes, then season. Serve with rice and lettuce.

CAPTAIN'S VEAL LIGHTS

1 3/4 lb. veal lights, 9 1/2 oz. soup vegetables (carrots, parsley root, celeriac, leek), 5 oz. lemons, 2/3 cup sour cream, 1 oz. flour, fat, 2/3 oz. capers, parsley sprigs, salt, pepper, prepared mustard, seasoning, thyme and lemon juice to taste

Wash, peel and rinse the vegetables. Cut into thin strips and fry them. Wash the lights and remove the windpipe. Cover with boiling salted water and cook until partly tender. Take them out. Allow to cool and cut into cubes. Add to the vegetables. Cover with stock from the lights so that only the lights are covered, then cook. Wash and scald the lemons, then peel them. Cut into half-slices, removing any pits. Add to the lights together with rinsed capers towards the end of cooking. Add the sour cream blended with the flour and seasoning. Cook for a while and combine with chopped parsley sprigs, then season.

VEAL LIGHTS DIFFERENTLY

1 3/4 lb. veal lights, 1/2 lb. soup vegetables (carrots, parsley root, celeriac, leek), 1/3 cup dry white wine, 3 1/2 oz. onions, fat, 1 oz. flour, 2—2 2/3 oz. ketchup, salt, pepper, garlic and lemon juice to taste

Wash, peel and rinse the vegetables. Cover with boiling salted water and cook. Wash the veal lights and cut out the windpipe. Cover with stock and cook. Take them out, cool and dice them. Peel, rinse and chop the onions finely. Fry them and add the flour. Brown them lightly. Blend with cold stock (1 1/4 cups), stirring briskly with an egg-whisk. Bring to a boil. Add the lights, ketchup and wine. Simmer over low heat for 6—8 minutes, then season. Serve with potatoes and salads.

BOILED BEEF

1 1/4 lb. boneless beef (shoulder, shank, breast, rump), 3/4 lb. soup vegetables (carrots, parsley root, celeriac, leek, savoy cabbage), onion, 2 dried mushrooms, 1 1/3 oz. butter, salt, pepper and seasoning to taste

Wash the meat and place it in boiling salted water. Cover and cook over low heat. Peel and rinse the onion. Brown it on the grill plate. Add to the meat towards the end of cooking together with cleaned and rinsed vege-

tables and mushrooms. Take out the meat when tender. Cut the meat across the grain into wide slices. Arrange on a platter. Surround with cut up vegetables. Dot with butter. Serve at once with boiled potatoes and soured cucumbers.

BOILED BEEF WITH HORSERADISH

1 1/4 lb. boneless beef (shoulder, shank, breast, rump), 3/4 lb. soup vegetables (carrots, parsley root, celeriac, leek savoy cabbage), onion, 2/3 cup sour cream, 2 egg yolks, 1 2/3 oz. horseradish (grated), 3 1/2 oz. hard cheese, salt, pepper, lemon juice and fat for oven-proof dish or pan

Cook the meat as above. Cut against the grain into wide slices. Arrange in a greased dish or pan. Pour seasoned sour cream blended with horseradish and egg yolks over it. Sprinkle with grated cheese and bake. Serve with scooped out potato balls and salads.

BRAISED ROAST BEEF

1 1/4 lb. boneless beef (round, shoulder, rump), 5 oz. onions, fat, 2/3 oz. flour, salt, pepper, allspice and bay leaf to taste

Wash the meat and remove any fibres. Pound with a mallet. Dredge with salt and flour. Brown on all sides. Add peeled, rinsed and diced onions. Fry lightly. Sprinkle with water and simmer covered over low heat. Add water when necessary. Towards the end of cooking add the seasoning. Take out the meat when tender. Cut diagonally against the grain into thin slices. Arrange on a platter. Add the remaining flour blended with a small amount of water to the sauce. Cook for a while and force through a strainer. Add seasoning and pour over the meat. Serve with potatoes, macaroni, kasha, beets, string beans and salads.

ROAST BEEF WITH VEGETABLES

1 1/4 lb. boneless beef (round, shoulder, rump), 2 2/3 oz. onions, 2 2/3 oz. carrots, 2 2/3 oz. celeriac, 2 2/3 oz. parsley root, 1 1/3 oz. canned

peas, 1 1/3 oz. tomato paste, 2/3 oz. flour, salt, pepper, barbecue sauce or seasoning, fat

Wash the meat and remove any veins. Pound with a mallet. Dredge with salt and flour. Brown on all sides. Sprinkle with water and simmer covered over low heat. Wash, peel and rinse the vegetables. Cut them into thin strips and add to the meat towards the end of cooking. Take out the meat when tender. Cut diagonally against the grain into thin slices. Arrange on a platter. Add the remaining flour blended with a small amount of water to the sauce together with the peas and tomato paste. Cook for a while and season. Pour over the meat. Serve with potatoes and salads.

HUSSAR'S ROAST BEEF

1 1/4 lb. boneless beef (round), 5 oz. onions for stuffing, 2—2 2/3 oz. onions for simmering, 1—1 1/3 oz. grated whole-wheat bread, egg yolk, 1/3 cup sour cream, 2/3 oz. flour, salt and pepper to taste, fat

Wash the meat and remove any veins. Pound with a mallet. Dredge with salt and flour. Brown on all sides together with peeled, rinsed and finely chopped onions. Sprinkle with water and simmer covered over low heat. Add water when necessary. Take out the meat when tender. Cut into slices, leaving every other slice partly uncut. Peel, rinse and chop the onions finely. Fry them and combine with the egg yolks and bread. Add seasoning. Place the stuffing in the pockets formed in the meat and arrange in a dish or pan. Combine the sauce with the sour cream blended with the remaining flour. Cook for a while and force through a strainer. Add seasoning. Pour over the meat and simmer for several minutes. Serve with potatoes, cabbage and salads.

CLOISTER ROAST BEEF

1 1/4 lb. boneless beef (round, shoulder, rump), 1/3 cup dry red wine, 2—2 2/3 oz. onions, 5 oz. plum jam, 2/3 oz. flour, 1 oz. almonds, salt, pepper, lemon juice and cloves to taste

Blanch the almonds. Wash the meat and remove any veins. Pound with a mallet. Cover with the almonds. Dredge with salt and flour. Brown in very hot fat together with peeled, rinsed and diced onions. Sprinkle with water and simmer covered over low heat with a small amount of cold water. Take out the meat when tender. Cut diagonally against the grain into thin slices and arrange on a platter. Force the sauce through a strainer. Add the jam and ground seasoning. Simmer for several minutes and pour over the meat. Serve with rice and cauliflower.

BEEF HU-HU

1 1/4 lb. boneless beef (shoulder, rump, shank), fat, 1/3 oz. flour, 5 oz. onions, 2 dried cèpe mushrooms, salt pepper, cloves, pimento, curry powder, prepared mustard, ground paprika, garlic, sugar and sherry to taste

Wash the meat and remove any veins. Cut into cubes. Dredge with salt and flour. Brown in very hot fat together with peeled, rinsed and diced onions. Sprinkle with water. Add soaked mushrooms that have been cut into thin strips. Simmer until tender. Towards the end add the remaining seasoning. Serve with scooped out potato balls and lettuce.

BEEF IN GINGER SAUCE

1 1/4 lb. boneless beef (shoulder, rump, shank), fat, 2/3 oz. flour, 5 oz. onions, 3 1/2 oz. ketchup, 4 prunes, salt, pepper, ginger, garlic and ground paprika to taste

Wash the meat and remove any veins. Cut into cubes. Dredge with the seasoning and flour. Brown in very hot fat together with peeled, rinsed and diced onions. Sprinkle with water and simmer covered over low heat. Towards the end add ketchup and soaked and pitted prunes. Combine the tender meat with the remaining flour blended with a small amount of cold water and seasoning. Simmer for several minutes and season. Serve with rice and salads.

BEEF GOULASH

1 lb. boneless beef (shoulder, shank, breast, rump), fat, 5 oz. onions, 2/3 oz. flour, 2/3 oz. tomato paste, salt, pepper, allspice, bay leaf and caraway seed to taste

Wash the meat and remove any veins. Cut into large cubes. Dredge with seasoning and flour. Brown in very hot fat together with peeled, rinsed and diced onions. Sprinkle with water and simmer covered over low heat. Towards the end add the seasoning and the remaining flour blended with a small amount of cold water. Add the tomato paste and seasoning. Serve with potatoes, macaroni, noodles, kashas and salads.

GOULASH WITH BEER

1 lb. boneless beef (shoulder, shank, breast, rump), fat, 2 2/3 oz. onions, 2/3 oz. flour, lager beer, 1/3 cup sour cream, 5 oz. farmer's cheese, salt, pepper and lemon rind to taste

Wash the meat and remove any veins. Cut into large cubes. Dredge with seasoning and flour. Brown in very hot fat together with peeled, rinsed and diced onions. Sprinkle with beer and simmer covered over low heat. Towards the end add sour cream blend with the remaining flour, then season. Add diced farmer's cheese. Serve with noodles and salads.

BEEF GOULASH WITH WINE

1 lb. boneless beef, fat, 5 oz. onions, 1 1/3 oz. tomato paste, dry red wine, salt, pepper, garlic and seasoning to taste, 2/3 oz. flour

Wash the meat and cut into cubes. Dredge with seasoning and flour. Brown in very hot fat together with peeled, rinsed and diced onions. Sprinkle with wine and simmer until tender. Towards the end add the tomato paste and the remaining flour blended with a small amount of cold water, then season.

ROLLED BEEF ZRAZY

1 lb. boneless beef (round), fat, 2/3 oz. flour, 1/3 cup sour cream, 1 1/3 oz. onions, 1 1/3 oz. pork fat, 1 2/3 oz. dill pickles, 1 1/3 oz. kiełbasa, 2—2 2/3 oz. onions for simmering, salt, pepper, marjoram and seasoning

Wash the meat and remove any veins. Cut diagonally against the grain into 4 wide slices. Pound with a mallet that has been dipped in water into thin strips. Dredge with seasoning and set aside in the refrigerator for 30 minutes. Peel and rinse the onions. Cut into thin strips together with the pork fat, pickles and kiełbasa, then season. Divide the stuffing into 4 portions. Wrap it in the meat slices and tie them up with thread. Sprinkle with seasoning and flour. Brown in very hot fat together with peeled, rinsed and diced onions. Sprinkle with water and simmer covered over low heat. Add water when necessary. When tender combine the meat with sour cream blended with the flour. Simmer for a while and season. Serve with potatoes, buckwheat kasha, beets and salads.

ROLLED BEEF ZRAZY WITH MUSHROOMS

1 lb. boneless beef (round), fat, 2/3 oz. flour, 1/3 cup sour cream, 5 oz. mushrooms, 1 2/3 oz. onions, 1/3—2/3 oz. breadcrumbs, egg yolk, parsley sprigs, 3 tablespoons dry white wine, salt, pepper and seasoning

Prepare the meat (as above). Clean, rinse and chop the onions and mushrooms finely. Fry them and combine with the egg yolk, chopped parsley sprigs and breadcrumbs, then season. Wrap this in strips of meat and tie them up with thread. Dredge with seasoning and flour. Brown in very hot fat. Sprinkle with water and simmer covered over low heat. Towards the end add the wine. Combine the remaining flour with the sour cream and add to the zrazy. Simmer for a while and season. Serve with potatoes, buckwheat kasha, dill pickles and salads.

ROLLED BEEF ZRAZY À LA ZAGŁOBA

1 lb. boneless beef (round), fat, 2/3 oz. flour, 3 1/2 oz. white kiełbasa, 1 1/3 oz. horseradish (grated), 1/3 oz. grated whole-wheat bread, 1 ta-

blespoon sour cream, 3 1/2 oz. onions, 1 oz. tomato paste, salt, pepper and nutmeg to taste

Prepare the zrazy (as in Rolled Beef Zrazy). Remove the skin from the kiełbasa and dice it. Combine with the horseradish, bread and sour cream, then season. Roll this in meat strips and tie up with thread. Dredge with seasoning and flour. Brown in very hot fat together with peeled, rinsed and diced onions. Sprinkle with water and simmer over low heat. Towards the end add the tomato paste and the remaining flour blended with a small amount of cold water. Take out the meat when tender. Force the sauce through a strainer and season. Pour over the meat. Serve with potatoes, noodles, kasha and salads.

POUNDED BEEF ZRAZY

1 lb. boneless beef (round), fat, 2/3 oz. flour, 1/3 coup sour cream, 1 oz. tomato paste, 2 2/3 oz. onions, salt, pepper, nutmeg and seasoning to taste

Wash the meat and remove any veins. Cut diagonally against the grain into 4 slices. Pound them lightly with a mallet that has been dipped in water. Dredge with seasoning and flour. Brown in very hot fat together with peeled, rinsed and diced onions. Sprinkle with water and simmer covered over low heat. Towards the end add the tomato paste and sour cream blended with the remaining flour, then season. Serve with potatoes, beets and salads.

RASCAL'S BEEF ZRAZY

1 lb. boneless beef (round), fat, 1/3 oz. flour, 3 1/2 oz. thin frankfurters, 1 1/3 oz. horseradish (grated), 3 1/2 oz. hard cheese, salt, pepper, sugar and lemon juice to taste

Prepare the zrazy (as in Pounded Beef Zrazy). Dredge with seasoning and flour. Brown in heated fat. Sprinkle with water and simmer covered

over low heat. Clean, rinse and dice the mushrooms. Add to the zrazy towards the end of cooking. Remove the skins, if any, from the frankfurters. Cut them into slices. Add to the zrazy together with the horseradish and season. Sprinkle with grated cheese and bake. Serve with rice and salads.

BEEF ZRAZY À LA AMBASSADOR

1 lb. boneless beef (round), fat, 1/3 oz. flour, 1/3 cup dry red wine, egg yolk, 1/3—2/3 oz. grated whole-wheat bread, 1 2/3 oz. ketchup, 3 1/2 oz. canned peas, salt, pepper and nutmeg to taste

Prepare the zrazy (as in Pounded Beef Zrazy). Dredge with seasoning and flour. Brown in very hot fat. Sprinkle with water and simmer covered over low heat. Towards the end add the peas and wine. Combine the ketchup with the egg yolk and add to the zrazy. Sprinkle with the bread and seasoning, then bake. Serve with rice and salads.

PAN-BROILED FILLET OF BEEF

3/4 lb. fillet of beef, fat, 2/3 oz. flour, salt and pepper to taste

Wash the meat, remove the outer skin and excess fat. Cut diagonally against the grain into 8 pieces. Pound lightly with a mallet. Dredge with seasoning and flour. Place in very hot fat and fry on both sides, leaving the meat rare inside. Serve with potatoes, French fries, string beans, cauliflower and salads.

GENERAL'S FILLET OF BEEF

3/4 lb. fillet of beef, fat, 2/3 oz. flour, 2/3 cup sour cream, 2 2/3 oz. onions, 1 oz. ham, 1 1/3 oz. canned peppers, 1 1/3 oz. dill pickles, 1—1 1/3 oz. tomato paste, parsley sprigs, salt, pepper, prepared mustard, ground paprika, sugar and seasoning to taste

Prepare the meat and fry (as above). Peel, rinse and chop the onions finely, then fry them. Cut the ham, peppers and pickles into strips. Add to the onions together with the tomato paste, sour cream and chopped parsley sprigs. Pour over the meat and simmer for several minutes. Season to taste. Serve with potatoes, cauliflower and salads.

FILLET OF BEEF À LA HENRY

3/4 lb. fillet of beef, fat, 2/3 oz. flour, 3 1/2 oz. mushrooms, 3 1/2 oz. tomatoes, 1 2/3 oz. dill pickles, 1 2/3 oz. ketchup, 1/3 cup sour cream, parsley sprigs, salt, pepper and seasoning to taste

Prepare and fry the fillet of beef (as in Pan-broiled Fillet of Beef). Wash, scald and peel the tomatoes. Cut them into pieces. Cut the pickles into half-slices. Clean and rinse the mushrooms. Cut them into thin strips and fry them. Add to the fillet of beef together with the tomatoes, pickles, sour cream, ketchup and chopped parsley sprigs. Simmer for several minutes. Season to taste. Serve with scooped out potato balls, boiled savoy cabbage and salads.

FILLET OF BEEF À LA SAPIEHA

3/4 lb. fillet of beef, fat, 2/3 oz. flour, French bread for toast, 5 oz. goose liver pâté; sauce: 3/4 cup pan drippings from poultry roast, 1/3 cup Madeira wine, 3 1/2 oz. mushrooms, 2/3 oz. fat, 2/3 oz. flour for roux, 2/3 oz. capers, salt, pepper, curry powder and seasoning to taste

Prepare and fry the fillets of beef (as in Pan-broiled Fillet of Beef). Cut the bread into 1/2 in. slices. Remove the crust. Spread pâté over the bread and cover with the fillet of beef. Arrange on a platter. Clean, rinse and chop the mushrooms finely, then fry them. Heat the fat and blend it with the flour. Fry without browning. Blend with cold stock, stirring briskly with an egg-whisk. Bring to a boil. Add the wine and rinsed capers. Cook over low heat for several minutes. Season and pour over the fillet

of beef. Serve with Cracow buckwheat kasha (q.v.), cauliflower and lettuce.

Note: Prepare this fillet of beef only when roast chicken juice is available, e.g. from the day before.

EDITOR'S FILLET OF BEEF

3/4 lb. fillet of beef, fat, 2/3 oz. flour, 3 1/2 oz. mushrooms, 3 1/2 oz. ketchup, 1 2/3 oz. prunes, parsley sprigs, salt and pepper to taste

Prepare and fry the fillet of beef (as in Pan-broiled Fillet of Beef). Wash, soak and cook the prunes. Force them through a strainer. Clean and rinse the mushrooms. Cut them into thin strips. Fry them and add to the fillet of beef together with the prune paste, ketchup and chopped parsley sprigs. Simmer for several minutes and season.

MINISTER'S BEEF STEAK

3/4 lb. fillet of beef, fat, 2/3 oz. flour, 1 oz. butter, 4 slices of canned pineapple, 4 halves of stewed or bottled peaches, 1 1/2 tablespoons rum, salt and pepper to taste

Rinse the fillet of beef. Remove the outer skin and excess fat. Cut against the grain into 4 pieces. Form into 1 in. thick circles with your hand and a knife. Dredge with pepper and flour. Fry in very hot fat for 2—3 minutes, leaving the inside pink. When done on one side, place the pineapple rings on the fried side, so that the meat soaks in the fruit aroma. Towards the end of frying add the butter. When done arrange the steaks on a platter. Place a peach half in each pineapple ring. Pour rum over this. Serve at once with French fries, asparagus and lettuce.

WROCŁAW BEEF STEAK

3/4 lb. fillet of beef, fat, 2/3 oz. flour, 2—2 2/3 oz. hard cheese, 2—2 2/3 oz. smoked ham, 1 2/3 oz. ketchup, salt and pepper to taste

Prepare and fry the steaks (as above). Surround with ham and cheese slices. Pour ketchup over and bake in a hot oven. Serve with French fries, cauliflower, canned peas and salads.

CAPTAIN'S BEEF STEAK

3/4 lb. fillet of beef, 2—2 2/3 oz. onions, 1 2/3 oz. canned peppers, 1 tablespoon olive oil, 2 egg yolks, 2/3 oz. tomato paste, fat, breadcrumbs, salt, pepper and ground paprika to taste

Wash the meat and mince together with the peppers. Combine with chopped onions, tomato paste, egg yolks and olive oil, then season. Make round 1 in. thick steaks from this mixture. Coat them with breadcrumbs and place in very hot fat. Brown on both sides, then continue frying over low heat for several minutes. Serve with potatoes, cauliflower and mizeria (q.v.).

GENERAL'S BEEF STEAK

3/4 lb. fillet of beef, 2—2 2/3 oz. onions, 1 2/3 oz. dill pickles, 1 1/3 oz. marinated mushrooms, 2/3 oz. capers, 2 egg yolks, 1 tablespoon olive oil, fat, salt, pepper, prepared mustard, ground paprika and seasoning to taste

Wash the meat and mince it. Chop the pickles and mushrooms finely together with peeled and rinsed onions. Combine with the meat, egg yolks, rinsed capers and olive oil, then season. Make 1 1/2 in. thick steaks from this mixture. Place them in very hot fat and brown on both sides, then continue frying over low heat for several minutes. Serve with French fries, canned peas and salads.

FILLET OF BEEF WITH MUSHROOMS

3/4 lb. fillet of beef, 2/3 oz. flour, fat, 1/2 lb. mushrooms, 1 2/3 oz. ketchup, salt and pepper to taste

Rinse the meat and remove the outer skin and excess fat. Cut diagonally against the grain into 4 pieces. Pound with a mallet that has been dipped in water into 5 in. long and 1/4 in. thick strips. Dredge with seasoning and flour. Fry on both sides for 2—3 minutes, leaving the inside slightly pink. Clean and rinse the mushrooms. Cut them into slices and fry them. Surround the meat slices with these and sprinkle with ketchup. Serve with French fries, string beans, Brussels sprouts and salads.

TOURNEDOS POLISH STYLE

3/4 lb. fillet of beef, fat, 2/3 oz. flour, French bread for toast, 5 oz. mushrooms, 1 1/3 oz. ketchup, 2—2 2/3 oz. smoked ham, 4 apples (sour), 3 1/2 oz. fried cranberries, 1 oz. horseradish (grated), salt, pepper, sugar and lemon juice to taste

Wash and peel the apples. Cut in half and remove the cores. Cook them in syrup made of sugar and water. Allow to cool. Take out the apples and fill with seasoned cranberries combined with the horseradish. Clean and rinse the mushrooms. Cut them into thin strips and fry them. Combine with the ketchup. Cut off the crust from the bread and cut it into 1 in. slices. Hollow out the insides, leaving the bottoms. Fry them and fill with mushrooms. Wash the meat and remove the outer skin and excess fat. Cut against the grain into 8 pieces. Pound lightly with a mallet that has been dipped in water. Dredge with seasoning and flour. Fry on both sides. Arrange on the toast slices. Cover with slices of fried ham. Place the apples alongside. Serve with French fries, canned peas and cauliflower.

FILLET OF BEEF SHASHLIK

3/4 lb. fillet of beef, fat, 2/3 oz. flour, 3 1/2 oz. onions, 3 1/2 oz. tomatoes, 1 2/3—2 oz. pork fat, 4 mushrooms (small), 7 oz. rice, 1 2/3 cups broth, 1 1/3 oz. tomato paste, 2 oz. onions for the rice, salt, pepper and ground paprika to taste

Rinse the rice and cover it with boiling broth. Bring to a boil, stirring constantly. Place in a hot oven for 20 minutes. Peel, rinse and chop the

onions finely. Fry them and combine with the rice and tomato paste. Fry for a while, stirring constantly. Season and arrange on a platter. Rinse the meat and remove the outer skin and excess fat. Cut into 3/4 in. squares 1/4 in. thick. Sprinkle with pepper and set aside for an hour. Peel and rinse the onions. Cut them into slices together with the pork fat and tomatoes. Clean and rinse the mushrooms. Place the meat on skewers alternately with the pork fat, tomatoes, onions and mushrooms. Dredge with seasoning and flour. Place in very hot fat and fry on both sides. When done arrange on the rice. Serve with soured cucumbers and salads.

STEAK WITH CAVIAR

1 lb. boneless steak, fat, 1/3 oz. flour, 1 oz. caviar, dry white wine, 1 2/3 oz. onions, 2 oz. celeriac, 1 2/3 oz. carrots, 1 tablespoon olive oil, salt, pepper and lemon juice to taste

Wash, peel and grate the vegetables coarsely. Combine with olive oil and seasoning. Surround the meat with them and set aside in the refrigerator for several hours. Remove the vegatables from the meat. Pour fat over it and dredge with flour. Brown in very hot fat and bake, basting with wine. Towards the end add the caviar. Take out the meat when tender. Cut diagonally into thin slices. Pour the seasoned sauce over this. Serve with scooped out potato balls, cauliflower and salads.

STEAK POLISH STYLE

1 lb. boneless steak, fat, pork fat, horseradish (grated), egg yolk, 1 oz. almonds, salt, pepper and lemon juice to taste, ketchup

Wash the meat and rub it with seasoning and lemon juice. Set aside in a cool place for an hour. Blanch the almonds and grind them. Combine with the horseradish and egg yolks, then season. Cover the steak with this. Wrap in thin strips of pork fat. Pour fat over the meat. Bake, basting with water, then with the pan drippings. When done cut into thin slices

and arrange on a platter. Combine the sauce with ketchup and season. Pour over the meat. Serve with French fries, cauliflower and lettuce.

RUMPSTEAK

1 lb. boneless beef (rump), or boneless steak, fat, 2/3 oz. flour, salt and pepper to taste

Wash the meat and remove any veins. Cut into 3/4 in. thick slices. Pound with a mallet that has been dipped in water. Shape into oval steaks with your hand and a knife. Dredge with salt, pepper and flour. Fry in very hot fat on both sides for 3—4 minutes. Serve with French fries. Brussels sprouts and salads.

BEEF ENTRECÔTE

1—1 1/4 lb. boneless beef entrecôte, fat, 2/3 oz. flour, 1 1/3 oz. ketchup, 1/3 cup dry red wine, salt, pepper and garlic to taste

Wash the meat and cut into portions. Pound lightly with a mallet that has been dipped in water. Dredge with seasoning and flour. Brown in very hot fat. Add crushed garlic, ketchup and wine. Simmer for several minutes and season.

BEEF RAGOUT WITH MUSHROOMS

1 lb. boneless beef, fat, 5 oz. mushrooms, 5 oz. onions, 1 1/3 oz. tomato paste, 1/3 cup sour cream, 2/3 oz. flour, parsley sprigs, salt, pepper and garlic to taste

Wash the meat and cut into large cubes. Dredge with seasoning and flour. Brown in very hot fat. Sprinkle with water and simmer covered over low heat. Clean, rinse and dice the mushrooms and onions. Fry them and add to the meat towards the end of cooking together with the sour cream

blended with the remaining flour and tomato paste. Simmer for several minutes. Combine with chopped parsley sprigs and season.

COOKED BEEF TONGUE

Beef tongue, 1/2 lb. soup vegetables (carrots, parsley root, celeriac, leek); brine: 2 cups water, 1/6 oz. saltpetre, 1/6 oz. sugar, 1 2/3 oz. salt, bay leaf, allspice, cloves, coriander and rosemary

Soak the tongue in cold water for 2 hours. Scrub it with a brush and cut out the salivary glands located on both sides at the base of the tongue. Arrange the tongue in a stoneware dish. Cover with the brine and set aside in a cool place (40°—48°F) for 10 days, turning it over from time to time. Take out the tongue and wash it thoroughly. Place it in boiling water and bring to a boil. Towards the end of cooking add cleaned and rinsed vegetables. Take out the tongue when done and remove the outer skin. Cut into portions. Serve with potatoes and various sauces, such as horseradish sauce or pickle sauce, and salads.

BEEF TONGUE POLISH STYLE

Beef tongue, 1/2 lb. soup vegetables (carrots, parsley root, celeriac, leek), 1 2/3 oz. almonds, 1 2/3 oz. raisins, 1 1/3 oz. prunes, 3 tablespoons dry red wine, 1 oz. butter, 1 oz. flour, salt, sugar, lemon juice, lemon rind and caramel syrup

Soak the tongue in cold water for 2 hours. Scrub it with a brush under running water. Cut out the salivary glands located on both sides at the base of the tongue. Place it in boiling water and cook. Towards the end of cooking add cleaned and rinsed vegetables. Take out the tongue when tender and remove the outer skin. Cut into portions. Blanch the almonds and grind them. Wash and soak the prunes. Cut them into thin strips. Heat the fat and blend it with the flour. Fry this without browning and blend with cold stock (1 cup), stirring briskly with an egg-whisk. Bring to a boil. Add the prunes, almonds, wine and caramel syrup. Cook for several minutes and season. Pour over the tongue and simmer for a while. The sauce should be sweet-sour. Serve with potatoes and salads.

WARSAW BEEF TRIPE

2 lb. beef tripe, stock from beef bones and vegetables, 1/2 lb. soup vegetables (carrots, parsley root, celeriac, leek), fat, 1 oz. flour, 2 oz. onions, 1 2/3 oz. hard cheese, 2/3 oz. butter, 1/3 oz. breadcrumbs, salt, pepper, bay leaf, allspice, ground paprika, ginger, seasoning and marjoram to taste

Clean and wash the tripe. Soak it in cold water for 2 hours. Cover with boiling water and cook for 10 minutes. Drain it and rinse. Cover with water again and cook for 4 hours. Cut the tripe into strips. Place in the stock together with cleaned and rinsed vegetables that have been cut into strips and fried. Add the seasoning and cook for a while. Peel, rinse and dice the onions, then fry them. Add the flour. Fry without browning. Combine with the tripe. Cook for 3—4 minutes, then season. Before serving, cover with browned breadcrumbs blended with melted butter. Sprinkle with grated cheese.

LVOV BEEF TRIPE

2 lb. tripe, stock from beef bones and vegetables, 1/2 lb. soup vegetables (carrots, parsley root, celeriac, leek), 5 oz. savoy cabbage, fat, 1/3 cup sour cream, 1 oz. flour, 1 2/3 oz. onions, 1/3 oz. breadcrumbs, 2/3 oz. butter, 1 1/3 oz. hard cheese, salt, pepper, bay leaf, allspice, ground paprika, ginger, seasoning and nutmeg to taste

Cook the tripe as above. Clean and rinse the vegetables without cabbage. Cut them into strips and fry them. Cover with the stock. Add tripe cut into strips and diced savoy cabbage. Cook until tender together with the bay leaf and allspice. Peel, rinse and dice the onions, then fry them. Add the flour. Fry without browning. Combine with the tripe, sour cream and grated cheese. Bring to a boil and season. Before serving top with browned breadcrumbs blended with melted butter.

LAMB RAGOUT WITH TOMATOES

1—1 1/2 lb. lamb with bones (brisket, shoulder), 1/2 lb. soup vegetables (carrots, parsley root, celeriac, leek), 7 oz. tomatoes, 1 oz. fat, 1 oz. flour, 2/3 oz. capers, parsley sprigs, salt, sugar and lemon juice to taste

Wash the meat and cover it with boiling salted water. Bring to a boil and cook covered until tender. Towards the end add cleaned and rinsed vegetables. Take out the meat when tender. Remove the bones and cut into portions. Arrange on a platter. Wash and scald the tomatoes. Remove the skins and cut into pieces. Surround the meat with them. Heat the fat and blend with the flour. Fry without browning. Blend with cold stock (1 1/4 cups), stirring briskly with an egg-whisk. Bring to a boil. Add rinsed capers and cook for 5 minutes. Season this and pour over the meat. Simmer for a while. Serve with scooped out potato balls and salads.

ROAST LAMB WITH SOUR CREAM

1—1 1/4 lb. boneless lamb (leg), fat, 1 2/3 oz. pork fat, 2 2/3 oz. onions, 2/3 oz. flour, 2/3 oz. capers, 1/3 cup vinegar, salt, pepper, sugar and lemon juice

Wash the meat and remove any veins. Cover with boiling vinegar blended with water (1 cup) and seasoning. Set aside in a cool place for 24 hours, turning over often. Take it out of the brine and lard with thin strips of pork fat. Sprinkle with water and simmer covered over low heat. Take out the meat when tender. Add the sour cream blended with the remaining flour to the sauce. Cook for a while and force through a strainer. Add rinsed capers and season to taste. Pour over the meat cut into portions. Simmer for several minutes and season. Serve with rice, Ćwikła (q.v.) and salads.

ROAST LAMB WITH VEGETABLES

1—1 1/4 lb. boneless lamb (leg), fat, 2/3 oz. flour, 3 1/2 oz. ketchup, 2 2/3 oz. onions, 2 2/3 oz. carrots, 2 2/3 oz. celeriac, 2 2/3 oz. parsley

sprigs, 3 1/2 oz. mushrooms, 1 2/3 oz. pork fat, 1/3 cup vinegar, salt, pepper and sugar to taste

Prepare the meat as above. Lard with thin strips of pork fat. Dredge with salt and flour. Brown in very hot fat. Sprinkle with water and simmer covered over low heat. Clean and rinse the vegetables and mushrooms. Cut them into strips and fry them lightly. Add to the meat towards the end of cooking. Take out the meat when tender and cut into portions. Add the remaining flour to the sauce after blending it with a small amount of cold water and ketchup. Season this and pour over the meat. Serve with potatoes, Ćwikła (q.v.) and salads.

LAMB FRICASSEE

1—1 1/4 lb. boneless lamb (leg), fat, 2/3 oz. flour, 1/3 cup sour cream, 5 oz. mushrooms, 2 2/3 oz. onions, 2/3 oz. capers, 1 2/3 oz. sour stewed or bottled cherries, salt, pepper and lemon juice to taste

Wash the meat and cut into cubes, 5 pieces to a serving. Dredge with seasoning and flour. Brown in very hot fat. Sprinkle with water and simmer covered over low heat. Clean, rinse and dice the onions and mushrooms. Fry them. Add to the meat towards the end of cooking together with rinsed capers. When tender, combine the meat with the sour cream blended with the remaining flour and preserves. Cook for a while and season.

CHEF'S LAMB

1 lb. boneless lamb (shoulder), fat, 2/3 oz. flour, 2 2/3 oz. onions, 1 1/3 oz. tomato paste, 1 2/3 oz. canned peppers, 1 1/3 oz. canned peas, 1 2/3 oz. flour for noodles, 1/2 egg, salt, pepper, ground paprika, garlic and seasoning to taste

Wash the meat and cut into cubes, allowing 4 pieces to a serving. Dredge with seasoning and flour. Brown in very hot fat together with peeled and

rinsed onions. Sprinkle with water and simmer covered over low heat. Sift the flour and blend it with the egg and water until a hard dough is formed. Grate the dough coarsley. Add to the meat towards the end of cooking together with the tomato paste, peas, pepper strips, seasoning and the remaining flour blended with a small amount of cold water, then season. Serve with scooped out potato balls and salads.

LAMB CUTLET SAUTÉ

1 1/4—1 1/2 lb. lamb (rib), fat, 2/3 oz. flour, 1/3 cup vinegar, water, salt, sugar, pepper, garlic and rosemary to taste

Wash the meat and separate it from the spine bones. Remove the outer skin and veins. Cover with boiling vinegar blended with water (1 cup) and seasoning. Set aside in a cool place for several hours. Take out the meat and cut into cutlets, allowing 2 per serving, leaving one rib bone for each. Remove the outer skin from each bone and remove the remaining meat for a length of 3/4 in. Pound the meat with a mallet that has been dipped in water, shaping it into 1/2 in. thick ovals. Rub with salt with garlic. Dredge with seasoning and flour. Fry in heated fat on both sides, then continue frying over low heat for several minutes. Serve with potatoes, sauces, mizeria (q.v.) or lettuce.

LAMB CUTLET POLISH STYLE

1 1/4—1 1/2 lb. lamb (rib), fat, 2/3 oz. flour, 2/3 cup sour cream, 7 oz. apples, 1 1/3 oz. horseradish (grated), 1/3 cup vinegar, water, salt, pepper, sugar and lemon juice to taste

Prepare and fry the cutlets (as above). Wash, peel and rinse the apples. Cut them in half, removing the cores and cut into pieces. Combine with sour cream, horseradish and seasoning. Pour over the cutlets. Simmer for several minutes and season.

MANAGER'S LAMB STEAK

1 lb. boneless lamb (leg), fat, 2/3 oz. flour, 2 garlic bulbs, 3 1/2 oz. ketchup, salt, sugar and pepper to taste, butter

Wash the meat and remove the outer skin and veins. Sprinkle with salt and pepper. Set aside in a cool place for 2 hours. Cut against the grain into portions. Pound with a mallet that has been dipped in water. Shape into 1/2 in. thick oval steaks with your hand and a knife. Dredge with flour and brown on both sides. Divide the garlic into cloves. Peel and scald it, then drain. Fry in butter together with sugar. Add to the cutlets together with ketchup. Simmer for several minutes and season.

GENERAL'S LAMB FILLET

1 lb. boneless lamb (leg), 1 1/3 oz. pork fat, 1 1/3 oz. smoked ham, 1/3 cup dry red wine, 1 1/3 oz. tomato paste, fat, 2/3 oz. flour, 1 2/3 oz. canned peppers, salt, garlic, pepper and sugar

Wash the meat and remove the outer skin and veins. Rub with seasoning and set aside in a cool place for 2 hours. Cut against the grain into 8 pieces. Pound with a mallet that has been dipped in water. Shape into elongated leaves with your hand and a knife. Lard each fillet with thin strips of pork fat and ham. Dredge with pepper and flour. Fry in very hot fat, leaving the inside pink. Add ground paprika, tomato paste and wine. Simmer for several minutes and season. Serve with rice, potatoes and pea purée.

WROCŁAW LAMB ZRAZY

1 lb. boneless lamb (leg), fat, 2/3 oz. flour for meat, 1 1/4—1 3/4 lb. potatoes, 5 oz. canned peppers, 5 oz. mushrooms, 1 oz. butter or margarine, 1 oz. flour for sauce, 1 cup stock from bones, 1/3 cup sour cream, parsley sprigs, salt, pepper, garlic and seasoning to taste

Wash the meat and remove the outer skin and veins. Cut against the grain into 8 pieces. Pound with a mallet that has been dipped in water. Shape into 1/2 in. thick ovals with your hand and a knife. Dredge with seasoning and flour. Brown on both sides. Wash, peel and rinse the potatoes. Cut them into slices and fry, several at a time, in fat. Arrange on a platter alternately with the lamb zrazy, pepper strips and sliced and fried mushrooms, sprinkling everything with the seasoning. Heat the butter and blend with the flour. Fry this without browning. Blend with cold stock, stirring briskly with an egg-whisk. Bring to a boil and cook for several minutes. Combine the sauce with the sour cream and chopped parsley sprigs. Season this and pour over the meat, then bake. Serve with salads.

MINCED LAMB ZRAZY POLISH STYLE

3/4 lb. boneless lamb (shoulder), 1 2/3 oz. onions, 2/3—1 oz. dried cèpe mushrooms, egg, 1 2/3 oz. bread without crust, fat, 2/3 cup sour cream, 2/3 oz. flour

Wash, soak and cook the mushrooms. Wash the meat and mince it together with peeled and rinsed onions and bread that has been soaked in water, then squeezed out. Combine with the egg and minced mushrooms, then season. Shape this mixture into 8 oval zrazy. Coat them with flour and fry on both sides until golden brown. Arrange on a platter. Pour sour cream and mushroom stock over. Simmer for several minutes and season.

LAMB SHASHLIK

3/4 lb. boneless lamb (leg), fat, 2/3 oz. flour, 3 1/2 oz. pork fat, 1 2/3 oz. onions for sprinkling, 3 1/2—5 oz. onions for skewers, salt, pepper, garlic and lemon juice to taste

Wash the meat and remove any veins. Rub with garlic crushed with salt. Cut into 3/4 by 3/4 in. squares 1/2 in. thick. Pound lightly with a mallet

that has been dipped in water. Sprinkle with finely chopped onions. Sprinkle with lemon juice and set aside for 4 hours. Place the meat pieces on skewers alternately with slices of pork fat and onions. Sprinkle with seasoning and flour. Fry in very hot fat on both sides. Serve with rice and tomato salad.

ROAST WILD BOAR

1 lb. wild boar ham or shoulder, fat, 2 2/3 oz. onions, 2/3 oz. flour, 1/3 cup vinegar, 3/4 cup water, 2/3 cup sour cream, 1 1/3 oz. tomato paste, salt, pepper, juniper berries, bay leaf, allspice, nutmeg and sugar to taste

Wash the meat and remove any veins. Cover with boiling vinegar blended with water and seasoning. Set aside in a cool place for 24 hours. turning over often. Take the meat out and dry it. Dredge with flour. Brown in very hot fat together with peeled, rinsed and diced onions. Sprinkle with water and marinade. Simmer covered over low heat. Towards the end add the tomato paste and sour cream blended with the remaining flour. Take out the meat when tender and cut against the grain into portions. Pour the strained and seasoned sauce over. Serve with potatoes, Ćwikła (q.v.) and salads.

ROAST WILD BOAR WITH ALMONDS

1 lb. wild boar ham or shoulder, fat, 1/3 oz. flour, 1/3 cup vinegar, 3/4 cup water, 1 2/3 oz. almonds, 1 1/3 oz. horseradish (grated), 1 oz. grated whole-wheat bread, 2/3 cup sour cream, salt, pepper, sugar and lemon juice

Wash the meat and remove any veins. Cover with boiling vinegar blended with water and seasoning, and set aside in a cool place for 24 hours. turning over often. Take out the meat and dry it. Dredge with flour and brown in very hot fat. Sprinkle with water and simmer covered over low heat. Blanch the almonds and brown them lightly in an oven. Take out the meat when tender and cut diagonally into portions. Add the sour

cream and bread to the sauce, then season. Pour over the meat. Sprinkle with almonds and bake. Serve with scooped out potato balls and salads.

WILD BOAR STEAK

1 lb. wild boar ham or shoulder, fat, 2/3 oz. flour, 7 oz. onions, 1 1/3 oz. walnut meats, salt, pepper and garlic to taste

Wash the meat and remove any veins. Cut into portions and pound with a mallet that has been dipped in water. Shape into 1/2 in. thick steaks. Dredge with seasoning and flour and fry on both sides. Peel and rinse the onions. Cut them into half-slices and fry them. Scald the walnuts and chop them. Add to the steaks together with the onions. Simmer for several minutes and season. Serve with potatoes in all forms and salads.

WILD BOAR FILLETS

1 lb. wild boar ham or shoulder, fat, 2/3 oz. flour, 1 2/3—2 oz. smoked ham, 3 tablespoons sour cream, 1 lb. fresh mushrooms (cèpes), 2 2/3 oz. onions, juniper berries, salt and pepper to taste

Clean and wash the mushrooms. Cut them into slices. Peel, rinse and dice the onions. Fry them and add the mushrooms. Simmer for 6—8 minutes, stirring often. Wash the meat and remove any veins. Cut against the grain into 8 pieces. Pound with a mallet that has been dipped in water. Shape into elongated leaves with your hand and a knife. Lard each fillet with thin strips of ham. Dredge with seasoning and flour. Fry on both sides. Surround with mushrooms blended with sour cream. Simmer for several minutes and season. Serve with potatoes and salads.

WILD BOAR ZRAZY

1 lb. wild boar ham or shoulder, fat, 2/3 oz. flour, 1 1/4 lb. sauerkraut, 2/3 oz. dried cèpe mushrooms, 2 2/3 oz. onions, salt, pepper and caraway seed to taste

Wash the meat and remove any veins. Cut against the grain into 8 pieces. Pound with a mallet that has been dipped in water. Shape into ovals with your hand and a knife. Dredge with seasoning and flour. Fry on both sides. Wash, soak and cook the mushrooms. Take them out and cut into strips. Chop the sauerkraut. Cover with meat and mushroom stock and simmer over low heat until tender. Peel, rinse and dice the onions. Fry them and add the remaining flour. Brown this lightly. Combine with the sauerkraut and simmer for several minutes more, then season. Add to the zrazy and simmer for a while. Season again. Serve with potatoes.

WILD BOAR GOULASH

1 lb. wild boar shoulder, fat, 2/3 oz. flour, 3 1/2 oz. onions, 1 1/3 oz. tomato paste, 2 dried cèpe mushrooms, 2—3 prunes, 1 1/3 oz. almonds, salt, pepper, juniper berries, paprika and seasoning to taste

Wash the meat and remove any veins. Cut into cubes. Dredge with seasoning and flour. Brown in very hot fat together with peeled, rinsed and diced onions. Sprinkle with water and simmer covered over low heat. Blanch the almonds. Wash and soak the prunes. Remove the pits and cut into strips together with soaked mushrooms. Add to the meat towards the end of cooking together with the almonds, tomato paste and ground seasoning. Blend the remaining flour with a small amount of cold water. Add to the meat and bring to a boil, then season. Serve with potatoes and salads.

ROAST VENISON

1 lb. boneless leg or shoulder, fat, 2/3 oz. flour, 1 2/3 oz. smoked pork fat, 1 2/3 oz. prunes, 1/3 cup sour cream, 1/3 cup vinegar, 3/4 cup water, salt, pepper, juniper berries and seasoning to taste

Wash the meat and remove any veins. Cover with boiling vinegar blended with water and seasoning. Set aside in a cool place for 24 hours, turning over often. Take the meat out and dry it. Lard with thin strips

of pork fat. Sprinkle with seasoning and flour and brown in heated fat. Sprinkle with water and the marinade and simmer covered over low heat. Towards the end add soaked prunes. Take out the meat when tender and cut diagonally into portions. Combine the sauce with sour cream blended with the remaining flour. Bring to a boil and pour through a strainer. Season and pour over the meat. Serve with potatoes and fried beets.

ROYAL ROAST VENISON

1 lb. boneless leg or shoulder, fat, 2/3 oz. flour, 1/3 cup dry red wine, 1 1/3 oz. raisins, 1 2/3 oz. cranberry preserves, 2 2/3 oz. lemon, 2/3 oz. butter, 2/3 oz. flour for the sauce, 1/3 cup vinegar, 3/4 cup water, salt, pepper and lemon juice to taste

Wash the meat and remove any veins. Cover with boiling vinegar, water and seasoning. Set aside in a cool place for 24 hours, turning over often. Take the meat out and dry it. Dredge with seasoning and flour and brown in very hot fat. Sprinkle with water and simmer covered over low heat. Take out the meat when tender and cut against the grain into portions. Wash the lemon and scald it. Peel it and cut into half-slices, removing any pits. Heat the butter and blend with the flour. Fry without browning and blend with cold strained sauce (3/4 cup). Combine with the wine and bring to a boil. Add rinsed raisins, the lemon and cranberries. Cover the meat and simmer for 5 minutes, then season. Serve with scooped out potato balls and lettuce.

VENISON GOULASH

1 lb. boneless meat, fat, 2/3 oz. flour, 2 2/3 oz. onions, 5 oz. sour apples, 1 1/3 oz. plum jam, 1 2/3 oz. almonds, 2/3 oz. grated whole-wheat bread, 1/3 cup vinegar, 3/4 cup water, salt, juniper berries, rosemary and pepper to taste

Wash the meat and remove any veins. Cut into cubes. Cover with boiling vinegar blended with water and seasoning and set aside in a cool place

for 2 hours. Dry it and dredge with seasoning and flour. Brown in very hot fat together with peeled, rinsed and diced onions. Sprinkle with water and simmer covered over low heat. Blanch the almonds. Wash and peel the apples. Cut them in halves, removing the cores. Cut them into pieces. Add to the meat towards the end of cooking together with the almonds, jam, bread and seasoning. Serve with scooped out potato balls and salads.

VENISON STEAK

1 lb. boneless leg, fat, 2/3 oz. flour, 1/3 cup dry white wine, 5 oz. apples, 5 oz. tomatoes, salt, pepper, sugar and lemon juice to taste

Wash the meat and remove any veins. Cut against the grain into portions. Pound with a mallet that has been dipped in water. Shape into 1/2 in. thick oval steaks with your hand and a knife. Dredge with seasoning and flour and brown in very hot fat on both sides. Wash, scald and peel the tomatoes. Wash and peel the apples. Cut them in halves, removing the cores. Cut into pieces together with the tomatoes and add to the steaks. Sprinkle with wine and simmer for several minutes, then season. Serve with French fries, cauliflower and salads.

ROLLED VENISON ZRAZY

3/4 lb. boneless leg, 3 1/2 oz. pork fat, 3 1/2 oz. smoked ham, 2—2 2/3 oz. dill pickles, 1 oz. ketchup, fat, 2/3 oz. flour, 1/3 cup sour cream, salt, pepper and thyme to taste

Wash the meat and cut against the grain into 4 wide slices. Pound with a mallet that has been dipped in water. Sprinkle with seasoning. Spread ketchup over the meat. Cover with strips of pork fat and ham. Place pieces of the pickles in the middle. Roll up the meat slices and tie them up with thread. Dredge with flour and brown in very hot fat. Sprinkle with water and simmer covered over low heat. Towards the end add the sour cream blended with the remaining flour, then season. Serve with potatoes, macaroni, Ćwikła (q.v.) and salads.

HARE OR RABBIT WITH SOUR CREAM

Saddle and thighs, 1/3 cup sour cream, 13 cup vinegar, 3/4 cup water, 1 2/3 oz. onions for marinade, 2 2/3 oz. onions for simmering, 1 2/3 oz. pork fat, 2/3 oz. flour, salt, sugar, pepper, seasoning and marjoram to taste

Peel, rinse and chop the onions finely. Cover with vinegar and water and bring to a boil. Season and cover the washed meat. Set aside in the refrigerator for 24 hours. Take out the meat and lard with thin strips of pork fat. Dredge with seasoning and flour and brown in very hot fat together with peeled, rinsed and diced onions. Sprinkle with water and simmer covered over low heat. Towards the end add sour cream blended with the remaining flour and season. Serve with potatoes and fried beets.

WROCŁAW HARE OR RABBIT

Saddle and thighs, 1/3 cup sour cream, 1/3 cup vinegar, 3/4 cup water, 1 2/3 oz. onions, 3 1/2 oz. mushrooms, 5 oz. peppers, 1 oz. horseradish (grated), 2/3 oz. raisins, fat, 2/3 oz. flour, salt, pepper, sugar and lemon juice to taste

Prepare the meat as above. Take it out and dry it. Dredge with seasoning and flour. Brown in very hot fat. Sprinkle with water and simmer covered over low heat. Clean, rinse and dice the peppers and mushrooms. Add to the meat towards the end of cooking. Take out the meat when tender and cut into portions. Add sour cream blended with the remaining flour, the horseradish and rinsed raisins to the sauce. Simmer for a while and season. Pour over the meat. Serve with potatoes and salads.

HARE OR RABBIT WITH CHERRIES

Saddle and thighs, 1/3 cup vinegar, 1/3 cup water, 1 2/3 oz. onions, 1/3 cup dry red wine, 5 oz. sour cherries, 1 oz. raisins, 2/3 oz. prunes, 2/3 oz. dried apricots, 1/3 oz. wheat flour, 1/3 oz. potato starch, salt, pepper and sugar to taste

Prepare the meat (as in Hare or Rabbit with Sour Cream). Take out the meat and dry it. Dredge with seasoning and flour and brown in very hot fat. Sprinkle with water and simmer covered over low heat. Towards the end add rinsed sour cherries, prunes and apricots. Take out the meat when tender and cut into portions. Combine the sauce with the wine and potato starch blended with a small amount of cold water. Cook for a while and force through a strainer. Add rinsed raisins and season. Cover the meat and continue simmering for a while. Serve with potatoes and salads.

BARRISTER'S HARE OR RABBIT

Saddle and thighs, 1/3 cup vinegar, 3/4 cup water, 1 2/3 oz. onions, 7 oz. mushrooms, 3 1/2 oz. smoked ham, 1 1/2 tablespoons cognac, 1 1/3 oz. walnut meats, 3 1/2 oz. hard cheese, fat, 1/3 oz. flour, salt, pepper and sugar to taste

Prepare the meat (as in Hare or Rabbit with Sour Cream). Take it out and dry it. Dredge with seasoning and flour, then brown in very hot fat. Sprinkle with water and simmer covered over low heat. Take out the meat when tender and cut into portions. Arrange on a greased platter. Blanch the walnuts and grind them. Clean and rinse the mushrooms. Cut them into strips and fry them. Surround the meat with them and add strips of ham. Sprinkle with cognac, walnuts, grated cheese and seasoning, then bake. Serve with rice and lettuce.

ROAST PHEASANT

Pheasant, fat for baking, 3 1/2 oz. pork fat, parsley sprigs, salt and nutmeg to taste

Wash the drawn pheasant. Rub with seasoning and set aside in a cool place for an hour. Place rinsed parsley sprigs inside the bird and tie up the legs. Cover the bird with thin strips of pork fat and tie up with thread. Pour fat over and bake, basting with water, then with the pan drippings. Towards the end of baking remove the pork fat and brown to a golden

brown. Take out the bird when done and place on a wooden board. Allow to cool and cut off the thighs. Slice each one across into 2—3 pieces. Cut the breast into pieces, removing the bones partly. Arrange the portioned meat on a platter, allowing a piece of the thigh and of the breast for each portion. Skim the fat off the sauce and season it, then pour over the meat. Heat in an oven. Serve with French fries, cranberries, compote and lettuce.

ROYAL PHEASANT

Pheasant, fat for baking, 3 1/2 oz. pork fat, 2 egg yolks, 2/3—1 oz. powdered chocolate, salt, cinnamon and white pepper to taste

Wash the drawn pheasant. Rub with seasoning and set aside in a cool place for an hour. Tie up the legs. Cover the bird with thin strips of pork fat and tie up with thread. Pour fat over and bake, basting with water, then with the pan drippings. Towards the end of baking remove the pork fat. Spread egg yolks over the pheasant. Sprinkle with the chocolate and bake until tender. When done cut as above and arrange on a platter. Skim the fat off the sauce and season it, then pour over the meat and heat. Serve with French fries, compote and lettuce.

PHEASANT PRELATIC STYLE

Pheasant, fat for pheasant, 3 1/2 oz. pork fat, 5 oz. boneless veal, 1 2/3 oz. ketchup, 2 egg yolks, 1 1/3 oz. walnut meats, 2/3 cup dry white wine, salt and pepper to taste

Wash the drawn pheasant. Rub with seasoning and set aside in a cool place for an hour. Blanch the walnuts and grind them. Combine with minced veal, egg yolks and ketchup, then season. Fill the inside of the bird and tie up the legs. Cover the bird with thin strips of pork fat and tie up with thread. Pour fat over and bake, basting with wine, then with the pan drippings. Take out the pheasant when done and cut into portions. Arrange on a platter and pour seasoned sauce over, then heat. Serve with French fries, compote and lettuce.

PHEASANT STEW

Pheasant, fat, 1/3 cup sour cream, 2/3 oz. flour, 5 oz. onions, 1 1/3 oz. tomato paste, salt, pepper and ground paprika to taste

Wash the drawn pheasant and cut into small pieces. Fry lightly together with peeled, rinsed and finely chopped onions. Sprinkle with water and simmer until tender. Towards the end add tomato paste and sour cream blended with flour, then season. Serve with rice, noodles and salads.

PHEASANT GOULASH

Pheasant, fat, 2/3 cup dry white wine, 1 1/3 oz. tomato paste, 5 oz. onions, 1 lb. scooped out potato balls, 1/2 lb. scooped out carrot balls, milk, 3 1/2 oz. hard cheese, fresh dill, salt, pepper and ground paprika

Wash the drawn pheasant and cut into pieces. Fry lightly together with peeled, rinsed and finely chopped onions. Sprinkle with water and simmer over low heat. Cook the potatoes and carrots in separate pots along with some milk and drain them. Combine with the meat, tomato paste and chopped dill. Season and sprinkle with grated cheese, then bake. Serve with salads.

ROAST BLACK OR WOOD GROUSE

Black or wood grouse (a young bird), fat for baking, 5—7 oz. pork fat, 2/3 cup dry white wine, 1 1/4 lb.—1 3/4 lb. vinegar, 3 1/2 oz. onions, pepper, juniper, sugar, cloves, allspice and bay leaf

Since black or wood grouse meat tends to be tough the tenderizing period is longer. After killing the birds hang them in a well-aired place for several days. When tender, pluck, singe and draw the birds. Wash them and cut off the necks and wings (scald older birds with a solution of boiling wine, water and vinegar blended with peeled and chopped onions and seasoning). Keep in this marinade in a cool place for three days. Take

them out, dry them and rub with seasoning. Lard densely with 1 1/2 in. thick strips of pork fat. Pass the pork fat through the skin so that it is visible on both sides. Pour fat over the meat and brown it. Sprinkle with the marinade and bake until tender. Take out when done and cut into portions so that each portion consists of a piece of leg and a piece of breast. Arrange on a platter. Skim the fat off the sauce and season it. Pour over the meat. Serve the remaining sauce in a sauceboat. Serve with French fries and compote.

BLACK OR WOOD GROUSE OLD POLISH STYLE

Black or wood grouse (young birds), fat for baking, 5—7 oz. pork fat, 2/3 cup dry white wine, 1 1/4—1 3/4 lb. vinegar, 3 1/2 oz. onions, 2/3 cup sour cream, 5 oz. mushrooms, 2/3 oz. butter for baking, 3 1/2 oz. walnut meats, 2 egg yolks, 5—7 oz. smoked ham, 2/3 oz. parsley sprigs, salt, pepper, juniper berries, sugar, cloves, allspice and bay leaf

Prepare the birds (as above). Blanch the almonds and grind them. Clean, rinse and chop the mushrooms finely. Fry them and combine with walnuts, egg yolks, minced ham and chopped parsley sprigs. Season this and stuff the birds. Tie up the legs. Cover with thin strips of pork fat and tie up with thread. Pour fat over and bake, basting with water, then with the pan drippings. Take out when done and cut into portions so that each portion consists of a piece of leg, a piece of breast and some stuffing. Arrange on a platter. Pour seasoned sauce over and heat. Serve with potatoes and salads.

ROAST WILD GOOSE OR DUCK

Goose or duck (young birds), fat for baking, 5—7 oz. pork fat, 1 cup dry white wine, 1/3 cup vinegar, water, 3 1/2 oz. onions, salt, pepper, marjoram, thyme and seasoning to taste

Peel and rinse the onions. Cut them into half-slices. Cover with wine, vinegar and water. Add the seasoning and bring to a boil. Wash the drawn

birds and cover with the marinade. Set aside in a cool place for several days, turning over several times. Cut the pork fat into 1 1/2 in. long strips. Lard thickly along the breasts and legs, 3—4 rows on each side. Pour fat over and bake, basting with the marinade, then with the pan drippings. Take out when done and cut into portions, so that each portion consists of a piece of leg and a piece of breast. Arrange on a platter. Skim the fat off the pan drippings and season them. Pour over the meat. Serve with potatoes and fried red cabbage.

HETMAN'S WILD GOOSE OR DUCK

Goose or duck (young birds), fat for baking, 5—7 oz. pork fat, 1 cup dry white wine, 1/3 cup vinegar, water, 3 1/2 oz. onions, 1/3 cup orange juice, 1/3 cup lemon juice, 1 1/3 oz. prepared mustard, 2—2 2/3 oz. gingerbread, salt, pepper, sugar, cloves and marjoram to taste

Prepare the birds (as above). Tie up the legs and pour fat over. Bake, basting with water, then with the pan drippings. Towards the end add mustard, lemon juice and orange juice. Take out the birds when done and cut into portions so that each portion consists of a piece of leg and a piece of breast. Arrange on a platter. Pour the sauce through a strainer and combine with grated gingerbread. Simmer for several minutes and season. Pour over the meat and heat. Serve with scooped out potato balls, apple compote and lettuce.

ROAST QUAIL OR PARTRIDGE

4 quail or partridges, fat for baking, 7 oz. pork fat, parsley sprigs, juniper berries, salt and pepper to taste

Wash the drawn birds and rub with seasoning. Set aside in a cool place for an hour. Place parsley sprigs inside the birds. Tie up the legs and cover with thin strips of pork fat. Tie up with thread and pour fat over. Bake, basting with water, then with the pan drippings. Towards the end remove the pork fat and brown the birds. When done cut lengthwise into

halves. Arrange on a platter. Skim the fat off the pan drippings and season them. Pour over the meat. Serve with French fries, salads and compote.

HUNTER'S QUAIL OR PARTRIDGE

4 quail or partridges, fat for baking, 7 oz. pork fat, 7 oz. mushrooms, 1 2/3 oz. tomato paste, 2/3 cup dry white wine, 2/3 oz. capers, 1 oz. raisins, 1 oz. smoked ham, salt, pepper, thyme and marjoram to taste

Wash the drawn birds and rub with seasoning. Set aside in a cool place for an hour. Tie up the legs and cover with thin strips of pork fat. Tie up with thread and pour fat over. Bake, basting with wine. Clean, rinse and cut the mushrooms into strips. Add to the birds towards the end of baking together with tomato paste, strips of ham, rinsed capers, rinsed raisins and seasoning. Towards the end of baking remove the pork fat and brown the birds. Take them out and cut lengthwise into halves. Pour seasoned sauce over. Serve with boiled potatoes and salads.

BACHELOR'S QUAIL OR PARTRIDGE

4 quail or partridges, fat for baking, 1 3/4 lb. apples, 7 oz. pork fat, 2/3 cup sour cream, 1 2/3 oz. walnut meats, salt, pepper, marjoram and lemon juice to taste

Wash the drawn birds and rub with seasoning. Set aside in a cool place for an hour. Tie up the legs and cover with thin strips of pork fat. Pour fat over and bake, basting with water, then with the pan drippings. Blanch the walnuts and grind them. Wash, peel and rinse the apples. Cut them in half, removing the cores. Cut them into pieces and add to the meat towards the end of baking. When done remove the pork fat and brown the birds. Take them out and cut in half, removing the bones partly. Add sour cream to the apples along with finely chopped pork fat. Season this and cover the birds with the mixture. Sprinkle with ketchup and walnuts, then bake. Serve with French fries and salads.

ROAST HAZEL GROUSE

2 hazel grouse, 5—7 oz. pork fat, milk, fat for baking, salt, pepper and nutmeg to taste

Wash the drawn hazel grouse. Place in milk and set aside in the refrigerator for 24 hours. Take them out and tie up the legs. Cover with thin strips of pork fat and tie up with thread. Pour fat over and bake, basting with water, then with the pan drippings. Take out when done and cut lengthwise into halves. Arrange on a platter. Pour seasoned sauce over and heat. Serve with potatoes, compote and lettuce.

ROAST WOOD-PIGEON

2 wood-pigeons, 5—7 oz. pork fat, fat for baking, 3 1/2 oz. hard cheese, 2 egg yolks, parsley sprigs, salt and pepper to taste

Wash the drawn birds. Cut the pork fat into 3/4 in. long strips. Lard the birds thickly along the breasts and legs, 3—4 rows on each side. Pour fat over and bake, basting with water, then with the pan drippings. When done, spread egg yolks over the meat. Sprinkle with grated cheese and bake. Serve with scooped out potato balls and compote.

ROAST COOT

Coot, soured milk, 5 oz. pork fat, fat for baking, 2/3 cup sour cream, 1—1 1/3 oz. grated whole-wheat bread, salt, pepper and juniper berries to taste

Wash the drawn bird. Immerse in beaten soured milk and set aside in the refrigerator for several hours. Take it out and dry it. Rub with seasoning and tie up the legs. Cut the pork fat into 3/4 in. long strips. Lard the bird thickly along the breast and legs, 3—4 rows on each side. Pour fat over and bake, basting with water, then sour cream. Take out the bird when done and cut into portions. Add bread and seasoning to the sauce and simmer for a while. Pour over the meat and heat. Serve with potatoes and lettuce.

Poultry

STUFFED CHICKEN POLISH STYLE I

2 chickens, 1 1/3 oz. butter for basting, 2—2 2/3 oz. French bread, chicken livers, 1 1/3 oz. butter, 1—2 eggs, parsley sprigs, salt and pepper to taste

Wash the drawn chickens. Break off the breast bone. With your fingers pull off the skin loose from the breasts to the wings and back. Cut off the necks and place the wings on the back. Rub with seasoning and set aside in a cool place for an hour. Soak the bread in milk or water, then squeeze it out and mince it. Blend the butter with the egg yolks and combine with the bread, chopped parsley sprigs, finely chopped livers and beaten egg whites. Season the stuffing and place it in a thin layer under the skin. Place the remaining stuffing inside the birds. Tie up the legs, baste with butter and bake for around 40 minutes. When browned sprinkle with water, then with the pan drippings. When done cut the chickens lengthwise into halves. Arrange on a platter and pour seasoned sauce over. Garnish with lettuce. Serve with scooped out potato balls, mizeria (q.v.), tomato salad and cauliflower.

STUFFED CHICKEN POLISH STYLE II

2 chickens, 1 1/3 oz. butter, 3 1/2—5 oz. yeast babka, 1 2/3 oz. raisins, 2 egg yolks, milk, salt and nutmeg to taste

Prepare the cleaned chickens (as above). Break the babka into small pieces and sprinkle with milk. Combine with the egg yolks, rinsed raisins and nutmeg. Place the stuffing under the skin in a thin layer. Place the remaining stuffing inside the chickens. Tie up the legs, baste with butter and bake for around 40 minutes. When browned sprinkle with water, then with the pan drippings. When done cut lengthwise into halves. Arrange on a platter and pour with seasoned sauce, then garnish. Serve with French fries, asparagus, cauliflower and salads.

STUFFED CHICKEN À LA SAPIEHA

2 chickens, 1 1/3 oz. butter, 5 oz. chicken livers, 3 1/2 oz. pork fat, 2 oz. onions, 1—2 eggs, 1—1 1/3 oz. breadcrumbs, 1 2/3 oz. raisins, 1/3—

2/3 oz. grated whole-wheat bread, 1/3 cup dry white wine, salt, pepper and seasoning to taste

Prepare the cleaned chickens (as in Stuffed Chicken Polish Style I). Peel, rinse and slice the onions. Dice the pork fat and render it down partly. Remove the outer skin from the livers and fry them lightly. Combine with the onions and brown lightly. Allow to cool and mince. Combine with the egg yolks, breadcrumbs, rinsed raisins and beaten egg whites, then season. Place this stuffing under the skin in a thin layer. Place the remaining stuffing inside the birds and tie up the legs. Baste with butter and bake. When the skin turns brown sprinkle with wine, then with the pan drippings. Towards the end of baking sprinkle with the bread. When done cut lengthwise into halves. Arrange on a platter and pour the seasoned sauce over, then garnish. Serve with scooped out potato balls, asparagus, cauliflower and salads.

CHICKEN STUFFED WITH BRAINS

2 chickens, 1 1/3 oz. butter, 5—7 oz. brains, 3 1/2 oz. mushrooms, egg yolk, 1 2/3 oz. onions, fat for the brains, parsley sprigs and onions, salt and pepper to taste

Prepare the cleaned chickens (as in Stuffed Chicken Polish Style I). Remove the outer skin from the brains. Rinse and chop them. Clean, rinse and chop the onions and mushrooms finely, then fry them. Add the brains and continue frying for several minutes, stirring often. Towards the end of frying add the egg yolk. Combine with chopped parsley sprigs and season. Place the stuffing under the skin in a thin layer. Place the remaining stuffing inside the chickens and tie up the legs. Baste with butter and bake for around 40 minutes. When browned sprinkle with water, then with the pan drippings. When done cut lengthwise into halves. Pour seasoned sauce over and garnish. Serve with French fries, cauliflower and salads.

WROCŁAW STUFFED CHICKEN

2 chickens, 1 1/3 oz. butter, 1/2 lb. apples, 3 1/2 oz. raisins, 1 1/3 oz. butter for apples, 2 egg yolks, salt, pepper and nutmeg to taste

Wash the cleaned chickens. Break off the breast bones. Cut off the necks and place the wings on the back. Wash the apples and cut them in halves, removing the cores. Grate them coarsely and fry in butter with rinsed raisins. Combine with the egg yolks and season. Place this stuffing inside the chickens and tie up the legs. Baste with butter and bake. When browned baste with water, then with the pan drippings. Cut the baked chickens lengthwise into halves. Arrange on a platter. Pour seasoned sauce over and garnish. Serve with French fries and salads.

BARBECUED CHICKEN

2 chickens or one hen, parsley sprigs, 1 2/3 oz. butter, 1 2/3 oz. ketchup, salt and pepper to taste

Wash the cleaned hen or chickens. Place the wings on the back. Rub with seasoning and set aside in a cool place for an hour. Rinse the parsley sprigs and place them inside the birds. Tie up the legs. Arrange on a spit, baste with butter and bake in a hot oven. While baking baste with melted fat and ketchup. When done cut into portions, removing the parsley sprigs. Serve with French fries, cauliflower, peas, tomato salad and mizeria (q.v.).

ROAST CHICKEN

2 chickens or one hen, parsley sprigs, 3 1/2—5 oz. pork fat, salt, poultry seasoning (savory, marjoram, mint, sage, coriander, thyme) to taste

Prepare the chickens (as above). Rub with salt and poultry seasoning. Set aside in a cool place for an hour. Rinse the parsley sprigs and place them inside the chickens. Cover the birds with thin strips of pork fat and tie up with thread. Bake in a hot oven (450°F) for around 30 minutes. While baking baste with water, then with the pan drippings. Towards the end of baking remove the pork fat and brown the chickens. When done, cut the chickens into portions. Arrange on a platter and pour seasoned sauce over. Arrange pieces of pork fat on top and garnish with parsley

sprigs or lettuce. Serve with French fries, boiled potatoes, cauliflower, asparagus, peas and salads.

SUNSHINE CHICKEN

2 chickens or one hen, 1 1/3 oz. butter, 2—2 2/3 oz. almonds, 3 table-spoons orange liqueur, salt and white pepper to taste

Wash the cleaned chickens or hen. Cut off the necks and wings. Cut each chicken into halves. Rub with seasoning and set aside in a cool place for an hour. Blanch the almonds and grind them. Combine with the liqueur and melted butter. Spread over the chicken meat and wrap in aluminium foil, two pieces at a time. Bake in a hot oven for around 50 minutes. Serve with French fries, cauliflower and salads.

ROAST CHICKEN À LA RADZIWIŁŁ

2 chickens or one hen, 1 1/3 oz. butter, 1 2/3 oz. ketchup, 1/3 cup sour cream, 1 oz. grated horseradish, 1 oz. raisins, salt, sugar and lemon juice to taste

Wash the cleaned chickens or hen. Cut off the necks and wings and cut each chicken into halves. Rub with salt and sprinkle with lemon juice. Set aside in a cool place for an hour. Pour butter over and bake in a hot oven. In the middle of baking pour ketchup over. Combine the sour cream with the horseradish and rinsed raisins. Pour over the chickens towards the end of baking. Season the chickens when tender. Serve with scooped out potato balls, tomato salad and lettuce.

CHICKEN WITH APRICTOS

2 chickens or one hen, 1 1/3 oz. butter, 3 tablespoons olive oil, can of apricots, 3 tablespoons brandy, salt and nutmeg to taste

Wash the cleaned chickens or hen. Cut off the necks and wings and cut each chicken lengthwise into halves. Brown in oil, then pour off the oil. Add butter and salt. Simmer over low heat basting with brandy and apricot juice. When tender transfer the chickens to a platter. Add the apricots to the sauce and bring to a boil, then season. Pour over the chickens and serve at once with lettuce.

CHICKEN Á L' OPÉRA

2 chickens or one hen, 1 2/3 oz. butter, 3 1/2 oz. celeriac, 3 1/2 oz. parsley root, 3 1/2 oz. onions, 3 1/2 oz. canned peas, 1 2/3 oz. canned peppers, 3 1/2 oz. ketchup, salt, pepper and curry powder to taste

Wash the cleaned chickens or hen. Cut off the necks and wings and cut lengthwise into halves. Rub with seasoning and set aside in a cool place for an hour. Pour butter over and bake for around 50 minutes in a hot oven, basting with water, then with the pan drippings. Wash and peel the vegetables. Cut them into strips. Add to the chickens towards the end of baking. Chop the peppers and add to the chickens together with canned peas, ketchup and seasoning. Simmer over low heat for several minutes and season. Serve with rice, tomato salad or other salads.

BACHELOR'S CHICKEN

2 chickens or one hen, 1 2/3 oz. butter, 3/4 lb. peaches, 5 oz. canned peppers, 3 tablespoons rum, salt, white pepper and lemon juice to taste

Wash cleaned chickens or hen. Cut off the necks and wings and cut lengthwise into halves. Rub with seasoning and set aside in a cool place for an hour. Baste with butter and brown on both sides. Sprinkle with water and simmer covered until tender. Wash the peaches and remove the pits. Mash together with the peppers and add to the chickens towards the end of cooking. When tender arrange the chickens on a platter. Pour the seasoned sauce blended with rum over the meat. Serve with rice and lettuce.

CHICKEN IN COQUILLES

1/2 chicken or hen, 1 oz. butter, 2/3 cup thick sour cream, 3 1/2 oz. hard cheese, 3 1/2 oz. carrots, 3 1/2 oz. onions, 3 1/2 oz. celeriac, 3 1/2 oz. parsley root, 1 2/3 oz. canned peppers, 2/3 oz. capers, 1 1/3 oz. butter for vegetables, salt, pepper and curry powder to taste

Wash the chicken or hen halves. Rub with seasoning and set aside in a cool place for an hour. Baste with butter and brown on both sides. Sprinkle with water and simmer covered over low heat for around 45 minutes. Take out the chicken when tender and separate the meat from the bones, then cut into strips. Wash, peel and rinse the vegetables, then cut them into strips. Fry them lightly in butter and add to the chicken sauce. Simmer until tender, stirring often. Combine with the meat, rinsed capers and finely chopped peppers, then season. Transfer to coquilles. Pour seasoned sour cream over, sprinkle with grated cheese and bake. Serve at once.

CHICKEN STEW

2 chickens or one hen, 2—2 2/3 oz. fat, 2/3—3/4 cup sour cream, 5 oz. mushrooms, 3 1/2 oz. onions, 3 1/2 oz. canned peas, 1 2/3 oz. canned peppers, 1 1/3 oz. tomato paste, 1 oz. flour, parsley sprigs, salt, pepper, ground paprika and prepared mustard to taste

Wash the cleaned chickens or hen. Cut into pieces (use the necks and wings for soup). Dredge with flour and salt. Brown in very hot fat together with finely chopped onions. Sprinkle with water or stock. Simmer covered over low heat together with mushroom strips. Towards the end of cooking add tomato paste. When the meat is tender add peas and sour cream blended with flour. Bring to a boil. Combine with chopped parsley sprigs and chopped peppers, then season. Serve with noodles, rice or scooped out potato balls.

ROYAL CHICKEN

Chicken, 1 2/3 oz. butter, champagne or dry white wine, 1/2 lb. oranges, 1 2/3 oz. raisins, salt, white pepper, lemon juice, lemon and orange rind to taste

Wash the cleaned chicken and tie up its legs. Rub with seasoning and set aside in a cool place for an hour. Brown it and bake for around 60 minutes, basting with champagne or wine, then with the pan drippings. When tender cut the chicken into portions, removing the bones partly. Transfer to the pan once more. Wash, scald and peel the oranges. Cut into cubes, removing any pits. Add to the chicken together with rinsed raisins, seasoning and grated rind. Simmer for a while and season. Serve with French fries and compote.

ADMIRAL'S CHICKEN

Hen, 3 tablespoons olive oil, 1 2/3 oz. flour, 1/3 cup sour cream, 3 1/2 oz. mushrooms, 1 2/3 oz. smoked ham, 5 oz. tomatoes, parsley sprigs, salt, pepper, seasoning and curry powder to taste

Wash the cleaned hen. Rub with seasoning and set aside in a cool place for an hour. Cut into portions. Dredge with flour and brown on all sides. Sprinkle with broth and simmer covered over low heat. Wash, scald and peel the tomatoes, then cut them into pieces. Clean and rinse the mushrooms. Cut them into strips together with the ham. Add to the hen towards the end of cooking together with tomatoes and sour cream. When the hen is tender add chopped parsley sprigs and season. Serve with rice, potatoes, lettuce or tomato sald.

CHICKEN FILLET SAUTÉ

2 chicken breasts, 2—2 2/3 oz. fat, 2/3 oz. butter, 1—1 1/3 oz. flour, salt and pepper to taste

Wash the chicken breasts and pull down the skin. Cut the breasts along the breast bone and collar bone. Separate the meat from the rib bones. Clean the fillets of skin and tendons. Cut off the wider end of the wing bone. Pound the meat with a mallet that has been dipped in water, shaping the fillets into elongated leaves. Dredge with seasoning and flour. Fry in very hot fat on both sides, then continue frying over low heat. When done skim off the fat. Add butter and melt it. Serve with French fries, cauliflower, string beans, tomatoes or mizeria (q.v.).

GENERAL'S CHICKEN FILLET

2 chicken breasts, 2—2 2/3 oz. fat, 1 oz. flour, 5 oz. ketchup, 1 2/3 oz. raisins, 3 1/2 oz. hard cheese, salt and pepper to taste

Prepare the fillets (as above). Dredge with seasoning and flour. Fry on both sides. Sprinkle with rinsed raisins, ketchup and grated cheese. Bake in heated oven. Serve with French fries, peas and salads.

CHICKEN ZRAZY POLISH STYLE

2 chicken breasts, 1 2/3—2 oz. fat, 1 oz. flour, 8 whitebread toast slices, 3 eggs, 1 oz. ham, 2/3 oz. canned peas, 5 oz. goose-liver pâté, fat for toast, salt and pepper to taste

Wash the chicken breasts and pull down the skin. Separate the meat from the bones. Clean the fillets of any remaining skin. Divide the meat into 8 pieces. Pound with a mallet that has been dipped in water, shaping them into circles. Dredge with seasoning and flour and fry on both sides. Fry the toast slices on both sides. Spread the pâté on them and arrange the zrazy on top. Place in a warm oven. Wash the eggs and break them into a dish. Beat with an egg-whisk and blend with strips of ham, peas, chopped parsley sprigs and seasoning. Heat the fat in a frying pan. Add the egg mixture and fry on both sides. Transfer to a pastry board. With a round cookie-cutter cut out 8 small omelets and arrange them on the meat. Transfer this to a platter and garnish. Serve with cauliflower and French fries.

CHICKEN SHASHLIK

2 chicken breasts, 3 1/2 oz. smoked bacon, 5 oz. peppers, 5 oz. onions, fat, salt and pepper to taste

Wash the chicken breasts and remove the skin and bones. Rub with seasoning and set aside in a cool place. Peel, rinse the onions and cut them into slices. Clean, rinse the peppers and bake them lightly in an oven. Peel them and cut into pieces together with the chicken and bacon which has been lightly pounded with a mallet. Place the chicken, peppers, bacon, onions etc. on skewers. Sprinkle with seasoning, pressing down with your hand. Place in very hot fat and brown, then continue frying over low heat. Serve with rice and soured cucumbers or tomato salad.

CHICKEN LIVERS WITH APPLES

1 lb. chicken livers, milk, 1/2 lb. apples, 3 1/2 oz. onions, fat, 1/3—2/3 cup dry white wine, salt, pepper and marjoram to taste

Wash the livers and soak them in milk. Set aside in a cool place for several hours. Remove the outer skin and cut the larger pieces in half. Fry on both sides. Wash and peel the apples. Cut them in half, removing the cores. Cut them into pieces together with peeled onions. Fry this and add to the livers. Add wine and sprinkle with seasoning. Simmer over low heat for around 6—8 minutes, then add salt. Serve with potatoes, rice and salads.

ROAST DUCK WITH APPLES

Duck, 1 2/3—2 oz. fat, 2 lb. cooking apples, salt, sugar and marjoram to taste

Wash the cleaned duck and cut off the neck and wings. Rub with seasoning and set aside in a cool place for an hour. Wash the apples and cut them in half, removing the cores. Cut them into pieces and stuff the duck

with them, setting aside some of the apple pieces. Tie up the duck or fasten it closed. Pour fat over and bake for 60—80 minutes, basting with water, then with the pan drippings. Turn the duck over often while baking. Take it out when done and cut into portions, removing the bones partly. Arrange on a platter. Skim the fat off the sauce. Add the remaining apples to the sauce. Sprinkle with sugar and marjoram. Simmer over low heat for several minutes. Cover the duck with this and garnish. Serve with potatoes, red cabbage and salads.

GENERAL'S ROAST DUCK I

Duck, 1 2/3—2 oz. fat, 3 1/2 oz. almonds, 5 oz. lemons, 3 1/2 oz. ketchup, marjoram and sugar to taste

Wash the cleaned duck and cut off the neck and wings. Rub with seasoning and set aside in a cool place for an hour. Pour fat over, sprinkle with wine and bake for 60—80 minutes, basting with the pan drippings. Take out the duck when tender and cut into portions, removing the bones partly. Arrange on a platter. Blanch the almonds. Wash the lemons, scald them and peel them. Cut them into half-slices, removing any pits. Sprinkle the duck with seasoning and lemons. Pour ketchup over. Sprinkle with sugar and bake. Serve with scooped out potato balls and salads.

GENERAL'S ROAST DUCK II

Duck, 1 2/3—2 oz. fat, 2/3—3/4 cup dry red wine, 3 tablespoons orange juice, 3 tablespoons rum, 3 1/2 oz. cranberry preserve, salt, pepper and cinnamon to taste

Wash the cleaned duck and cut off the neck and wings. Rub with seasoning and set aside in a cool place for an hour. Pour fat over, sprinkle with wine and bake for 60—80 minutes, basting with the pan

drippings. Towards the end add orange juice, rum, cranberries and ground cinnamon. Take out the duck when tender and cut into portions, removing the bones partly. Arrange on a platter. Strain the sauce and skim off the fat, then season it. Pour over the duck. Serve potatoes and salads.

ROAST DUCK WITH CHERRIES

Duck, 1 2/3—2 oz. fat, 1 cup dry red wine, 3/4 lb. sour cherries, 2/3 oz. flour, salt, white pepper and sugar to taste

Wash the cleaned duck and cut off the neck and wings. Rub with seasoning and set aside in a cool place for an hour. Baste with fat and sprinkle with wine. Bake for 60—80 minutes, basting with the pan drippings. Towards the end add rinsed cherries. Take out the meat when tender and cut into portions, removing the bones partly. Arrange on a platter. Add flour blended with a small amount of water to the sauce. Cook for a while and pour through a strainer, then season. Pour over the duck and bake. Serve with potatoes, rice and salads.

ROYAL ROAST DUCK

Duck, 1 2/3—2 oz. fat, 1 lb. plums (Damson), 2/3 cup strong tea, 3 tablespoons rum, 2—3 egg whites, salt, pepper, sugar and lemon juice to taste

Wash the cleaned duck and cut off the neck and wings. Rub with seasoning and set aside in a cool place for an hour. Pour fat over, sprinkle with tea and bake for 60—80 minutes, basting with the pan drippings. Towards the end add washed and pitted plums. Take out the duck when tender and cut into portions, removing the bones partly. Arrange on a platter. Allow the sauce to cool and pour it through a strainer. Combine with rum and season. Combine with beaten egg yolks. Cover the duck with this and bake. Serve with rice and salads.

CASTELLAN'S ROAST DUCK

Duck, 1 2/3—2 oz. fat, 2/3 cup Madeira wine, 3 1/2 oz. ham, 3 1/2 oz. thin frankfurters, 5 oz. onions (green or shallot), salt, pepper, sugar, lemon juice and juniper berries to taste

Wash the cleaned duck and cut off the neck and wings. Rub with seasoning and set aside in a cool place for an hour. Baste with fat, sprinkle with water and bake for 60—80 minutes, basting with the pan drippings. Peel and rinse the onions. Cut them into pieces and fry lightly. Add to the duck towards the end of baking together with sliced frankfurters, strips of ham and seasoning. Take out the duck when tender and cut into portions, removing the bones partly. Arrange on a platter. Skim the fat off the sauce and season it. Pour over the duck. Serve with rice and salads.

CAPUCHIN'S ROAST DUCK

Duck, 1 2/3—2 oz. fat, 2/3—3/4 cup dry red wine, 3 1/2 oz. white beans, 1 1/3 oz. tomato paste, 5 oz. onions (green or shallot), fat for onions, 1 1/3 oz. raisins, salt, pepper and marjoram

Wash the cleaned duck and cut off the neck and wings. Rub with seasoning and set aside in a cool place for an hour. Baste with fat, sprinkle with wine and bake for 60—80 minutes, basting with the pan drippings. Sort and rinse the beans. Cover with water and bring to a boil. Set aside for 2 hours. Cook the beans in the same water. Peel and rinse the onions. Cut them into pieces and fry them lightly. Add to the duck towards the end of baking together with the beans, tomato paste and rinsed raisins. Take out the duck when tender and cut into portions, removing the bones partly. Arrange on a platter. Skim the fat off the sauce and season it. Pour over the duck. Serve with scooped out potato balls and salads.

ROAST DUCK WITH MUSHROOMS

Duck, 1 2/3—2 oz. fat, 2/3 cup sour cream, 1/2 lb. mushrooms, 1 1/3 oz. tomato paste, 2/3 oz. flour, salt, pepper, seasoning and garlic

Wash the cleaned duck and cut off the neck and wings. Rub with seasoning and set aside in a cool place for an hour. Baste with fat, sprinkle with sour cream and bake for around 60—80 minutes, basting with the pan drippings. Clean and rinse the mushrooms and cut them into strips. Add to the duck towards the end of baking together with tomato paste. Take out the duck when tender and cut into portions, removing the bones partly. Arrange on a platter. Add flour blended with a small amount of cold water. Cook for a while and season. Pour over the duck. Serve with rice and salads.

ROAST DUCK WITH PEACHES

Duck, 1 2/3—2 oz. fat, 1 lb. stewed or bottled peaches, 2 egg yolks, 1 2/3 oz. ketchup, 3 tablespoons orange liqueur, salt, lemon juice and white pepper to taste

Wash the cleaned duck and cut off the neck and wings. Rub with seasoning and set aside in a cool place for an hour. Baste with fat, sprinkle with water and bake for 60—80 minutes, basting with the pan drippings. Take out the duck when tender and cut into portions, removing the bones partly. Arrange on a platter. Surround with peaches cut into pieces. Pour over ketchup blended with liqueur, egg yolks and seasoning, then bake. Serve with rice and lettuce.

WROCŁAW ROAST DUCK

Duck, 1 2/3—2 oz. fat, 1 lb. apples, 3 1/2 oz. prunes, 1 2/3 oz. raisins, 3 1/2 oz. lemons, 3 1/2 oz. stewed or bottled peaches, 3 tablespoons cognac, salt, pepper and lemon juice to taste

Wash the cleaned duck and cut off the neck and wings. Rub with seasoning and set aside in a cool place for an hour. Wash the apples and cut them into pieces, removing the cores. Stuff the duck with them. Sew up the duck or fasten it closed. Baste with fat and bake for 60—80 minutes, sprinkling with water, then with the pan drippings. When tender,

cut the duck into portions, removing the bones and apples partly. Arrange on a platter. Wash and soak the prunes. Remove the pits, cook the prunes and force them through a strainer. Wash, scald and peel the lemons. Cut them into half-slices. Skim the fat off the sauce. Combine the sauce with the lemons, prune paste, cognac and peaches cut into cubes. Simmer for several minutes and season. Pour over the duck and bake. Serve with scooped out potato balls and lettuce.

ROAST DUCK MASURIAN STYLE

Duck, 1 2/3—2 oz. fat, 2/3 cup sour cream, 1 1/3 oz. dried cèpe mushrooms, 2 2/3 oz. onions, fat for onions, 2 egg yolks, parsley sprigs, salt, pepper and marjoram

Wash the cleaned duck and cut off the neck and wings. Rub with seasoning and set aside in a cool place for an hour. Wash, soak and cook the mushrooms. Take them out and chop them. Baste the duck and bake it 60—80 minutes, sprinkling with mushroom stock, then with sour cream. Peel, rinse and chop the onions finely, then fry them. Take out the duck when tender and cut into portions, removing the bones partly. Arrange on a platter. Combine the sauce with the onions and simmer for 5 minutes. Skim the fat off the sauce and pour it through a strainer. Combine with mushrooms and egg yolks, then season. Pour over the duck and bake. Serve with potatoes and salads.

BELVEDERE ROAST DUCK

Duck, 1 2/3—2 oz. fat, 2/3 cup dry white wine, 7 oz. oranges, 1 1/3 oz. tomato paste, 1 1/3 oz. raisins, salt, pepper, sugar and lemon juice to taste

Wash the cleaned duck and cut off the neck and wings. Rub with seasoning and set aside in a cool place for an hour. Pour fat over and bake for around 60—80 minutes, basting with wine, then with the pan drippings. Wash, scald and peel the oranges. Cut them into cubes, removing

the pits. Combine with the duck towards the end of baking. Take out the duck when tender and cut into portions removing the bones partly. Arrange on a platter. Combine the sauce with tomato paste and rinsed raisins. Simmer for several minutes and season. Pour over the duck and bake. Serve with potatoes and salads.

POZNAŃ DUCK

Duck, 1 2/3—2 oz. fat, 2/3 cup dry red wine, 1 1/4 lb. red cabbage, 7 oz. grapes, 2 2/3 oz. pork fat, 2 2/3 oz. onions, 2/3 oz. flour, salt, pepper, sugar and lemon juice to taste

Wash the cleaned duck and cut off the neck and wings. Rub with seasoning and set aside in a cool place for an hour. Baste with fat and brown on all sides. Simmer, sprinkling with wine. Clean, rinse and cut the cabbage into thin slices, removing the tick pieces. Sprinkle with water and simmer over low heat until tender. Peel, rinse and cut the onions finely. Cut the pork fat into cubes and render it down partly. Combine with the flour and brown lightly. Combine with the cabbage and halved grapes. Skim the fat off the sauce and combine it with the pork fat mixture. Bring to a boil and season. Take out the duck when tender and cut into portions, removing the bones partly. Surround with the cabbage and bake. Serve with potatoes and mizeria (q.v.).

DUCK IN GOLD SAUCE

Duck, 1/2 lb. soup vegetables (carrots, parsley root, celeriac, leek), 5 oz. marinated agaric mushrooms, 3 1/2 oz. gherkins, 2/3 oz. fat, 2/3 oz. flour, salt, pepper, sugar, bay leaf, allspice and saffron

Wash the cleaned duck and cut off the neck and wings. Cover with boiling water and cook the duck over low heat. Wash, peel, rinse and cut up the vegetables. Add to the duck in the middle of cooking together with seasoning. Take out the duck when tender and cut into portions, removing the bones partly. Arrange on a platter. Heat the fat and blend it

with the flour. Fry it without browning. Blend with cold strained stock (1 cup) and bring to a boil. Add the mushrooms and strips of gherkins. Cook for several minutes and season. Pour over the duck and bake. Serve with rice, scooped out potato balls and salads.

DUCK FRICASSEE

Duck, 3/4 lb. soup vegetables (carrots, parsley root, celeriac, leek), 2/3 cup sour cream, 3 1/2 oz. mushrooms, 3 1/2 oz. duck livers, 2/3 oz. fat, 2/3 oz. grated whole-wheat bread, salt, pepper, curry powder and seasoning to taste

Wash the cleaned duck and cut off the neck and wings. Cover with boiling salted water and bring to a boil over low heat. Wash, peel and rinse the vegetables. Cut them up and add to the duck towards the end of cooking. Clean and rinse the mushrooms. Cut them into strips and fry together with the livers. Allow to cool and mince. Combine with the sour cream and bread, then season. Take out the duck when tender and cut into portions, removing the bones partly. Arrange on a platter. Pour the sauce over and bake. Serve with rice and salads.

DUCK STEW

Duck, 1 2/3—2 oz. fat, 2/3 cup sour cream, 5 oz. onions, 1 1/3 oz. tomato paste, 2/3 oz. flour, parsley sprigs, salt, pepper, ground paprika and allspice to taste

Wash the cleaned duck and rub it with seasoning. Set aside in a cool place for an hour. Cut into pieces and brown in very hot fat together with finely chopped onions. Sprinkle with water and simmer until tender. Towards the end add tomato paste. When tender combine the meat with sour cream blended with flour. Bring to a boil and add chopped parsley sprigs, then season. Serve with potatoes, macaroni, noodles and salads.

DUCK GOULASH

Duck, 5 oz. smoked bacon, 1 oz. dried cèpe mushrooms, 2/3 cup dry red wine, 2/3 oz. flour, 2/3 oz. fat, salt, pepper and marjoram to taste

Wash the cleaned duck and rub with seasoning. Set aside in a cool place for an hour. Wash, soak and cook the mushrooms. Cut them into strips. Cut the duck into pieces. Cut the bacon into cubes and partly render it down. Add the duck and brown it. Cover with the mushroom and wine stock and simmer until tender. Heat the fat and blend with flour. Fry without browning. Combine with the duck towards the end of simmering, then season. Add the mushrooms. Serve with potatoes and salads.

ROAST GOOSE I

Goose (young), goose fat, 1 lb. cooking apples, salt, pepper and marjoram to taste

Wash the cleaned goose and cut off the neck and wings. Rub with seasoning and set aside in a cool place for an hour. Wash and peel the apples. Cut them in half, removing the cores. Cut them into pieces and stuff the goose with this. Sew it up or fasten it closed. Pour fat over and bake for around 2 hours, basting with water, then with the pan drippings. When tender cut the goose into portions, removing the bones partly. Surround with apples. Skim the fat off the sauce and season it. Pour over the duck. Serve with potatoes, salads and fried cabbage.

ROAST GOOSE II

Goose (young), goose fat, 7 oz. onions, 3 1/2 oz. prepared mustard, salt, pepper, marjoram and thyme to taste

Wash the cleaned goose and cut off the neck and wings. Rub with seasoning and set aside in a cool place for an hour. Pour fat over and brown

together with peeled and diced onions. Sprinkle with water and bake for around 2 hours, basting with the pan drippings. Towards the end of baking spread mustard over the goose and brown it. Take out the goose when tender and cut into portions, removing the bones partly. Arrange on a platter. Skim the fat off the sauce and season it. Pour over the goose. Serve with potatoes and fried cabbage.

GOOSE POLISH STYLE I

Goose (young), goose fat, 1 1/3 oz. dried cèpe mushrooms, 3 1/2 oz. ketchup, 1 lb. sauerkraut, salt, pepper, caraway seed, seasoning and marjoram to taste

Wash the cleaned goose and cut off the neck and wings. Rub with seasoning and set aside in a cool place for an hour. Wash, soak and cook the mushrooms, then chop them. Pour fat over the goose and bake for around 2 hours, basting with mushroom stock, then with the pan drippings. Dice the cabbage and cover it with a small amount of mushroom stock. Bring to a boil and combine with chopped mushrooms, then season. Cut the goose into portions, removing the bones partly. Arrange in a dish alternately with cabbage. Pour ketchup over and bake. Serve with potatoes and salads.

GOOSE POLISH STYLE II

Goose (young), goose fat, 5 oz. white beans, 2—2 2/3 oz. prunes, 1 1/3 oz. raisins, 2 2/3 oz. onions, 2/3 oz. fat, salt, pepper, garlic and basil to taste

Wash the cleaned goose and cut off the neck and wings. Rub with seasoning and set aside in a cool place for an hour. Pour fat over and bake for around 2 hours, basting with water, then with the pan drippings. Take out the goose when tender and cut into portions, removing the bones partly. Sort and rinse the beans. Cover with water and bring to a boil. Set aside for 2 hours. Cook the beans in the same water. Wash, soak and

cook the prunes, then force them through a strainer. Combine the beans with the prune paste, rinsed raisins and finely chopped fried onions, then season. Surround the goose and bake for around 6—8 minutes. Serve with potatoes and salads.

GOOSE POLISH STYLE III

Goose (young), goose fat, 3 1/2 oz. goose livers, 7 oz. apples, 1 2/3 oz. raisins, milk, parsley sprigs, 3 2/3 oz. onions, 2/3 oz. butter, 2 white rolls, salt, pepper and nutmeg to taste

Wash the cleaned goose and cut off the neck and wings. Peel, rinse and chop the onions finely. Fry together with the livers. Allow to cool and mince together with the rolls that have been soaked in milk and squeezed out. Wash and peel the apples. Cut them in half, removing the cores. Grate them coarsely and combine with the prepared mixture, rinsed raisins and chopped parsley sprigs. Season to taste and stuff the goose with this. Sew it up or fasten it closed. Pour fat over and bake for 2 hours, basting with water, then with the pan drippings. Take out the goose when tender and cut into portions. Arrange on a platter. Skim the fat off the sauce and season it. Pour over the goose. Serve with potatoes and salads.

GOOSE LITHUANIAN STYLE

Goose (young), goose fat, 2/3 cup sour cream, 1 1/3 oz. dried cèpe mushrooms, 3 1/2 oz. onions, salt, pepper, garlic, seasoning, juniper berries and marjoram to taste

Wash the cleaned goose and cut off the neck and wings. Rub with seasoning and set aside in a cool place for an hour. Wash, soak and cook the mushrooms. Pour fat over the goose and bake for around 2 hours, basting with mushroom stock, then with the pan drippings. Peel, rinse and chop the onions finely. Add to the goose towards the end of baking together with chopped mushrooms, ground seasoning and

sour cream. When tender cut the goose into portions, removing the bones partly. Arrange on a platter. Skim the fat off the sauce and season it. Pour over the goose. Serve with potatoes and salads.

GOOSE WITH CABBAGE

Goose (young), goose fat, 1 1/4—1 3/4 lb. white cabbage, 2/3 cup sour cream, 3 1/2 oz. onions, 1 1/3 oz. tomato paste, 1 1/3 oz. fat for onions, 2/3 oz. flour, salt, pepper and marjoram to taste

Wash the cleaned goose and cut off the neck and wings. Rub with seasoning and set aside in a cool place for an hour. Pour fat over and bake for around 2 hours, basting with water, then with the pan drippings. Remove any damaged leaves from the cabbage. Rinse it and cut into cubes. Add to the goose towards the end of baking together with sour cream and tomato paste. When tender cut the goose into portions, removing the bones partly. Peel, rinse and chop the onions finely. Fry and combine with flour. Brown this lightly and add to the cabbage. Bring to a boil and season. Surround the goose and simmer for several minutes. Serve with potatoes and salads.

GOOSE WITH TOMATOES

Goose (young), goose fat, 2/3 cup sour cream, 1 2/3 oz. tomato paste, 1 2/3 oz. raisins, 5 oz. onions, salt, pepper, seasoning and marjoram to taste

Wash the cleaned goose and cut off the neck and wings. Rub with seasoning and set aside in a cool place for an hour. Pour fat over and bake for around 2 hours, basting with water, then with the pan drippings and sour cream. Peel, rinse and chop the onions finely. Add to the goose towards the end of baking together with the tomato paste and rinsed raisins. When tender, cut the goose into portions, removing the bones partly. Arrange on a platter. Skim the fat off the sauce and season it. Serve with scooped out potato balls and salads.

GOOSE COUNTRY STYLE

Goose (young), goose fat, 1 cup sour cream, 5 oz. French bread, 5 oz. onions, 2/3 oz. butter, 2—3 hard-boiled eggs, 3 1/2 oz. goose livers, parsley sprigs, salt, pepper and thyme to taste

Wash the cleaned goose and cut off the neck and wings. Rub with seasoning and set aside in a cool place for an hour. Peel, rinse and chop the onions finely, then fry them. Cut the crust off the bread and cut it into cubes. Dry it in an oven and combine with the onions, minced eggs, minced livers, chopped parsley sprigs and sour cream (2/3 cup), then season. Stuff the goose with this and sew it up or fasten it closed. Pour fat over and bake for around 2 hours, basting with water, then with the pan drippings. Towards the end of baking add the remaining sour cream. When tender cut the goose into portions, removing the bones partly. Skim the fat off the sauce and season it. Serve with potatoes and salads.

UHLAN'S GOOSE

Goose (young), goose fat, 3/4 cup dry red wine, 3 1/2 oz. carrots, 5 oz. celeriac, 3 1/2 oz. parsley root, 3 1/2 oz. onions, 1 2/3 oz. plum jam, 1 1/3 oz. grated whole-wheat bread, salt, pepper, caramel syrup, cloves, sugar and lemon juice to taste

Wash the cleaned goose and cut off the neck and wings. Rub with seasoning and set aside in a cool place for an hour. Wash, peel and rinse the onions and vegetables, then chop them finely. Baste the goose with fat and brown together with the vegetables. Pour water over and bake for around 2 hours. Towards the end of baking add the wine, plum jam, bread and seasoning. When tender cut the goose into portions, removing the bones partly. Arrange on a platter. Skim the fat off the sauce and season it. Pour over the goose. Serve with potatoes and tomato salad.

GOOSE STEW POLISH STYLE

Goose (young), goose fat, 2/3 cup sour cream, 1 1/3 oz. dried cèpe mushrooms, 1/3—2/3 oz. flour, parsley sprigs, salt and pepper to taste

Wash the cleaned goose and cut off the neck and wings. Rub with seasoning and set aside in a cool place for an hour. Wash, soak and cook the mushrooms. Cut the goose into pieces and brown it. Cover with mushroom stock and simmer until tender. Combine with sour cream blended with flour, chopped mushrooms and chopped parsley sprigs. Simmer for a while and season. Serve with potatoes and salads.

GOOSE LIVER SHASHLIK I

3/4—1 lb. goose livers, 1 lb. smoked bacon, salt and pepper to taste

Rinse and dry the livers. Cut the larger pieces in half. Cut the bacon into thin strips. Pound them with a mallet and wrap around the livers. Sprinkle with seasoning and place on skewers. Place in a hot oven and bake. Serve with rice and salads.

GOOSE LIVER SHASHLIK II

1/2—3/4 lb. goose livers, 3 1/2 oz. pork fat, 3 1/2 oz. onions, 1/2 lb. mushrooms (small), 1 2/3 oz. almonds, fat for frying, salt and pepper to taste

Rinse and dry the livers. Cut the larger pieces in half. Blanch the almonds and grind them. Peel and rinse the onions, then cut them into strips together with the pork fat. Clean and rinse the mushrooms. Place them on skewers alternately with pork fat, livers and onions. Sprinkle with seasoning, pressing down with your hand. Place in very hot fat and brown on both sides, then continue frying over low heat. Arrange the fried shashliks on cooked and seasoned rice. Sprinkle with almonds. Serve with tomato salad.

GOOSE LIVERS WITH ONIONS

1 lb. goose livers, 7 oz. onions, 2/3—1 oz. flour, fat for frying, salt and pepper to taste

Rinse and dry the livers. Cut the larger pieces into slices. Peel and rinse the onions. Cut them into half-slices. Fry them and transfer to a plate. Dredge the livers with pepper and flour. Fry in very hot fat. Sprinkle with one tablespoon of water. Add onions, simmer lightly and season. Serve with potatoes and salads.

BAKED GOOSE LIVERS

1 lb. goose livers, 1/3 cup Madeira wine, 3 1/2 oz. pork fat, 3 1/2 oz. onions, 2/3—1 oz. flour, fat for frying, salt, pepper, ginger and seasoning to taste

Rinse and dry the livers. Cut the larger pieces in half. Lard with thin strips of pork fat. Peel and rinse the onions. Cut them into half-slices. Fry them and transfer to a plate. Dredge the livers with seasoning and flour. Baste with fat and bake. Cover with the onions, sprinkle with wine and simmer for a while. Serve with potatoes and salads.

GOOSE LIVER FILLETS

1/2 lb. goose livers, fat for frying, 8 slices of toast from French bread, 1 oz. butter, 5 oz. chicken or poultry pâté, 1—1 1/3 oz. flour, 5 oz. mushrooms, 2/3 oz. butter for mushrooms, 2/3 cup sour cream, parsley sprigs, salt and pepper to taste

Rinse and dry the livers. Cut the larger pieces in half. Clean, rinse and chop the mushrooms finely. Fry them and sprinkle with flour (1/3 oz.). Fry for a while, add sour cream and bring to a boil. Combine with chopped parsley sprigs and season to taste. Dredge the livers with seasoning and flour. Fry in very hot fat. Spread butter on the toast and fry. Place the pâté and livers on the toast. Add the sauce and bake in a hot oven. Serve with scooped out potato balls, cauliflower and salads.

GOOSE GIZZARD GOULASH

1 1/4—1 1/2 lb. gizzards, 7 oz. soup vegetables (carrots, parsley root, celeriac, leek), 1 1/3 oz. tomato paste, 3 1/2 oz. onions, fat, 1 oz. flour, salt, pepper, seasoning, marjoram and ground paprika to taste

Wash the cleaned gizzards. Cover them with boiling salted water and cook covered over low heat. Wash, peel and rinse the vegetables. Add them to the gizzards towards the end of cooking. Take out the gizzards when tender and cut them into smaller pieces. Combine with strained stock (1 2/3 cups). Peel, rinse and dice the onions, then fry them. Combine with flour and fry lightly. Combine with the gizzards. Cook for a while and season. Serve with potatoes and salads.

GOOSE GIZZARD TRIPE

1 3/4 lb. goose gizzards, 1/2 lb. soup vegetables (carrots, parsley root, celeriac, leek), 3 1/2 oz. onions, 1 1/3 oz. fat, 1 oz. flour, salt, pepper, allspice, bay leaf, seasoning, ginger, marjoram and nutmeg to taste

Wash the cleaned gizzards and cover with boiling salted water. Cook covered over low heat. Take them out and cut into strips. Wash, peel and rinse the vegetables. Cut them into strips. Cover with gizzard stock and cook. Peel, rinse and dice the onions. Fry them and blend with flour. Brown lightly. Combine with the vegetables and gizzards. Cook for a while and season.

STUFFED GOOSE NECK

Goose neck, 3 1/2 oz. chicken or poultry livers, 5 oz. boneless veal, 1 2/3 oz. hardened French bread, 5 oz. soup vegetables (carrots, parsley root, celeriac, leek), milk, 3 1/2 oz. onions, 1 1/3 oz. fat, egg, 1 2/3 oz. pork fat, salt pepper, allspice, bay leaf and nutmeg to taste

Clean the goose neck thoroughly, then wash it. Remove the outer skin and cook the neck together with cleaned and rinsed vegetables. Take out the neck when tender and separate the meat from the bones. Wash the veal and cut it into pieces. Brown it in fat together with onions, livers and pork fat. Sprinkle with water or stock and simmer until tender. Towards the end of cooking add bread broken into small pieces. When tender allow the meat to cool and mince it twice, together with the meat

from the goose neck. Combine with the egg and season. Stuff the skin of the neck loosely and sew up on both sides. Pierce in several places and place in the stock together with the seasoning. Simmer for around 40 minutes. Take out when done and cut diagonally into strips. Serve with potatoes and salads.

ROULADE OF GOOSE

Goose (young), 1/2 lb. boneless pork, 7 oz. goose livers, 2 2/3—3 1/2 oz. hardened French bread, milk, 1 2/3 oz. pork fat, 1—2 eggs, 5 oz. mushrooms, 2/3 oz. butter for mushrooms, goose fat, salt, pepper and marjoram to taste

Wash the cleaned goose and cut off the neck and wings. Place on a chopping board breast down. With a sharp knife slice along the backbone, separating the skin and meat from the bones. Cut strips of meat from the breast. Lightly even out the more muscled places and shape into a rectangle. Clean, rinse and chop the mushrooms finely, then fry them. Soak the bread in milk and squeeze it out. Mince twice together with the pork and livers. Combine with the eggs, mushrooms and diced and scalded pork fat, then season. Place this mixture on the strip of goose meat. Tie this up as you would a ham and baste with fat. Wrap in aluminium foil and bake for around 70 minutes. When done, cut the roulade into portions. Skim the fat off the sauce and season it. Pour over the roulade. Serve with potatoes, Sautéed Cabbage (q.v.) and tomato salad.

ROAST TURKEY

Turkey (young), fat for baking, salt and pepper to taste

Wash the drawn turkey and remove the tendons from the legs, slicing the skin near the knee joint. Press the turkey breast firmly with your hand, so that it flattens out. Cut off the neck, rub with seasoning and set aside in a cool place for 2 to 3 hours. Place the turkey in a baking pan backside down. Baste with fat and brown. Bake, basting with water,

then with the pan drippings. Take out the turkey when done and place on a board. Allow to cool lightly. Cut off the thighs and cut each thigh across into pieces. Cut off strips of meat diagonally from the breast, beginning with the shoulder joint. Arrange the portioned meat on a platter, so that each portion contains a piece of meat from the thigh and from the breast. Skim the fat off the sauce and season it. Pour over the turkey. Heat in the oven. Serve with French fries, cranberries and compote.

Note: The length of baking time depends on the weight of the turkey. Generally 30 minutes is allowed per 2 lbs. weight.

TURKEY POLISH STYLE I

Turkey (young), fat for baking, 1 2/3 oz. hardened French bread, milk, 3 1/2 oz. turkey livers, 1 2/3 oz. raisins, 2 eggs, 2/3—1 oz. breadcrumbs, 1 1/3 oz. butter, salt, pepper, nutmeg and cloves to taste

Prepare the turkey (as above). Rinse the livers and remove the outer skin. Cover with milk and set aside in a cool place for several hours. Soak the bread in milk and squeeze it out. Mince together with the livers. Combine with butter, beaten egg yolks, rinsed raisins and beaten egg whites, alternately adding breadcrumbs. Season this. Place the stuffing in a thin layer under the skin around the throat. Fill the throat as well and sew it up. Pour fat over and brown. Bake, basting with water, then with the pan drippings. When done cut as above, adding a piece of the stuffing to each portion. Serve with French fries, cranberries and compote.

TURKEY POLISH STYLE II

Turkey (young), fat for baking, 5 oz. yeast babka, 1 2/3 oz. raisins, 2—3 egg yolks, 1 2/3 oz. butter, 3 tablespoons sour cream or milk, salt, pepper, sugar, lemon and orange rind to taste

Prepare the turkey (as in Roast Turkey). Moisten the babka with cream or milk and crumble it. Combine with butter blended with egg yolks,

rinsed raisins and grated rinds, then season. Place the mixture in a thin layer under the skin around the throat. Fill the throat as well and sew it up. Pour fat over and brown. Bake, basting with water, then with the pan drippings. Cut the turkey up when done (as in Roast Turkey), adding a piece of stuffing to each portion. Serve with French fries, fruit salads and compote.

TURKEY WITH NUTS

Turkey (young), fat for baking, 5 oz. walnut meats, 1 2/3 oz. almonds, 1 2/3 oz. raisins, 3 tablespoons sour cream, 1 2/3 oz. butter, parsley sprigs, salt, pepper, sugar and lemon juice to taste

Prepare the turkey (as in Roast Turkey). Blanch the nuts and almonds. Grind them, then add butter, sour cream, rinsed raisins and chopped parsley sprigs. Simmer for a while and season. Place the stuffing in a thin layer under the skin around the throat. Fill the throat as well and sew it up. Pour fat over and bake, basting with water, then with the pan drippings. Cut the turkey when done (as in Roast Turkey), adding a piece of the stuffing to each portion. Serve with French fries, lettuce and compote.

WARSAW TURKEY

Turkey (young), fat for baking, 3 1/2 oz. turkey livers, 7 oz. mushrooms, 1 oz. butter for mushrooms, 2 eggs, 1 2/3 oz. breadcrumbs, parsley sprigs, milk, salt, pepper and thyme to taste

Prepare the turkey (as in Roast Turkey). Rinse the livers and remove the outer skin. Soak in milk for several hours. Clean, rinse and chop the mushrooms finely, then fry them. Combine with chopped livers, egg yolks, chopped parsley sprigs, beaten egg whites and breadcrumbs. Season this. Place the stuffing in a thin layer under the skin around the throat. Fill the throat as well and sew it up. Pour fat over and bake, basting with water, then with the pan drippings. When done cut up (as in Roast Turkey), adding a piece of stuffing to each portion. Serve with French fries, fruit salads and compote.

CARDINAL'S TURKEY

Turkey (young), fat for baking, milk, 5 oz. mushrooms, 2/3 oz. lobster butter for mushrooms, 3 1/2 oz. turkey livers, 3 1/2 oz. lobster tails, 1 2/3 oz. hardened French bread, 2 eggs, salt and pepper to taste

Prepare the turkey (as in Roast Turkey). Rinse the livers and remove the outer skin. Soak in milk for several hours. Clean, rinse and chop the mushrooms finely, then fry them. Mince the livers together with bread that has been soaked in milk and squeezed out. Combine with the mushrooms, chopped lobster tails, egg yolks and beaten egg whites, then season. Place the stuffing in a thin layer under the skin around the throat. Fill the throat as well and sew it up. Pour fat over and brown. Bake, basting with water, then with the pan drippings. When done, cut it up (as in Roast Turkey), adding a piece of stuffing to each portion. Serve with French fries, lettuce and compote.

CHEF'S TURKEY I

Turkey (young), fat for baking, 7 oz. mushrooms, 1/2 lb. peppers, fat for mushrooms, 1 lb. cauliflower, 3 tablespoons dry red wine, 1 1/3 oz. butter for roux, 1 1/3 oz. flour, 2 cups milk, egg yolk, 3 1/2 oz. hard cheese, salt, pepper, nutmeg and sugar

Prepare the turkey (as in Roast Turkey). Pour fat over and brown. Bake, basting with water, then with the pan drippings. When done cut up (as in Roast Turkey). Arrange on a platter. Clean, rinse and chop the peppers and mushrooms finely, then fry them. Clean and rinse the cauliflower. Cover with boiling salted water with sugar and cook. Surround the turkey with this. Sprinkle with mushrooms and peppers. Heat the butter and blend with the flour. Fry without browning. Blend with cold milk, stirring briskly with an egg-whisk and cook for a while. Combine with the egg yolk and season. Pour over the turkey, sprinkle with grated cheese and bake. Serve with scooped out potato balls and lettuce.

CHEF'S TURKEY II

Turkey (young), fat for baking, 3 1/2 oz. carrots, 5 oz. celeriac, 3 1/2 oz. parsley root, 3 1/2 oz. onions, 1 lb. tomatoes, 2/3 cup sour cream, 1/3—2/3 oz. flour, parsley sprigs, salt, pepper, seasoning and curry powder to taste

Prepare the turkey (as in Toast Turkey). Baste with fat and brown. Bake, basting with water, then with the pan drippings. Wash, peel and rinse the vegetables. Cut them into strips and add to the turkey towards the end of baking. Take out the turkey when done and cut it up (as in Roast Turkey). Arrange on a platter. Add sour cream blended with the flour to the sauce. Bring to a boil and season. Wash, scald and peel the tomatoes. Cut them into pieces and surround the turkey with them. Blend the sauce with chopped parsley sprigs and pour over the turkey, then bake. Serve with scooped out potato balls and lettuce.

CASTELLAN'S TURKEY

Turkey (young), fat for baking, 1/3 cup sour cream, 1 cup dry white wine, 5 oz. mushrooms, 5 oz. celeriac, 3 1/2 oz. onions, 5 oz. parsley root, 5 oz. carrots, 1 1/3 oz. tomato paste, salt and pepper to taste

Prepare the turkey (as in Roast Turkey). Pour fat over and brown. Bake, basting with water and wine towards the end. Clean and rinse the vegetables and mushrooms. Cut them into strips and add to the turkey towards the end of baking. Take out the turkey when done and cut it up (as in Roast Turkey). Arrange on a platter. Combine the sauce with tomato paste and simmer for a while, then season. Cover the turkey with the vegetables and mushrooms and with the sauce. Pour seasoned sour cream over and bake. Serve with scooped out potato balls and lettuce.

TURKEY OLD TOWN STYLE

Turkey (young), fat for baking, 3/4 cup dry white wine, 7 oz. mushrooms, 5 oz. thin frankfurters, parsley sprigs, 3 1/2 oz. hard cheese, 1 2/3 oz. walnuts meats, salt, pepper, thyme and tarragon to taste

Prepare the turkey (as in Roast Turkey). Baste with fat and brown. Bake, sprinkling with water, then with wine and the pan drippings. Blanch the almonds and grind them. Clean, rinse and cut the mushrooms into strips. Add to the turkey meat towards the end of baking. Cut the turkey when done (as in Roast Turkey). Arrange on a platter. Remove the outer skin, if any, from the frankfurters. Cut them into slices and add to the sauce. Simmer for a while and season. Surround the turkey with this. Sprinkle with walnuts and grated cheese, then bake. Serve with French fries and lettuce.

GENERAL'S TURKEY

Turkey (young), fat for baking, can of peaches, 1/3 cup rum, salt, white pepper and lemon juice to taste

Prepare the turkey (as in Roast Turkey). Pour fat over and bake, basting with water, then with the pan drippings. Towards the end of baking add the rum and part of the juice from peaches. Take out the turkey when done and cut it up (as in Roast Turkey). Arrange on a platter. Surround with peaches. Skim the fat off the sauce and season it. Pour over the turkey. Serve with French fries and compote.

WROCŁAW TURKEY

Turkey (young), fat for baking, 5 oz. prunes, 3 1/2 oz. almonds, 2 egg yolks, parsley sprigs, salt, pepper and lemon juice to taste

Prepare the turkey (as in Roast Turkey). Pour fat over and brown. Bake, basting with water, then with the pan drippings. Add soaked and pitted prunes in the middle of baking. Blanch the almonds and grind them. Take out the turkey when done and cut it up (as in Roast Turkey). Arrange on a platter. Pour over strained sauce combined with the almonds, egg yolks, chopped parsley sprigs and seasoning, then bake. Serve with French fries, lettuce, cauliflower and compote.

TURKEY STEW

1/2 turkey (back part), fat for frying, 1 cup sour cream, 5 oz. onions, 1 1/3 oz. tomato paste, 2/3 oz. flour, parsley sprigs, salt, pepper, seasoning and ground paprika to taste

Wash the meat and cut it into pieces. Dredge with seasoning and flour, then brown. Add finely chopped onions and fry lightly. Sprinkle with water and simmer covered over low heat until tender. Towards the end add tomato paste. Blend the sour cream with the flour and combine with the meat. Simmer for a while. Add chopped parsley sprigs and season. Serve with noodles, rice and salads.

TURKEY FRICASSEE

1/2 turkey (back part), 3/4 lb. soup vegegables (carrots, parsley root, celeriac, leek), 1 1/3 oz. butter or margarine, 1 1/3 oz. flour, 1/3 cup sour cream, egg yolk, parsley sprigs, salt, nutmeg, sugar and lemon juice to taste

Wash the meat and cut into portions. Cover with boiling salted water and cook covered over low heat. Wash, peel and rinse the vegetables. Add them to the turkey towards the end of cooking. Take out the meat when tender and arrange on a platter, removing the bones partly. Heat the butter and blend it with the flour. Fry this without browning. Blend with cold strained stock (1 2/3 cups) and bring to a boil, stirring briskly with an egg-whisk. Combine with the egg yolk, sour cream and chopped parsley sprigs. Season to taste. Pour over the turkey and heat in an oven. Serve with rice and lettuce.

TURKEY ENTRECÔTE

Turkey (young, front part), fat for frying, 2/3 oz. butter, 3 1/2 oz. bread for toast, 2/3 oz. breadcrumbs, 2/3 oz. flour, 1—2 eggs, salt and pepper to taste

244

Wash the turkey breast and pull down the skin. Slice the breast along the bone together with the collar bone. Separate the meat from the bones. Remove any membrane and tendons from the fillets. Pound the meat with a mallet that has been dipped in water, shaping the slices into elongated leaves. Cut the bread into thin slices, then into 1 1/2—2 in. long strips. Combine with breadcrumbs. Dredge the meat with seasoning and flour. Add to beaten eggs and place on toast slices, evening out the edges with your hand and a knife. Fry in heated fat on both sides, then continue frying over low heat. When done pour off the fat, add butter and melt it. Serve with French fries, cauliflower, peas and salads.

TURKEY FILLET SAUTÉ

Turkey (young, front part), fat for frying, 2/3 oz. butter, 2/3—1 oz. flour, salt and pepper to taste

Wash the turkey breast and pull down the skin. Slice the breast along the bone together with the collar bone. Separate the meat from the bones. Remove any membrane and tendons from the fillets. Pound with a mallet that has been dipped in water, shaping them into elongated leaves. Dredge with salt, pepper and flour. Place in very hot fat and brown on both sides, then continue frying over low heat for several minutes. Pour off the fat, add butter and melt it. Serve with French fries, cauliflower, asparagus, peas and salads.

TURKEY MEDALLIONS SAUTÉ

Turkey (young, front part), fat for frying, 2/3 oz. butter, 2/3 oz. flour, salt and pepper to taste

Wash the meat and pull down the skin. Slice the breast along the bone together with the collar bone. Separate the meat from the bones. Remove membranes and tendons from the fillets and divide into portions. Pound with a mallet that has been dipped in water, shaping them into ovals.

Dredge with seasoning and flour. Place in very hot fat and brown on both sides, then continue frying over low heat for several minutes. When done pour off the fat, add butter and melt it. Serve with French fries, cauliflower, tomato salad, mizeria (q.v.) (cucumber salad) and salads.

ROYAL TURKEY CUTLETS

Turkey (young, front part), 3 1/2 oz. French bread, sour cream, 3 egg yolks, 1 1/3 oz. raisins, parsley sprigs, 2 2/3 oz. almonds, fat, salt and nutmeg to taste

Wash the meat and pull down the skin. Slice the breast along the bone together with the collar bone. Separate the meat from the bones. Cut the bread up finely and sprinkle with sour cream. Set aside for 6 to 8 minutes. Mince together with the meat. Combine with the egg yolks, rinsed raisins and chopped parsley sprigs, then season. Blanch the almonds and grind them. Form cutlets from this mixture and coat with almonds. Pour fat over and wrap in aluminium foil. Bake in a hot oven. Serve with French fries, lettuce, tomato salad, cauliflower and salads.

ROAST GUINEA HEN

Guinea hen (young), fat for baking, 5 oz. pork fat, salt, lemon juice and 2 teaspoons ginger

Wash the drawn guinea hen. Rub it with seasoning and set aside in a cool place for an hour. Cut the pork fat into 1 1/2 in. long strips. Lard densely in even rows along the breast and thighs, 3—4 rows on each side. Pour fat over and bake, basting with water, then with the pan drippings. Take out when done and cut so that each portion contains a piece of thigh and a piece of breast. Arrange on a platter. Pour seasoned sauce over and heat. Serve with potatoes, mizeria (q.v.) (cucumber salad) and compote.

WROCŁAW GUINEA HEN

Guinea hen (young), fat for baking, 5 oz. pork fat, 5 oz. mushrooms, 1 2/3 oz. hardened French bread, 2 egg yolks, butter for mushrooms, parsley sprigs, milk, 1 1/3 oz. horseradish (grated), salt, pepper and lemon juice to taste

Wash the drawn guinea hen. Rub it with seasoning and set aside in a cool place for an hour. Clean, rinse and chop the mushrooms finely, then fry them. Soak the bread in milk and squeeze it out. Mince it and combine with the mushrooms, egg yolks and chopped parsley sprigs, then season. Stuff the bird and tie up the legs. Lard with thin strips of pork fat 1 1/2 in. long. Lard densely in even rows along the breast and thighs, 3—4 rows on each side. Pour fat over and bake, basting with water, then with the pan drippings. Take out when done and cut so that each portion contains a piece of thigh, breast and stuffing. Arrange on a platter. Pour seasoned sauce over and heat. Serve with potatoes, lettuce and compote.

GENERAL'S GUINEA HEN I

Guinea hen (young), fat for baking, 1 2/3 oz. almonds, 3 1/2 oz. ketchup, 5 oz. smoked ham, parsley sprigs, salt, pepper and lemon juice to taste

Wash the drawn guinea hen. Rub with seasoning and set aside in a cool place for an hour. Blanch the almonds. Lard the guinea hen densely and thickly, then tie up the legs. Spread ketchup blended with chopped parsley sprigs. Cover with thin strips of ham and tie up with thread. Pour fat over and bake, basting with water, then with the pan drippings. Take out when done and cut into portions, so that each portion consists of a piece of thigh and a piece of breast. Arrange on a platter. Pour seasoned sauce over and heat. Serve with French fries, tomato salad and compote.

GENERAL'S GUINEA HEN II

Guinea hen (young), fat for baking, 5 oz. pork fat, 1 oz. dried cèpe mushrooms, egg yolk, salt, pepper, prepared mustard and ginger to taste

Wash the drawn guinea hen. Rub it with seasoning, tie up the legs and set aside in a cool place for an hour. Wash, soak and cook the mushrooms. Take them out and mince them. Combine with the egg yolk and season. Spread over the guinea hen. Cover with thin strips of pork fat and tie up with thread. Pour fat over and bake, basting with water, then with the pan drippings. Take out when done and cut into portions, so that each portion consists of a piece of thigh and a piece of breast. Arrange on a platter. Pour seasoned sauce over and heat. Serve with potatoes, cauliflower and salads.

BELVEDERE GUINEA HEN

Guinea hen (young), fat for baking, 5 oz. pork fat, 2/3 cup sour cream, 1 2/3 oz. horseradish (grated), 1 2/3 oz. raisins, salt, pepper, sugar, lemon juice, lemon and orange rind to taste

Prepare and lard the guinea hen (as in Roast Guinea Hen). Pour fat over and bake, basting with water, then with the pan drippings. Blend the sour cream with the horseradish, rinsed raisins and grated lemon and orange rinds. Add to the guinea hen towards the end of baking. Take out when done and cut into portions so that each portion consists of a piece of thigh and a piece of breast. Arrange on a platter. Pour seasoned sauce over and heat. Serve with scooped out potato balls and lettuce.

Eggs

CODDLED EGGS

8 eggs, salt and vinegar to taste

Wash the eggs, break each one into a saucer and slip onto the surface of lightly salted boiling water. Be careful not to let the egg white separate from the yolk. Cook for 3—4 minutes, or until the egg white is firm, enclosing the yolk. Take the egg out with a spoon and drain. Serve with sauces or baked.

EGGS OLD TOWN STYLE I

4 hard-boiled eggs, 1 2/3 oz. grated horseradish, 1 tablespoon sour cream for horseradish, 1 oz. ham, 1 oz. canned peas, 1 oz. canned peppers, 2 1/2 oz. mayonnaise, 3 tablespoons sour cream, lettuce, salt, pepper, sugar and lemon juice to taste

Combine the horseradish with the sour cream and season. Place on egg halves. Arrange the eggs on a platter covered with lettuce leaves. Cut the ham and peppers into strips. Combine with the peas, mayonnaise and sour cream, then season. Pour over the eggs and garnish.

EGGS OLD TOWN STYLE II

4 hard-boiled eggs, 3 1/2 oz. cooked beef, 3 1/2 oz. dill pickles, 3 1/2 oz. canned peas, 1 2/3 oz. mayonnaise, 2 tablespoons thick sour cream, 1/3 cup whipping cream, fresh dill, lettuce, salt, pepper, sugar and lemon juice to taste

Cut the meat and pickles into cubes. Combine with the peas, mayonnaise and sour cream, then season. Arrange on a platter covered with lettuce leaves. Add egg halves, yolk side down. Garnish with whipped cream blended with chopped dill and seasoning.

SEYM EGGS I

4 hard-boiled eggs, 7 oz. boneless baked duck (breast), 5 oz. chicken livers, 2 oz. onions, fat, 1 1/3 oz. ketchup, 3 1/2 oz. cooked potatoes, 1 2/3 oz. cooked carrots, 3 1/2 oz. cooked cauliflower, 1 2/3 oz. canned zucchini, 3 1/2 oz. mayonnaise, lettuce, salt, pepper, sugar and lemon juice to taste

Peel, rinse and chop the onions finely. Wash the livers and cut the larger pieces in half. Fry them, adding the onions towards the end. Allow to cool and mince the livers. Combine with ketchup and season. Cut the potatoes, carrots and zucchini into cubes. Add cauliflower broken up into rosettes. Combine with the mayonnaise and season. Arrange on a platter covered with lettuce. Add egg halves covered with strips of duck meat. Press the prepared mixture through a pastry bag onto the eggs and garnish.

SEYM EGGS II

4 hard-boiled eggs, 2/3 oz. caviar, 8 thin strips of smoked salmon, 3 1/2 oz. mushrooms, fat for mushrooms, 7 oz. cooked rice, 2/3 oz. ketchup, 1 oz. mayonnaise, fresh dill, lettuce, salt and pepper to taste

Clean, rinse and chop the mushrooms finely. Fry them and allow to cool. Combine with the rice, ketchup, mayonnaise and chopped dill, then season. Shape into 8 balls and wrap with strips of salmon. Arrange on a platter covered with lettuce. Place egg halves with caviar on top and garnish.

EGGS IN TARTARE SAUCE

4 hard-boiled eggs, 3 1/2 mayonnaise, 3 tablespoons sour cream, 1 2/3 oz. dill pickles, 1 oz. marinated mushrooms, 2/3 oz. capers, lettuce, salt, pepper, seasoning, ground paprika, sugar and prepared mustard to taste

Slice off the top of the wider part of the eggs. Arrange the eggs on a platter covered with lettuce leaves. Chop the pickles finely together with the mushrooms. Combine with the mayonnaise, sour cream and rinsed capers. Season to taste and pour over the eggs. Cover with the cut off tops and sprinkle with ground paprika.

CRACOW EGGS

4 hard-boiled eggs, 5 oz. cooked cauliflower, 1 1/3 oz. almonds, 1/3 cup thick sour cream, 1 oz. grated horseradish, parsley sprigs, 2/3 oz. ketchup, lettuce, salt, pepper, sugar and lemon juice to taste

Blanch the almonds. Cut the eggs in half and arrange on a platter covered with lettuce leaves. Sprinkle with chopped almonds and surround with crumbled up cauliflower. Combine the sour cream with horseradish, chopped parsley sprigs and seasoning. Pour over the eggs. Sprinkle with ketchup and garnish.

EGGS IN ASPIC

2 hard-boiled eggs, 1 cup broth or meat and vegetable stock, 2 2/3 oz. cooked veal or chicken, 1 2/3 oz. lobster tails, 1 1/3 oz. canned peas, 1 2/3 oz. tomatoes, 1/6 oz. tomato paste, 1/2 egg white, 1/2 oz. gelatin, salt and lemon juice to taste

Blend the broth with the tomato paste, egg white and seasoning. Bring to a boil, stirring. Add gelatin that has been soaked in cold boiled water and dissolve it. Season and strain through a linen cloth. Pour some of the aspic into individual serving molds and allow to set. Place tomato slices on the aspic. Add egg halves, yolk side down. Sprinkle with strips of meat, peas and lobster tails. Cover with the remaining aspic and allow to set once more. Dip the molds in hot water for a moment. Take out the eggs with the aspic. Arrange on a platter and garnish.

GARNISHED EGGS

4 hard-boiled eggs, 5 oz. chicken livers, fat for livers, 1 1/3 oz. mayonnaise, 8 thin strips of smoked salmon, 8 slices of French bread toast, fat for toast, 1 2/3 oz. lemon, 2 2/3 oz. tomatoes, parsley sprigs, salt and pepper to taste, lettuce

Wash the livers and cut the larger pieces in half. Fry them, allow to cool and mince. Combine with mayonnaise and season. Arrange the toast slices on a platter covered with lettuce leaves. Add egg halves wrapped with strips of salmon, leaving the narrower ends uncovered. Garnish with tomato pieces, lemon and parsley sprigs.

GARNISHED EGGS WITH HAM OR SMOKED FILLET OF BEEF

4 hard-boiled eggs, 2/3 oz. dried mushrooms, 2 2/3 oz. onions, fat for onions, 8 strips of ham or smoked fillet of beef, 2/3 oz. pickled plums, 5 oz. canned peas, 7 oz. dill pickles, 5 oz. tomatoes, 2—2 2/3 oz. mayonnaise, parsley sprigs, mayonnaise for garnishing, salt and pepper to taste

Wash, soak and cook the mushrooms. Peel, rinse and chop the onions finely, then fry them. Cut the eggs in half and take out the yolks. Mince the yolks them together with the mushrooms. Combine with the onions and season. Stuff the egg whites with this. Wash, scald and peel the tomatoes. Cut them into pieces. Combine with the peas, chopped parsley sprigs, mayonnaise and diced dill pickles, then season. Arrange the salad on a platter. Add egg halves wrapped in strips of ham or fillet of beef, with the narrower end of the egg uncovered. Garnish with mayonnaise, plums and parsley sprigs.

GARNISHED EGGS IN SALMON

4 hard-boiled eggs, 8 thin strips of salmon, 2 2/3 oz. lemons, 1 2/3 oz. tomatoes, 1 2/3 oz. mayonnaise, 3 1/2 oz. cooked potatoes, 2 2/3 oz. cooked carrots, 2 2/3 oz. cooked celeriac, 1 2/3 oz. canned peas, 2 2/3 oz. apples, parsley sprigs, mayonnaise for garnishing, lettuce, salt, pepper and prepared mustard to taste

Wash, and peel the apples. Cut them in half, removing the cores. Cut into cubes together with the potatoes, carrots, pickles and celeriac. Combine with the mayonnaise, peas and chopped parsley sprigs, then season. Arrange on a platter covered with lettuce leaves. Add egg halves wrapped in strips of salmon, with the narrower end uncovered. Garnish with mayonnaise, tomato pieces, lemon slices and parsley sprigs.

EGGS WITH SARDINE FILLING

4 hard-boiled eggs, 1/2 can of sardines, 1 oz. mayonnaise, 1 2/3 oz. lemons, 2/3 oz. canned peppers, lettuce, salt and pepper to taste

Cut the eggs in half and take out the yolks, taking care not to damage the whites. Blend the egg yolks with the sardines. Combine with the mayonnaise and season. Fill the egg whites with this and garnish with lemon and peppers. Transfer onto a platter covered with lettuce leaves.

EGGS WITH HERRING FILLING

4 hard-boiled eggs, 1 2/3 oz. herring fillets, 1 tablespoon sour cream, chives, 1 oz. canned peppers, 1/3 oz. canned peas, lettuce, salt and pepper to taste

Cut the eggs in half and take out the yolk, taking care not to damage the whites. Blend the egg yolks with finely chopped herring fillets, sour cream and chopped chives, then season. Fill the egg whites. Arrange on a platter covered with lettuce leaves.

EGGS WITH MUSHROOM FILLING

4 hard-boiled eggs, 1 1/3 oz. lobster tails, 2 2/3 oz. mushrooms, fat for baking, 1 oz. mayonnaise for stuffing, 3 1/2 oz. mayonnaise for spread-

ing, 1 tablespoon sour cream, 1 1/3 oz. tomatoes, parsley sprigs, fresh dill, lettuce, salt, pepper and lemon juice to taste

Clean, rinse and chop the mushrooms finely. Fry them and allow to cool. Combine with chopped lobster tails, mashed egg yolks and mayonnaise, then season. Fill the egg whites and arrange on a platter on lettuce leaves. Blend the remaining mayonnaise with cream and chopped parsley sprigs and pour over the eggs.

EGG ÉCLAIRS

8 eggs, 1 oz. flour, 2—2 2/3 oz. breadcrumbs, 1 2/3 oz. hard cheese, 1 1/3 tablespoons milk, 2 eggs, fat, salt and vinegar to taste

Cook the eggs (as in Coddled Eggs) and take them out with a special spoon. Drain of water and sprinkle with flour. Dip in egg beaten with milk and coat with breadcrumbs mixed with grated cheese. Fry on all sides in very hot fat. Serve with boiled potatoes.

EGG DAINTIES

8 eggs, 9 1/2 oz. mushrooms, fat for mushrooms, 3 1/2 oz. ketchup, 3 1/2 oz. hard cheese, 3 1/2 oz. ham, parsley sprigs, salt, pepper and vinegar to taste

Clean, rinse and cut the mushrooms into strips. Fry them and combine with chopped parsley and ham pieces, then season. Cook the eggs (as in Coddled Eggs) and arrange on the mushrooms. Pour ketchup over this. Sprinkle with pepper and grated cheese, then bake.

CARDINAL'S EGGS

8 eggs, 3 1/2 oz. lobster tails, 3 1/2 oz. mushrooms, fat for mushrooms, 2/3 oz. fat, 2/3 oz. flour, 1 cup broth, 1/3 cup sour cream, fresh dill, 1 2/3 oz. hard cheese, salt, curry powder and vinegar to taste

Heat the fat and blend with flour. Fry without browning. Dilute in a little cold broth, stirring briskly with an egg-whisk. Bring to a boil. Clean, rinse and chop the mushrooms finely. Fry them and combine with the sauce, lobster tails, sour cream nad chopped dill, then season. Cook the eggs (as in Coddled Eggs). Pour the sauce over, sprinkle with grated cheese and bake in a hot oven.

CLUB EGGS

8 eggs, 1 1/4—1 3/4 lb. cooked home-made macaroni, 5 oz. thin frankfurters, 7 oz. onions, fat, 1 cup sour cream, egg yolk, parsley sprigs, salt, pepper and vinegar to taste

Remove the outer skin, if any, from the frankfurters. Cut them into strips. Combine with the macaroni and fat, then season. Transfer to a greased pan and even out the surface. Cook the eggs (as in Coddled Eggs) and arrange on the macaroni. Peel and rinse the onions. Cut them into half-slices. Fry and combine with the sour cream, egg yolk and chopped parsley sprigs. Season this, pour over the eggs and bake.

EGGS POLISH STYLE

8 hard-boiled eggs, 1 2/3 oz. hardened French bread, milk, 1 2/3 onions, fat, 2/3 oz. raisins, parsley sprigs, 3/4 cup sour cream (thick), 2—2 2/3 oz. famer's cheese, 1 1/3 oz. horseradish (grated), salt, pepper, sugar and lemon juice to taste

Combine the sour cream with the horseradish and season. Peel, rinse and chop the onions finely, then fry them. Soak the bread in milk and squeeze it out. Cut the eggs in half and take out the yolks, taking care not to damage the whites. Mince the yolks together with the bread. Combine with the onions, chopped parsley sprigs and rinsed raisins. Season to taste. Fill the egg whites and arrange in a greased pan. Pour sour cream over this. Sprinkle with cheese that has been forced through a strainer and bake.

CLOISTER EGGS

8 hard-boiled eggs, 1 2/3 oz. walnut meats, 1 lb. boneless cooked fish, 3 1/2 oz. prepared mustard, raw egg yolk, 3 1/2 oz. hard cheese, fat, salt, pepper and sugar to taste

Blanch the walnuts and grind them. Cut the eggs in half and take out the yolks, taking care not to damage the whites. Mince the yolks and combine with the walnuts. Season to taste and fill the whites. Arrange in a greased pan. Surround with fish cut into cubes. Pour seasoned mustard blended with the egg yolk over the eggs. Sprinkle with grated cheese and bake.

BASIC STUFFED EGGS

8 hard-boiled eggs, 2 2/3 oz. onions, 1 2/3 oz. hardened French bread, milk, egg, parsley sprigs or fresh dill, fat, breadcrumbs, salt and pepper

Cool the hard-boiled eggs and cut them lengthwise into halves. Take out the eggs from the shells, taking care not to damage the shells. Peel, rinse and chop the onions finely. Fry them and mince together with the eggs and bread that has been soaked in milk and squeezed out. Combine with the egg and chopped parsley sprigs, then season. Fill the egg shells with this stuffing. Sprinkle with breadcrumbs and press down with your hand. Place in very hot fat, egg-side down, and brown.

STUFFED EGGS

8 hard-boiled eggs, 5 oz. mushrooms, 1 2/3 oz. ketchup, parsley sprigs, fat, breadcrumbs, salt and pepper to taste

Clean, rinse and chop the mushrooms finely, then fry them. Cool the hard-boiled eggs and cut them lengthwise into halves, taking care not to damage the shells. Take out the eggs and chop them. Combine with the mushrooms, ketchup and chopped parsley sprigs, then season. Fill the egg shells with this stuffing. Sprinkle with breadcrumbs and press down with your hand. Place in intensely heated fat, egg-side down, and brown.

STUFFED EGGS POLISH STYLE

8 hard-boiled eggs, 1 oz. dried cèpe mushrooms, 1 1/3 oz. horseradish (grated), egg yolk, parsley sprigs, fat, breadcrumbs, salt and pepper to taste

Wash, soak and cook the mushrooms, then take them out. Cool the hard-boiled eggs and cut them legnthwise into halves. Take out the eggs from the shells, taking care not to damage the shells. Mince together with the mushrooms. Combine with the horseradish, egg yolk and chopped parsley sprigs, then season. Fill the egg shells with this stuffing. Sprinkle with breadcrumbs and press down with your hand. Place in very hot fat, egg-side down, and brown.

EGG CUTLETS

4 hard-boiled eggs, raw egg, 1 2/3 oz. hardened French bread, milk, 1 2/3 oz. ham, 1 2/3 oz. hard cheese, 1 2/3 oz. walnut meats (optional), parsley sprigs, fat, breadcrumbs, salt, pepper to taste

Blanch the walnuts and grind them. Soak the bread in milk and squeeze it out. Mince together with the eggs and ham. Combine with the raw egg, walnuts, grated cheese and chopped parsley sprigs, then season. Shape this mixture into 4 oval cutlets. Dredge with breadcrumbs and place in very hot fat. Fry on both sides, then continue frying over low heat for several minutes.

SCRAMBLED EGGS WITH MUSHROOMS

8 eggs, 7 oz. mushrooms, 1 1/2 tablespoons milk, 1—1 1/3 oz. fat, parsley sprigs, salt and pepper to taste

Clean, rinse and cut the mushrooms in half, then into strips. Fry them. Wash the eggs and break them into a dish. Blend with milk and pour into the mushrooms. Add chopped parsley sprigs and seasoning. Fry slowly, stirring to make sure the eggs set evenly.

CHEF'S SCRAMBLED EGGS I

8 eggs, 1—1 1/3 oz. fat, 1 2/3 oz. horseradish (grated), 1 1/3 oz. walnut meats, 1 1/2 tablespoons sour cream, salt and pepper to taste

Blanch the walnuts and grind them. Wash the eggs and break them into a dish. Combine with sour cream, walnuts and horseradish. Pour into heated fat in a frying pan and fry slowly, stirring to make sure the eggs set evenly.

CHEF'S SCRAMBLED EGGS II

8 eggs, 1 1/3 oz. fat, 5—7 oz. onions (green or shallot), 1—1 1/3 oz. tomato paste, 1 1/2 tablespoons sour cream, salt and pepper to taste

Peel, rinse and cut the onions into pieces. Fry lightly together with the tomato paste. Wash the eggs and break them into a dish. Combine with sour cream. Pour into the onions and fry slowly, stirring to make sure the eggs set evenly.

SCRAMBLED EGGS WITH TOMATOES

8 eggs, 1—1 1/3 oz. fat, 1 1/2 tablespoons milk, 7 oz. tomatoes, parsley sprigs, salt and pepper to taste

Wash and scald the tomatoes. Peel them and cut into pieces. Wash the eggs and break them into a dish. Combine with milk. Pour into heated fat in a frying pan. Add tomatoes and fry slowly, stirring to make sure the eggs set evenly. Towards the end add chopped parsley sprigs and season.

CARDINAL'S SCRAMBLED EGGS

8 eggs, 1—1 1/3 oz. fat, 1 can sardines, 1 oz. capers, 1 cup milk, salt and pepper to taste

Rinse the capers and soak them in water for several minutes. Wash the eggs and break them into a dish. Combine with milk and seasoning. Pour into heated fat in a frying pan and fry slowly so that the eggs set evenly. Towards the end add drained capers and crumbled sardines.

SCRAMBLED EGGS WITH CAVIAR

8 eggs, 1—1 1/3 oz. fat, 1 1/2 tablespoons light cream, 1 oz. caviar, parsley sprigs, salt and nutmeg to taste

Wash the eggs and break them into a dish. Combine with sour cream. Pour into heated fat in a frying pan and fry, stirring to make sure the eggs set evenly. Towards the end add caviar and chopped parsley sprigs, then season.

FRIED EGGS

8 eggs, 1—1 1/3 oz. fat, salt and pepper to taste

Heat the fat in a frying pan, in individual serving dishes or in a pan that fries eggs separately. Carefully break in the washed eggs. Sprinkle with seasoning and fry slowly until the whites set.

FRIED EGGS IN SOUR CREAM WITH TOMATOES

8 eggs, 1—1 1/3 oz. fat, 1 1/2 tablespoons light cream, 7 oz. tomatoes, 1 2/3 oz. hard cheese, salt, pepper and nutmeg to taste

Heat the fat in a frying pan or in individual serving dishes. Wash the tomatoes and scald them. Peel them and cut into pieces. Place in the

frying pan. Add the cream and carefully break in the washed egg. Sprinkle with seasoning and grated cheese. Cook slowly until the egg whites set.

FRIED EGGS POLISH STYLE

8 eggs, 1—1 1/3 oz. fat, 1/3 cup sour cream, 1 1/3 oz. grated horseradish, salt, pepper and sugar to taste

Blend the sour cream with the horseradish and season. Heat the fat in a frying pan or in individual serving dishes. Carefully break in washed eggs. Cover with the sour cream. Place in a hot oven and bake until the egg whites set.

GENERAL'S FRIED EGGS

8 eggs, 1—1 1/3 oz. fat, 3 1/2 oz. pickled plums from wine, 3 1/2 oz. ketchup, 1 1/3 oz. walnut meats, salt and pepper to taste

Blanch the walnuts and grind together with pitted plums. Combine with ketchup and season. Transfer to greased individual serving dishes. Carefully break in washed eggs. Sprinkle with salt and pepper. Bake in a hot oven until the egg whites set.

FRIED EGGS WITH MUSHROOMS

8 eggs, 1—1 1/3 oz. fat, 1 lb. fresh mushrooms (cèpes), 2 2/3 oz. onions, 1/3 cup sour cream, 3 1/2 oz. hard cheese, salt and pepper to taste

Clean, rinse and dice the onions and mushrooms. Fry the onions lightly. Add the mushrooms and simmer until tender. Towards the end add the sour cream and season. Place in greased individual serving dishes. Carefully break in the washed eggs. Sprinkle with salt, pepper and grated cheese. Bake in a hot even until the egg whites set.

NATURAL OMELET

2 eggs, 1 tablespoon sour cream, water or milk, fat, salt to taste

Wash the eggs and break them into a dish. Add the sour cream, milk or water and salt to taste. Stir until blended. Pour into heated fat in a frying pan and fry slowly without stirring. When the omelet sets on the bottom, fold both sides towards the centre with a spatula. Transfer onto a warmed platter or plate and serve at once.

OMELET WITH MUSHROOMS

2 eggs, 1 tablespoon sour cream, milk or water, 3 1/2 oz. mushrooms, parsley sprigs, fat, salt and pepper to taste

Clean, rinse and cut the mushrooms into slices. Fry them and combine with chopped parsley sprigs, then season. Make the omelet (as in Natural Omelet). When it sets on the bottom, spread with the above mixture and fold both sides towards the centre with a spatula. Transfer to a heated platter and serve at once.

OMELET WITH HAM

2 eggs, 1 tablespoon sour cream, milk or water, 2/3 oz. canned peas, 1 teaspoon chopped parsley sprigs, fat, salt and pepper to taste

Make the omelet (as in Natural Omelet). When it fries on the bottom, spread strips of ham on it. Sprinkle with peas, parsley sprigs and pepper. Fold both sides towards the centre with a spatula. Transfer to an ovenproof platter. Baste with fat and bake.

WROCŁAW OMELET

2 eggs, 1 tablespoon sour cream, milk or water, 3 1/2 oz. onions, 2/3 oz. tomato paste, fat, 1 oz. hard cheese, salt and pepper to taste

Peel, rinse and cut the onions into half-slices. Fry them without browning. Combine with tomato paste and grated cheese, then season. Make the omelet (as in Natural Omelet). When it fries on the bottom, spread the filling on it and fold both sides towards the centre with a spatula. Arrange on a platter or plate and serve at once.

OMELET WITH BRAINS

2 eggs, 1 tablespoon sour cream, milk or water, 3 1/2 oz. veal or pork brains, 1 2/3 oz. onions, egg yolk, fat, salt and pepper to taste

Rinse the brains, remove the outer skin and chop them. Peel, rinse and chop the onions finely. Fry them without browning and combine with the brains. Fry 3—4 minutes, stirring constantly. Add the egg yolk and continue frying for a while, then season. Make the omelet (as in Natural Omelet). When it fries on the bottom, spread the brains on it and fold both sides towards the centre with a spatula. Transfer to a heated platter or plate and serve at once.

CARDINAL'S OMELET

2 eggs, 1 tablespoon sour cream, milk or water, 1 2/3 oz. mushrooms, 1 2/3 oz. lobster tails, fresh dill, salt and pepper to taste

Clean, rinse and cut the mushrooms into slices. Fry them in butter. Combine with the lobster tails and chopped dill, then season to taste. Make the omelet (as in Natural Omelet). When the omelet fries on the bottom, spread the filling on it and fold both sides towards the centre with a spatula. Transfer to a heated platter or plate and serve at once.

OMELET WITH FRANKFURTERS

2 eggs, 1 tablespoon sour cream, milk or water, 1 2/3 oz. thin frankfurters, 2 oz. smoked bacon, 1 oz. hard cheese, fat. salt and pepper to taste

Remove the skins, if any, from the frankfurters and cut them into slices. Dice the bacon and render it down partly. Add the frankfurters and fry them lightly. Make the omelet (as in Natural Omelet). When it fries on the bottom, spread the filling on it and fold both sides towards the centre with a spatula. Transfer to a greased oven-proof platter. Sprinkle with grated cheese and bake.

BURGHER'S OMELET

2 eggs, 1 tablespoon sour cream, milk or water, 1 2/3 oz. boneless roasted chicken, 2 oz. apples, 2/3 oz. raisins, fat, salt, pepper, curry powder and lemon juice to taste

Wash, peel and halve the apples, removing the cores. Dice them together with the chicken meat. Combine with rinsed raisins, season and simmer for a while. Make the omelet (as in Natural Omelet). When it fries on the bottom, spread the filling on it and fold both sides towards the centre with a spatula. Transfer to a heated platter or plate and serve at once.

WARSAW OMELET

2 eggs, 1 tablespoon sour cream, milk or water, 1 2/3 oz. stewed peaches, 1 2/3 oz. boneless roasted chicken, 2 tablespoons sour cream, 2/3 oz. walnut meats, fat, salt and pepper to taste

Blanch the walnuts and grind them. Dice the peaches and chicken meat. Combine with the sour cream and walnuts. Simmer for 3—4 minutes and season. Make the omelet (as in Natural Omelet). When it fries on the bottom, spread the filling on it and fold both sides towards the centre with a spatula. Transfer to a heated platter or plate and serve at once.

SPONGE OMELET

2 eggs, 2/3 oz. confectioners' sugar, 1/3 oz. flour, 2/3 oz. chocolate, 1/2 teaspoon vanilla extract, fat, salt to taste

Grease an oven-proof platter and sprinkle with flour. Wash the eggs and break them. Separate the egg yolks from the whites. Beat the whites until stiff, adding the sugar towards the end. Gently stir in the egg yolks and vanilla extract, alternately adding the flour. Transfer to a platter and even out the surface and sides. Bake in an oven. When done sprinkle with confectioners' sugar and grated chocolate. Serve at once.

OMELET WITH PINEAPPLE

2 eggs, 1 tablespoon sour cream, milk or water, 1 2/3 oz. farmer's cheese, 2/3 oz. raisins, 1 oz. canned pineapple, egg yolk, 2/3 oz. chocolate, fat, salt and sugar to taste

Blend the egg yolk with confectioners' sugar, then with ground farmer's cheese. Combine with rinsed raisins and finely chopped pineapple. Make the omelet (as in Natural Omelet). When it fries on the bottom, spread the filling on it and fold both sides towards the centre with a spatula. Transfer to a greased over-proof platter. Sprinkle with grated chocolate and bake.

SWEET OMELET I

2 eggs, 1 tablespoon sour cream, milk or water, 2 2/3 oz. farmer's cheese, egg yolk, 2/3 oz. butter, 2/3 oz. confectioners' sugar, 1/3 oz. raisins, 1 tabelspoon cognac, fat, salt to taste
Sauce: 2/3 cup milk, 2 egg yolks, 1—1 1/3 oz. confectioners' sugar, 2/3 oz. butter, salt and vanilla extract to taste

Blend the butter with the sugar and egg yolk. Combine with minced farmer's cheese, rinsed raisins and cognac. Make the omelet (as in Natural Omelet). When it fries on the bottom, spread the filling on it and fold both sides towards the centre with a spatula. Transfer to a greased oven-proof platter. Bring the milk to a boil. In the top of a double boiler blend the egg yolks with sugar. Gradually add the hot milk in a thin drizzle, stirring briskly with an egg-whisk. Pour hot water into the bottom pot of the double boiler. Beat egg yolk mixture until it thickens. Keep the water near boiling point, but do not let it boil. Add the butter piece by piece, stirring constantly. Add the salt and vanilla. Pour the sauce over the omelet and bake.

Note: The sauce is for 4 omelets.

SWEET OMELET II

2 eggs, 1 tablespoon sour cream, milk or water, 2—2 2/3 oz. orange jam, 1 oz. pickled plums, 1/3 oz. raisins, fat, salt to taste

Sauce: 2/3 cup dry red wine, lemon rind, cinnamon, cloves, sugar, 2/3 oz. raisins, 1 level teaspoon potato starch

Pit the plums and cut them into strips. Combine with the jam and rinsed raisins. Make the omelet (as in Natural Omelet). When it fries on the bottom, spread the filling on it and fold both sides towards the centre with a spatula. Transfer to a greased oven-proof platter. Add sugar and spices to the wine and bring to a boil, then strain. Blend the potato starch with a small amount of cold water and add in a thin drizzle to the hot wine, stirring briskly with an egg-whisk. Bring to a boil and add the rinsed raisins. Pour over the omelet and bake.

Notes: The sauce is for 4 omelets.

SPECIAL OMELET I

3 egg whites, 1 oz. confectioners' sugar, 2/3 oz. almonds, 1/2 tablespoon flour, fat, salt and lemon rind to taste

Blanch the almonds and grind them. Beat the egg whites until stiff along with the salt, adding the sugar towards the end. Gently stir in the almonds, sifted flour and grated lemon rind. Pour into heated fat in a frying pan and smooth out the surface. Place in a hot oven and bake. Serve sprinkled with confectioners' sugar.

SPECIAL OMELET II

2 eggs, 1 oz. confectioners' sugar, 5 oz. apples, 1/3—2/3 oz. butter, 1 oz. sugar, 1 tablespoon dry white wine, 1 tablespoon Maraschino liqueur, 1/2 talbespoon flour, 1/3—2/3 oz. chocolate, fat, salt to taste

Wash, peel and halve the apples, removing the cores. Cut into slices. Add the wine, butter and sugar. Fry lightly until translucent. Wash the eggs and break them. Separate the yolks from the whites. Blend the egg yolks with the sugar. Combine with the liqueur and stiffly beaten egg whites, adding the flour alternately. Pour into heated fat in a frying pan and smooth out the surface. Place in a hot oven and bake. Spread the filling on the omelet and fold it. Sprinkle with grated chocolate and serve at once.

APPLE SOUFFLÉ

1 lb. apples, 5 egg yolks, 2 oz. confectioners' sugar for egg yolks, 1 1/3 oz. butter, 1/3 oz. flour for egg yolks, 2 egg whites, 1/6 oz. flour for egg whites, 1 oz. confectioners' sugar, vanilla extract

Wash, peel and halve the apples, removing the cores. Grate the apples coarsely and combine with the flour and butter blended with the sugar and egg yolks. Transfer to a dish and cover with stiffly beaten egg whites blended with flour and sugar, then bake.

APRICOT SOUFFLÉ

3 1/2 oz. apricot jam, 1/2 lb. stewed apricots, 2 egg yolks, 1 1/3 oz. almonds, 3—4 egg whites, 1 1/3 oz. confectioners' sugar, fat

Cut the apricots in halves and remove the pits. Arrange on a greased oven-proof platter. Blanch the almonds and grind them. Heat the jam and combine it with the egg yolks. Pour over the aprictos. Sprinkle with the almonds. Decorate with egg whites stiffly beaten with sugar and bake.

PRUNE SOUFFLÉ

7 oz. prunes, 5 oz. almonds, 2—3 egg whites, 2—2 2/3 oz. confectioners' sugar, lemon juice, 4 egg whites, 1 2/3 oz. confectioners' sugar

Wash and soak the prunes. Cook them and force through a strainer. Blanch the almonds and grind them. Blend with the egg whites and sugar. Sprinkle with lemon juice and transfer to a greased pan. Smooth out the surface and dry the mixture in an oven. Beat the egg whites until stiff, adding confectioners' sugar towards the end. Combine with the prune paste, arrange on the prepared mixture and bake. Take out of the oven and serve at once.

WHOLE-WHEAT BREAD SOUFFLÉ

3 1/2 oz. grated whole-wheat bread, 1 2/3 oz. butter, 4 eggs, 1 2/3 oz. confectioners' sugar for egg yolks, 1 oz. confectioners' sugar for egg whites, 1 oz. raisins, 1/3 cup dry white wine, 1 1/3 oz. cocoa, cinnamon, cloves, fat and breadcrumbs

Combine the bread with the wine and allow to soak for 10 minutes. Blend the butter with the sugar, adding the egg yolks one by one. Combine with cocoa, ground spices, rinsed raisins, bread and stiffly beaten egg whites with sugar. Transfer to a greased pan sprinkled with breadcrumbs and bake.

FARINA SOUFFLÉ

1 2/3 oz. farina, 2 1/2 oz. farmer's cheese, 3 1/2 oz. apples, 4 eggs, 1 2/3 oz. confectioners' sugar, salt, ground cinnamon, fat and breadcrumbs

Wash, peel and halve the apples, removing the cores. Grate finely and combine with minced farmer's cheese, egg yolks blended with sugar, stiffly beaten egg whites, alternately adding farina, then season. Transfer to a greased pan sprinkled with breadcrumbs and bake.

FARMER'S CHEESE SOUFFLÉ

7 oz. farmer's cheese, 1 2/3 oz. butter or margarine, 4 eggs, 1 2/3 oz. raisins, 1 2/3 oz. breadcrumbs, 1 2/3 oz. confectioners' sugar, 1 teaspoon baking powder, 1 teaspoon vanilla extract, fat and breadcrumbs for pan

Grease the pan and sprinkle with breadcrumbs. Blend the butter with the sugar, egg yolks and minced farmer's cheese. Combine with rinsed raisins, vanilla extract and baking powder. Stir lightly with stiffly beaten egg whites, alternately adding breadcrumbs. Fold the mixture into the pan and bake for around 50 minutes in a moderate oven. When done remove from the pan. Pour red wine sauce over the soufflé and serve at once.

VANILLA PUDDING

3 1/2 oz. flour, 1 2/3 oz. butter, 3 1/2 oz. confectioners' sugar, 5 eggs, 1 cup milk, 1 2/3 oz. raisins, vanilla bean to taste, fat and breadcrumbs

Bring the milk, butter and finely ground vanilla to a boil. Add flour and stir with a wooden spoon until smooth. Remove the batter from heat. Add the egg yolks one by one and sugar, stirring constantly. Stir lightly with stiffly beaten egg whites and rinsed raisins. Transfer to a greased pan sprinkled with breadcrumbs. Cover tightly and cook for around 50 minutes in water. When done remove from the pan and sprinkle with vanilla sugar.

WALNUT PUDDING

3 1/2 oz. walnut meats, 1 2/3 oz. breadcrumbs, 1 2/3 oz. butter, 4 eggs, 1 2/3 oz. confectioners' sugar, lemon rind and orange rind to taste, fat and breadcrumbs for pan

Blanch the walnuts and grind them. Blend the butter with the sugar, egg yolks, grated lemon and orange rinds. Stir lightly with stiffly beaten egg whites, alternately adding breadcrumbs and walnuts. Grease the pan and sprinkle with breadcrumbs. Fold in the mixture and close tightly. Cook in water for around 60 minutes. Remove the pudding from the pan when done and cooled.

Cereals,
Noodles,
Patties

DRY ROASTED BUCKWHEAT KASHA

7 oz. buckwheat kasha, 1 2/3 cups water, 2/3 oz. fat, 1/2 egg white, salt

Sift the kasha and clean of unnecessary particles. Pour into a pan and combine with the egg white. Dry in a moderate oven stirring often. Add fat and kasha to boiling salted water and bring to a boil, stirring. Cover it and keep in a moderate oven for two hours, stirring with a fork from time to time. Instead of roasting the kasha in an oven it can be cooked in a double boiler, adding water as needed to the lower pan.

BUCKWHEAT KASHA WITH FARMER'S CHEESE

1/2 lb. buckwheat kasha, 2 cups water, 2/3 oz. fat, 1/2 egg white, 3 1/2 oz. onions, fat for onions, 1/2 lb. farmer's cheese, 2/3 cup sour cream (thick), fat and breadcrumbs for pan, salt, pepper to taste

Make the kasha (as above). Peel, rinse and dice the onions. Fry them and combine with minced farmer's cheese and kasha. Season to taste. Transfer the kasha into a greased oven-proof pan sprinkled with breadcrumbs. Smooth out the surafce. Pour seasoned sour cream over this and bake.

FARMER'S BUCKWHEAT KASHA

7 oz. buckwheat kasha, 1 2/3 cups meat stock, 1/2 egg white, 1/2 lb. potatoes, 7 oz. apples, 3 1/2 oz. pork fat, 2 2/3 oz. onions, fat and bread-crumbs for pan, salt, pepper and marjoram to taste

Make the kasha (as in Dry Roasted Buckwheat Kasha). Wash, peel and rinse the potatoes. Cover them with boiling salted water and cook covered. Drain and allow the water to evaporate. Wash, peel and halve the apples, removing the cores. Cut them into pieces. Peel, rinse and dice the onions together with the pork fat. Render the pork fat down partly. Add the onions and fry them. Combine with the kasha, minced potatoes

and apples. Season to taste. Transfer the kasha to a greased oven-proof pan sprinkled with breadcrumbs. Even out the surface and bake.

DRY ROASTED PEARL BARLEY

7 oz. pearl barley, ca. 1 2/3 cups water, 1 oz. fat, salt

Rinse, strain and drain the kasha. Pour it into boiling salted water with fat. Stir, then bring to a boil, stirring constantly. Cover and cook in the top of a double boiler for around 2 hours. Add water to the lower pan as necessary.

PEARL BARLEY WITH MUSHROOMS

7 oz. pearl barley, ca. 1 2/3 cups water, 1 oz. fat, 1 2/3 oz. dried cèpe mushrooms, 1/3 cup sour cream, 2 egg yolks, 3 1/2 oz. hard cheese, 3 tablespoons ketchup, fat, breadcrumbs, salt and pepper to taste

Make the kasha (as above). Wash, soak and cook the mushrooms. Mince them and combine with the kasha. Season to taste. Transfer to a greased oven-proof pan sprinkled with breadcrumbs. Even out the surface. Pour sour cream blended with egg yolks over this. Sprinkle with grated cheese and ketchup, then bake.

CAPTAIN'S PEARL BARLEY

7 oz. pearl barley, ca. 1 2/3 cups water, 1 oz. fat, 5 oz. smoked bacon, 3 1/2 oz. onions, 1 2/3 oz. tomato paste, 1 2/3 oz. hard cheese, fat and breadcrumbs, salt and pepper to taste

Make the kasha (as in Dry Roasted Pearl Barley). Peel, rinse and chop the onions finely. Dice the bacon and render it down partly. Add the onions and fry them lightly. Combine with tomato paste and simmer for a while. Combine with the kasha and season to taste. Transfer to

a greased oven-proof pan sprinkled with breadcrumbs. Smooth out the surface, sprinkle with grated cheese and bake.

PEARL BARLEY DOMINICAN STYLE

7 oz. pearl barley, ca. 1 2/3 cups water, 1 oz. fat, 7 oz. roasted chicken, 5 oz. mushrooms, 3 1/2 oz. prunes, fat for mushrooms, 1 2/3 oz. hard cheese, fat and breadcrumbs, salt, pepper and lemon juice to taste

Make the kasha (as in Dry Roasted Pearl Barley). Clean and rinse the mushrooms. Cut them into slices and fry them. Wash and soak the prunes. Cook them and force through a strainer. Combine with finely chopped chicken meat. Season to taste. Grease an oven-proof dish and sprinkle with breadcrumbs. Arrange in layers: kasha, mushrooms, kasha, chicken meat and kasha. Sprinkle with grated cheese and bake.

PEARL BARLEY OLD POLISH STYLE

7 oz. pearl barley, ca. 1 2/3 cups water, 1 oz. fat, 7 oz. white beans, 3 1/2 oz. onions, 1 oz. fat, 5 oz. kiełbasa, 1 1/3 oz. tomato paste, 2/3 cup thick sour cream, fat and breadcrumbs for pan, salt, pepper, marjoram and seasoning to taste

Make the kasha (as in Dry Roasted Pearl Barley). Sort the beans and rinse them. Cover with cold water and bring to a boil. Set aside for 2 hours. Cook in the same water. Peel, rinse and dice the onions. Fry them and combine with the beans, tomato paste and strips of kiełbasa. Season to taste. Transfer the seasoned kasha to a greased pan sprinkled with breadcrumbs, making a layer of beans in the middle. Smooth out the surface. Pour sour cream over this and bake.

ROYAL BUCKWHEAT GROATS

7 oz. buckwheat groats, ca. 1 1/4 cups milk, 2 egg yolks, 1 2/3 oz. butter, 3 1/2 oz. sour cherry preserves, 1 2/3 oz. raisins, 2—2 2/3 oz. sugar, vanilla bean, salt

Sift the kasha and pour into a dish or a pan. Combine with egg yolks and dry in an oven, stirring often to prevent burning. Pour the cooled kasha into boiling milk with butter. Place in a larger pan with hot water and cook for 30—40 minutes. Add water when necessary to the lower pan. When cooked combine the kasha with sugar, rinsed raisins, sour cherry preserves and finely chopped vanilla bean. Add salt and mix thoroughly. Place in a moderate oven for 5 minutes.

BUCKWHEAT GROATS À LA KRZESZOWICE

7 oz. buckwheat groats, ca. 1 1/4 cups milk, 1 1/3 oz. butter, 1/2 egg white, 3/4 lb. apples, 1 1/3 oz. butter for apples, 2—2 2/3 oz. sugar, 2 egg yolks, 1 1/2 tablespoons banana liqueur, salt sugar for pan

Make the kasha (as in Royal Buckwheat Groats). Wash, peel and halve the apples, removing the cores. Grate coarsely and fry in butter, stirring constantly. Allow to cool lightly. Combine with egg yolks blended with sugar and liqueur, then add salt. Transfer the kasha to a pan rinsed in cold water and sprinkled with sugar, making a layer of the above mixture in the middle. Smooth out the surface and bake.

EDITOR'S FARINA

7 oz. farina, ca. 1 2/3 cups milk, 1 1/3 oz. butter, egg, 5 oz. dried peaches or apricots, 1/2 lb. bananas, 2 2/3—3 1/2 oz. confectioners' sugar, 3 tablespoons Cherry Cordial, 2/3—1 1/3 oz. butter for basting, salt, breadcrumbs for pan

Soak the peaches or apricots. Cook in a small amount of water and force through a strainer. Sift the kasha and pour into a dish or a pan. Combine with the egg and dry in an oven, stirring often to prevent burning. Add butter to boiling milk. Add cooled kasha and stir. Bring to a boil and cover. Place the dish with the kasha in a larger pan with boiling water and cook for around 40 minutes. Add water to the lower pan when necessary. Combine the kasha with the peaches and transfer to a greased

pan sprinkled with breadcrumbs. Wash the bananas and cut them into slices. Sprinkle with sugar and pour the Cherry Cordial over this. Set aside for an hour. Place this on the kasha. Baste with butter and bake.

GENERAL'S FARINA

7 oz. farina, ca. 1 2/3 cups milk, 3 tablespoons Maraschino liqueur, egg, 1/2 lb. bananas, 2 egg yolks, 3 1/2 oz. confectioners' sugar, 2/3 cup whipping cream, 1 oz. confectioners' sugar for cream, salt and vanilla extract to taste, fat and breadcrumbs for pan

Make the kasha (as above). Wash and peel the bananas. Place in a blender together with the sugar and vanilla extract. Turn on the blender for 30 seconds. Combine bananas with the kasha and season to taste. Transfer to a greased pan sprinkled with breadcrumbs. Smooth out the surface and bake. Allow to cool and surround with whipped cream with sugar.

FARINA DESSERT

7 oz. farina, ca. 3 tablespoons milk. 1 1/3 oz. butter, egg. 1 oz. powdered chocolate, 1 2/3 oz. raisins, 1 2/3 oz. figs, 1 2/3 oz. dates, 1 2/3 oz. walnut meats, 3 1/2 oz. confectioners' sugar, salt and vanilla extract to taste, fat and breadcrumbs for pan

Make the farina (as in Editor's Farina). Blanch the walnuts and chop together with the figs and dates. Combine with rinsed raisins and sugar. Combine with the kasha. Transfer to a greased pan sprinkled with breadcrumbs and even out the surface. Sprinkle with chocolate and bake.

RICE WITH HAM

1/2 lb. rice, 2 cups poultry stock, 4 eggs, 3 1/2 oz. ham or kiełbasa, 3 1/2 oz. canned peas, 3 1/2 oz. hard cheese, salt and pepper to taste, fat and breadcrumbs for pan

Rinse the rice and cover it with the stock. Stir, cover and cook this. Season and transfer to a greased pan sprinkled with breadcrumbs. Smooth out the surface and surround with the peas and strips of ham. Sprinkle with seasoning. Pour beaten eggs over this. Sprinkle with grated cheese and bake.

RICE OLD POLISH STYLE

1/2 lb. rice, 2 cups poultry stock, 3 1/2 oz. prunes, 2 2/3 oz. dried cèpe mushrooms, 1/3 cup sour cream, egg yolk, parsley sprigs, salt, pepper and lemon juice to taste, fat and breadcrumbs for pan

Rinse the rice and cover with stock. Stir, cover and cook this. Wash the mushrooms and prunes. Soak in separate dishes and cook them. Dice them, combine with the rice and season. Transfer to a greased pan sprinkled with breadcrumbs and even out the surface. Over this pour sour cream combined with the egg yolk, chopped parsley sprigs and seasoning, then bake.

CASTELLAN'S RICE

1/2 lb. rice, 2 cups poultry stock, 1 lb. carrots, 1/3 cup sour cream, egg yolk, 1 2/3 oz. raisins, 5 oz. farmer's cheese, salt, pepper and sugar to taste, fat and breadcrumbs for pan

Rinse the rice and cover it with stock. Stir, cover and cook this. Wash, peel and rinse the carrots. Cover with boiling salted water and cook. Allow to cool and mash the carrots. Combine with the sour cream, egg yolk and rinsed raisins. Season to taste. Arrange the rice in a greased pan sprinkled with breadcrumbs, making a layer of carrots in the middle. Sprinkle with grated cheese and bake.

RICE MASURIAN STYLE

1/2 lb. rice, 2 cups water or meat stock, 1/2 lb. smoked bacon (cooked), 1/2 lb. prunes, 2 2/3 oz. hard cheese, salt, pepper and lemon juice to taste, fat and breadcrumbs for pan

Rinse the rice and cover it with boiling water. Stir, cover and cook for 15 minutes, then season. Wash and soak the prunes. Remove the pits and cook the prunes, then sprinkle with lemon juice. Grease a pan and sprinkle it with breadcrumbs. Arrange the rice in it alternating with strips of bacon and prunes. Even out the surface, sprinkle with grated cheese and bake.

RICE WITH RAISINS

7 oz. rice, 1 2/3 cups milk, 1 1/3 oz. butter, vanilla bean, salt, 3 1/2 oz. raisins, 3—4 egg yolks, 1 2/3 oz. butter for egg yolks, 2—2 2/3 oz. confectioners' sugar, 1 tablespoon Maraschino liqueur

Rinse the rice in warm water, strain and drain it. Cover with plenty of boiling water. Cook for 2 minutes, strain and drain it. Cover with boiling milk. Add rinsed raisins, butter, finely chopped vanilla bean and salt. Stir, cover and cook for around 20 minutes over low heat. Blend the butter and sugar, adding the egg yolks one by one. Combine with the liqueur and cooled rice. Transfer to a pan that has been rinsed with cold water. Even out the surface and allow to cool. Before serving place the pan in hot water for several seconds. Transfer the rice to a platter and garnish.

RICE WITH APPLES

7 oz. rice, 1 2/3 cups milk, 3/4 lb. apples, 3 egg yolks, 1 1/3 oz. butter, 1 2/3 oz. confectioners' sugar, vanilla bean, lemon juice to taste

Sauce: 1 cup milk, 3—4 egg yolks, 2—2 2/3 oz. confectioners' sugar, 1 oz. butter, vanilla bean

Rinse the rice in warm water and strain it. Cover with plenty of boiling water. Cook for 2 minutes and strain. Cover with boiling milk and stir. Add butter, finely chopped vanilla bean and salt. Cook covered over low heat for around 20 minutes. Sauce: Bring the milk to a boil together with finely chopped vanilla bean and strain. Blend the egg yolks with the sugar. Gradually add the hot milk in a thin drizzle, stirring with an egg-whisk. Place the dish with the egg yolks in a larger pan with boiling water and heat, stirring constantly until the sauce thickens. Keep the water in the pan near boiling point, but do not let it boil. When the sauce thickens remove from heat and add the butter piece by piece. Combine with the rice. Wash, peel and rinse the apples. Halve them, removing the cores. Grate them coarsely and combine with egg yolks blended with the sugar and lemon juice. Rinse the pan with cold water. Arrange the rice in it alternately with the apples. Smooth the surface and set aside to cool. Before serving place the pan in hot water for several seconds. Transfer the rice to a platter.

BASIC BLINY

3/4 lb. flour, 2 2/3 cups milk, 1 2/3 oz. butter or margarine, 2 eggs, 1 oz. yeast, 1/3 oz. sugar, fat for frying, salt to taste

Blend the milk (1/3 cup) with the yeast mixed with sugar and flour (1/3 oz.) and let this rise. Combine with the remaining milk, sifted flour and egg yolks. Add salt and knead well. Combine the dough with melted butter, then with stiffly beaten egg whites. Let this rise. Grease 5 1/2 in. skillets and place 1/2 in. thick pieces of the dough in them. Fry on both sides or bake in a hot oven. When done pour melted butter over and serve at once.

BLINY LITHUANIAN STYLE

7 oz. wheat flour, 7 oz. buckwheat flour, 2 2/3 cups milk, 1 1/3 oz. yeast, 1 2/3 oz. butter or margarine, 3 eggs, 2/3 oz. confectioners' sugar, fat for frying, salt to taste

Blend milk (1/3 cup) with the yeast mixed witth sugar and wheat flour (1/3 oz.) and let this rise. Combine with the eggs, the remaining sifted flour and milk. Knead well. Towards the end add melted butter and salt. Proceed as in Basic Bliny.

BEER BLINY

3/4 lb. flour, bottle of lager beer, 5—6 eggs, fat for frying, salt to taste

Wash the eggs and break them, separating the yolks from the whites. Beat the yolks until light in color. Combine with the beer, alternately adding sifted flour. Add salt and combine with stiffly beaten egg whites. Proceed as in Basic Bliny.

FARMER'S BLINY

1 lb. potatoes, 5 oz. buckwheat flour, 5 oz. farmer's cheese, 1 cup milk, 3—4 eggs, fat for frying, salt and pepper to taste

Wash, peel and rinse the potatoes. Cover with boiling salted water until 3/4 covered. Cook covered. Strain and allow the water to evaporate. When cooled mash together with the farmer's cheese. Combine with the flour, milk, egg yolks and stiffly beaten egg whites. Season to taste. Proceed as in Basic Bliny.

PEASANT'S BLINY

1 1/2 lb. potatoes, 5 oz. hardened French bread, 1 cup sour cream, 3 eggs, 1 oz. yeast, 1/3 oz. sugar, 1 2/3 oz. flour, fat for frying, salt to taste

Wash, peel and rinse the potatoes. Grate them finely. Cut the bread into cubes. Combine with the potatoes, sour cream, egg yolks and yeast blended with sugar. Add salt and combine with stiffly beaten egg whites. Allow to rise. Proceed as in Basic Bliny.

BASIC NOODLES

3/4 lb. flour, 2/3 cup — 3/4 cup water, 2 eggs, 2/3 oz. fat, salt to taste

Sift the flour into a bowl. Add the eggs, water and salt. Blend thoroughly and knead with a spoon. All these ingredients may be put in a blender and blended for 30 seconds. Drop long noodles from a metal spoon into boiling salted water with fat. Stir so that they do not cling to the bottom and cook covered. Strain and pour boiling water over them. Drain on a strainer. Serve with sauces or butter and sugar. They may also be sprinkled with grated farmer's cheese.

CHEESE NOODLES

1/3 lb. flour, 1 cup milk, 1 2/3 oz. butter or margarine, 3 1/2 oz. hard cheese, 4 eggs, 2/3 oz. fat for cooking, 1 1/3 oz. butter for basting, salt

Bring the milk to a boil together with the butter. Add sifted flour and stir. Add the eggs one by one, kneading well. Towards the end add grated cheese and salt. Set aside in a cool place for an hour. Shape into long noodles with a metal spoon and drop into boiling salted water with fat. Cook, strain and pour butter over.

CAPTAIN'S NOODLES

1/2 lb. flour, 1 cup milk, 1 2/3 oz. butter or margarine, 3 1/2 oz. ham, 1 1/3 oz. almonds, 3 eggs, fat for cooking, salt and pepper to taste

Blanch the almonds and grind them. Bring the milk to a boil together with the butter. Add sifted flour and knead well until it does not stick to the sides. Combine with the almonds, minced ham, stiffly beaten egg whites and seasoning. Shape long noodles with a metal spoon and drop into boiling salted water with fat. Bring to a boil and strain. Serve with melted butter or Béchamel Sauce.

PUFFS À LA HENRY

Dough: 7 oz. flour, ca. 1 1/4 cups water, 3 1/2 oz. butter or margarine, 5 eggs, salt to taste

Filling: 7 oz. poultry pâté, 3 1/2 oz. mushrooms, 2/3 oz. fat, 1/2 can sardines

Sauce: 1 oz. butter or margarine, 2/3 oz. flour, 1 cup milk, egg yolk, 1 2/3 oz. hard cheese, salt and nutmeg to taste

Bring the water to a boil together with the butter and salt. Add sifted flour, remove from heat and break down all lumps. Place over heat again and heat lightly, stirring until smooth and shiny. Remove the pot and allow the dough to cool lightly. Add eggs one by one, kneading well. Grease a cookie sheet and press the dough onto it through a pastry bag, makking small puffs. Bake in a hot oven for around 10 minutes. If taken out of the oven too quickly they fall easily. Clean and rinse the mushrooms. Chop them finely and fry them. Allow to cool and mince together with the pâté and sardines. Season to taste. Cut the puffs in half and put in the filling. Join the halves and arrange on a pan. Heat the fat and blend with the flour. Fry without browning. Gradually add hot milk, stirring briskly with an egg-whisk. Bring to a boil and combine with egg yolks. Season and pour over the puffs. Sprinkle with grated cheese and bake.

MUSHROOM NOODLES

Dough; 7 oz. flour, ca. 1 1/4 cups water, 3 1/2 oz. butter or margarine, 5 eggs, salt to taste.

Filling: 1 1/3 oz. dried mushrooms, 2/3 oz. fat for cooking, 1 1/3 oz. butter for puffs, 1/3 oz. breadcrumbs

Make the dough (as above). Wash, soak and cook the mushrooms. Mince them or chop them finely. Combine with the dough. Drop long noodles from a metal spoon into boiling salted water with fat and cook covered. Strain the noodles and divide into portions. Pour browned breadcrumbs blended with melted butter over.

Note: The noodles may also be cooked without mushrooms.

ROBBER'S NOODLES

1 1/4 lb. potatoes, 1 oz. breadcrumbs, 3 hard-boiled eggs, 3 1/2 oz. onions, fat for onions, 2 eggs, 5 oz. flour, parsley sprigs, 2/3 oz. fat for cooking, 1 1/3 oz. butter for noodles, salt and pepper to taste

Wash, peel and rinse the potatoes. Cover with boiling salted water and cook, then strain and allow the water to evaporate. Peel, rinse and chop the onions finely. Fry them and allow to cool. Mince together with the potatoes and eggs. Combine with sifted flour, breadcrumbs, eggs and chopped parsley sprigs. Season to taste. With a metal spoon shape into long noodles and drop into boiling salted water with fat. Cook and strain them. Divide into portions and pour butter over. Serve at once.

NOODLES SILESIAN STYLE

2 1/2 lb. potatoes, 2 oz. potato starch, 1 2/3 wheat flour, 2 eggs, fat for cooking, salt to taste

Wash, peel and rinse the potatoes. Cover with boiling salted water. Cook and strain. Allow the water to evaporate, cool and mash. Combine with sifted flour, starch and eggs. Knead the dough quickly. Make into noodles 1—1 1/3 oz. each. Cook a few at a time in boiling salted water with fat. When done remove with a special spoon and strain. Pour butter or pork fat cracklings over the noodles.

POTATO NOODLES

1 3/4 lb. potatoes, 3 tablespoons sour cream, 3 1/2 oz. flour, 3 eggs, 1 1/3 oz. butter or margarine, 1 oz. yeast, fat for frying, salt and pepper to taste

Wash, peel and rinse the potatoes. Cover with boiling salted water and cook, then drain and allow the water to evaporate. When cool mash them and combine with yeast blended with the sour cream, sifted flour, eggs

and melted butter, then season. Shape into long noodles with a metal spoon and drop into hot fat to fry. Take out with a special spoon and drain of fat. Serve at once.

BELVEDERE DUMPLINGS

1/2 lb. flour, 1 2/3 oz. butter or margarine, 3 eggs, 3 1/2 oz. ham or kieł-basa, 2/3 oz. fat for cooking, salt to taste

Wash the eggs and break them. Separate the yolks from the whites. Blend the yolks with butter. Combine with sifted flour, finely chopped ham and stiffly beaten egg whites. Add salt. Shape into round dumplings and drop into boiling salted water with fat. Cook them, then remove with a spoon and drain. Divide into portions and pour butter over. Serve at once.

ZAKOPANE DUMPLINGS

1 1/4 lb. potatoes, 3 1/2 oz. bryndza (a soft sheep's cheese), 2 2/3 oz. onions, fat for onions, 5 oz. flour, 2 eggs, 1 1/3 oz. butter for top, 1/3 oz. breadcrumbs, salt and pepper

Wash, peel and rinse the potatoes. Cover with boiling salted water and cook, then drain and allow the water to evaporate. When cool mince together with the bryndza. Peel, rinse and chop the onions finely. Fry them and combine with the potatoes, eggs, and sifted flour, then season. Drop from a metal spoon into boiling salted water and cook. Take them out with a spoon. Blend melted butter with browned breadcrumbs and pour over the dumplings.

ZIĘBICE DUMPLINGS

1/2 lb. breadcrumbs, 2/3 cup sour cream, 2 eggs, 1 1/3 oz. butter or margarine, 1 2/3 oz. hard cheese, 3 1/2 oz. kiełbasa, 2 2/3 oz. onions, 1 2/3 oz. flour, salt

Peel, rinse and chop the onions finely. Fry them and blend with bread-crumbs, sour cream, grated cheese, minced kiełbasa, egg yolks and stiffly beaten egg whites, then season. Shape into round dumplings and roll them in flour. Drop into boiling salted water and cook. When done take them out and drain them. Pour pork fat cracklings over the dumplings.

YEAST DUMPLINGS

1/2 lb. flour, 1 cup milk, 1—2 eggs, 1 1/3 oz. butter or margarine, 2/3 oz. yeast, 2/3 oz. fat for cooking, 1 1/3 oz. butter for top, bread-crumbs, salt

Add crumbled yeast to warm milk together with eggs, sifted flour, melted butter and salt. Knead well, until the dough becomes smooth and shiny. Set aside to let it rise. Shape into long dumplings with a metal spoon and drop them into boiling salted water with fat. Cook and take them out with a special spoon. Blend browned breadcrumbs with melt-ed butter and pour over the dumplings. Serve at once.

POTATO DUMPLINGS WITH MEAT

Dough: 2 lb. potatoes, 1/2 lb. flour, egg, salt to taste
Filling: 3/4 lb. boneless beef, 7 oz. soup vegetables (carrots, parsley root, celeriac, leek), 3 1/2 oz. onions, 2/3 oz. fat, egg, salt and pepper to taste, 1 1/3 oz. butter or margarine for top, 2/3 oz. breadcrumbs

Wash the meat and cover with boiling salted water. Cook, adding cleaned and rinsed vegetables towards the end. Peel, rinse and chop the onions finely. Fry them and combine with minced meat. Season to taste. Wash, peel and rinse the potatoes. Cover with boiling salted water and cook them. Drain and allow the water to evaporate. Cool and mash them. Com-bine with sifted flour and egg. Add salt and quickly knead the dough. Di-vide into parts and shape into 1/2—2 in. thick rolls. Cut into pieces and flatten. Place the filling on each piece and shape into balls. Drop into

boiling salted water. When done take out with a spoon and drain. Pour browned breadcrumbs blended with butter over the dumplings.

Note: Do not store the dough too long as it tends to become thin quickly and dissolves during cooking.

WROCŁAW POTATO DUMPLINGS I

Dough: 2 lb. potatoes, 1/2 lb. flour, egg, salt to taste
Filling: 1/2 lb. hard cheese, 5 oz. smoked ham or kiełbasa, sat, pepper and ketchup to taste, 1 1/3 oz. butter or margarine for top, 2/3 oz. breadcrumbs

Grate the cheese finely and combine with ground ham and ketchup. Season to taste. Continue as above.

WROCŁAW POTATO DUMPLINGS II

Dough: 2 lb. potatoes, 1/2 lb. flour, egg, salt to taste
Filling: 5 oz. mushrooms, 2 2/3 oz. onions, 7 oz. boneless pork or veal, 1 1/3 oz. fat, 2 2/3 oz. hard cheese, salt and pepper to taste, 1 1/3 oz. butter or margarine for top, 2/3 oz. breadcrumbs

Clean, rinse and chop the onions and mushrooms finely. Fry them together with the minced meat. Sprinkle with water and simmer until tender. Allow to cool and combine with finely grated cheese. Season to taste. Continue as in Potato Dumplings with Meat.

POTATO DUMPLINGS WITH MUSHROOMS

Dough: 2 lb. potatoes, 1/2 lb. flour, egg, salt to taste
Filling: 3 1/2 oz. dried cèpe mushrooms, 3 1/2 oz. onions, 2/3 oz. fat, egg yolk, salt and pepper to taste, 1 1/3 oz. butter or margarine for top, 2/3 oz. breadcrumbs

Wash and soak the mushrooms, then cook and mince them. Peel, rinse and chop the onions finely. Fry them and combine with the mushrooms and egg yolk. Season to taste. Proceed as in Potato Dumplings with Meat.

POTATO DUMPLINGS WITH ONIONS

Dough: 2 lb. potatoes, 1/2 lb. flour, egg, salt to taste
Filling: 3 1/2 oz. onions, 1 oz. fat, 2 2/3 oz. hard cheese, egg yolk, salt and pepper to taste, 3 1/2 oz. pork fat for cracklings

Peel, rinse and dice the onions. Fry them and allow to cool. Combine with grated cheese and egg yolk. Season to taste. Proceed as in Potato Dumplings with Meat.

POTATO DUMPLINGS LITHUANIAN STYLE I

Dough: 2 lb. potatoes, 5 oz. flour, 3 1/2 oz. farina, egg, salt to taste
Filling: 3/4 lb. sauerkraut, 1 1/3 oz. dried mushrooms, 2 2/3 oz. onions, 2/3 oz. fat, salt, pepper and caraway seed to taste, 5 oz. pork fat for cracklings

Drain the sauerkraut of juice. Cover with water and cook. Wash and soak the mushrooms, then cook and mince them. Peel, rinse and dice the onions. Fry them and combine with sauerkraut and mushrooms. Season to taste. Wash, peel and rinse the potatoes. Cover with boiling salted water and cook. Drain them and allow the water to evaporate. Cool and mash, then combine with farina. Set aside for 20 minutes. Combine with flour and eggs, then season. Proceed as in Potato Dumplings with Meat.

POTATO DUMPLINGS LITHUANIAN STYLE II

Dough: 2 lb. potatoes, 5 oz. hardened French bread, 7 oz. flour, 2 eggs, parsley sprigs, salt to taste

Filling: 3 1/2 oz. buckwheat kasha, 1 1/3 oz. dried cèpe mushrooms, 2 2/3 oz. onions, fat for onions, 3 1/2 oz. pork fat for cracklings, salt

Sort the kasha and rinse it. Cover with boiling salted water (3/4 cup) and bring to a boil, stirring. Place kasha on top of a double boiler and cook. Wash, soak and cook the mushrooms. Take them out and mince them. Peel, rinse and chop the onions finely. Fry them and combine with the kasha and mushrooms, then season. Wash, peel and rinse the potatoes. 3/4 cover with boiling water. Cook and drain them, then allow the water to evaporate. Mash them and combine with bread cubes, eggs, flour and chopped parsley sprigs, then season. Proceed as in Potato Dumplings with Meat.

POTATO DUMPLINGS WITH PLUMS

Dough: 2 lb. potatoes, 1/2 lb. flour, egg, salt to taste
Filling: 1 lb. fruit, 1 1/3 oz. butter, breadcrumbs, salt and sugar to taste

Wash, peel and rinse the potatoes. Cover with boiling water and cook covered. Drain and allow to cool. Mince the potatoes and combine with sifted flour and egg, then add salt. Knead the dough and divide into parts. Shape into a 1/2 in. thick roll. Cut into pieces and flatten. Place some of the fruit on each piece and shape into balls. Cook in boiling salted water. Take out when done and sprinkle with sugar, then pour browned breadcrumbs blended with butter over the dumplings.

POTATO DUMPLINGS WITH PLUMS OR PEACHES

Dough: 2 lb. potatoes, 7 oz. farmer's cheese, 1/2 lb. flour, 2 eggs
Filling: 1 3/4 lb. fruit, 1 1/3 oz. butter, breadcrumbs, salt and sugar to taste

Wash the fruit and remove pits. Divide into pieces. Wash, peel and rinse the potatoes. Cover with boiling salted water and cook. Drain and allow to cool. Mince together with the farmer's cheese. Combine with sifted flour and eggs, then add salt. Proceed as above.

POTATO DUMPLINGS WITH STRAWBERRIES

Dough: 2 lb. potatoes, 1/2 lb. flour, egg, salt
Filling: 1 lb. strawberries, 1 1/3 oz. breadcrumbs for fruit, 1 1/3 oz.
butter, breadcrumbs for top, sugar

Sort the strawberries and rinse them. Discard the stems and sprinkle
with breadcrubms. Proceed as in Potato Dumplings with Plums or Peaches.

DUMPLINGS WITH STRAWBERRIES

Dough: 7 oz. flour, 3 1/2 oz. breadcrumbs, 1/2 cup milk, 1 2/3 oz. but-
ter, 3 egg yolks, salt, flour as needed
Filling: 1 lb. strawberries, 1 1/3 oz. breadcrumbs, 1 1/3 oz. butter for
top, breadcrumbs for top, sugar

Sort the strawberries and rinse them. Discard the stems and sprinkle
with breadcrumbs. Blend the butter with the egg yolks and combine with
breadcrumbs, sifted flour and milk. Add salt and knead the dough. Shape
into balls on a pastry board sprinkled with flour. Place some of the fruit
inside each ball. Cook in boiling salted water. Take them out when done
and drain. Pour browned breadcrumbs blended with melted butter over
the dumplings and sprinkle with sugar.

DUMPLINGS WITH CHEESE

Dough: 13 1/2 oz. farmer's cheese, 2 2/3 oz. farina, 3 1/2 oz. flour,
egg, salt
Filling: 1/2 lb. plum jam, 1 oz. butter, 2/3 oz. breadcrumbs, 1 2/3 oz.
sugar

Mince farmer's cheese and combine with sifted flour, farina and egg.
Add salt and knead the dough. Shape into balls and fill with plum jam.
Cook in boiling salted water. When done take the dumplings out with
a special spoon. Brown breadcrumbs and blend with melted butter, then
pour over the dumplings. Sprinkle with sugar.

DUMPLINGS WITH BREAD

1/2 lb. flour, 2 loaves French bread, 1 cup milk, 1 2/3 oz. raisins, 2 eggs, 1 oz. yeast, 1 2/3 oz. candied orange peel, 1 2/3 oz. flour for dredging, 1/3 oz. butter for top, 2/3 oz. breadcrumbs, salt, vanilla-flavoured sugar

Cut the bread into small cubes and dry in an oven. Beat the milk with an egg-whisk together with the eggs. Combine with sifted flour and yeast blended with sugar. Cover with a cloth and set aside to let it rise. Combine with rinsed raisins, toasts and grated orange rind, then add salt. Shape into balls on a pastry board sprinkled with flour. Cook in boiling salted water. When done take the dumplings out with a spoon and drain. Brown breadcrumbs and blend with melted butter, then pour over the dumplings. Sprinkle with vanilla-flavoured sugar.

OFFICER'S DUMPLINGS

Dough: 5 oz. flour, 1 cup milk, 1 2/3 oz. butter, 3—4 eggs, salt
Filling: 1 1/4 lb. peaches or apricots, 7 oz. apritcots for sauce, 1 1/3 confectioners' sugar, 1/3 cup thick sour cream

Bring the milk to a boil together with the butter. Add sifted flour. Keep over low heat until dough becomes translucent, stirring briskly with a wooden spoon. Allow to cool slightly and add eggs one by one, stirring constantly. Add salt. Shape into balls and fill with pieces of peach. Drop into boiling salted water and cook. Take out the dumplings and drain them. Wash the apricots and remove pits. Place them in a blender together with sugar and cream. Turn on blender for 30 seconds. Before serving pour the sauce over dumplings.

KOŁDUNY (MEAT DUMPLINGS) LITHUANIAN STYLE I

Dough: 3/4 lb. flour, egg, 2/3 cup water, salt
Filling: 1/2 lb. leg of lamb, 3 1/2 oz. fillet of beef, 3 1/2 oz. beef suet or bone marrow, 1 2/3 oz. onions, 2/3 oz. fat for cooking, 1 1/3 oz. butter for top, salt, pepper, garlic and marjoram to taste

Wash the meat and remove outer skin and tendons. Chop finely with a cleaver together with the suet or bone marrow and onions. Add several tablespoons of cold broth or water and season. Mix until smooth. Sift flour onto a pastry board and add an egg. Work the dough with a knife, adding water in a thin drizzle. Make a loose dough, kneading carefully with your hands. Divide into parts and roll it out. Cut out circles with a wine glass. Place a piece of filling the size of a walnut on one circle. Cover with another circle and press the edges together. Cook for several minutes in boiling salted water with fat or in broth. When done take the kołduny out with a spoon and drain. Pour butter over.

KOŁDUNY (MEAT DUMPLINGS) LITHUANIAN STYLE II

Dough: 3/4 lb. flour, egg, ca. 2/3 cup water, salt
Filling: 3/4 lb. fillet of beef, 3 1/2 oz. bone marrow, 1/3 oz. onions, 1 cup sour cream, 1 2/3 oz. hard cheese, fat for frying, salt, pepper, garlic and marjoram to taste

Make the kołduny as above. Fry them uncooked in fat on both sides. Transfer to a greased pan and add seasoned sour cream. Sprinkle with grated cheese and bake. Serve as soon as they are out of the oven.

COUNT TYSZKIEWICZ'S KOŁDUNY (MEAT DUMPLINGS)

Dogh: 3/4 lb. flour, egg, ca. 2/3 cup water, salt
Filling: 1/2 lb. smoked ham, 1 2/3 oz. dried mushrooms, 2 2/3 oz. onions, fat for onions, egg, fat for cooking, 1 1/3 oz. butter or margarine for top, salt and pepper to taste

Wash and soak the mushrooms, then cook and chop them. Peel, rinse and dice the onions, then fry them. Combine with minced ham, the egg and mushrooms. Season to taste. Proceed as in Kołduny Lithuanian Style.

CARDINAL'S CROQUETTES

3 1/2 oz. rice, 5 oz. mushrooms, 1 oz. lobster butter, 3 1/2 oz. lobster tails, egg, fresh dill, egg and breadcrumbs for frying, salt and pepper to taste, fat for frying

Rinse the rice and cover with boiling salted water. Cook and drain it. Clean, rinse and chop the mushrooms finely, then fry them. Combine with the rice, egg, lobster tails and chopped dill. Season to taste. Make 1 1/4 in. thick rolls from the mixture and slice them into 3—4 in. long pieces. Dip in beaten egg and cover with breadcrumbs. Fry on all sides in very hot fat, then continue frying over low heat for several minutes. Serve with all kinds of sauces, salads, or with borsch (q.v.) or bouillon.

ROYAL CROQUETTES

1 1/4 lb. mushrooms, 1 2/3 oz. butter or margarine, 5 oz. ham or kiełbasa, 2 egg yolks, 1 2/3 oz. hard cheese, 1 1/3 oz. breadcrumbs, egg and breadcrumbs for coating, salt, pepper to taste, fat for frying

Clean, rinse and chop the mushrooms finely. Fry them and combine with minced ham, grated cheese, egg yolks and breadcrumbs. Season to taste. Continue as above.

CROQUETTES À LA RADZIWIŁŁ

1/2 lb. boneless roasted game meat, 1/2 lb. poultry livers, 1 oz. butter, 1 2/3 oz. hardened French bread, 3 tablespoons sour cream, 2 egg yolks, 1 oz. raisins, egg, breadcrumbs, salt and pepper to taste, fat for frying

Rinse and fry the livers. Soak the bread and squeeze out the liquid. Mince together with the meat and livers. Combine with sour cream, egg yolks and rinsed raisins. Season to taste. Proceed as in Cardinal's Croquettes.

CROQUETTES WITH MEAT

1 1/4 lb. boneless beef, 1/2 lb. soup vegetables (carrots, parsley root, celeriac, leek), 1 2/3 oz. hardened French bread, 3 1/2 oz. onions, egg, 2/3 oz. fat, egg and breadcrumbs for coating, salt and pepper to taste, fat for frying

Wash the meat, cover with boiling salted water and cook. Towards the end add cleaned and rinsed vegetables. Peel and chop the onions finely, then fry them. Soak the bread and squeeze out the liquid. Mince it together with the meat. Combine with onions and egg. Season to taste. Proceed as in Cardinal's Croquettes.

CROQUETTES LITHUANIAN STYLE

7 oz. rice, 5 oz. ham, 1 1/3 oz. dried cèpe mushrooms, 1 2/3 oz. hard cheese, egg, parsley sprigs, egg and breadcrumbs for coating, salt and pepper to taste, fat for frying

Rinse the rice and cover it with boiling salted water. Cook and drain it. Wash, soak and cook the mushrooms. Chop them and combine with the rice, minced ham, grated cheese, chopped parsley sprigs and egg. Season to taste. Proceed as in Cardinal's Croquettes.

WROCŁAW CROQUETTES

1 1/4 lb. sauerkraut, 7 oz. roast pork, 3 1/2 oz. onions, 2/3 oz. fat, 1/3 cup sour cream, 2/3 oz. dried cèpe mushrooms, 2/3—1 oz. flour, breadcrumbs, salt and pepper to taste, fat for frying

Wash, soak and cook the mushrooms. Mince them with the meat. Slice the cabbage and cover it with mushroom stock. Cook this, then allow the water to evaporate. Peel, rinse and chop the onions finely. Fry them lightly and blend with the flour. Brown lightly and combine with the cabbage, mushrooms and meat. Season to taste. Shape into croquettes 1 1/2 in. thick and 1 1/2—3 in. long. Roll them in breadcrumbs. Proceed as in Cardinal's Croquettes.

ROBBER'S CROQUETTES

1 1/4 lb. potatoes, 7 oz. roast pork, 3 1/2 oz. onions, 7 oz. peppers, 1 1/3 oz. tomato paste, egg, breadcrumbs, salt, pepper and ground paprika to taste, fat for frying

Wash, peel and rinse the potatoes. 3/4 cover with boiling salted water and cook. Drain them and mince together with the meat. Clean, rinse and dice the onions and peppers. Fry them lightly, stirring constantly. Towards the end add tomato paste. Combine with the potato mixture and egg, then season. Proceed as in Cardinal's Croquettes.

CROQUETTES WITH CABBAGE AND MUSHROOMS

Batter: 7 oz. flour, 3/4 cup milk, 3/4 cup water, 2—3 eggs, 2/3—1 oz. pork fat, salt to taste
Filling: 1 3/4 lb. sauerkraut, 1 1/3 oz. dried cèpe mushrooms, 3 1/2 oz. onions, 2/3 oz. fat, 2 eggs and breadcrumbs for coating, salt, pepper, fat for frying

Wash the eggs and break them into a blender. Add flour, water and salt and turn on blender for 30—40 seconds. Heat a frying pan and grease with pork fat. Add a thin layer of batter, spreading it evenly on the frying pan. Fry the batter, browning it lightly. When done place the crêpes on a plate turned upside down. Wash, soak and cook the mushrooms. Slice the cabbage and cover it with mushroom stock. Cook this and allow the water to evaporate. Peel, rinse and chop the onions finely. Fry them and combine with the cabbage and chopped mushrooms, then season. Arrange the crêpes so that they overlap and brush the edges with crêpe batter. Place the filling on these and roll up. Cut into 3 1/2 in. pieces. Coat with beaten eggs and breadcrumbs. Fry in very hot fat, then lower the heat and continue frying. Serve with all kinds of sauces and salads.

CROQUETTES WITH EGGS

Batter: 7 oz. flour, 3/4 cup milk, 3/4 cup water, 2—3 eggs, 2/3—1 oz. pork fat, salt to taste
Filling: 7 oz. onions, 1 oz. fat, 5 oz. farmer's cheese, 4 hard-boiled eggs, parsley sprigs, 2 eggs and breadcrumbs for coating, salt, pepper, fat for frying

Peel, rinse and cut the onions into half-slices. Fry them and combine with grated cheese, chopped parsley sprigs and chopped eggs, then season. Proceed as above.

CROQUETTES WITH APPLES

2 lb. apples, 2 egg yolks, 2 oz. sugar, cinnamon, vanilla extract and fresh orange rind to taste, 1 1/3 oz. flour, 3 1/2 oz. breadcrumbs, 2 eggs and breadcrumbs for coating, fat for frying

Wash, peel and halve the apples, removing the cores. Grate them finely. Add sugar, grated orange rind, cinnamon and vanilla. Fry this, stirring often. Combine with egg yolks and breadcrumbs. Shape into croquettes and roll in flour. Coat with beaten eggs and breadcrumbs. Fry on all sides until golden. Serve with sour cream.

CROQUETTES WITH PRUNES

1 lb. prunes, 1 2/3 oz. hardened French bread, 3 1/2 oz. almonds, lemon rind to taste, 2 1/3 oz. breadcrumbs, 1 2/3 oz. confectioners' sugar, 3/4 cup milk, fat for frying, 1 1/3 oz. confectioners' sugar for dusting

Wash, soak and cook the prunes. Force them through a strainer and allow the water to evaporate. Soak the bread in milk and squeeze it out, then mince it. Blanch the almonds and grate together with the lemon rind. Combine with prunes, bread, sugar and eggs. Shape into cro-

quettes and coat them with beaten eggs and breadcrumbs. Fry in very hot fat until golden. Serve dusted with confectioners' sugar mixed with cinnamon.

CROQUETTES WITH FARMER'S CHEESE

1 lb. farmer's cheese, 2—3 eggs, 2 oz. confectioners' sugar, 1 2/3 oz. raisins, 1 1/3 oz. flour, 1 1/3 oz. breadcrumbs, fat for frying, vanilla extract

Wash the eggs and break them, separating the yolks from the whites. Blend the yolks with sugar and combine with minced farmer's cheese, rinsed raisins, vanilla and stiffly beaten egg whites, alternately adding flour. Shape into croquettes and roll in breadcrumbs. Fry in very hot fat on all sides until golden.

CROQUETTES WITH RICE AND APPLES

5 oz. rice, 1—1 1/3 cups milk, 2/3 oz. butter, 2 oz. confectioners' sugar, 2 eggs, 1 1/3 oz. breadcrumbs, salt, vanilla bean and orange rind to taste, fat for frying

Rinse the rice in warm water and drain it. Cover with plenty of boiling water and cook for 2 minutes, then drain it. Cover with boiling milk and add salt, butter, finely chopped vanilla bean and grated orange rind. Stir and cook covered over low heat for 15 minutes. Wash, peel and halve the apples, removing the cores. Grate coarsely and combine with cooled rice, eggs and sugar. Shape into a 1 in. thick roll and cut into 3 in. long pieces. Fry in lightly heated fat on all sides until golden.

TARTELETTES WITH BRAINS

Dough: 1/2 lb. flour, 5 oz. butter or margarine, 2 egg yolks, salt to taste
Filling: 1 lb. brains, 2 2/3 oz. onions, 2/3 oz. fat, 2 egg yolks, salt and pepper to taste

Rinse the brains, remove the outer skin and chop. Peel, rinse and dice the onions. Fry them lightly and add the brains. Fry for 3—4 minutes, stirring constantly. Add egg yolks and seasoning and continue frying for a while. Sift the flour onto a pastry board. Cut in butter with a knife. Add egg yolks and salt and knead the dough quickly. Set aside in a cool place for 30 minutes. Line individual fluted tart shells with the dough, pressing it firmly to the sides. Bake lightly in an oven. 3/4 fill with the brains and cover with round dough tops, carefully closing the edges. Place in a hot oven and bake.

TARTELETTES WITH MEAT

Dough: 1/2 lb. flour, 5 oz. butter or margarine, 2 egg yolks, salt to taste
Filling: 1 lb. boneless beef, 7 oz. soup vegetables (carrots, parsley root, celeriac, leek), 2 2/3 oz. onions, 2 hard-boiled eggs, 2/3 oz. fat, salt and pepper to taste

Wash the meat, cover it with boiling water and cook. Towards the end add cleaned vegetables and salt. Peel, rinse and chop the onions finely. Fry them and combine with the meat and eggs. Season to taste. Proceed as above.

GENERAL'S TARTELETTES

Dough: 5 oz. flour, 5 oz. farmer's cheese, 5 oz. butter or margarine, 1/2 teaspoon baking powder, salt to taste
Filling: 7 oz. mushrooms, 2/3 oz. fat, 5 oz. ham, 2—3 oz. ketchup, parsley sprigs, salt and pepper to taste

Clean, rinse and chop the mushrooms finely. Fry them and combine with minced ham, chopped parsley sprigs and ketchup. Season to taste. Sift the flour onto a pastry board. Cut minced cheese and butter into flour with a knife and add salt and baking powder. Knead the dough. Line individual fluted tart shells with the dough, add the filling and bake.

KULEBIAK WITH FISH

Butter dough: 1/2 lb. butter or margarine, 1 2/3 oz. flour
Basic dough: 7 oz. flour, 1/2 egg, salt, 1 teaspoon vinegar, water
Filling: 3/4 lb. fish (cleaned and drawn), 7 oz. soup vegetables (carrots, parsley root, celeriac, leek), 1 2/3 oz. rice, 2 2/3 oz. onions, 2/3 oz. fat, parsley sprigs, egg for brushing, salt and pepper to taste

Wash and peel the vegetables. Cover with boiling salted water and cook them. Towards the end add the fish. Rinse the rice and cover with plenty of boiling salted water. Cook it and drain. Peel, rinse and chop the onions finely, then fry them.
Butter dough: Sift the flour onto a pastry board. Cut in butter with a knife and mix well. Shape into a square and chill.
Basic dough: Sift the flour onto a pastry board. Break in an egg and mix the dough with a knife, adding water and vinegar in a thin drizzle. With your hand carefully knead into a loose dough. Cover with a cloth and set aside for 15 minutes. Roll the dough out into a square twice as big as the butter dough square. Place the butter dough in the middle and fold into an envelope. Roll the dough away from you into a rectangle. Fold it up into 3 parts. Roll up in a cloth and place in the refrigerator for 15 minutes. Repeat folding and rolling process 3 more times every 20 minutes. Divide the dough into two parts: one smaller, the other larger. Roll out into 1/2 in. thick rectangles. Place the following filling in layers on the smaller rectangle: rice, boned cut up fish and rice. Sprinkle each layer with seasoning, onions and chopped parsley sprigs. Leave a 1/2 in. wide rim around the filling. Cover with the larger piece of dough and close up the edges. Brush with beaten egg and bake in a hot oven. Serve as a hot hors-d'oeuvre.
Note: Yeast dough may also be used.

KULEBIAK À LA SAPIEHA

Butter dough: 1/2 lb. butter or margarine, 1 2/3 oz. flour
Basic dough: 7 oz. flour, 1/2 egg, salt, 1 teaspoon vinegar, water
Filling: 3/4 lb. sauerkraut, 1 oz. dried cèpe mushrooms, 3 1/2 oz. smoked ham, 2 2/3 oz. onions, 2/3 oz. fat, egg for coating, salt and pepper

Wash, soak and cook the mushrooms. Slice the cabbage and cover it with mushroom stock, then cook uncovered. Peel, rinse and dice the onions, then fry them and combine with the cabbage, chopped mushrooms and strips of ham, then season. If the filling is moist, roll it in fried crêpes before rolling it up in the dough. Proceed as above.

Note: Yeast dough may also be used.

KULEBIAK À LA RADZIWIŁŁ I

Butter dough: 5 oz. butter or margarine, 1 2/3 oz. flour
Basic dough: 7 oz. flour, 1/2 egg, salt, 1 teaspoon vinegar, water
Filling: 1/2 lb. boned roast chicken, 2 hard-boiled eggs, 5 oz. smoked ham, parsley sprigs, salt, pepper, egg for coating

Cut the meat, ham and eggs into cubes and combine with chopped parsley sprigs, then season. Proceed as in Kulebiak with fish.

Note: Yeast dough may also be used.

KULEBIAK À LA RADZIWIŁŁ II

Butter dough: 1/2 lb. butter or margarine, 1 2/3 oz. flour
Basic dough: 7 oz. flour, 1/2 egg, salt, 1 teaspoon vinegar, water
Filling: 3 1/2 oz. dried cèpe mushrooms, 1 can anchois, 5 oz. lobster tails, 2 hard-boiled egg yolks, parsley sprigs, salt, pepper, egg for coating

Wash, soak and cook the mushrooms. Mince them and combine with chopped anchois, lobster tails, egg yolks forced through a strainer and finely chopped parsley sprigs, then season. Proceed as in Kulebiak with Fish.

KULEBIAK POLISH STYLE

Butter dough: 1/2 lb. butter or margarine, 1 2/3 oz. flour
Basic dough: 7 oz. flour, 1/2 egg, salt, 1 teaspoon vinegar, water

Filling: 1/2 lb. thin frankfurters, 2 hard-boiled eggs, 1 2/3 oz. hardened French bread, milk, parsley sprigs, 1 oz. raisins, egg for coating, salt and pepper

Remove outer skins, if any, from the frankfurters and cut them into slices. Soak the bread in milk and squeeze it out. Mince together with the eggs and combine with the frankfurters, chopped parsley sprigs and rinsed raisins. Season to taste. Proceed as in Kulebiak with Fish.

KULEBIAK LITHUANIAN STYLE

Dough: 1/2 lb. wheat flour, ca. 2/3 cup milk, 2/3 oz. yeast, 1 2/3 oz. butter or margarine, 2 egg yolks, 1 teaspoon sugar, fat for greasing baking sheet or pan, salt
Filling: 3 1/2 oz. buckwheat kasha, 2 2/3 oz. onions, 2/3 oz. fat, 7 oz. roast pork, egg for brushing, salt and pepper to taste

Rinse the kasha and cover with boiling salted water (3/4 cup). Bring to a boil, stirring. Cook the kasha until tender in the top of a double boiler. Peel, rinse and chop the onions finely. Fry them and combine with the kasha and finely diced meat. Season to taste. Blend the yeast with sugar and part of the warm milk. Set aside in a warm place for 30 minutes. Gradually pour into sifted flour together with the remaining milk and egg yolks. Knead the dough, forcing in as much air as possible. When the dough does not stick to your hands and the sides of the dish, gradually add melted fat, kneading constantly. Cover the dough with a cloth and set aside to let it rise. Place the dough on a pastry board and pull out into a rectangle with your hands. Smooth it out with a rolling pin. Place the filling along the longer end of the rectangle and roll it up lengthwise. Place on a greased baking sheet. Arrange strips of dough on top of the kulebiak. Brush with beaten egg, prick with a fork and bake in a hot oven. Cut into pieces and serve.

LASAGNE NOODLES

3/4 lb. flour, 2 eggs, ca. 3 tablespoons water, salt

Sift the flour onto a pastry board. Make a well in the centre, break in the eggs and add water. Mix with a knife. Make a stiff dough, kneading well. Divide into parts and roll out thinly. Allow for it to dry. Sprinkle with flour and roll it up. Cut into 3/4 in. wide strips. Cut these across into squares and scatter on the pastry board. Drop the noodles into boiling salted water and stir. Cover, cook and drain them. Pour warm water over and drain the noodles.

LASAGNE NOODLES WITH CABBAGE

Dough: 3/4 lb. flour, 2 eggs, ca. 3 tablespoons water, salt
Filling: 1 oz. dried cèpe mushrooms, 1 lb. sauerkraut, 2/3 oz. onions, 2/3 oz. flour, 1 2/3 oz. fat, salt, pepper and caraway seed to taste, fat and breadcrumbs

Make the lasagne noodles as above. Wash, soak and cook the mushrooms. Slice the cabbage and cover with mushroom stock. Cover and bring to a boil. Uncover for a while, then continue cooking covered. Peel, rinse and chop the onions finely. Fry without browning. Add flour and brown lightly. Combine with drained cabbage, lasagne noodles and chopped mushrooms. Season to taste. Transfer to a greased oven-proof pan sprinkled with breadcrumbs. Smooth out the surface and bake.

LASAGNE NOODLES LITHUANIAN STYLE I

Dough: 3/4 lb. flour, 2 eggs, ca. 3 tablespoons water, salt
Filling: 7 oz. kiełbasa, 2/3 cup sour cream, 2 egg yolks, egg, 3 1/2 oz. onions, fat for onions, salt and pepper to taste, fat and breadcrumbs

Make the lasagne noodles as in Lasagne Noodles. Peel, rinse and chop the onions finely. Fry them and combine with the noodles, strips of kiełbasa and sour cream blended with the egg and egg yolks. Season to taste. Transfer to a greased oven-proof pan sprinkled with breadcrumbs and bake.

LASAGNÉ NOODLES LITHUANIAN STYLE II

Dough: 1/2 lb. flour, 2 eggs, ca. 3 tablespoons water, salt
Filling: 7 oz. ham or kiełbasa, 1 1/3 oz. dried cèpe mushrooms, 3 1/2 oz.
hard cheese, salt and pepper to taste, fat and breadcrumbs

Make the lasagne noodles as in Lasagne Noodles. Wash, soak and cook the mushrooms. Cut them into strips together with the ham. Combine with the lasagne noodles and season to taste. Transfer to a greased oven-proof pan sprinkled with breadcrumbs. Even out the surface, sprinkle with grated cheese and bake.

HOMEMADE MACARONI

3/4 lb. flour, 2 eggs, ca. 3 tablespoons water, 1 1/3 oz. butter, salt

Sift the flour onto a pastry board. Make a well in the centre and break in the eggs. Add water and mix with a knife. Make a stiff dough, kneading well. Divide into parts and roll out thinly. Allow for it to dry. Sprinkle with flour and rool it up, moving it to the edge of the pastry board. Cut it up finely and scatter on the pastry board. Drop the macaroni into boiling salted water and stir. Cover, cook and drain it. Pour hot water over it and drain. Transfer to a platter or divide into portions. Pour butter over the macaroni.

HOMEMADE MACARONI WITH HAM

Dough: 3/4 lb. flour, 2 eggs, ca. 3 tablespoons water, salt
Filling: 1/2 lb. ham or kiełbasa, 1 1/3 oz. butter or margarine, 2 2/3 oz.
hard cheese, parsley sprigs, salt and pepper to taste, fat and breadcrumbs

Make the macaroni as above. Combine with strips of ham, butter, grated cheese, seasoning and chopped parsley sprigs. Transfer to a greased baking pan sprinkled with breadcrumbs. Smooth out the surface and bake.

Note: 7 oz. of store-bought macaroni or spaghetti may be used instead of homemade macaroni.

HOMEMADE MACARONI WITH LOBSTER

Dough: 3/4 lb. flour, 2 eggs, ca. 3 tablespoons water, salt
Filling: 5 oz. mushrooms, 1 oz. butter or margarine, 5 oz. lobster tails,
2/3 cup sour cream, salt and pepper to taste, fat and breadcrumbs

Make the macaroni as in Homemade Macaroni. Clean, rinse and cut the
mushrooms into slices. Fry them and combine with the macaroni and
lobster tails. Season to taste. Transfer to a greased oven-proof pan
sprinkled with breadcrumbs. Even out the surface. Pour seasoned sour
cream over this and bake.

HOMEMADE MACARONI WITH MUSHROOMS

Dough: 3/4 lb. flour, 2 eggs, ca. 3 tablespoon water, salt
Filling: 1/2 lb. mushrooms, 1 1/3 oz. tomato paste, 1 1/3 oz. fat, 3 1/2
oz. hard cheese, salt, pepper, thyme and tarragon to taste, fat and bread-
crumbs for baking pan or dish

Make the macaroni as in Homemade Macaroni. Clean and rinse the
mushrooms. Cut them into slices and fry them. Combine with tomato
paste, macaroni and seasoning. Transfer to a greased oven-proof dish
sprinkled with breadcrumbs. Smooth out the surface, sprinkle with
grated cheese and bake.

Note: 7 oz. of store-bought macaroni or spaghetti may be used instead of homemade
macaroni.

FARMER'S HOMEMADE MACARONI

Dough: 3/4 lb. flour, 2 eggs, ca. 3 tablespoons water, salt
Filling: 5 oz. kiełbasa, 3 1/2 oz. white beans, 1 1/3 oz. tomato paste,
1 oz. fat, 1 2/3 oz. hard cheese, salt, pepper and marjoram to taste, fat
and breadcrumbs for baking pan or dish

Make the macaroni as in Homemade Macaroni. Sort the beans, rinse
them and cover with cold water. Bring to a boil and set aside for 2 hours.

Cook in the same water and drain them. Combine with macaroni, strips of kiełbasa, fat and tomato paste. Season to taste. Transfer to a greased oven-proof dish sprinkled with breadcrumbs. Smooth out the surface, sprinkle with grated cheese and bake.

HOMEMADE MACARONI WITH ONIONS

Dough: 3/4 lb. flour, 2 eggs, ca. 3 tablespoons water, salt
Filling: 1/2 lb. onions, fat for onions, 4 eggs, 1 2/3 oz. ketchup

Make the macaroni as in Homemade Macaroni. Peel and rinse the onions and cut them into half-slices. Fry them and combine with the macaroni. Season to taste. Transfer to greased oven-proof individual serving dishes. Break in the eggs, sprinkle with grated cheese, pour ketchup over this and bake.

Note: 7 oz. of store-bought macaroni or spaghetti may be used instead of homemade macaroni.

CRÊPES WITH EGGS

Dough: 7 oz. flour, ca. 3/4 cup milk, ca. 3/4 cup water, 2 eggs, 1 oz. pork fat, salt to taste
Filling: 4 hard-boiled eggs, 1 2/3 oz. hardened French bread, 2/3 cup milk, 2 2/3 oz. hard cheese, 2 2/3 oz. onions, fat for onions, parsley sprigs, salt and pepper to taste, fat for frying

Wash the eggs and break them into a blender. Add milk, water and salt. Turn on the blender for 30—40 seconds. Or: pour milk into a dish, break in the eggs and add salt. Beat well with an egg-whisk. Gradually add sifted flour, beating with the egg-whisk until all lumps disappear and air bubbles form on the surface of the dough. Thin down the dough until it can form a thin layer in a frying pan. Heat the frying pan and grease it with pork fat. Pour in a thin layer of the dough, spreading it evenly in the frying pan. Fry until light brown. When done place the crêpes on a plate turned upside down. Peel, rinse and dice the onions, then fry·them. Soak the bread in milk with water. Mince together with the eggs. Combine with onions, grated cheese and chopped parsley sprigs. Season to taste. Place some of the filling on each crêpe and roll up. Fry on both sides until light brown. Pour ketchup or tomato sauce over the crêpes and serve with salads.

CRÊPES WITH MUSHROOMS

Dough: 7 oz. flour, ca. 3/4 cup milk, ca. 3/4 cup water, 3 eggs, 1 oz. pork fat, salt to taste
Filling: 1 lb. fresh cèpe mushrooms, 2 2/3 oz. onions, 1 oz. fat, 2/3 oz. breadcrumbs, parsley sprigs, salt and pepper to taste, fat for frying

Clean the mushrooms thoroughly and wash them, then cut into slices. Peel, rinse and dice the onions. Fry them lightly. Add the mushrooms and simmer until tender. Combine with breadcrumbs and chopped parsley sprigs. Season to taste. Proceed as in Crêpes with Eggs.

CRÊPES WITH POULTRY LIVERS

Dough: 7 oz. flour, 3/4 cup milk, 3/4 cup water, 3 eggs, 1 oz. pork fat, salt to taste
Filling: 1 lb. poultry livers, 5 oz. onions, 2 hard-boiled eggs, 1 oz. fat, 3 tablespoons sour cream, salt and pepper to taste, fat for frying

Rinse the livers and remove the outer skin (they may be soaked in milk). Cut into smaller pieces and fry. Peel, rinse and chop the onions finely, then fry them. Allow to cool and mince together with the livers and eggs. Add sour cream and season to taste. Proceed as in Crêpes with Eggs.

CRÊPES WITH CABBAGE AND MUSHROOMS

Dough: 7 oz. flour, 3/4 cup milk, 3/4 cup water, 3 eggs, 1 oz. pork fat, salt to taste

Filling: 1 lb. sauerkraut, 2 2/3 oz. onions, 1 oz. dried cèpe mushrooms, 1/3—2/3 oz. flour, 1 1/3 oz. fat, salt, pepper and caraway seed to taste, fat

Wash, soak and cook the mushrooms. Slice the cabbage and cover it with mushroom stock, then cook it. Peel, rinse and chop the onions finely. Fry them and combine with the flour. Brown this lightly and combine with sauerkraut from which the liquid has evaporated. Add chopped mushrooms and seasoning. Simmer for a while and season to taste. Proceed as in Crêpes with Eggs.

CRÊPES LITHUANIAN STYLE

Dough: 7 oz. flour, 3/4 cup milk, 3/4 cup water, 3 eggs, 1 oz. pork fat, salt to taste
Filling: 1 3/4 lb. cabbage, 2 2/3 oz. onions, 1 1/3 oz. fat, 2 hard-boiled eggs, 3 1/2 oz. farmer's cheese, salt and pepper to taste, fat for frying

Clean, rinse and dice the cabbage. Cover with a small amount of boiling salted water and cook. Drain it. Mince the eggs together with the cheese. Peel, rinse and chop the onions. Fry it. Combine with the cabbage, eggs and cheese. Season to taste. Proceed as in Crêpes with Eggs.

CRÊPES WITH POULTRY

Dough: 7 oz. flour, 3/4 cup milk, 3/4 cup water, 3 eggs, 1 oz. pork fat, salt to taste
Filling: 3/4 lb. boned roast chicken, 5 oz. canned peas, 1 2/3 oz. ketchup, 1 2/3 oz. farmer's cheese, egg yolk, salt and pepper to taste, fat for frying
Sauce: 1 cup milk, 2/3 oz. butter, 2/3 oz. flour, 1 2/3 oz. walnut meats, 1 2/3 oz. farmer's cheese, egg yolk, salt and pepper to taste

Mince the meat and combine with the peas and ketchup, season to taste. Place this on the prepared crêpes (as in Crêpes with Eggs). Fry and place

on an oven-proof dish. Blanch the walnuts and grind them. Melt the butter and blend with flour without browning. Add cold milk, stirring briskly with an egg-whisk and bring to a boil. Add the walnuts and egg yolks. Pour this over the crêpes, sprinkle with crumbled cheese and bake.

GENERAL'S PATTIES

Butter dough: 1/2 lb. butter or margarine, 1 2/3 oz. flour
Basic dough: 7 oz. flour, 1/2 egg, 1 teaspoon vinegar, salt, water
Filling: 7 oz. hard cheese, 5 oz. ham, 1 2/3 oz. ketchup, 2 egg yolks, fresh dill, 1/2 egg for coating, salt and pepper to taste

Make the dough as in Kulebiak with Fish. Mince the ham and combine with grated cheese, ketchup, egg yolks and chopped dill. Season to taste. Roll into 1/2 in. thickness and cut out circles 2 1/2 in. in diameter. Place some of the filling on one circle, cover with another and close the edges tightly. Brush with egg, sprinkle with grated cheese and bake.

PATTIES WITH ONIONS

Butter dough: 1/2 oz. butter or margarine, 1 2/3 oz. flour
Basic dough: 7 oz. flour, 1/2 egg, 1 teaspoon vinegar, salt, water
Filling: 2 2/3 oz. rice, 2 2/3 oz. onions, 2/3 oz. butter, 2 hard-boiled eggs, 1 2/3 oz. hard cheese, 1 1/3 oz. ketchup, 1/2 egg for coating, 1 1/3 oz. hard cheese for top, salt, pepper and sugar to taste

Rinse the rice and cover with plenty of boiling salted water. Cook and drain it. Peel, rinse and chop the onions finely. Fry them and combine with the rice, minced eggs, ketchup and grated cheese. Season to taste. Make the dough as in Kulebiak with Fish. Roll into 1/2 in. thickness and cut into 3—4 in. wide strips. Place some of the filling along each strip and roll up, leaving 1/2 in. wide strip unrolled. Close the edges up and cut diagonally into 1 1/2—2 in. pieces. Brush with beaten egg, sprinkle with grated cheese and bake.

PATTIES WITH MEAT

Cream puff paste: 1/2 lb. flour, 7 oz. butter or margarine, 1/3 cup sour cream, 1/2 egg, 2 egg yolks, salt
Filling: 1 lb. boneless beef, 7 oz. soup vegetables (carrots, parsley root, celeriac, leek), 2 2/3 oz. onions, 2/3 oz. fat, 2 hard-boiled eggs, 1/2 egg for coating, 1 1/3 oz. hard cheese, salt and pepper to taste, fat for baking sheet

Sift the flour onto a pastry board. Cut in butter. Add egg yolks, egg, sour cream and salt. Knead the dough quickly, cover with a cloth and place in the refrigerator for 10—12 hours. Wash the meat and cover with boiling salted water, then cook. Towards the end add cleaned vegetables. Peel, rinse and dice the onions. Fry them and combine with minced meat and minced eggs. Season to taste. Roll the dough out to 1/4 in. thickness and cut into squares. Place some of the filling in the centre of each square and fold diagonally. Close up so that the bottom protrudes 1/4 in. Brush with beaten egg, sprinkle with grated cheese and bake.
Note: These patties can also be made from yeast dough, tart dough or plain puff paste.

WROCŁAW PATTIES

Dough: 1/2 lb. flour, 2/3 cup milk, 1 2/3 oz. butter or margarine, 2/3 oz. yeast, egg, 1/2 teaspoon sugar and salt to taste, fat for baking sheet
Filling: 1/2 lb. thin frankfurters, 2 2/3 oz. grated horseradish, egg yolk, 1/2 egg for brushing, salt, sugar and lemon juice to taste

Remove the outer skin, if any, from the frankfurters. Cut 3/4 of each frankfurter lengthwise. Fill with seasoned horseradish blended with egg yolk. Proceed as in Wrocław Patties.

PIEROGI WITH MEAT I

Dough: 3/4 lb. flour, egg, 2/3 cup water, salt
Filling: 1 lb. boneless beef, 3 1/2 oz. onions, 2/3 oz. fat, 7 oz. soup vegetables (carrots, parsley root, celeriac, leek), 2 eggs, parsley sprigs, 2/3 oz. fat for cooking, 3 1/2 oz. pork fat, salt and pepper to taste

Sift the flour onto a pastry board. Break in an egg and cut the dough with a knife, adding water in a thin stream. Make a loose dough, kneading well with your hand. Divide into parts and cover with a damp cloth. Wash the meat, place in boiling salted water and cook. Towards the end add cleaned and rinsed vegetables. Peel, rinse and dice the onions. Fry them and combine with minced meat, hard-boiled and chopped eggs and chopped parsley sprigs, then season. If the mixture is too tough add meat stock. Roll the dough into 1 1/2 in. thickness. Cut out circles with a glass or special cutter. Place some of the filling on each circle and fold in half. Close the edges, taking care not to allow any filling to get between the edges (in which case the pierogi break open during cooking). Arrange the pierogi on a pastry board sprinkled with flour. Drop several at a time into boiling salted water with fat and stir. Cover the pot and bring water to a boil. When the pierogi surface, remove cover and cook for a while. Take out with a special spoon when done and pour pork fat cracklings over.

PIEROGI WITH MEAT II

Dough: 3/4 lb. flour, egg, 2/3 cup water, salt
Filling: 3/4 lb. boneless pork, 5 oz. mushrooms, 3 1/2 oz. onions, 1 oz. fat, egg, breadcrumbs, 2/3 oz. fat for cooking, 3 1/2 oz. pork fat, salt and pepper to taste

Clean and rinse the onions and mushrooms. Cut them into cubes together with the meat. Fry lightly, sprinkle with water and simmer until tender. Allow to cool and mince. Break in an egg, add breadcrumbs and season. Proceed as above.

PIEROGI WITH SAUERKRAUT

Dough: 3/4 lb. flour, egg, 2/3 cup water, salt
Filling: 3/4 lb. sauerkraut, 1/2 lb. boneless pork, 3 1/2 oz. onions, egg, 2/3 oz. fat for cooking, 3 1/2 oz. pork fat, salt and pepper to taste

Slice the cabbage and cover with a small amount of stock from bones, then cook. Wash the meat and cut into pieces, then brown it. Add diced onions and simmer until tender. Allow to cool and mince. Combine with sauerkraut drained of liquid and egg, then season. Proceed as in Pierogi with Meat I.

PIEROGI CARPATHIAN STYLE

Dough: 3/4 lb. flour, egg, 2/3 cup water, salt
Filling: 1 lb. peppers, 3 1/2 oz. onions, 3 1/2 oz. hard cheese, egg, 2/3 oz. tomato paste, breadcrumbs, 1 oz. fat, 2/3 oz. fat for cooking, 3 1/2 oz. pork fat, salt, pepper and ground paprika to taste

Clean, rinse and chop the onions and peppers finely. Fry lightly and simmer until tender. Combine with egg, grated cheese and breadcrumbs, then season. Proceed as in Pierogi with Meat I.

PIEROGI WITH RICE AND CHEESE

Dough: 3/4 lb. flour, egg, 2/3 cup water, salt
Filling: 3 1/2 oz. rice, 1/2 lb. farmer's cheese, 2 hard-boiled eggs, 2 2/3 oz. onions, 2/3 oz. fat, parsley sprigs, 2/3 oz. fat for cooking, 1 1/3 oz. fat for top, salt and pepper to taste

Rinse rice and cover with salted water (1 1/4 cups). Cook covered over low heat for 15 minutes. Peel, rinse and dice the onions. Fry them and combine with minced farmer's cheese, cooled rice, chopped eggs and chopped parsley sprigs, then season. Proceed as in Pierogi with Meat I.

AMATEUR'S PIEROGI

Dough: 3/4 lb. flour, egg, 2/3 cup water, salt
Filling: 3/4 lb. mushrooms, 3 1/2 oz. lobster tails, 2 egg yolks, 1 oz. breadcrumbs, parsley sprigs, fat for mushrooms and for cooking, butter for top, salt and curry powder to taste

Clean, rinse and dice the mushrooms. Fry them and combine with the lobster tails, egg yolks, breadcrumbs and chopped parsley sprigs, then season. Proceed as in Pierogi with Meat. Pour butter over the pierogi.

PUFFS WITH MUSHROOMS

Dough: 5 oz. flour, 2 2/3 oz. butter or margarine, 1 cup milk or water, 4—5 eggs, 1/2 teaspoon baking powder, salt
Filling: 3/4 lb. mushrooms, 3 1/2 oz. onions, fat for onions and mushrooms, 2 egg yolks, salt and pepper to taste, fat for greasing baking sheet

Bring the water or milk to a boil together with the butter. Add salt and sifted flour. Remove from heat and break down all lumps. Place over heat again and heat lightly, stirring constantly until the dough becomes smooth and shiny. Remove from heat and allow the dough to cool slightly. Break in the eggs one by one, mixing well. Towards the end add baking powder and mix again. Grease the baking sheet and sprinkle with flour. Force the dough through a pastry bag onto the sheet to make puffs. Bake in a preheated (350° F) oven for 25—30 minutes, without opening the oven for the first 10—15 minutes. Remove the puffs from the sheet and cut into halves with a sharp knife. Clean, rinse and chop the mushrooms and onions finely. Fry them and combine with egg yolks. Season to taste. Fill the puffs and heat in the oven before serving.

PUFFS WITH CABBAGE

Dough: 5 oz. flour, 2 2/3 oz. butter or margarine, 1 cup milk or water, 4—5 eggs, 1/2 teaspoon baking powder, salt
Filling: 1/2 lb. sauerkraut, 1 oz. dried mushrooms, 1 2/3 oz. kiełbasa, 2 oz. onions, 2/3 oz. fat, salt and pepper to taste, fat for baking sheet

Wash, soak and cook the mushrooms. Slice the cabbage and cover with meat and mushroom stock. Cook, then allow the water to evaporate. Peel, rinse and dice the onions. Fry them and combine with the cabbage,

chopped mushrooms and strips of kiełbasa. Season to taste. Make the puffs as above and allow to cool. Cut them in halves and fill with cabbage. Heat in the oven before serving.

USZKA (RAVIOLI) WITH MUSHROOMS

Dough: 3/4 lb. flour, egg, ca. 2/3 cup water, salt
Filling: 2 2/3—3 1/2 oz. dried cèpe mushrooms, 2 2/3 oz. onions, fat
for onions, 1 oz. breadcrumbs, egg yolk, 2/3 oz. fat for cooking, salt and
pepper to taste

Wash, soak, cook and mince the mushrooms. Peel, rinse and dice the onions. Fry them and combine with the mushrooms, breadcrumbs and egg yolk, then season. Sift the flour onto a pastry board. Break in an egg and mix the dough with a knife, adding a thin stream of water. Make a loose dough, kneading well with your hand. Roll out the dough thinly and cut into 1 1/2 in. squares. Place some of the filling in the centre of each square and fold over diagonally. Close the edges and press opposite ends together. Drop into boiling salted water with fat. When they surface take out with a spoon and drain. Serve with clear borsch or broth.

USZKA (RAVIOLI) WITH MEAT

Dough: 3/4 lb. flour, egg, ca. 2/3 cup water, salt
Filling: 3/4 lb. boneless beef, 7 oz. soup vegetables (carrots, parsley
root, celeriac, leek), 2 2/3 oz. pork fat, 2 2/3 oz. onions, 1/2 hardened
French bread, egg yolk, 2/3 oz. fat for cooking, salt and pepper to taste

Wash the meat and cover with boiling salted water. Cook the meat. Towards the end add cleaned and rinsed vegetables. Soak the bread and squeeze out the liquid. Mince together with the cooled meat. Cut the pork fat and peeled onions into cubes. Fry them and combine with the meat and egg yolk, then season. Proceed as above.

BELVEDERE USZKA (RAVIOLI) I

Dough: 3/4 lb. flour, egg, ca. 2/3 cup water, salt
Filling: 1/2 lb. lobster tails, fresh dill, 1 1/3 oz. almonds, 2/3 oz. fat for
cooking

Rinse and chop the dill finely. Combine with lobster tails and blanched ground almonds. Proceed as in Uszka with Mushrooms. Serve with broth.

BELVEDERE USZKA (RAVIOLI) II

Dough: 3/4 lb. flour, egg, ca. 2/3 cup water, salt
Filling: 4 hard-boiled eggs, 2 2/3 oz. hard cheese, 1 1/3 oz. butter, parsley
sprigs, fat for cooking, salt and pepper to taste

Blend the butter with grated cheese and chopped parsley sprigs. Combine with minced eggs, then season. Proceed as in Uszka with Mushrooms. Serve with clear borsch or broth.

Vegetables

BUTTERED BRUSSELS SPROUTS

1 3/4 lb. Brussels sprouts, butter, breadcrumbs, salt and sugar to taste

Clean and rinse Brussels sprouts. Cover them with boiling salted water with sugar and bring to a boil covered. Uncover for 10-15 minutes, then continue cooking covered. When tender drain and transfer to a bowl. Pour browned breadcrumbs blended with melted butter over the Brussels sprouts.

WROCŁAW BRUSSELS SPROUTS

1 1/2 lb. Brussels sprouts, 3 1/2 oz. onions (green or shallot), 1 2/3 oz. smoked ham, 2/3 oz. dried cèpe mushrooms, 1/3 cup sour cream, 1 2/3 oz. ketchup, 2-3 oz. hard cheese, salt, pepper and sugar to taste

Clean and rinse the Brussels sprouts. Cover with boiling salted water with sugar and bring to a boil covered. Uncover for 10 minutes and continue cooking covered, then drain. Peel, rinse and fry the onions. Sprinkle with confectioners' sugar and brown. Wash, soak an cook the mushrooms. Chop them and combine with Brussels sprouts, onions and strips of ham. Blend sour cream with ketchup and pour over the Brussels sprouts. Season to taste. Sprinkle with grated cheese and bake.

SAUTÉÉD BEETS

1 1/2 lb. beets, 2 2/3 oz. onions, fat, 2/3 oz. flour, 2/3 cup sour cream, salt, sugar and lemon juice to taste

Scrub the beets with a brush under running water. Wash them and cover with boiling water. Cook covered or bake in an oven. Take them out and allow to cool. Peel and grate them finely or coarsely. Peel, rinse and chop the onions finely. Fry them and combine with flour. Brown lightly and combine with the beets and sour cream. Simmer over low heat for several minutes. Season to taste.

CAPTAIN'S BEETS

1 1/2 lb. beets, 3 1/2 oz. pork fat, 2 2/3 oz. onions, 1 oz. flour, 2/3 cup dry red wine, salt, sugar and lemon juice to taste

Scrub the beets with a brush under running water. Wash them and cover with boiling water. Cook covered or bake in an oven. Take them out and allow to cool. Peel and grate them finely or coarsely. Peel, rinse and chop the onions finely. Dice the pork fat and render it down partly. Add onions and fry lightly. Combine with flour and brown lightly. Combine with beets and wine and simmer over low heat for several minutes. Season to taste.

BELVEDERE BEETS

1 1/2 lb. beets, 3 1/2 oz. onions, 2/3 oz. flour, 3 1/2 oz. raisins, olive oil, 1/3 cup ketchup, salt, sugar and lemon juice to taste

Scrub the beets with a brush under running water. Wash them and cover with boiling salted water. Cook covered or bake in an oven. Allow to cool, peel and grate them finely. Peel, rinse and chop the onions finely. Fry them and combine with flour. Fry this, browning lightly, and combine with the beets, ketchup and rinsed raisins. Simmer over low heat for several minutes. Season to taste.

ĆWIKŁA (BEET SALAD)

1 1/2 lb. beets, 1 2/3 oz. grated horseradish, 5 oz. apples, 3 tablespoons dry red wine, salt, sugar and lemon juice to taste

Scrub the beets with a brush under running water. Wash them and cover with boiling water. Cook covered or bake in an oven. Allow to cool, peel and grate them finely. Wash, peel and halve the apples, removing the cores. Grate coarsely and combine with the beets, horseradish and wine. Season to taste. Transfer to a jar. Cover and leave in the refrigerator for several hours.

CAPTAIN'S BROAD BEANS

1 3/4 lb. broad beans (young), 1 1/3 oz. butter, 1/3 cup ketchup, parsley sprigs, salt, pepper and curry powder to taste

Rinse the beans, cover with boiling water and cook covered. Add salt towards the end. Drain, peel and transfer the beans to a dish. Add melted butter, ketchup and chopped parsley sprigs. Simmer for several minutes. Season to taste.

WROCŁAW BROAD BEANS

1 1/2 lb. broad beans (young), 5 oz. smoked bacon, 5 oz. onions, 3 table-spoons dry white wine, parsley sprigs, salt and pepper to taste

Rinse the beans, cover with boiling water and cook covered. Add salt towards the end. Drain and peel the beans. Peel, rinse and dice the onions finely. Dice the bacon and render it down partly. Add onions and brown this. Combine with the beans and wine, then simmer for several minutes. Season to taste. Combine with chopped parsley sprigs before serving.

FRIED ONIONS

1 1/4 lb. onions, fat, 1 1/3 oz. flour, ketchup, salt and pepper to taste

Peel, rinse and cut the onions into thick slices. Dredge with seasoning and flour. Fry in very hot fat on both sides, then continue frying over low heat for several minutes. Sprinkle with ketchup before serving.

ONIONS IN PASTRY

1 1/4 lb. onions, fat, 3 1/2 oz. flour, 2 eggs, sour cream, salt and pepper to taste

Sift the flour and pour into a blender. Add eggs and enough sour cream to make a thick batter. Add salt and turn on the blender for 30 seconds. Peel, rinse and cut the onions into thick slices. Sprinkle with seasoning and dip into the batter. Place in very hot fat and brown on both sides, then continue frying over low heat for several minutes.

ONIONS À LA VOIVODE

1 1/4 lb. onions (green or shallot), fat, 7 oz. apples, 1/3 cup ketchup, salt, pepper and lemon juice to taste

Peel and rinse the onions, then scald and drain them. Wash, peel and halve the apples, removing the cores. Grate them coarsely and combine with onions, ketchup, fat and seasoning. Simmer for several minutes. Season to taste.

STUFFED ONIONS

8 large onions, 1 1/3 oz. dried cèpe mushrooms, 1 2/3 oz. rice, 1 1/3 oz. tomato paste, 1 oz. raisins, fat, parsley sprigs, sour cream, salt and pepper to taste

Peel and rinse the onions. Slice off the tops and hollow out the centres with a special spoon, leaving the sides thick. Cover with boiling salted water, cook for several minutes and drain. Sprinkle with seasoning. Wash, soak and cook the mushrooms. Cut them into strips. Rinse the rice and cover with plenty of boiling salted water. Cook until partly tender and strain. Combine with tomato paste, mushrooms, rinsed raisins and chopped parsley sprigs. Season to taste and fill the onions. Arrange in a greased dish or pan. Pour seasoned sour cream over the onions and bake.

CHIVE SALAD WITH SOUR CREAM

7 oz. chives, 3/4 cup sour cream, 2 hard-boiled eggs, salt

Wash the chives well and drain. Cut them up, combine with sour cream and chopped eggs, then season.

CHIVE SALAD WITH FARMER'S CHEESE

7 oz. chives, 5 oz. cucumbers, 5 oz. farmer's cheese, 1/3 cup sour cream, salt to taste

Wash the chives well, drain and cut them up. Wash, peel and cut the cucumbers into half-slices. Combine with chives, farmer's cheese forced through a strainer and sour cream. Season to taste.

CHIVE SALAD WITH PLUMS

7 oz. chives, 5 oz. stewed plums, 1/3 cup ketchup, 3 tablespoons sour cream, salt to taste

Wash the chives well, drain and cut them up. Remove the pits from the plums and cut them into strips. Combine with chives, ketchup and sour cream. Season to taste.

CHIVE SALAD WITH MAYONNAISE

7 oz. chives, 3 1/2 oz. radishes, 1 1/3 oz. tomato paste, 5 oz. mayonnaise sauce, fresh dill, salt and sugar to taste

Wash the chives well, drain and cut them up. Clean, rinse and cut the radishes into half-slices. Combine with tomato paste, mayonnaise, chopped dill and chives. Season to taste.

BUTTERED ENDIVE

1 3/4 lb. endive, butter, breadcrumbs, salt and sugar to taste

Clean the endive of damaged leaves and cut out the bitter pulp from the base of the roots. Rinse, cover with boiling salted water with sugar

and cook for 15 minutes. **Drain and arrange** on a platter. Pour browned breadcrumbs blended with melted butter over the endive.

GENERAL'S ENDIVE

8 thick endives, 8 slices smoked ham, butter, 3 1/2 oz. hard cheese, 1 2/3 oz. ketchup, salt, sugar and pepper to taste

Clean the endive of damaged leaves and cut out the bitter pulp from the base of the roots. Rinse, cover with boiling salted water with sugar and cook for 15 minutes. Drain and sprinkle with pepper. Roll up in ham slices and arrange in a greased dish or pan. Sprinkle with grated cheese and ketchup, then bake.

CHEF'S ENDIVE

1 3/4 lb. endive, 5 oz. canned peppers, 3 tablespoons dry red wine, 7 oz. mushrooms, fat, parsley sprigs, salt, pepper, sugar and nutmeg to taste

Clean the endive of damaged leaves and cut out the bitter pulp from the base of the roots. Rinse, cover with boiling salted water with sugar and cook for 15 minutes. Drain and arrange in a greased dish or pan. Clean, rinse and chop the mushrooms finely. Fry them and combine with mashed peppers, wine and chopped parsley sprigs. Season to taste, pour over the endive and bake.

ENDIVE SALAD I

3/4 — 1 lb. endives, 1 2/3 oz. chives, 1 1/2 tablespoons olive oil, salt, sugar and lemon juice to taste

Clean the endive of damaged leaves and cut out the bitter pulp from the base of the roots. Rinse and slice it thinly together with the chives. Combine with olive oil and season.

ENDIVE SALAD II

3/4 lb. endives, 3 1/2 oz. canned peas, 1 2/3 oz. ketchup, 1 1/2 table-spoons olive oil, 5 oz. apples, salt, sugar and lemon juice to taste

Clean the endive of damaged leaves and cut out the bitter pulp from the base of the roots. Rinse and slice it thinly. Wash the apples and halve them, removing the cores. Grate coarsely, combine with peas, endives, ketchup and olive oil, then season.

ENDIVE SALAD III

3/4 lb. endives, 5 oz. oranges, 1 2/3 oz. walnut meats, 4 oz. cream cheese, salt, sugar and lemon juice

Clean the endive of damaged leaves and cut out the bitter pulp from the base of the roots. Rinse and slice it thinly. Wash and scald the oranges with boiling water, then peel and dice them. Blanch the walnuts and chop them. Combine with oranges, cream cheese and endives, then season.

ENDIVE SALAD IV

3/4 lb. endives, 3 1/2 oz. mayonnaise sauce, 3 tablespoons sour cream, 3 1/2 oz. stewed peaches, 5 oz. apples, 5 oz. tomatoes, salt, sugar, pepper and lemon juice to taste

Clean the endive of damaged leaves and cut out the bitter pulp from the base of the roots. Rinse and slice it thinly. Wash the apples and halve them, removing the cores. Wash and scald the tomatoes with boiling water. Peel them and cut into cubes together with the apples and peaches. Combine with mayonnaise and sour cream, then season.

ENDIVE SALAD V

3/4 lb. endives, 1 1/2 tablespoons olive oil, 3 1/2 oz. soured agaric mushrooms, 1 2/3 oz. ham, 1 2/3 oz. ketchup, parsley sprigs, salt, pepper, sugar and lemon juice to taste

Clean the endive of damaged leaves and cut out the bitter pulp from the base of the roots. Rinse and slice it thinly. Cut the mushrooms and ham into thin strips. Combine with endives, olive oil, ketchup and chopped parsley sprigs, then season.

BOILED STRING BEANS

1 1/2 lb. string beans, butter, breadcrumbs, salt and sugar to taste

Remove strings from the beans and cut off the ends. Rinse and cover with boiling salted water with sugar. Cook uncovered for around 30 minutes. Drain when tender and arrange on a platter. Brown breadcrumbs, blend with melted butter and pour over the beans.

STRING BEANS POLISH STYLE

1 1/2 lb. string beans, 2/3 cup sour cream, 2 hard-boiled eggs, fat, 2 egg yolks, parsley sprigs, salt, pepper and sugar to taste

Remove strings from the beans and cut off the ends. Rinse and cover with boiling salted water with sugar. Cook uncovered for around 30 minutes. Drain when tender and sprinkle with chopped parsley sprigs and chopped eggs. Blend fat and sour cream with egg yolks and seasoning, then bake.

STRING BEANS À L'OPÉRA

1 1/2 lb. string beans, 5 oz. smoked bacon, 3 1/2 oz. onions (green or shallot), 3 1/2 oz. ketchup, 3 tablespoons dry red wine, 3 1/2 oz. thin frankfurters, salt, pepper and sugar to taste

Remove strings from the beans and cut off the ends. Rinse and cover with boiling salted water with sugar. Cook uncovered for around 30 minutes. Remove outer skin, if any, from the frankfurters and cut into slices. Peel and rinse the onions. Cut the bacon into cubes and render it down partly. Add onions and fry. Combine with drained beans, frankfurters, ketchup and wine. Simmer for several minutes and season.

ADMIRAL'S STRING BEANS

1 1/2 lb. string beans, fat, 5 oz. canned peppers, 1 teaspoon dry red wine, salt, pepper and sugar to taste

Remove strings from the beans and cut off the ends. Rinse and cover with boiling salted water with sugar. Cook uncovered for around 30 minutes. Drain and pour over fat and wine blended with mashed peppers and seasoning. Simmer for several minutes and season to taste.

WROCŁAW WHITE BEANS

3/4 lb. white beans, fat, 3 1/2 oz. ketchup, parsley sprigs, 2 egg yolks, salt, pepper and marjoram to taste

Sort, rinse and cover the beans with water. Bring to a boil and set aside for 2 hours. Cook in the same water and drain. Combine with ketchup, egg yolks, fat, chopped parsley springs and seasoning. Simmer for several minutes and season.

WHITE BEANS DOMINICAN STYLE I

1/2 lb. white beans, fat, 1/2 lb. kiełbasa, 3 1/2 oz. onions, 2/3 oz. flour, 2/3 cup sour cream, parsley sprigs, salt, pepper, ground paprika and seasoning to taste

Sort, rinse and cover the beans with water. Bring to a boil and set aside for 2 hours. Cook in the same water. Remove the outer skin

from the kiełbasa, cut into half-slices and fry lightly. Peel, rinse and chop the onions finely, then fry them. Add flour and brown lightly. Combine with the beans, kiełbasa, sour cream and chopped parsley sprigs. Simmer for several minutes and season.

WHITE BEANS DOMINICAN STYLE II

1/2 lb. white beans, fat, 1 1/3 oz. tomato paste, 5 oz. mushrooms, 5 oz. peppers, 3 tablespoons dry red wine, salt, papper, marjoram and thyme to taste

Sort, rinse and cover the beans with water. Bring to a boil and set aside for 2 hours. Cook in the same water and drain. Clean the mushrooms and peppers and rinse them. Dice, fry them and combine with tomato paste, beans, wine and seasoning. Simmer for several minutes and season.

WHITE BEANS POLISH STYLE

1/2 lb. white beans, fat, 2 2/3 oz. onions, 5 oz. white kiełbasa (scalded), 2/3 oz. flour, 2/3 oz. dried cèpe mushrooms, 2/3 oz. capers, salt and pepper

Sort, rinse and cover the beans with water. Bring to a boil and set aside for 2 hours. Cook in the same water. Wash, soak and cook the mushrooms. Take them out and dice them. Peel, rinse and chop the onions finely. Fry them and blend with flour. Brown lightly. Combine with the beans, mushrooms, rinsed capers and kiełbasa cut into half-slices. Simmer for several minutes and season.

ROYAL GREEN PEAS I

1 1/2 lb. green peas, butter, 1 2/3 oz. walnut meats, 3 egg yolks, parsley sprigs, salt, sugar and pepper to taste

Sort, rinse and cover the peas with a small amount of boiling salted water with sugar. Cook covered for around 15 minutes, then drain. Blanch the walnuts and chop them. Combine with the peas, egg yolks, chopped parsley sprigs and butter. Fry for several minutes, stirring constantly, and season.

ROYAL GREEN PEAS II

1 1/4 lb. green peas, butter, 1/3 cup sour cream, 3 1/2 oz. lobster tails, 1 2/3 oz. almonds, 2/3 oz. fresh dill, salt, pepper and sugar to taste

Sort, rinse and cover the peas with a small amount of boiling salted water with sugar. Cook covered for around 15 minutes, then drain. Blanch the almonds and combine with the peas, sour cream, lobster tails and chopped dill. Season and simmer for 4 minutes.

BARRISTER'S GREEN PEAS

1 1/4 lb. green peas, butter, 5 oz. ham, 1 1/3 oz. tomato paste, 2/3 oz. capers, 1/3 cup sour cream, parsley sprigs, salt, pepper and sugar to taste

Sort, rinse and cover the peas with a small amount of boiling salted water with sugar. Cook covered for around 15 minutes, then drain. Combine with the butter, minced ham, tomato paste, sour cream, rinsed capers and chopped parsley sprigs. Simmer for several minutes and season.

BUTTERED CAULIFLOWER

Cauliflower, butter, breadcrumbs, salt, sugar and vinegar

Clean the cauliflower and rinse in water with a little vinegar. Place in boiling salted water with sugar and cook uncovered. Take out when tender and drain. Arrange on a round platter. Pour browned breadcrumbs with melted butter over the cauliflower.

CAULIFLOWER IN PASTRY

Cauliflower, fat, 3 1/2 oz. flour, 2 eggs, milk, fat, salt, sugar and vinegar to taste

Clean the cauliflower and rinse in water with a little vinegar. Place in boiling salted water with sugar and cook uncovered. Take out when tender and divide into pieces. Sift the flour and place it in a blender together with the eggs. Add enough milk to make a thick batter, then add salt. Dip the cauliflower in the batter and place in very hot fat. Brown on both sides, then continue frying over low heat for several minutes.

FRIED CAULIFLOWER

Cauliflower, fat, 1 1/3 oz. flour, 2 — 3 eggs, breadcrumbs, salt, sugar and vinegar to taste

Clean the cauliflower and rinse in water with a little vinegar. Place in boiling salted water with sugar and cook uncovered. Take out when tender and divide into pieces. Dredge with flour and coat with beaten eggs and breadcrumbs. Place in very hot fat and brown on all sides, then continue frying over low heat for several minutes.

BOILED WHITE OR SAVOY CABBAGE

1 1/2 lb. white or savoy cabbage, 1 1/3 oz. butter or margarine, 2/3 oz. breadcrumbs, salt and sugar to taste

Remove damaged leaves from cabbage, rinse it and divide into 4 parts. Cover with boiling salted water with sugar and cook covered. Uncover for a while, then continue cooking covered. Take out the cabbage when tender, drain it and cut out the stem. Arrange cabbage on a platter. Pour browned breadcrumbs with melted butter over it.

SAUTÉED WHITE OR SAVOY CABBAGE

1 1/2 lb. white or savoy cabbage, fat, 2 2/3 oz. onions, 2/3 oz. flour, salt, pepper, sugar, garlic and lemon juice to taste

Remove damaged leaves from cabbage, rinse it and shred thinly, removing the stem and thick veins. Add fat and cover with a small amount of boiling salted water with sugar. Bring to a boil covered. Uncover for a while, then continue cooking covered. Peel, rinse and chop the onions finely. Fry them and blend with flour. Fry without browning and combine with the cabbage. Simmer for several minutes, then season.

WHITE OR SAVOY CABBAGE WITH SOUR CREAM

1 1/2 lb. white or savoy cabbage, fat, 2 oz. onions, 1/3 cup sour cream, 2/3 oz. flour, 5 oz. tomatoes, 5 oz. apples, parsley sprigs, salt, pepper, sugar and lemon juice to taste

Remove damaged leaves from cabbage, rinse it and shred thinly, removing the stem and thick veins. Add fat and cover with a small amount of boiling salted water with sugar. Bring to a boil covered. Uncover for a while, then continue cooking covered. Wash and scald the tomatoes with boiling water, then peel them. Wash, peel and halve the apples, removing the cores. Cut them into pieces together with the tomatoes. Peel, rinse and chop the onions finely. Fry them lightly. Add flour and fry without browning. Combine with the cabbage, sour cream, tomatoes, apples and chopped parsley sprigs. Simmer for several minutes and season.

OFFICER'S WHITE OR SAVOY CABBAGE

1 1/2 lb. white or savoy cabbage, fat, 2 2/3 oz. onions, 1/2 lb. apples, 1/3 cup dry white wine, 1 1/3 oz. raisins, 2/3 oz. flour, salt, pepper, sugar and lemon juice to taste

Remove damaged leaves from cabbage, rinse it and shred thinly, removing the stem and thick veins. Add fat and cover with a small amount of boiling salted water with sugar. Bring to a boil covered. Uncover for a while, then continue cooking covered. Wash, peel and halve the apples, removing the cores. Grate them coarsely and add to the cabbage together with rinsed raisins and wine. Peel, rinse and chop the onions finely. Fry them lightly and combine with flour. Fry without browning and combine with the cabbage. Simmer for several minutes and season.

UHLAN'S WHITE OR SAVOY CABBAGE

1 1/2 lb. white or savoy cabbage, fat, 3 1/2 oz. onions, 1/3 cup sour cream, 5 oz. canned peppers, 1 1/3 oz. tomato paste, parsley sprigs, 2/3 oz. flour, 1 oz. raisins, salt, pepper and sugar to taste

Remove damaged leaves from cabbage, rinse it and shred thinly, removing the stem and thick veins. Add fat and cover with a small amount of boiling salted water with sugar. Bring to a boil covered. Uncover for a while, then continue cooking covered until tender. Peel, rinse and chop the onions finely, then fry them. Add flour and brown lightly. Combine with the cabbage, mashed peppers, tomato paste, sour cream, rinsed raisins and chopped parsley sprigs, then season.

WHITE OR SAVOY CABBAGE IN PASTRY

1 1/2 lb. white or savoy cabbage, fat, 3 1/2 oz. flour, egg, milk, salt, sugar and pepper to taste

Remove damaged leaves from cabbage, rinse it and divide into 4 parts. Cover with boiling salted water with sugar and bring to a boil covered. Uncover for a while, then continue cooking covered until crisp. Take it out, drain and remove the stem. Wash the egg and break it into a blender. Add milk and sifted flour. Turn on the blender for 30 seconds. Make a thick batter and add salt. Sprinkle the cabbage

with pepper and dip in the batter. Place in very hot fat and fry to a light golden colour. Continue frying over low heat for several minutes.

BREADED WHITE OR SAVOY CABBAGE

1 1/2 lb. white or savoy cabbage, fat, 1 oz. flour, 2 eggs, breadcrumbs, salt, pepper and sugar to taste

Remove damaged leaves from cabbage, rinse it and divide into 4 parts. Cover with boiling salted water with sugar and bring to a boil covered. Uncover for a while, then continue cooking covered until crisp. Take it out, drain and remove the stem. Dredge with pepper and flour. Coat with beaten eggs and breadcrumbs. Place in heated fat and fry until golden. Continue frying over low heat for several minutes.

BELVEDERE WHITE OR SAVOY CABBAGE

1 1/2 lb. white or savoy cabbage, fat, 1 1/3 oz. dried mushrooms, 2 hard-boiled eggs, 3 1/2 oz. hard cheese, 2 — 2 2/3 oz. ham or kiełbasa, 5 oz. prunes, 2 egg yolks, 1 1/3 oz. horseradish (grated), salt, sugar, pepper and lemon juice to taste

Remove damaged leaves from cabbage, rinse it and divide into 4 parts. Cover with boiling salted water with fat and bring to a boil covered. Uncover for a while, then continue cooking covered until crisp. Take it out, drain and remove the stem. Wash, soak and cook the mushrooms. Take them out and mince together with the eggs and ham, then season. Place between cabbage leaves and press down with your hand. Arrange in a greased oven-proof dish. Wash, soak and cook the prunes. Force them through a strainer and combine with egg yolks and horseradish. Season to taste, pour over the cabbage and bake.

GOŁĄBKI (STUFFED CABBAGE) WITH MEAT AND RICE

1 head white or savoy cabbage, 5 oz. rice, 3 1/2 oz. onions, 7 oz. pork or veal, parsley sprigs or fresh dill, fat, 1 1/3 oz. tomato paste, 1 cup broth, 2/3 cup sour cream, salt and pepper

Remove damaged leaves from cabbage. Cut out the stem and rinse. Cover with plenty of boiling water and cook until the leaves are tender. Take out the cabbage and separate the leaves. Cut off the thick veins without damaging the leaves. Rinse the rice and cover with boiling salted water. Cook until slightly tender and drain. Peel, rinse and dice the onions, then fry them. Wash and mince the meat. Combine it with the onions, rice and chopped greens, then season. Place the filling on the leaves. Fold the edges to the middle and roll up. Arrange on a platter covered with cabbage leaves. Cover with broth and cook covered until tender. Towards the end add sour cream blended with tomato paste and seasoning. When tender arrange the gołąbki on a platter and pour with seasoned sauce.

Note: Buckwheat, pearl barley or hulled barley kasha may be used instead of rice.

FARMER'S GOŁĄBKI (STUFFED CABBAGE)

1 head white or savoy cabbage, 7 oz. smoked ham, 3 1/2 oz. hardened French bread, milk, 7 oz. mushrooms, fat, 2 eggs, parsley sprigs, 1 cup sour cream, salt, pepper and nutmeg to taste

Cook the cabbage as above. Soak the bread in milk, squeeze it out and mince it. Clean, rinse and chop the mushrooms finely. Fry them and combine with the bread, strips of ham, chopped parsley sprigs, egg yolks and stiffly beaten egg whites, then season. Place the filling on cabbage leaves, fold the edges into the centre and roll up. Arrange in a dish covered with cabbage leaves. Cover with seasoned sour cream and simmer covered over low heat.

SEYM WHITE OR SAVOY CABBAGE

1/2 white or savoy cabbage, 5 oz. white kiełbasa, fat for deep-fat frying
Batter: 5 oz. flour, 2/3 cup water, 2 2/3 oz. butter or margarine, 5 eggs, 1 teaspoon baking powder, salt, pepper, curry powder and sugar to taste

Remove damaged leaves from cabbage, rinse it and divide into parts. Cover with boiling salted water with sugar and cook until crisp. Take it out, drain and remove the stem. Wash the kiełbasa, cover with boiling water and heat in ca. 200° F for around 15 minutes. Take out when done and remove the outer skin. Mince it together with the cabbage. Bring the water to a boil together with the butter. Add flour, stirring constantly. Remove from heat and break down all lumps. Place over heat again and heat slightly, stirring constantly until the batter becomes smooth and shiny. Remove pot from heat. Add eggs one by one to the heated batter, mixing until smooth. Combine the batter with the cabbage mixture and season. With a metal spoon place in very hot fat so that the cabbage floats easily. Fry until light golden. When done take out with a special spoon and drain of fat.

WHITE OR SAVOY CABBAGE SALAD

3/4 lb. white or savoy cabbage, 5 oz. apples, 1 1/2 tablespoons olive oil, 3 1/2 oz. cucumbers, parsley sprigs, salt, pepper, sugar, lemon juice and prepared mustard to taste

Remove damaged leaves from cabbage, rinse it and shred thinly, removing the stem and thick veins. Wash the apples and halve them, removing the cores. Grate them coarsely. Wash, peel and cut the cucumbers into half-slices. Combine with the cabbage, apples, olive oil and chopped parsley sprigs, then season.

WHITE OR SAVOY CABBAGE SALAD WITH PLUMS

3/4 lb. white or savoy cabbage, 5 oz. plums, 1 2/3 oz. almonds, 1/3 cup sour cream, parsley sprigs, salt, sugar, pepper and lemon juice

Remove damaged leaves from cabbage, rinse it and shred thinly, removing the stem and thick veins. Blanch the almonds. Wash the plums, remove pits and cut into strips. Combine with the cabbage, sour cream, almonds and chopped parsley sprigs, then season.

WHITE OR SAVOY CABBAGE SALAD WITH CHERRIES

3/4 lb. white or savoy cabbage, 5 oz. sour cherries, 1 2/3 oz. walnut meats, parsley sprigs, 1/3 cup sour cream, salt, sugar and pepper to taste

Remove damaged leaves from cabbage, rinse it and shred thinly, removing the stem and thick veins. Blanch the walnuts and chop them. Rinse the cherries, remove pits and combine with the cabbage, walnuts, sour cream and chopped parsley sprigs, then season.

WHITE OR SAVOY CABBAGE SALAD
WITH TOMATOES

3/4 lb. white or savoy cabbage, 5 oz. tomatoes, 2 hard-boiled eggs, 1/3 cup sour cream, fresh dill, salt, pepper, sugar and lemon juice to taste

Remove damaged leaves from cabbage, rinse it and shred thinly, removing the stem and thick veins. Wash and scald the tomatoes with boiling water and peel them. Dice them together with the eggs. Combine with the cabbage, sour cream and chopped dill, then season.

MANAGER'S WHITE OR SAVOY CABBAGE SALAD

3/4 lb. white or savoy cabbage, 3 1/2 oz. mayonnaise sauce, 3 table-spoons sour cream, 3 1/2 oz. canned peas, 1 2/3 oz. canned peppers, parsley sprigs, salt, pepper, sugar and lemon juice to taste

Remove damaged leaves from cabbage, rinse it and shred thinly, removing the stem and thick veins. Combine with the mayonnaise, sour cream, chopped parsley sprigs, strips of peppers and peas, then season.

STEWED RED CABBAGE

1 3/4 lb. red cabbage, fat, 3 1/2 oz. pork fat, 3 1/2 oz. onions, 2/3 oz. flour, salt, sugar and lemon juice to taste

Remove damaged leaves from cabbage, rinse it and shred thinly, removing the stem and thick veins. Add fat, sprinkle with water and simmer over low heat, stirring occasionally. Peel, rinse and chop the onions finely. Dice the pork fat and render it down partly. Add onions, fry lightly and combine with flour. Brown lightly and add to the cabbage. Simmer for several minutes, then season.

MANAGER'S RED CABBAGE

1 3/4 lb. red cabbage, fat, 3/4 cup red currant juice, 1 2/3 oz. raisins, 2/3 oz. flour, salt, pepper and lemon juice to taste

Remove damaged leaves from cabbage, rinse it and shred thinly, removing the stem and thick veins. Add fat, sprinkle with juice and simmer covered over low heat, stirring often. Heat the fat, combine with flour and fry, browning lightly. Combine with the cabbage and rinsed raisins. Simmer for several minutes, then season.

RED CABBAGE WITH GRAPES

1 1/2 lb. red cabbage, 7 oz. grapes, dry red wine, 2/3 oz. flour, salt, pepper, sugar and lemon juice to taste

Remove damaged leaves from cabbage, rinse it and shred thinly, removing the stem and thick veins. Add fat, sprinkle with wine and

simmer covered over low heat, stirring often. Heat the fat and combine with the flour. Fry without browning and combine with the cabbage and halved grapes. Simmer for several minutes, then season.

RED CABBAGE WITH RAISINS

1 3/4 lb. red cabbage, dry red wine, 3 1/2 oz. raisins, fat, 2/3 oz. flour, 2—2 2/3 oz. sour cherry jam, salt, pepper and lemon juice to taste

Remove damaged leaves from cabbage, rinse it and shred thinly, removing the stem and thick veins. Add fat, sprinkle with wine and simmer covered over low heat, stirring often. Heat the fat, combine with flour and fry without browning. Combine with the cabbage, rinsed raisins and jam. Simmer for several minutes, then season.

RED CABBAGE WITH PEPPERS

1 1/4 lb. red cabbage, 1/2 lb. peppers, 2 2/3 oz. onions, fat, 2/3 oz. flour, 2—2 2/3 oz. gooseberries, salt, sugar, pepper and lemon juice to taste

Remove damaged leaves from cabbage, rinse it and shred thinly, removing the stem and thick veins. Sprinkle with water, add fat and simmer covered over low heat. Clean, rinse and dice the onions and peppers. Fry them lightly and simmer until tender. Heat fat and blend with flour. Fry without browning and combine with the cabbage, peppers and grated gooseberries. Simmer for several minutes and season.

RED CABBAGE POLISH STYLE I

1 3/4 lb. red cabbage, fat, 2/3 oz. flour, 3 1/2 oz. cranberry preserves, 3 1/2 oz. red currants, salt and sugar to taste

Remove damaged leaves from cabbage, rinse it and shred thinly, removing the stem and thick veins. Add fat, sprinkle with water and simmer covered over low heat. Heat the fat and blend with the flour. Fry without browning and combine with the cabbage, cranberries and currants forced through a strainer. Simmer for several minutes, then season.

RED CABBAGE POLISH STYLE II

1 1/2 lb. red cabbage, fat, dry red wine, 5 oz. prunes, 5 oz. lemons, salt, sugar, cloves and lemon juice to taste

Remove damaged leaves from cabbage, rinse it and shred thinly, removing the stem and thick veins. Add fat, sprinkle with wine and simmer covered over low heat. Wash the prunes and cover with a small amount of water. Cook them and force through a strainer. Wash the lemons, scald and peel them. Dice them, removing the pits. Heat the fat and blend with the flour. Fry without browning and combine with the cabbage, prunes, lemons and seasoning. Simmer for several minutes, then season.

ROYAL RED CABBAGE

1 3/4 lb. red cabbage, fat, 2/3 oz. flour, dry red wine, salt, nutmeg, sugar, lemon and orange juice, and lemon and orange rind to taste

Remove damaged leaves from cabbage, rinse it and shred thinly, removing the stem and thick veins. Add fat, sprinkle with wine and simmer covered over low heat. Heat the fat and combine with the flour. Fry without browning and combine with the cabbage, grated rinds, lemon and orange juice. Simmer for several minutes, then season.

RED CABBAGE SALAD WITH APPLES I

3/4 lb. red cabbage, 5 oz. apples, 2 2/3 oz. raisins, 1 1/2 tablespoons olive oil, salt, sugar and lemon juice to taste

Remove damaged leaves from cabbage, rinse it and shred thinly, removing the stem and thick veins. Wash the apples and halve them, removing the cores. Grate them coarsely and combine with the cabbage, olive oil and rinsed raisins, then season.

RED CABBAGE SALAD WITH APPLES II

3/4 lb. red cabbage, 5 oz. apples, 3 1/2 oz. lemons, 1/3 cup dry red wine, 2 egg yolks, salt, sugar and lemon juice to taste

Remove damaged leaves from cabbage, rinse it and shred thinly, removing the stem and thick veins. Wash the apples and halve them, removing the cores, then grate coarsely. Bring the wine to a boil and gradually pour into egg yolks beaten with sugar, stirring briskly with an egg-whisk. Wash, scald and peel the lemons. Dice them, remove the pits and combine with the sauce, apples and cabbage, then season.

RED CABBAGE SALAD WITH PEACHES

3/4 lb. red cabbage, 7 oz. peaches, 1 2/3 oz. walnut meats, 1 1/2 tablespoons olive oil, salt, pepper, sugar and lemon juice to taste

Remove damaged leaves from cabbage, rinse it and shred thinly, removing the stem and thick veins. Blanch and grind the walnuts. Wash the peaches, remove the pits and dice them. Combine with the cabbage, olive oil and walnuts, then season.

RED CABBAGE SALAD WITH PEPPERS

3/4 lb. red cabbage, 1 1/2 tablespoons olive oil, 7 oz. peppers, 1 2/3 oz. ketchup, hard-boiled egg, salt, pepper, sugar and lemon juice to taste

Remove damaged leaves from cabbage, rinse it and shred thinly, removing the stem and thick veins. Clean, rinse and cut the peppers

into strips. Combine with olive oil and ketchup, then season. Divide into portions and sprinkle with chopped egg.

STEWED SAUERKRAUT

1 1/4 lb. sauerkraut, 3 1/2 oz. pork fat, 3 1/2 oz. onions, 2/3 oz. flour, meat stock, salt, pepper, caraway seed, sugar and seasoning to taste

Press out the juice from the sauerkraut, shred it and cover with stock. Cook covered. Uncover for a while, then continue cooking covered over low heat for around 50 minutes. Peel, rinse and chop the onions finely. Dice the pork fat and render it down partly. Add the onions and fry lightly. Combine with flour and brown lightly. Combine with the sauerkraut and seasoning. Simmer for several minutes, then season.

SAUERKRAUT OLD POLISH STYLE

1 1/4 lb. sauerkraut, fat, 2/3 oz. flour, 2/3 oz. dried cèpe mushrooms, 1 1/3 oz. prunes, 3 1/2 oz. pork fat, salt, pepper, sugar and seasoning to taste

Wash and soak the prunes, then cook and force them through a strainer. Wash, soak and cook the mushrooms. Take them out and cut into strips. Squeeze out the juice from the sauerkraut and shred it. Add fat, cover with water and bring to a boil covered. Uncover for a while, then continue cooking covered over low heat for around 50 minutes. Dice the pork fat, render it down partly and combine with the flour. Fry, browning lightly, and combine with the sauerkraut, prunes and mushrooms. Simmer for several minutes, then season.

SAUERKRAUT WITH RAISINS

1 1/4 lb. sauerkraut, fat, 2/3 oz. flour, 1/3 cup dry white wine, 3 1/2 oz. raisins, salt, pepper and sugar to taste

Press out the juice from the sauerkraut and shred it. Add fat, cover with water and bring to a boil covered. Uncover for a while, then cook covered over low heat for around 50 minutes. Heat the fat and blend it with the flour. Fry, browning lightly, and combine with the cabbage, wine and rinsed raisins. Simmer for several minutes, then season.

SAUERKRAUT DAINTIES I

Dough: 1/2 lb. flour, 1 cup milk, 3 eggs, 2 egg yolks, 2/3 oz. yeast, salt, 1/3 oz. sugar, egg for top, fat
Filling: 1 lb. sauerkraut, fat, 2/3 oz. flour, 2/3 oz. capers, 3 1/2 oz. kiełbasa, salt, pepper and seasoning to taste

Dice the sauerkraut, sprinkle with water and add fat. Bring to a boil covered. Uncover for a while and cook covered for around 50 minutes. Heat the fat and blend it with the flour. Fry, browning lightly, and combine with the sauerkraut, rinsed raisins and minced kiełbasa. Simmer for several minutes, then season. Bring the milk to a boil and pour gradually into the sifted flour (3 1/2 oz.), stirring briskly. Allow to cool and combine with the yeast mixed with the sugar. Set aside in a warm place 30 minutes. Beat the eggs and egg yolks with an egg-whisk and combine with the dough. Add the remaining flour and salt. Knead the dough and set aside to let it rise. Roll out into 1/4 in. thickness and cut out circles with a glass. Make a hollow in the centre of each circle and place filling in it. Brush with beaten egg and arrange on a greased baking sheet. Allow for the dough to rise again. Place in a moderate oven and bake.

SAUERKRAUT DAINTIES II

Dough: 1/2 lb. flour, 3 1/2 oz. margarine, 7 oz. soft cheese, salt, egg for top, fat, caraway seed
Filling: 3/4 lb. sauerkraut, fat, 2 hard-boiled eggs, 2/3 oz. dried cèpe mushrooms, 2 2/3 oz. onions, 2/3 oz. flour, salt, pepper and seasoning to taste

Dice the sauerkraut, and soaked and chopped mushrooms and fat. Sprinkle with water and simmer covered over low heat. Peel, rinse and chop the onions finely. Fry them and add flour. Brown lightly and combine with the sauerkraut. Simmer for several minutes and combine with minced eggs, then season. Sift the flour onto a pastry board. Cut in the fat and cheese. Make into a dough quickly and set aside in the refrigerator for an hour. Roll out the dough into 1 1/2 in. thickness and cut out circles with a glass. Place filling on one and cover with another circle. Arrange on a greased baking sheet. Brush with beaten egg and sprinkle with caraway. Bake in a hot oven.

BIGOS OLD POLISH STYLE

1 3/4 lb. sauerkraut, 7 oz. veal, 7 oz. boneless pork, 3 1/2 oz. smoked bacon, 5 oz. kiełbasa, fat, 2/3 oz. flour, 3 tablespoons dry red wine, 1 1/3 oz. tomato paste, 2—3 dried cèpe mushrooms, 2/3 oz. prunes, salt, pepper, sugar, garlic, marjoram and seasoning to taste

Press the juice out from the sauerkraut and shred it. Add soaked and chopped mushrooms, then pitted prunes cut into strips. Cover with boiling salted water and bring to a boil covered. Uncover for a while, then cook covered over low heat for around 50 minutes. Wash the meat and remove any veins. Cut into cubes together with the bacon and peeled and rinsed onions. Render the bacon down partly and add the meat. Fry lightly, add the onions and brown lightly. Sprinkle with water and simmer covered over low heat. Remove the outer skin from the kiełbasa, cut lengthwise, then into slices. Fry the kiełbasa lightly. Heat the fat and blend with the flour. Fry, browning lightly, and combine with the cabbage, meat, kiełbasa, tomato paste, wine and seasoning. Simmer for several minutes, then season.

MARINER'S BIGOS

1 1/4 lb. sauerkraut, fat, 3 1/2 oz. onions, 2/3 oz. flour, 5 oz. thin frankfurters, 1/2 lb. boneless pork, 1/2 lb. peppers, 1 1/3 oz. tomato

*paste, 5 oz. mushrooms, salt, pepper, ground paprika, seasoning, marjo-
ram, sugar and curry powder to taste*

Press the juice out from the sauerkraut and shred it. Cover with
boiling water, add fat and bring to a boil covered. Uncover for a while,
then cook covered over low heat for around 50 minutes. Wash the
meat and dice it. Fry lightly, add seasoning and sprinkle with water.
Simmer until tender. Clean, rinse and dice the onions and mushrooms.
Fry them lightly and add to the meat halfway through the cooking
process. Heat the fat and blend with the flour. Fry without browning
and combine with the sauerkraut, meat, tomato paste and peeled frankfurters cut into slices. Simmer for several minutes, then season.

FARMER'S BIGOS

*1 3/4 lb. sauerkraut, 3 1/2 oz. white beans, 5 oz. kiełbasa, 1/2 lb.
fresh bacon, 3 1/2 oz. plums (Damson), 2 2/3 oz. onions, fat, 1/3 cup
sour cream, 2/3 oz. flour, salt, pepper, marjoram and seasoning to
taste*

Sort and rinse the beans. Cover with water and bring to a boil. Set
aside for 2 hours. Cook in the same water. Press the juice out from
the sauerkraut and dice together with the bacon. Cover with boiling
water and bring to a boil covered. Uncover for a while, then cook
covered over low heat for around 50 minutes. Wash the plums, remove
pits and cut into strips. Peel, rinse and chop the onions finely. Fry
them, add flour and brown lightly. Combine with the sauerkraut,
plums, beans, sour cream and kiełbasa cut into half-slices. Simmer for
several minutes, then season.

SAUERKRAUT SALAD I

*3/4 lb. sauerkraut, 1 1/2 tablespoons olive oil, 5—7 oz. apples, 2 2/3 oz.
onions, parsley sprigs, salt, sugar and pepper to taste*

Peel, rinse and dice the onions together with the sauerkraut. Wash the apples and halve them, removing the cores. Grate them coarsely and combine with the sauerkraut, chopped parsley sprigs and olive oil, then season.

SAUERKRAUT SALAD II

3/4 lb. sauerkraut, 1 1/2 tablespoons olive oil, 7 oz. tomatoes, 1 1/3 oz. chives, fresh dill, parsley sprigs, salt, pepper and sugar to taste

Wash the tomatoes and scald with boiling water. Peel them, cut into pieces and combine with shredded sauerkraut, chopped greens and olive oil, then season.

GENERAL'S SAUERKRAUT SALAD I

3/4 lb. sauerkraut, 1 1/2 tablespoons olive oil, 7 oz. tomatoes, 1 1/3 oz. raisins, 2 2/3 oz. ketchup, parsley sprigs, salt, pepper and sugar to taste

Dice the sauerkraut and combine with olive oil, rinsed raisins, chopped parsley sprigs and ketchup, then season.

GENERAL'S SAUERKRAUT SALAD II

3/4 lb. sauerkraut, 1 1/2 tablespoons olive oil, 3 1/2 oz. canned peppers, 3 1/2 oz. celeriac cooked with milk, 3 1/2 oz. apples, parsley sprigs, salt, sugar and pepper to taste

Wash the apples and halve them, removing the cores. Grate them coarsely together with the celeriac. Combine with chopped sauerkraut, chopped parsley sprigs and peppers cut into strips, then season.

WROCŁAW SAUERKRAUT SALAD

3/4 lb. sauerkraut, 1 1/2 tablespoons olive oil, 5 oz. radishes, parsley sprigs, hard-boiled egg, salt, pepper and sugar to taste

Clean, rinse and grate the radishes coarsely. Combine with chopped sauerkraut, olive oil, chopped parsley sprigs and egg, then season.

CARROTS AND PEAS

1 1/4 lb. carrots, 7 oz. canned peas, milk, 1/2 oz. flour, fat, parsley sprigs, salt and sugar to taste

Wash, peel and rinse the carrots. Dice them and cover with a small amount of boiling water with fat, salt and sugar. Cook covered. Heat the fat and combine with the flour. Fry without browning and combine with the carrots, peas and milk. Simmer for several minutes, season and combine with chopped parsley sprigs.

GENERAL'S CARROTS

1 1/4 lb. carrots, 1/2 lb. apples, fat, 1/3 cup dry white wine, salt, sugar, 1/2 oz. flour, lemon juice, lemon and orange rind to taste

Wash, peel and rinse the carrots. Dice them and cover with a small amount of boiling water with fat, salt and sugar, then cook covered. Wash and peel the apples. Rinse and halve them, removing the cores, then dice them. Heat the fat, blend with flour and fry without browning. Combine with the carrots, apples, wine and grated rinds. Simmer for several minutes, then season.

MASHED CARROTS

1 3/4 lb. carrots, 1/3 cup sour cream, 1—2 egg yolks, fat, 1/3—1 2/3 oz. flour, parsley sprigs, salt and sugar to taste

Wash, clean and peel the carrots. Rinse them and cover with boiling salted water with sugar. Cook covered, then force through a strainer. Heat the fat and blend with the flour. Fry without browning and com-

bine with the carrots and sour cream. Simmer for several minutes. Add egg yolks and chopped parsley sprigs, then season.

CARROT SALAD WITH HORSERADISH

3/4 lb. carrots, 1/3 cup sour cream (thick), 5 oz. apples, 1 1/3 oz. horseradish (grated), parsley sprigs, salt, sugar and lemon juice to taste

Wash, peel and rinse the carrots, then grate them finely. Wash the apples and halve them, removing the cores. Grate them coarsely and combine with the carrots, sour cream and chopped parsley sprigs, then season.

MINISTER'S CARROT SALAD I

3/4 lb. carrots, 1/3 cup whipping cream, 5 oz. oranges, 5 oz. walnut meats, salt, sugar and lemon juice to taste

Wash, scald and peel the oranges. Dice them, removing the pits. Blanch the walnuts and grind them. Wash, peel and rinse the carrots. Grate them finely and combine with the oranges, walnuts and whipped cream, then season.

MINISTER'S CARROT SALAD II

3/4 lb. carrots, 1/3 cup sour cream (thick), 1 2/3 oz. almonds, 5 oz. stewed peaches, 3 1/2 oz. lemons, salt, sugar and lemon juice to taste

Wash, scald and peel the lemons. Dice them, removing the pits. Wash, peel and rinse the carrots. Grate them finely and combine with the lemons, sour cream, diced peaches and blanched walnuts, then season.

FRIED CUCUMBERS OR SUMMER SQUASH I

2 lb. cucumbers or summer squash, fat, 1 1/3 oz. flour, 2 eggs, breadcrumbs, salt and pepper to taste

Wash, peel and rinse the cucumbers or summer squash. Cut them into 1/2 in. thick slices. Sprinkle with seasoning and set aside for 30 minutes. Drain and dredge with flour. Coat with beaten eggs and breadcrumbs. Place in very hot fat and fry on both sides until golden.

FRIED CUCUMBERS OR SUMMER SQUASH II

2 lb. cucumbers or summer squash, fat, 2 2/3 oz. onions, 2 oz. hardened French bread, milk, 1/2 lb. boneless pork, egg for mixture, 1 1/3 oz. flour, 2 eggs for coating, breadcrumbs, salt and pepper to taste

Wash, peel and rinse the cucumbers or summer squash. Cut into 1 1/2—2 in. thick slices. Make hollows in the centers, leaving some of the pulp on the bottom. Sprinkle with seasoning and set aside for 30 minutes. Peel, rinse and dice the onions, then fry them. Soak the bread in milk, squeeze it out and mince together with the meat. Combine with the onions and eggs, then season. Fill the cucumbers or squash. Dredge with flour and coat with beaten eggs and breadcrumbs. Place in very hot fat and brown on all sides until golden, then continue frying over low heat.

CUCUMBERS OR SUMMER SQUASH
WITH SOUR CREAM

1 1/4 lb. cucumbers or summer squash, 3/4 lb. tomatoes, 3/4 cup sour cream, 3 1/2 oz. onions, fat, 1/3 oz. flour, fresh dill, salt and pepper to taste

Wash and dice the cucumbers or summer squash together with the peeled and rinsed onions, then fry them lightly. Wash the tomatoes and scald with boiling water. Peel them and cut into pieces. Add to the vegetables. Cover with the sour cream blended with flour, chopped dill and seasoning. Simmer for 3—4 minutes.

OFFICER'S CUCUMBERS OR SUMMER SQUASH

1 3/4 lb. cucumbers or summer squash, 1/3 cup sour cream, 3—4 egg yolks, butter, parsley sprigs, salt and pepper to taste

Wash, peel and rinse the cucumbers or summer squash. Cut them into half-slices. Scald with boiling water and drain. Arrange in a greased pan or dish. Cover with sour cream blended with egg yolks, chopped parsley sprigs and seasoning. Bake in a hot oven.

MIZERIA (CUCUMBER SALAD)

1 lb. cucumbers, 1/3 cup sour cream (thick), fresh dill, salt, pepper, sugar and lemon juice to taste

Wash, peel and rinse the cucumbers. Cut them lengthwise, then into slices. Arrange on individual serving plates and pour seasoned sour cream over. Sprinkle with chopped dill.

CUCUMBER SALAD I

1 lb. cucumbers, 1 2/3 oz. chives, 3 1/2 oz. ketchup, salt and pepper to taste

Wash, peel and rinse the cucumbers. Cut into half-slices. Arrange on individual serving plates. Sprinkle with seasoning, ketchup and chopped chives.

CUCUMBER SALAD II

1 lb. cucumbers, 3 1/2 oz. radishes, 1 2/3 oz. tomato paste, 1 1/2 table-spoons olive oil, 2 2/3 oz. onions, salt, pepper and sugar to taste

Wash, peel and rinse the cucumbers. Cut them into half-slices. Clean, rinse and cut the radishes into half-slices. Peel, rinse and chop the

onions finely. Combine with the radishes, cucumbers, tomato paste and olive oil, then season.

CUCUMBER SALAD III

1 lb. cucumbers, 5 oz. canned peppers, 1 2/3 oz. walnut meats, parsley sprigs, fresh dill, salt, pepper and sugar to taste

Wash, peel and rinse the cucumbers. Cut them into half-slices. Combine with chopped greens and mashed peppers, then season. Divide into portions and sprinkle with blanched and ground walnuts.

CUCUMBER SALAD IV

1 lb. cucumbers, 1 1/2 tablespoons olive oil, 1 oz. almonds, 1 2/3 oz. pitted olives, 2/3 capers, parsley sprigs, salt, pepper, sugar and lemon juice to taste

Wash, peel and rinse the cucumbers. Cut them lengthwise, then into slices. Combine with the olives, rinsed capers, chopped parsley sprigs, olive oil and blanched almonds, then season.

BRAISED PEPPERS

2 lb. peppers, olive oil, 7 oz. onions, 1 1/3 oz. tomato paste, parsley sprigs, salt, sugar, pepper and ground paprika to taste

Clean, rinse and dice the peppers. Peel, rinse and chop the onions finely. Fry them lightly, add peppers and simmer covered until tender, stirring constantly. Towards the end add the tomato paste. Rinse the parsley sprigs and chop them finely. Combine with the peppers, then season.

BREADED PEPPERS

2 lb. peppers, 1 2/3 oz. flour, fat, 2—3 eggs, breadcrumbs, salt and pepper

Clean, rinse and bake the peppers lightly in an oven. Allow to cool and peel them. Cut them into halves and flatten out. Dredge with seasoning and flour. Coat with beaten eggs and breadcrumbs. Fry on both sides until golden, then continue frying for several minutes.

PEPPERS IN PASTRY

2 lb. peppers, fat, 1 2/3 oz. flour, 4 eggs, salt and ground paprika

Clean, rinse and bake the peppers lightly in an oven. Allow to cool and peel. Cut into halves and flatten out. Wash the eggs and separate the yolks from the whites. Beat the egg whites until stiff and combine with the egg yolks and sifted flour, then season. Dip the peppers in the batter, place on a greased baking sheet and bake.

WROCŁAW PEPPERS

2 lb. peppers, fat, 3 1/2 oz. onions, 1/2 lb. kiełbasa, 1 1/3 oz. tomato paste, 2 2/3 oz. white beans, 2/3 cup sour cream, 2/3 oz. flour, salt, pepper, ground paprika, marjoram and seasoning to taste

Sort and rinse the beans. Cover with water, bring to a boil and set aside for 2 hours. Cook in the same water. Clean and rinse the peppers. Dice them and simmer until tender. Remove the outer skin from the kiełbasa. Cut into half-slices and fry it. Peel, rinse and chop the onions finely. Fry them, add flour and brown lightly. Combine with the peppers, beans, tomato paste, sour cream and kiełbasa. Simmer for several minutes, then season.

PEPPERS WITH APPLES

3/4 lb. peppers, 5 oz. apples, 2 2/3 oz. onions, 1/3 cup sour cream (thick), parsley sprigs, salt, sugar and lemon juice to taste

Wash the apples and halve them, removing the cores. Grate them coarsely. Clean, rinse and dice the onions and peppers. Combine with the apples, sour cream and chopped parsley sprigs, then season.

PEPPERS WITH RAISINS, NUTS AND FIGS

3/4 lb. peppers, 3 tablespoons olive oil, 1 2/3 oz. raisins, 1 2/3 oz. walnut meats, 5 oz. figs, parsley sprigs, salt, sugar and lemon juice

Clean, rinse and cut the peppers into strips. Blanch the walnuts, chop them and combine with the peppers, rinsed raisins, olive oil, chopped parsley sprigs and ground figs, then season.

GENERAL'S PEPPER SALAD

1 lb. peppers, olive oil, 5 oz. stewed peaches, egg yolk, 1 2/3 oz. ketchup, parsley sprigs, salt, pepper, sugar and lemon juice to taste

Clean, rinse and cut the peppers into strips. Break down the peaches and place in a blender together with the egg yolk and ketchup. Turn it on for 30 seconds. Combine the mixture with peppers and chopped parsley sprigs, then season.

GDAŃSK PEPPER SALAD

3/4 lb. peppers, olive oil, 7 oz. oranges, 3 1/2 oz. lemons, 1 2/3 oz. ketchup, salt, honey, ginger and lemon juice to taste

Wash, scald and peel the oranges and lemons. Dice them, removing the pits. Clean, rinse and cut the peppers into strips. Combine with the oranges, lemons and olive oil. Season, divide into portions and pour ketchup over.

AMATEUR PEPPER SALAD

3/4 lb. peppers, 1/3 cup sour cream, 1/2 lb. bananas, 1 1/3 oz. raisins, salt, pepper, sugar and lemon juice to taste

Clean, rinse and cut the peppers into strips. Wash the bananas and scald with boiling water. Peel them, break them down and place in a blender. Add sour cream and turn on the blender for 30 seconds. Combine the mixture with the peppers and rinsed raisins, then season.

TOMATOES WITH SOUR CREAM

2 lb. tomatoes, fat, 1 cup sour cream, 2 lb. flour, parsley sprigs, 3 1/2 oz. hard cheese, salt and pepper to taste

Wash the tomatoes and scald them with boiling water. Peel them, cut into pieces and arrange in a greased dish or pan. Combine the sour cream with flour and chopped parsley sprigs, then season. Pour this over the tomatoes, sprinkle with grated cheese and bake.

TOMATOES IN PASTRY

2 lb. tomatoes, 5 oz. flour, 2 eggs, milk, salt and pepper to taste

Wash the tomatoes and scald them with boiling water. Peel them and cut into thick slices. Sprinkle with seasoning and set aside for 30 minutes. Wash the eggs and break them into a blender together with sifted flour and enough milk to make a thick batter. Turn on the blender for 30 seconds, then season the batter. Dip the tomatoes in the batter and fry on both sides.

STUFFED TOMATOES

8 tomatoes (large), fat, 1/3 cup sour cream, 2 2/3 oz. onions, 7 oz. thin frankfurters, 2 2/3 oz. hard cheese, 1 2/3 oz. horseradish (grated), salt and pepper

Wash the tomatoes and cut off the tops. Hollow out the centres with a special spoon. Sprinkle with seasoning and set aside in a cool place for 30 minutes. Peel, rinse and chop the onions finely. Fry them and combine with frankfurters cut into half-slices and horseradish, then season. Stuff the tomatoes. Combine the pulp from the hollowed tomatoes with sour cream and seasoning. Pour this over the tomatoes. Sprinkle with grated cheese and bake.

BELVEDERE RADISHES I

4 bunches radishes, 2/3 cup sour cream, butter, fresh dill, salt and sugar to taste

Wash, clean and rinse the radishes. Scald with boiling water, strain and drain. Fry lightly in butter. Pour over them seasoned sour cream blended with chopped dill. Simmer for several minutes, then season.

BELVEDERE RADISHES II

4 bunches radishes, 3 1/2 oz. ketchup, butter, 1 1/3 oz. raisins, salt, sugar and lemon juice to taste

Wash, clean and rinse the radishes. Scald with boiling water, strain and drain. Add butter, ketchup and rinsed raisins. Simmer for several minutes, then season.

RADISHES WITH CAULIFLOWER

4 bunches radishes, 7 oz. cooked cauliflower, 3 1/2 oz. ketchup, 3 1/2 oz. hard cheese, fresh dill, olive oil, salt and pepper to taste

Wash, clean and rinse the radishes. Scald with boiling water, strain and drain. Combine with crumbled cauliflower, chopped dill, ketchup and olive oil. Sprinkle with seasoning and grated cheese, then bake.

RADISHES POLISH STYLE

4 bunches radishes, 3 tablespoons ketchup, 3 tablespoons sour cream, olive oil, 3 1/2 oz. soured agaric mushrooms, 3 1/2 oz. cooked egg whites, salt, pepper and sugar to taste

Wash, clean and rinse the radishes. Cut them into half-slices and combine with the mushrooms cut into strips, ketchup and diced egg whites, then season.

AMATEUR RADISHES

4 bunches radishes, 1 can sardines, 3 1/2 oz. ketchup, 2/3 oz. capers, parsley sprigs, salt, pepper and lemon juice to taste

Wash, clean and rinse the radishes. Cut them into half-slices and combine with crumbled sardines, ketchup, rinsed capers and chopped parsley sprigs, then season.

TOSSED SALAD I

2 heads lettuce, 3 1/2 oz. cucumbers, 1 2/3 oz. radishes, 1 1/3 oz. chives, 2/3 cup sour cream, salt, pepper, sugar and lemon juice to taste

Remove damaged and yellowed leaves from lettuce. Rinse, drain and divide it. Arrange on individual plates. Wash, peel and rinse the cucumbers. Cut them into half-slices together with cleaned and rinsed radishes. Combine with chopped chives and sour cream. Season and pour over lettuce leaves.

TOSSED SALAD II

2 heads lettuce, 3 1/2 oz. canned peas, 3 1/2 oz. mayonnaise sauce, 3 tablespoons sour cream, fresh dill, salt and pepper to taste

Remove damaged and yellowed leaves from lettuce. Rinse, drain and divide it. Arrange on individual plates. Combine the peas with mayonnaise, sour cream and chopped dill. Season and pour over lettuce.

TOSSED SALAD III

2 heads lettuce, 3 1/2 oz. ketchup, 3 1/2 oz. lobster tails, 1 1/3 oz. olives (black), salt, pepper, sugar and lemon juice to taste

Remove damaged and yellowed leaves from lettuce. Rinse, drain and divide it. Arrange on individual plates. Sprinkle with seasoning, lobster tails, chopped olives and ketchup.

TOSSED SALAD IV

2 heads lettuce, 1 1/2 tablespoons olive oil, 5 oz. plums (Damson), hard-boiled egg, 1 2/3 oz. canned peppers, salt, pepper and lemon juice to taste

Remove damaged and yellowed leaves from lettuce. Rinse, drain and divide it. Arrange on individual plates. Wash the plums, remove pits and cut into strips together with the peppers. Combine with olive oil, season and pour over lettuce leaves. Sprinkle with chopped egg.

BREADED CELERIAC

1 3/4 lb. celeriac, fat, 2—3 eggs, 1 1/3 oz. flour, breadcrumbs, milk, salt and pepper to taste

Scrub the celeriac with a brush under running water. Peel, rinse and cover with boiling salted water with added milk. Cook until tender. Strain, drain and cut into 1/2 in. slices. Sprinkle with seasoning and flour. Coat with beaten eggs and breadcrumbs. Place in very hot fat and brown on both sides. Continue frying over low heat until done.

STUFFED CELERIAC

4 celeriacs (round), milk, 5 oz. mushrooms, 3 1/2 oz. ham, fat, 1 2/3 oz. ketchup, 2—2 2/3 oz. hard cheese, parsley sprigs, salt, pepper and milk

Scrub the celeriac with a brush under running water. Cover with boiling water with added milk and cook covered until partly tender. Strain, allow to cool and peel. Cut into halves and hollow out the centers with a special spoon, leaving the sides thick. Clean, rinse and chop the mushrooms finely. Fry them and combine with diced ham, chopped parsley sprigs and ketchup. Season and stuff the celeriac. Sprinkle with grated cheese, arrange in a greased pan or dish and bake.

CELERIAC POLISH STYLE

1 3/4 lb. celeriac, fat, 5 oz. prunes, 1 1/3 oz. horseradish (grated), 1/3 cup sour cream, 1 1/3 oz. raisins, salt, pepper, sugar and lemon juice to taste

Scrub the celeriac with a brush under running water. Peel, rinse and cook it. Take it out and cut into pieces. Arrange in a greased pan or dish. Wash and soak the prunes, remove the pits. Cook them, force through a strainer and combine with the horseradish, sour cream and rinsed raisins. Season and pour over the celeriac. Simmer for several minutes and season.

BOILED ASPARAGUS

1 3/4 lb. asparagus, butter, breadcrumbs, salt and sugar to taste

Wash the asparagus and remove lower hardened ends. Peel off fibrous outer skin. Place in cold water to prevent darkening. Tie up in bunches and place in boiling salted water with sugar. Cook covered. Take out when done and drain. Untie the bunches and arrange on a platter. Pour over browned breadcrumbs blended with melted butter.

ASPARAGUS WITH BÉCHAMEL SAUCE

1 3/4 lb. asparagus, fat, 2/3 oz. butter, 2/3 oz. flour, 1 cup milk, egg yolk, 3 1/2 oz. hard cheese, 1 2/3 oz. walnut meats, salt, sugar, white pepper or nutmeg to taste

Cook the asparagus (as above) and arrange on a greased platter. Heat the butter and blend with the flour. Fry without browning and combine with milk, stirring briskly with an egg-whisk. Cook for a while and allow to cool slightly. Combine with egg yolk, season to taste and pour over the asparagus. Sprinkle with blanched and chopped walnuts and grated cheese, then bake.

ASPARAGUS IN BATTER

1 3/4 lb. asparagus, fat, milk, 3—4 eggs, 1 2/3 oz. flour, salt, sugar and nutmeg to taste

Cook the asparagus (as in Boiled Asparagus). Wash the eggs, break them and separate the yolks from the whites. Beat the egg whites until stiff and combine with the egg yolks and sifted flour. Season to taste. Dip the asparagus in the batter, place on a greased baking sheet and bake.

ASPARAGUS À LA RADZIWIŁŁ

1 3/4 lb. asparagus, 8 slices smoked ham, 2 1/2 oz. ketchup, 4 egg whites, fat, salt, pepper and sugar to taste

Cook the asparagus (as in Boiled Asparagus). Sprinkle with seasoning and ketchup. Roll up in slices of ham and arrange on a greased platter. Cover with stiffly beaten egg whites and bake.

BOILED SPINACH

2 lb. spinach, butter, 2/3 oz. flour, 2/3 cup sour cream, salt and garlic to taste

Sort the spinach, clean and rinse it. Scald with boiling water, strain and drain. Mash it or chop with a cleaver. Heat the fat and combine with the flour. Fry without browning and combine with the spinach and sour cream. Simmer for several minutes and season to taste.

SPINACH POLISH STYLE

2 lb. spinach, butter, 2/3 oz. flour, 1/3 cup sour cream, 4 eggs, 3 1/2 oz. hard cheese, salt, pepper and garlic to taste

Sort the spinach, clean and rinse it. Scald with boiling water, strain and drain. Mash it or chop with a cleaver. Heat the fat and combine with the flour. Fry without browning and combine with the spinach and sour cream. Season to taste and break in the eggs. Sprinkle with seasoning and grated cheese, then bake.

MANAGER'S SPINACH

2 lb. spinach, butter, 2/3 oz. flour, 2 egg yolks, 1/3 cup ketchup, 2/3 oz. capers, salt, pepper and garlic to taste

Sort the spinach, clean and rinse it. Scald with boiling water, strain and drain, then mash it. Heat the fat and combine with the flour. Fry without browning and combine with the spinach, ketchup and rinsed capers. Simmer for several minutes, combine with the egg yolks and season to taste.

MASHED POTATOES

2 lb. potatoes, 1 1/3 oz. butter, 1/3 cup milk, parsley sprigs, 1—2 egg yolks (optional), salt to taste

Wash, peel and rinse the potatoes. 3/4 cover with boiling salted water and cook covered. Strain and allow the water to evaporate. Use a potato

masher. Combine the potatoes with hot milk and egg yolks. Season to taste. Divide into portions and sprinkle with chopped parsley.

POTATOES POLISH STYLE

2 lb. potatoes, fat, breadcrumbs, salt and pepper to taste

Wash, peel and rinse the potatoes. 3/4 cover with boiling salted water and cook covered. Strain and allow the water to evaporate. Cut into strips and fry in fat, sprinkling with breadcrumbs. Season to taste.

STUFFED POTATOES POLISH STYLE

12 large potatoes, 24 strips smoked bacon, 5 oz. onions, 7 oz. kiełbasa, 1 oz. tomato paste, fat, parsley sprigs, salt, pepper and garlic to taste

Wash, peel and rinse the potatoes. Hollow out the centres with a special spoon, leaving the sides thick. Cover with boiling salted water, cook until partly tender and strain. Sprinkle with seasoning. Peel, rinse and chop the onions finely. Fry them and combine with tomato paste and ground kiełbasa. Season to taste and stuff the potatoes. Pound the bacon with a mallet and arrange each two strips crosswise. Place potatoes in the centre and fold up the sides, securing the top with a toothpick. Arrange on a greased baking sheet and bake.

POTATO PANCAKES

3 lb. potatoes, 2 eggs, 1 2/3 oz. flour, fat, salt to taste

Wash, peel and rinse the potatoes. Grate them finely and drain of some of the juice. Combine the potato pulp with eggs and sifted flour. Season to taste. With a spoon place thin small pancakes in very hot fat. Fry on both sides until golden.

Cakes

YEAST CAKE WITH CRUMB TOPPING

Cake: 1 lb. flour, 3/4 cup milk, 7 oz. margarine, 3—4 eggs, 3 1/2—5 oz. confectioners' sugar, 1 1/3 oz. yeast, vanilla extract, salt, orange rind
Crumb topping: 3 1/2 oz. flour, 1 2/3 oz. margarine, 1 2/3 oz. confectioners' sugar, grease for baking pan

Make leaven from 1 2/3 oz. flour, yeast and milk. Allow it to rise. Wash and break the eggs. Separate the yolks from the whites. Blend the yolks with the sugar and combine with the leaven, remainig flour, salt, grated orange rind and vanilla extract. Knead the dough well, adding melted margarine towards the end. Combine with stiffly beaten egg whites. Roll the dough out into a rectangle and place it in a greased pan, filling it halfway. Even out the edges, brush the top with beaten egg, sprinkle with crumb topping and set aside for it to rise. Bake in a hot oven for around 40 minutes. Towards the end you can cover the cake with greased parchment paper or aluminium foil. The topping is made by combining flour with sugar and melted margarine, then crumbling the mixture.

FRUIT YEAST CAKE

1 lb. flour, 1 cup milk, 3 1/2 oz. confectioners' sugar, 3 1/2 oz. margarine, 3 eggs, 1 1/3 oz. yeast, 1 3/4 lb. fruit (cherries, sour cherries, plums or apples), fruit jelly, vanilla extract, fat for baking pan

Rinse the fruit and cut into halves, removing the pits. Peel the apples, cut them into pieces and drain. Make the dough as above and roll out into a 1/2 in. thick rectangle. Place in a greased pan and even out the edges. Arrange the fruit on top and set aside for it to rise. Bake in a hot oven for around 40 minutes. Allow to cool when done. Cover with nearly firm jelly, the same flavour as the fruit used for top, and allow it to set. Follow package directions when making the jelly.

YEAST CAKE SPECIAL

1 lb. flour, 1 cup milk, 3 1/2—5 oz. confectioners' sugar, 6 egg yolks, 1 2/3 yeast, 1/2 lb. margarine, 1/2 lb. nut filling, 1/2 lb. cheese filling, salt, orange rind, vanilla extract, fat for baking pan, chocolate icing

Make leaven from 1 2/3 oz. flour, yeast and milk. Allow it to rise. Blend egg yolks with sugar and combine with sifted flour, leaven, vanilla extract, grated orange rind and salt. Knead well, adding the melted fat towards the end. Roll out the dough and place in a greased pan. Cover with nut filling (q.v.), then with cheese filling and set aside for it to rise. Bake in a hot oven for around 60 minutes. When done, cover with chocolate icing (q.v.).

APPLE PIE

1/2 lb. flour, 3 1/2 oz. confectioners' sugar, 3 1/2 oz. butter or margarine, 2 egg yolks, 1 2/3 oz. raisins, 1—2 egg yolks for apples, 1 lb. apples, 2—2 2/3 oz. confectioners' sugar for apples, vanilla-flavoured confectioners' sugar for dusting, lemon rind

Sift the flour and cut in butter with a knife. Combine with the egg yolks blended with sugar and make the dough quickly. Set aside in a cool place for 30 minutes. Roll out into 3/4 in. thickness and place in a baking pan. Bake until golden. Wash, peel and halve the apples, removing the cores. Grate coarsely and fry with sugar until translucent. Combine with egg yolks, rinsed raisins and grated lemon rind. Place on the cake and bake in a hot oven. Allow to cool, dust with vanilla-flavoured confectioners' sugar and cut into pieces.

EGG-WHITE TART

7 oz. flour, 7 oz. confectioners' sugar, 5 oz. butter or margarine, 8 egg whites, 1 1/3 oz. cocoa, 1 2/3 oz. walnut meats, 1 teaspoon baking powder, salt, lemon rind, fat and breadcrumbs for baking pan

Blanch the walnuts and grind them. Beat the egg whites until stiff, adding confectioners' sugar towards the end. Combine with walnuts, grated lemon rind, salt, cocoa, sifted flour with baking powder and melted fat. Place in a greased pan sprinkled with breadcrumbs and even out the surface. Bake in a hot oven for around 40 minutes. Take out when done and allow to cool. Cut into two layers and fill with Russel Cream. Garnish and cover with lemon icing.

NUT TART

1/2 lb. flour, 3 1/2 oz. confectioners' sugar, 5 oz. butter or margarine, 2 egg yolks, 3/4 lb. nut filling, 5 oz. preserves

Sift the flour and cut in butter with a knife. Combine with egg yolks blended with sugar and make a dough quickly. Set aside in a cool place for 30 minutes. Divide into two parts and roll out. Place one part in a baking pan and bake until golden. Spread preserves on top and cover with nut filling (q.v.). Cut the remaining dough into strips and arrange in a lattice pattern on the nut filling. Bake in a hot oven for around 45 minutes. Allow to cool and cover with chocolate icing.

SPONGE CAKE

7 oz. flour, 3 1/2—5 oz. confectioners' sugar, 6—8 eggs, 1 2/3 oz. raisins, lemon rind, fat and breadcrumbs for pan

Wash the eggs and break them. Separate the yolks from the whites. Beat the egg whites until stiff, adding confectioners' sugar towards the end. Mix lightly with the egg yolks, grated lemon rind, alternating with sifted flour and rinsed raisins dredged with flour. Place in a greased pan sprinkled with breadcrumbs. Even out the surface and bake in a hot oven for around 45 minutes. When done allow to cool and take out of pan.

APPLE STRUDEL

Cake: 1/2 lb. flour, 3/4 cup water, egg, salt
Filling: 1 1/2 lb. apples, 1 oz. breadcrumbs, 2 oz. butter, 3 1/2 oz.
confectioners' sugar, orange rind, cinnamon, fat and breadcrumbs for
baking pan

Sift the flour onto pastry board. Make a well in the centre and pour
in warm water blended with egg and salt. Mix with a knife until the
liquid combines with the flour. Make a soft dough, pressing firmly with
your hand, until bubbles form and the dough is smooth and shiny. The
dough should be softer than for pierogi (q.v.). When kneaded set aside
covered for 2 hours so that it ferments. Place a flat plate upside down
in the centre of a table. Cover the table with a clean cloth and sift
flour over the cloth evenly. Place the dough on the plate and pull it
towards yourself with hands dredged with flour, adding flour to hands
as necessary. In order to pull out the dough well, it is best to do it with
another person. Pull out the dough as thin as possible, taking care
not to tear it. When the dough is pulled out allow for it to dry. Pour
browned breadcrumbs blended with melted butter (1 1/2 oz.) over the
dough. Wash, peel and halve the apples, removing the cores. Cut into
half-slices and combine with sugar, grated orange rind and cinnamon.
Arrange the apples on the dough and roll up, raising the cloth on one
side, at the same time bringing it up with your hands from the bottom.
Transfer the strudel onto a greased baking sheet sprinkled with breadcrumbs. Pour butter over it and bake in a hot oven for 25—30 minutes.
When done dust with confectioners' sugar and cut into portions. Serve
with sour-cherry juice and thick sour cream.

NUT STRUDEL

Cake: 1/2 lb. flour, 3/4 cup water, egg, salt
Filling: 7 oz. walnut meats, 1/3 cup sour cream, 1 2/3 oz. gingerbread,
1 2/3 oz. powdered chocolate, 2 egg yolks, 2 2/3 oz. confectioners' sug-
ar, 1 oz. butter, lemon and orange rind to taste, fat and breadcrumbs
for baking sheet and dough

Make the dough (as above). Blanch the walnuts and combine with sour cream, egg yolks, grated gingerbread, chocolate, sugar and grated rinds. Roll out the dough, pour over butter blended with browned bread-crumbs, spread with filling and roll up (as in Apple Strudel). Arrange on a greased baking sheet sprinkled with breadcrumbs and bake in a hot oven for 30 minutes.

FRUIT-AND-NUT STRUDEL

Cake: 1/2 lb. flour, 3/4 cup water, egg, salt
Filling: 2/3 cup sour cream, 2 egg yolks, 1 2/3 oz. butter or marga-rine, 2 2/3 oz. confectioners' sugar, 3 1/2 oz. gingerbread, 1 2/3 oz. raisins, 3 1/2 oz. walnut meats, 1 2/3 oz. figs, 1 2/3 oz. dates, 1 oz. butter for top, lemon and orange rind to taste, fat and breadcrumbs for baking sheet and dough

Make the dough (as in Apple Strudel). Blanch the walnuts, grind together with the gingerbread and combine with the sour cream, egg yolks blended with sugar, grated lemon and orange rind, melted butter and finely chopped fruits and nuts. Pour butter with breadcrumbs over the dough and spread fruit and nut mixture on top. Roll up (as in Apple Strudel) and arrange on a greased baking sheet sprinkled with bread-crumbs. Pour butter over and bake in a hot oven for around 30 min-utes.

APPLE TART

Cake: 1/2 lb. flour, 3 1/2 oz. butter or margarine, 2 2/3 oz. confection-ers' sugar, 2 egg yolks
Filling: 2 lb. apples, 3 1/2 oz. sugar, 2/3 oz. confectioners' sugar, 1 2/3 oz. raisins, egg, 1/3 oz. breadcrumbs, cinnamon to taste

Sift the flour and cut in butter with a knife. Combine with egg yolks blended with sugar. Knead quickly into a dough and set aside in a cool place for 30 minutes. Roll out and divide into two parts — one larger,

the other smaller. Spread larger part on a baking pan, making a 3/4 in. high rim. Bake in a hot oven until golden. Wash, peel and halve the apples, removing the cores. Grate coarsely and combine with bread-crumbs, rinsed raisins, sugar and ground cinnamon. Spread over lightly baked cake and even out the surface. Cover with remaining dough, brush with beaten egg, prick with a fork and bake in a moderate oven. When done allow to cool, dust with confectioners' sugar and cut into squares.

APRICOT TART

Cake: 1/2 lb. flour, 3 1/2 oz. margarine, 2 2/3 oz. confectioners' sugar, 2 egg yolks
Filling: 2 lb. apricots, 7 oz. sugar, 1 1/2 tablespoons rum, 4 egg whites, confectioners' sugar for top

Make the dough (as in Apple Tart) and bake. Wash the apricots and remove pits. Cut them up and cook in a small amount of water. Force through a strainer, add sugar and fry until as thick as jam, stirring frequently. Beat egg whites until stiff and combine with the hot paste and sugar. Spread on the cake. Cover with the remaining dough and bake in a moderate oven for around 30 minutes. Take out when done, cut into squares and dust with confectioners' sugar.

VILNA APPLE TART

Crêpe batter: 7 oz. flour, 3/4 cup milk, 3/4 cup water, 2—3 eggs, 2/3 oz. pork fat, salt to taste
Filling: 3 lb. apples, 1/2 lb. sugar, 3 1/2 oz. honey, 1 2/3 oz. raisins, fat and breadcrumbs for baking pan

Wash the eggs and break into a blender. Add milk, water and salt. Turn on blender for 30—40 seconds. Or: Pour milk into a dish, add eggs and salt and beat thoroughly with an egg-whisk. Add sifted flour, beating constantly with an egg-whisk until all the ingredients are blended and air bubbles appear on the surface of the batter. Thin down the batter

with water until it can thinly cover the bottom of a frying pan. Fry the crêpes until golden. Place the fried crêpes on a plate turned upside down. Wash, peel and halve the apples, removing the cores. Grate coarsely and combine with sugar. Fry them lightly, stirring frequently, until translucent. Grease a pan the size of the crêpes and sprinkle with breadcrumbs. Place crêpes on bottom of pan, covering the sides as well. Combine apples with honey and rinsed raisins. Spread over the crêpes and arrange in the pan, one on top of the other. Pour fat over them and bake in a hot oven. Serve hot with sour cream and sour-cherry juice.

PEACH TART

Cake: 1/2 lb. flour, 3 1/2 oz. margarine, 2 2/3 oz. confectioners' sugar, 2 egg yolks
Filling: 1 lb. stewed or bottled peaches, 1 cup milk, 1 cup cream, 1 2/3 oz. butter, 2/3 oz. cocoa, half a vanilla bean, 1—2 egg yolks, 1 2/3 oz. confectioners' sugar, 1/3 cup whipping cream, 2/3 oz. confectioners' sugar for cream, 2/3 oz. raisins, 1 oz. potato starch

Make the dough (as in Apple Tart) and roll it out. Arrange in a cake pan, covering the sides 1 1/4 in. high. Bake until golden, then allow to cool. Spread chopped peaches on cake. Bring the milk to a boil together with finely chopped vanilla, then strain. Combine cream with potato starch and gradually add to the hot milk, stirring with an egg-whisk. Bring to a boil. Blend egg yolks with sugar. Gradually add the hot mixture, beating with an egg-whisk and adding butter piece by piece. Pour over the peaches, smooth out the surface and allow to set. Just before serving garnish with whipped cream with sugar and cocoa and sprinkle with rinsed raisins.

STRAWBERRY TART

1/2 lb. ladyfingers, 1 lb. strawberries
Filling: 3/4 cup milk, 2/3 whipping cream, 1 2/3 oz. raisins, 1 1/2 tablespoons rum, 1 2/3 oz. confectioners' sugar for cream, 2—3 egg yolks, waffle cones

Rinse raisins and drain them. Cover with rum and set aside for 2 hours. Sort and rinse the strawberries and remove stems. Arrange in a pan on top of ladyfingers. Blend egg yolks with sugar. Gradually add hot milk, stirring briskly with an egg-whisk. Place pot or dish with egg yolks in a larger one with hot water and beat until mixture thickens. Allow the mixture to cool, stirring, and combine with whipped cream with sugar. Pour over the strawberries and smooth out the surface. Sprinkle with raisins and garnish with waffle cones.

YEAST BABKA WITH RAISINS

1 lb. flour, 1 cup milk, 3 1/2—5 oz. confectioners' sugar, 5 oz. margarine, 1 1/3 oz. yeast, 5 eggs, 3 1/2 oz. raisins, salt and vanilla extract to taste, fat and breadcrumbs for baking pan

Make leaven from 1 2/3 oz. flour, yeast and milk. Set aside to rise. Sift flour and add the leaven, egg yolks, salt and warm fat. Knead the dough thoroughly and set aside for it to rise. Combine with stiffly beaten egg whites, vanilla extract and rinsed, then dredged raisins. Transfer to a greased pan sprinkled with breadcrumbs. When the dough rises, place in a moderate oven and bake for around 50 minutes. When done, allow to cool slightly. Take cake out of pan and dust with vanilla-flavoured confectioners' sugar.

CHOCOLATE BABKA

1/2 lb. flour, 2/3 cup milk, 1 2/3 oz. powdered chocolate, 2 2/3 oz. confectioners' sugar, 1 2/3 oz. raisins, 1 oz. yeast, 4—5 eggs, salt, vanilla extract, fat and breadcrumbs for baking pan

Make leaven from 1 2/3 oz. flour, yeast and milk. Set aside to rise. Wash the eggs, break them and separate the yolks from the whites. Beat the yolks with sugar, chocolate and vanilla extract. Combine with the leaven, sifted flour and knead well. Combine with whipped egg whites and rinsed raisins which have been dredged with flour. Add

salt and transfer to a greased pan sprinkled with breadcrumbs. Smooth out the surface and bake in a moderate oven for around 45 minutes. When done, allow to cool slightly. Take cake out of pan and dust with vanilla-flaovoured confectioners' sugar.

SILESIAN BABKA

7 oz. all-purpose flour, 1 2/3 oz. potato starch, 5 oz. confectioners' sugar, 3 1/2 oz. margarine, 5 eggs, salt and vanilla extract, fat for baking pan

Wash the eggs and break into a bowl. Separate the yolks from the whites. Blend butter with sugar, adding egg yolks one by one. Combine with stiffly beaten egg whites, alternately adding sifted flour and potato starch. Add salt and vanilla extract. Transfer to a greased pan and bake in a moderate oven for around 50 minutes. Take out when done and allow to cool slightly. Dust with vanilla-flavoured confectioners' sugar.

SCALDED BABKA

1 lb. flour, 7 oz. margarine, 7 oz. confectioners' sugar, 1 1/3 cups milk, 10 egg yolks, 1 2/3 oz. raisins, 2 oz. almonds, 1 2/3—2 oz. yeast, salt, vanilla extract, candied orange rind, fat and breadcrumbs for baking pan

Make leaven from 1 2/3 oz. flour, yeast and 1/3 cup milk. Set aside to rise. Blend egg yolks with sugar. Scald 3 1/2 oz. flour with boiling milk. Blend well, breaking down any lumps. When cooled, combine with the leaven, egg yolks and remaining flour. Knead well. When the dough becomes smooth and shiny combine with melted fat and rinsed raisins dredged with flour, blanched grated almonds, vanilla extract, salt and grated orange rind. Transfer to a greased baking pan sprinkled with breadcrumbs. Smooth out the surface and set aside for it to rise. Bake in a moderate oven for around 50 minutes. Take out when done, cool slightly and cover with icing.

COFFEECAKE BABKA

3 1/2 oz. all-purpose flour, 3 1/2 oz. potato starch, 4 oz. confectioners' sugar, 4 oz. margarine, 3 tablespoons milk, 3 eggs, teaspoon baking powder, lemon extract, fat and breadcrumbs for baking pan

Combine flour and potato starch with baking powder and sift. Wash the eggs, break them and separate the yolks from the whites. Blend margarine with sugar, adding egg yolks one by one. Combine with milk, lemon extract and stiffly beaten egg whites, adding flour alternately. Transfer to a greased baking pan sprinkled with breadcrumbs. Bake in a moderate oven for around 40 minutes, raising the temperature towards the end. Allow the cake to cool, take out of pan and dust with confectioners' sugar.

BABKA WITH CREAM CHEESE

13 1/2 oz. flour, 7 oz. margarine, 1/3 cup sour cream, 3 1/2 oz. raisins, 7 oz. farmer's cheese, 1 1/2 tablespoons rum, 5 oz. confectioners' sugar, 3 eggs, orange rind, baking powder, fat and breadcrumbs for baking pan

Wash the eggs and break them. Blend with sugar and mix with sifted flour combined with baking powder, sour cream, rum, grated orange rind, minced farmer's cheese, melted fat and rinsed raisins dredged with flour. Transfer to a greased pan and bake in a moderate oven for around 60 minutes. Take out when done and allow to cool slightly. Cover with chocolate icing.

BREAD BABKA

1/2 lb. grated bread, 1/3 cup sour cream or dry white wine, 1/2 lb. confectioners' sugar, 8 eggs, fat, orange rind, cinnamon, cloves and nutmeg taste

Pour sour cream or wine over bread and set aside for 20 minutes. Wash the eggs, break them and separate the yolks from the whites. Blend egg yolks with sugar, grated orange rind, ground spices and stiffly beaten egg whites, alternately adding bread. Transfer to a greased baking pan and bake in moderate oven for around 50 minutes. When done, allow to cool, take out of pan and cover with chocolate icing.

PLAIN SPICE CAKE

1/2 lb. flour, 5 oz. margarine, 5—7 oz. confectioners' sugar, 3 1/2 oz. raisins, 5 eggs, 1 2/3 oz. walnut meats, 1 tablespoon rum, 1 1/3 oz. candied orange rind, baking powder

Blanch and grind the walnuts. Wash the eggs, break them and separate the yolks from the whites. Blend margarine with sugar, adding egg yolks one by one. Combine with walnuts, rum, grated orange rind, stiffly beaten egg whites, flour sifted with baking powder and rinsed raisins dredged in flour. Spread greased parchment paper in baking pan. Place dough in pan and smooth out the surface, then make a deep slit along the surface lengthwise. Bake in a hot oven for around 60 minutes. Allow to cool when done. Take out of pan together with the paper and dust with confectioners' sugar.

VILNA SPICE CAKE I

7 oz. flour, 5 oz. butter or margarine, 5 oz. honey, 4 eggs, 1 2/3 oz. raisins, 2/3 oz. coffee, cinnamon, cloves, baking powder

Blend butter with honey, adding eggs one by one. Combine with flour sifted with baking powder and rinsed raisins dredged in flour. Proceed as in Plain Fruitcake.

VILNA SPICE CAKE II

3 1/2 oz. grated whole-wheat bread, 1 2/3 oz. breadcrumbs, 5 oz. confectioners' sugar, 6—8 eggs, 1 2/3 oz. butter or margarine, 1 2/3 oz. raisins, cinnamon and cloves

Wash the eggs, break them and separate the yolks from the whites. Blend margarine with sugar, adding egg yolks one by one. Combine with stiffly beaten egg whites, alternately adding bread, breadcrumbs and ground spices. Combine with rinsed raisins dredged in flour. Proceed as in Plain Fruitcake.

CASTLE GINGERBREAD

13 1/2 oz. flour, 1/2 lb. honey, 3 tablespoons rum, 3—4 eggs, gingerbread spices (cloves, nutmeg, cinnamon, ginger), 1 1/6 oz. baking powder, fat and breadcrumbs for pan

Wash the eggs and break them into a bowl. Blend lightly with browned honey and combine with rum, ground spices and flour sifted with baking powder. Transfer to a greased baking pan sprinkled with bread-crumbs. Smooth out the surface and bake in a moderate oven for around 50 minutes.

SILESIAN GINGERBREAD

13 1/2 oz. flour, 13 1/2 oz. confectioners' sugar, 1/3 cup lager beer, 4 eggs, 1 2/3 oz. butter or margarine, gingerbread spices (cloves, nutmeg, cinnamon, ginger), 1 1/6 oz. baking powder, fat and breadcrumbs for pan

Sift flour with baking powder. Wash the eggs, break them and separate the yolks from the whites. Blend egg yolks with sugar and combine with flour, melted butter, beer, ground spices and stiffly beaten egg whites. Transfer to a greased baking pan sprinkled with breadcrumbs. Smooth out the surface and bake in a moderate oven for around 50 minutes.

HETMAN'S GINGERBREAD

1 lb. flour, 9 1/2 oz. honey, 5 oz. butter or margarine, 9 1/2 oz. con-fectioners' sugar, 3/4 cup sour cream, 3—4 eggs, 1 teaspoon ammonia,

fat and breadcrumbs for baking pan, gingerbread spices, (cloves, nutmeg, cinnamon, ginger)

Wash the eggs, break them and separate the yolks from the whites. Blend butter with sugar and browned honey, adding eggs one by one. Combine with sour cream, sifted flour, ammonia dissolved in a small amount of milk, stiffly beaten egg whites and ground spices. Transfer to a greased baking pan sprinkled with breadcrumbs. Smooth out the surface and bake in a moderate oven for around 50 minutes.

GINGERBREAD COOKIES POLISH STYLE

13 1/2 oz. flour, 1/3 cup milk, 3 tablespoons strong coffee, 3 1/2 oz. honey, 1 2/3 oz. yeast, 2 eggs, 1 2/3 oz. butter or margarine, gingerbread spices (cloves, nutmeg, cinnamon, ginger)

Make leaven from 1 2/3 oz. flour, yeast and milk. Set aside to rise. Wash the eggs and break them. Combine with sifted flour, lightly browned honey, melted butter, coffee, leaven and ground spices. Knead well. Roll out into 1/4 in. thickness and cut out cookies with a cookie cutter. Arrange on a greased baking sheet sprinkled with flour and set aside to rise. Bake in a hot oven. When done, allow to cool and cover with icing.

YEAST MAZURKA

1/2 lb. flour, 1/2 cup milk, 2 2/3 oz. butter or margarine, 2 2/3 oz. confectioners' sugar, 4 egg yolks, egg, 1 1/3 oz. sugar, 1 2/3 oz. raisins, 1 2/3 oz. almonds, 2/3—1 oz. yeast, vanilla extract, fat for baking pan

Make leaven from 1 2/3 oz. flour, yeast and milk. Set aside to rise. Blend egg yolks with sugar and combine with sifted flour, leaven and vanilla extract. Knead well, adding melted butter towards the end. Set aside for it to rise. Roll out into 1/2 in. thickness. Place in a greased

baking pan and set aside to let it rise again. Blanch and grind the almonds. Prick the dough in several places and brush with beaten egg. Place rinsed raisins in dough, sprinkle with almonds and sugar and cover with greased parchment paper. Bake in a moderate oven.

KNIGHT'S MAZURKA

Cake: 1 lb. flour, 1/2 lb. margarine, 3 1/2 oz. chocolate, 5 oz. confectioners' sugar, 4 egg yolks
Filling: 1/2 lb. almonds, 1/2 lb. confectioners' sugar, 1 1/2 tablespoons lemon juice, 3 tablespoons sour cream, vanilla extract

Sift the flour and cut in margarine with a knife. Combine with egg yolks blended with confectioners' sugar and melted chocolate. Knead quickly into a dough and set aside in a cool place for an hour. Roll out and divide into two squares. Place on a baking sheet and bake until golden. Blanch and grind the almonds. Blend them with sugar, sour cream, lemon juice and vanilla extract. Spread between cooled cake layers, press down with a wooden board and allow to set. Pour chocolate icing over the cake.

SUDETEN MAZURKA

1/2 lb. butter or margarine, 1/2 lb. flour, 7 oz. confectioners' sugar, 3 1/2 oz. walnut meats, 2 egg yolks, 5 egg whites, 1 lb. jam, lemon rind

Blanch and grind the walnuts. Sift the flour and cut in the butter. Combine with egg yolks blended with sugar (3 1/2 oz.). Knead quickly into a dough and set aside in a cool place for an hour. Roll out, place on à baking sheet and bake until golden. Spread jam over the top. Cover with stiffly beaten egg whites and smooth out the surface. Sprinkle with walnuts and bake in an oven.

RAISIN MAZURKA

9 1/2 oz. raisins, 1/2 lb. flour, 3 1/2 oz. almonds, 1/2 lb. confectioners' sugar, 1/3 cup sour cream, 3 1/2 oz. butter or margarine, 6 egg yolks, egg, candied orange rind, fat for baking sheet

Blanch and grind the almonds. Blend butter with sugar, adding eggs one by one. Combine with sifted flour, sour cream, almonds, grated orange rind and rinsed raisins. Transfer to a greased baking sheet. Smooth out the surface. Brush with beaten egg and bake in a moderate oven.

APPLE MAZURKA

Cake: 1/2 lb. flour, 3 1/2 oz. margarine, 2 2/3 oz. confectioners' sugar, 2 egg yolks
Filling: 2 lb. apples, 9 1/2 oz. sugar, 3 1/2 oz. raisins, 2/3 cup water, lemon juice to taste

Sift the flour and cut in margarine with a knife. Combine with egg yolks blended with sugar. Knead quickly into a dough and set aside in a cool place for an hour. Roll out into 1/2 in. thickness and arrange in a baking pan, covering the sides. Bake until golden. Wash, peel and halve the apples, removing the cores. Grate coarsely and combine with water and sugar. Cook, stirring frequently. Combine with rinsed raisins and lemon juice. Spread on cake, smooth out the surface and allow to set. Cover with white icing.

PRUNE MAZURKA

1/2 lb. prunes, 7 oz. hard chocolate, 1/3 cup dry red wine, 1/2 lb. almonds, 1 lb. confectioners' sugar, 2/3 oz. flour, 5 egg whites, lemon juice and lemon rind to taste, waffles or wafers

Wash the prunes, cover with wine and set aside for 4 hours. Remove pits and chop finely. Blanch and grind the almonds. Beat egg whites

until stiff and combine with sugar. Place bowl or pot with egg whites into a larger pot with hot water and beat until mixture thickens. Allow to cool, beating with an egg-whisk. Combine with melted chocolate, sifted flour, almonds, prunes, lemon juice and grated lemon rind. Transfer to a pan lined with wafers or waffles. Smooth out the surface and bake in a moderate oven. When done, allow to cool and cover with white icing.

POLISH MAZURKA

5 oz. all-purpose flour, 5 oz. potato starch, 13 1/2 oz. confectioners' sugar, 13 1/2 oz. margarine, 6—7 eggs, lemon rind and nutmeg to taste, fat and breadcrumbs for baking pan

Sift flour with potato starch. Wash the eggs, break them and separate the yolks from the whites. Blend margarine with sugar, adding egg yolks one by one. Combine with flour, grated lemon rind, ground nutmeg and stiffly beaten egg whites. Transfer to a greased baking pan sprinkled with breadcrumbs. Smooth out the surface and bake in a hot oven.

CHEESECAKE

Cake: 1/2 lb. flour, 3 1/2 oz. margarine, 2 2/3 oz. confectioners' sugar, 2 egg yolks
Filling: 1 3/4 lb. farmer's cheese, 1/2 lb. confectioners' sugar, 5 oz. butter or margarine, 1/3 cup sour cream, 6—8 egg yolks, 1 2/3 oz. raisins, 2 2/3 oz. walnut meats, 1 2/3 oz. figs, 1 2/3 oz. coffee, orange rind, lemon extract to taste, baking powder

Sift the flour and cut in margarine with a knife. Combine with egg yolks blended with sugar. Knead quickly into a dough and set aside in a cool place for an hour. Roll out, place in a baking pan and bake until golden. Blanch and grind the walnuts. Wash the eggs, break them and separate the yolks from the whites. Blend butter with sugar, adding

egg yolks one by one. Combine with minced cheese, sour cream, walnuts, rinsed raisins, finely chopped figs, baking powder, grated orange rind, lemon extract and ground coffee. Spread over cake top, smooth out and bake in a moderate oven.

CAPTAIN'S CHEESECAKE

2 lb. farmer's cheese, 9 1/2 oz. confectioners' sugar, 3 1/2 oz. butter or margarine, 6—8 eggs, 3 1/2 oz. walnut meats, 1 2/3 oz. candied orange rind, 1 oz. yeast, 1 1/2 tablespoons milk, vanilla extract, fat and breadcrumbs for baking pan

Blanch and grind the almonds and walnuts. Wash the eggs, break them and separate the yolks from the whites. Blend butter with sugar, adding egg yolks one by one. Combine with yeast dissolved in milk, vanilla extract, grated orange rind, minced cheese, almonds, walnuts and stiffly beaten egg whites. Transfer to a greased baking pan sprinkled with breadcrumbs. Smooth out the surface and bake in a moderate oven for 50 minutes.

REFRIGERATOR CHEESECAKE

1 lb. farmer's cheese, 1 cup whipping cream, 5 oz. butter or margarine, 1/2 lb. confectioners' sugar, 3 1/2 oz. hard chocolate, 1 1/2 tablespoons rum, 3 hard-boiled egg yolks, 3 1/2 oz. raisins, 1 2/3 oz. walnut meats, orange extract

Blanch and grind the walnuts. Blend butter with sugar and egg yolks forced through a strainer. Combine with minced cheese, grated chocolate, rinsed raisins, walnuts, orange extract, rum and whipped cream with sugar. Transfer to a pan rinsed in cold water and smooth out the surface. Set aside in the refrigerator for several hours. Transfer onto a platter and garnish.

NO-BAKE CHEESE DESSERT

1 lb. cream cheese, 3/4 cup cream, 1/2 lb. butter or margarine, 3 1/2 oz. canned pineapple, 3 1/2 oz. stewed or bottled apricots, 7 oz. confectioners' sugar, 1 2/3 oz. raisins, 1 2/3 oz. walnut meats, 3 egg yolks, 2/3 oz. gelatin

Blanch the walnuts and grind them. Blend butter with sugar, adding egg yolks one by one. Combine with cream, cream cheese, walnuts, rinsed raisins, diced pineapples, diced apricots and gelatin that has been soaked in cold water, then dissolved. Transfer to a pan rinsed in cold water and allow to set. Remove from pan, garnish with whipped cream and sugar and sprinkle with grated chocolate.

LAYERED CHEESE DESSERT

1 package orange-flavoured jelly, 2 egg yolks, 1 1/3 oz. confectioners' sugar, 1 oz. chocolate, 8 oz. strawberry-flavoured cream cheese, 1 2/3 oz. raisins, fresh lemon rind and orange rind to taste

Make jelly according to package directions. Pour into a square-shaped pan and allow to set. Blend egg yolks with sugar and grated lemon and orange rinds. Place dish or pot with egg yolks in a larger pot containing hot water and beat until mixture thickens. Add cream cheese with raisins and allow to cool, stirring. Fill round glasses alternately with diced jelly and cream cheese mixture, ending with a cone-shaped layer of cream cheese. Sprinkle with grated chocolate.

PASSOVER CHEESECAKE

2 lb. farmer's cheese, 7 oz. butter or margarine, 3 1/2 oz. raisins, 1 2/3 oz. walnut meats, 1 2/3 oz. figs, 2/3 cup sour cream, 3 hard-boiled egg yolks, 1/2 lb. confectioners' sugar, 1 2/3 oz. hard chocolate, 1 1/3 oz. candied orange rind, vanilla extract

Blanch and grind the walnuts. Blend butter with sugar and egg yolks forced through a strainer. Combine with minced cheese, sour cream, rinsed raisins, walnuts, strips of figs, grated orange rind and vanilla extract. Fold mixture into pan and allow to set in a cold place. Just before serving place pan in hot water for several seconds. Transfer to a platter and sprinkle with grated chocolate.

PĄCZKI (POLISH DOUGHNUTS)

3 1/2 oz. flour, 3/4 cup milk, 1 1/2 tablespoons rum, 3/4 tablespoons spirit, 3 1/2 oz. butter or margarine, 2 2/3 oz. confectioners' sugar, 3 eggs, 2 egg yolks, 1 1/3 oz. yeast, 7 oz. preserves or jam, salt, vanilla-flavoured confectioners' sugar, fat for frying

Make leaven from 1 2/3 oz. flour, yeast and milk. Set aside in a warm place to let it rise. Blend eggs and egg yolks with sugar and combine with sifted flour, leaven, rum, spirit and salt. Knead well, until dough becomes smooth and shiny and does not stick to sides of bowl. Towards the end add melted fat. Cover with a cloth and set aside to let it rise. When the dough begins to rise, take 1—1 1/3 oz. portions and shape into small circles. Place preserves or jam in the centres, fold up, press sides together and shape into balls. Arrange on a pastry board sprinkled with flour. Cover with a cloth and allow to rise. Heat fat in a skillet. Check whether the fat is hot enough by dropping in a piece of the dough. If it surfaces and browns quickly, the pączki can be fried. Brush off flour from the risen dough balls and place in fat, tops turned down, so that they swim freely. Cover and fry until browned on one side. Turn over and continue frying uncovered. When done take out and drain of fat on tissue paper. Dust with vanilla-flavoured confectioners' sugar and arrange on a platter.

PĄCZKI (DOUGHNUT) PUFFS

13 1/2 oz. flour, 1 2/3 cups milk, 8 eggs, 1 1/2 tablespoons rum, fat for frying, 13 1/2 oz. peaches, 1/3 cup Maraschino liqueur, 2 egg yolks, 5 oz. butter

Bring milk to a boil together with butter. Add sifted flour, stirring with a wooden spoon. Heat for a while, stirring constantly. When slightly cooled, add eggs one by one, stirring constantly. Towards the end add salt and rum. With a spoon make pączki (doughnuts) from the dough. Place in very hot fat and fry. Take out when done and drain on tissue paper. Scald and peel peaches. Remove pits, break fruit down and place in blender together with egg yolks. Add liqueur and turn on blender for 30 seconds. Pour over pączki and serve at once.

FRIED PASTRY TWISTS

3/4 lb. flour, 3 tablespoons sour cream, 1 1/2 tablespoons rum, 1 2/3 oz. butter or margarine, 2 eggs, 6 egg yolks, salt, fat for frying, vanilla-flavoured confectioners' sugar for dusting

Sift flour onto pastry board and cut in butter. Add egg yolks, eggs and sour cream. Knead well, adding salt and rum towards the end. Divide dough into parts, roll out very thinly, sprinkling with flour slightly. Cut into strips 1 1/4 in. wide and 3—4 in. long. Make a slit through the centre of each strip and pull one end through the opening, thus making a knot. Heat fat in pan. Check whether the fat is hot enough by dropping in a piece of the dough. If it surfaces and browns quickly, the twists can be fried. Place twists in hot fat and fry until golden, turning over in the fat. Take them out and drain on tissue paper. Arrange on a platter and dust with vanilla-flavoured confectioners' sugar.

CARNIVAL ROSES

3/4 lb. flour, 3 tablespoons sour cream, 1 1/2 tablespoons rum, 1 2/3 oz. butter or margarine, 2 eggs, 6 egg yolks, salt, fat for frying, vanilla-flavoured confectioners' sugar for dusting

Sift flour onto pastry board and cut in butter. Add egg yolks, eggs and sour cream. Knead well, adding salt and rum towards the end. Divide dough into parts and roll out very thinly. With a round cutter cut out

4 circles for each rose, making each circle smaller than the former. Make slits with a knife in 4—5 places equally apart. Stick together with egg white in the centres, 4 circles for each rose. Press down in the centre with your finger to keep them together. Proceed as in Fried Pastry Twists.

COCONUT COOKIES

3 1/2 oz. coconut flour, 3 1/2 oz. walnut meats, 2 2/3 oz. confectioners' sugar, 1 2/3 oz. potato starch, 1 2/3 oz. all-purpose flour, 5 eggs, 1 teaspoon baking powder, fat for baking sheet

Sift all-purpose and coconut flour together with potato starch and baking powder. Wash the eggs, break them and separate the yolks from the whites. Blend yolks with sugar and combine with stiffly beaten egg whites, alternately adding peeled and ground walnuts and flour. With a teaspoon place small balls on a greased baking sheet so that they do not touch and bake in a moderate oven.

AGA COOKIES

1/2 lb. flour, 1 2/3 oz. butter or margarine, 5 egg yolks, 1 1/2 table-spoon spirit, 2 2/3— 3 1/2 oz. walnut meats, 2/3—1 oz. hard chocolate, egg white, vanilla-flavoured confectioners' sugar for dusting

Blanch and grind the walnuts. Sift flour onto a pastry board and cut in butter with a knife. Combine with egg yolks and spirit. Knead into a dough quickly and set aside in a cool place for 30 minutes. Roll out and cut out cookies with cutter. Brush with egg white. Sprinkle with walnuts and grated chocolate. Bake in a hot oven. When done dust with vanilla-flavoured confectioners' sugar.

RAISIN COOKIES

1/2 lb. flour, 1/2 lb. confectioners' sugar, 2 2/3 oz. butter or margarine, 2 eggs, 2 2/3 oz. raisins, 1 1/2 tablespoons liqueur, cinnamon and cloves to taste

Rinse and drain raisins. Cover with liqueur and set aside for an hour. Wash the eggs and break them. Blend butter with sugar and ground spices. Add eggs and knead into a dough, adding sifted flour. Roll out into 1/8 in. thickness. With a round cutter cut out cookies. Spread icing over them and sprinkle with raisins. Bake in a hot oven.

WHOLE-WHEAT BREAD COOKIES

3 1/2 oz. grated whole-wheat bread or Pumpernickel, 3 1/2 oz. walnut meats, 3 1/2 oz. butter or margarine, 6—8 eggs, fat for cookie cups, 3 1/2 oz. sugar

Blanch and grind the walnuts. Wash the eggs, break them and separate the yolks from the whites. Blend butter with sugar, adding egg yolks one by one. Combine with walnuts, stiffly beaten egg whites and bread. Transfer to greased cookie cups and bake in a moderate oven. When done, pour icing over them.

BACHELOR'S EYES

1/2 lb. butter or margarine, 1/2 lb. flour, 2 2/3 oz. confectioners' sugar, 2 egg yolks, lemon rind, 1 1/3 oz. walnut meats, egg, vanilla-flavoured confectioners' sugar, preserved sour cherries

Whip 5 oz. butter, gradually adding the remaining melted butter and sugar. Add egg yolks one by one, beating constantly. Combine with sifted flour and grated lemon rind. Set aside in a cool place for an hour. Blanch and grind the walnuts. Make balls from the dough with a hole in the centre. Brush with beaten egg, sprinkle with walnuts and bake in a hot oven. When done dust with vanilla-flavoured confectioners' sugar. Place sour cherries in hollows.

APPLE COOKIES

5 oz. flour, 2 lb. apples, 3 1/2 oz. confectioners' sugar, 6—8 eggs, baking powder, vanilla-flavoured confectioners' sugar for dusting, fat for cookie cups

Wash, peel and halve the apples, removing the cores. Grate them coarsely. Wash the eggs, break them and separate the yolks from the whites. Beat the egg whites until stiff, adding confectioners' sugar towards the end. Combine with egg yolks and flour sifted with baking powder. Place dough in greased cookie cups, making a layer with the apple mixture in the middle. Place in a hot oven and bake. Towards the end reduce heat. When cooled, pour chocolate icing over the cookies.

HONEY COOKIES

1/2 lb. flour, 3 1/2 oz. confectioners' sugar, 3 1/2 oz. almonds, 7 oz. honey, 5 eggs, 1 2/3 oz. candied fruit rind, lemon and orange rind to taste, fat for baking sheet

Blanch and grind the almonds. Wash the eggs and break them. Blend with sugar, honey, grated rinds and sifted flour. Transfer to a greased baking sheet. Smooth out the surface, sprinkle with almonds and finely chopped candied fruit rind, then bake in a hot oven. When done cut into squares.

JAM OR MARMALADE COOKIES

9 1/2 oz. flour, 5 oz. butter or margarine, 2 eggs, 2 tablespoons sour cream, 5—7 oz. jam or marmalade, 1/2 teaspoon baking powder

Wash the eggs and break them. Sift flour together with baking powder and cut in butter with a knife. Combine with eggs and sour cream and knead into a dough quickly. Roll out into 1/4 in. thickness and cut into 1/2 in. squares. Spread jam or marmalade on top, fold over in half and press edges together. Arrange on a baking sheet and bake in a hot oven.

LONG-LASTING COOKIES

7 oz. potato starch, 5 oz. confectioners' sugar, 1 2/3 oz. almonds, 3 1/2 oz. butter or margarine, 6 eggs, vanilla extract, lemon and orange rind, fat for baking sheet

Blanch and grind the almonds. Blend butter with sugar, adding eggs one by one, alternately adding almonds. Combine with vanilla extract, grated rinds and sifted flour. Knead well. With a teaspoon drop small cookies onto a greased baking sheet, leaving equal spaces between. Bake in a moderate oven.

CRISPY COOKIES

9 1/2 oz. flour, 3 1/2 oz. butter or margarine, 1/2 cup milk, 2 egg yolks, 6 oz. baking powder, vanilla extract, lemon rind to taste, fat for baking sheet

Sift flour together with baking powder and cut in butter with a knife. Combine with egg yolks, milk, grated lemon rind and vanilla extract. Knead into a dough. Use a special cookie insert in the meat mincer. Put dough through mincer. As dough comes out, cut it into 2 in. long pieces. Place on a greased baking sheet so that they do not touch and bake in a hot oven until golden.

ONION COOKIES

1/2 lb. flour, 3 1/2 oz. poppyseed, 7 oz. butter or margarine, 5 oz. onions, 3—4 eggs, 6 oz. baking powder, egg for top, salt and pepper to taste

Scald poppyseed with boiling water, drain and strain. Peel, rinse and dice the onions finely, then fry them. Sift flour and baking powder onto a pastry board. Cut in butter with a knife. Combine with poppyseed, onions and eggs. Knead into a dough. Roll out into 1/4 in. thickness and cut out square cookies with a cutter. Brush with beaten egg. Arrange on a baking sheet so that they do not touch and bake in a hot oven.

KISSES

1/2 lb. confectioners' sugar, 1/2 lb. peaches, 5 egg whites

Wash the peaches and remove pits. Chop them finely, fry lightly and force through a strainer. Beat egg whites until stiff together with sugar. Add peach paste and blend well. Line baking pan or sheet with greased parchment paper. With a pastry bag press out small kisses and dry them in a warm oven.

CINNAMON COOKIES

1/2 lb. confectioners' sugar, 1/2 lb. flour, 1 2/3 oz. butter or margarine, 3 eggs, 1 2/3 oz. almonds, 1 teaspoon ground cinnamon, egg white, 5 cloves

Blanch the almonds. Wash the eggs. Blend butter with sugar, adding eggs one by one. Combine with cinnamon, ground cloves and sifted flour. Knead into a dough. Shape into balls the size of walnuts, placing an almond in each ball. Roll in egg white and bake in a hot oven.

GINGER COOKIES

5 oz. butter or margarine, 5 oz. flour, 3 1/2 oz. confectioners' sugar, 2 egg yolks, 1/2 teaspoon ground ginger, lemon rind to taste

Blend butter with sugar, adding egg yolks one by one. Combine with sifted flour, ginger and grated lemon rind. Knead into a dough. Roll into 1/8 in. thickness and with a cookie cutter cut out cookies the shape of a ginger root. Arrange on a baking sheet so that they do not touch and set aside in a cool place for 2 hours. Bake in a hot oven.

DEER HORNS

3/4 lb. flour, 3 1/2 oz. confectioners' sugar, 1 2/3 oz. butter or margarine, 2 egg yolks, 3 eggs, 3 tablespoons sour cream, fat for frying, vanilla-flavoured confectioners' sugar and lemon rind for top

Sift flour and cut in butter with a knife. Combine with eggs, egg yolks, sugar and sour cream. Knead into a dough. Shape into a roll and cut out 3 in. long pieces. Make diagonal slits on each side alternately. Heat the fat, drop in several cookies at a time and fry until golden. Take out when done and drain on tissue paper. Sprinkle with vanilla-flavoured confectioners' sugar and grated lemon rind.

CATS' TONGUES

3 1/2 oz. butter or margarine, 3 1/2 oz. confectioners' sugar, 3 1/2 oz. flour, egg, egg yolk, vanilla extract, fat for baking sheet

Grease baking sheet and sprinkle with flour. Blend butter with sugar and combine with egg, egg yolk, vanilla extract and sifted flour. Knead well. With a pastry bag press out long cookies onto the baking sheet so that they do not touch. Bake in a moderate oven. When done, remove from sheet while still hot and bend lightly on a rolling pin. Allow to cool.

CHERRY COOKIES

1/2 lb. confectioners' sugar, 1/2 lb. flour, 1/2 lb. butter or margarine, 10 egg yolks, 1 1/2 tablespoons rum, vanilla extract, Russel cream and stewed or bottled sour cherries for garnishing, fat for cookie cups

Blend egg yolks with sugar and vanilla extract. Add sifted flour, mixing well. Towards the end add melted butter and rum. Grease rectangular cups 3 in. long, 1 1/2 in. wide and 1 in. high. 3/4 fill with dough. Smooth out the surface and bake in a hot oven. When done, take out of cups and allow to cool. Garnish with cream and fruit.

MOUSE CAKES

1/2 lb. flour, 3 1/2 oz. butter or margarine, 4 egg yolks, 2 egg whites, 1 cup milk, 2 2/3 oz. confectioners' sugar, 2/3 oz. yeast, jam for top,

1 cup whipping cream, confectioners' sugar for cream, fat for special pan used for frying eggs separately

Blend egg yolks with sugar. Combine with ground yeast, milk and sifted flour. Knead well, adding melted fat towards the end. Mix lightly with stiffly beaten egg whites. Cover with a cloth and set aside to let it rise. Grease egg pan and 3/4 fill the individual moulds with the dough. Bake in a hot oven. When done, allow to cool. Brush with jam and arrange on a platter. Serve whipped cream with sugar separately.

CHEESE COOKIES

1 lb. farmer's cheese, 4 oz. flour, 2 2/3 oz. confectioners' sugar 1 2/3 oz. butter or margarine, 4—5 eggs, 3 tablespoons sour cream, salt, fat for frying, confectioners' sugar for top

Mince farmer's cheese and beat in eggs one at a time. Combine with sugar, sifted flour, sour cream, melted butter and salt. Knead well. Shape dough into balls, then flatten these lightly. Fry on both sides in very hot fat or bake in a hot oven. When done, dust with confectioners' sugar.

ALMOND COOKIES

7 oz. flour, 1 2/3 oz. shredded coconut, 7 oz. butter or margarine, 7 oz. confectioners' sugar, 3 1/2 oz. almonds, egg, 1/3 cup water, 1 tablespoon rum

Bring water to a boil. Add sifted flour and blend well. Add butter, sugar, shredded coconut and rum. Knead into a dough on a pastry board. Roll out to 1/8 in. thickness. With cookie cutters of various shapes cut out cookies. Blanch and grind almonds. Brush cookies with beaten egg and sprinkle with almonds. Arrange on a baking sheet so that they do not touch and bake in a hot oven.

MERINGUES I

13 1/2 oz. confectioners' sugar, 8 egg whites, whipped cream with confectioners' sugar and cocoa

Beat egg whites until stiff, adding 5—7 oz. sugar. Towards the end add the remaining sugar gradually. Line baking sheet with greased waxed paper. With a pastry bag press round cookies onto baking sheet at regular intervals. Sprinkle with confectioner's sugar. Place in a warm oven and dry for 2—3 hours. When dried, remove the cookies by lifting them with a knife. Join two in two with a layer of cream whipped with sugar and cocoa.

MERINGUES II

13 1/2 oz. sugar, 8 egg whites, 2 2/3 oz. lemon, 2 2/3 oz. almonds, 3/4 cup water, almond extract, cream filling

Blanch and grind the almonds. Add sugar to the water. Heat, stirring, until the sugar dissolves completely. Add lemon juice and cook covered over high heat. From time to time take out a small amount of the syrup with a spoon and pour it onto a plate. If the last drop ends in a thread, discontinue heating. Beat egg whites until stiff, gradually adding the hot syrup. Remove from heat and continue beating until cool. Combine with almonds and lemon juice. Line baking sheet with greased waxed paper. With a pastry bag press out triangular cookies onto the baking sheet at regular intervals. Sprinkle with confectioners' sugar and place in a warm oven for 2—3 hours. Remove from sheet when cool. Join in two with any cream filling.

JAM COOKIES WITH CREAM

7 oz. flour, 7 oz. butter or margarine, 7 oz. confectioners' sugar, 3 1/2 oz. almonds, 8 egg whites, 6 oz. baking powder, salt, lemon rind, 1 lb. jam, 2/3 cup whipping cream, 1 2/3 oz. confectioners' sugar

Sift flour together with baking powder. Blend butter with sugar and combine with blanched and ground almonds, grated lemon rind, salt and stiffly beaten egg whites, alternately adding flour. Transfer to a baking pan lined with greased waxed paper. Smooth out the surface and bake in a moderate oven. When done, remove the paper and slice cake into two parts. Fill with jam and press down lightly. Cut into triangles and garnish with cream whipped with sugar.

POLISH CUP CAKES

7 oz. flour, 7 oz. confectioners' sugar, 3 1/2 oz. cocoa, 1 2/3 oz. butter or margarine, 1 2/3 oz. raisins, 2 eggs, 3/4 cup milk, baking powder, lemon rind, fat and breadcrumbs for cups

Sift flour together with baking powder. Wash the eggs, break them and separate the yolks from the whites. Blend butter with sugar, adding eggs one by one. Combine with cocoa, milk, flour, rinsed raisins dredged in flour and grated lemon rind. Combine with stiffly beaten egg whites. Grease fluted cups and sprinkle with breadcrumbs. 3/4 fill each cup with the dough and bake in a moderate oven. When done, allow to cool and pour white icing over cakes.

RUSSEL CREAM PROFITEROLES

5 oz. flour, 2/3 cup water, 2 2/3 oz. butter, 5—6 eggs, fat, Russel Cream

Bring butter and water to a boil. Add sifted flour and a little salt, stirring constantly. Remove from heat and break down all lumps. Place saucepan with dough over low heat and stir constantly, until the dough becomes smooth and shiny. Remove from heat. Add eggs one by one to the hot dough, stirring constantly, until smooth. A blender may be used for mixing the dough. Grease baking sheet. With a pastry bag press out small balls at equal intervals onto the baking sheet. Bake in a hot oven. When done, allow to cool. Using a cookie-press with a small opening fill the cookies with Russel Cream.

EGG-YOLK CONES

1/2 lb. flour, 1 2/3 oz. butter or margarine, 1 2/3 oz. confectioners' sugar, 10 egg yolks, 1 tablespoon spirit, vanilla extract, egg yolk cream filling, chocolate icing

Sift flour onto a pastry board. Cut in butter with a knife. Combine with egg yolks, spirit and vanilla extract. Knead into a dough. Roll out to 1/8 in. thickness. Cut into strips 3/4 in. wide and 6—8 in. long. Roll them on metal cones in coils so that the edges overlap. Brush with beaten egg. Arrange on a baking sheet at equal intervals and bake in a hot oven. When done, remove cookies from cones and allow to cool. Fill with cream and pour chocolate icing over ends.

YEAST BUNS

1 lb. flour, 3 1/2 oz. confectioners' sugar, 3 1/2 oz. butter or margarine, 3/4 cup milk, 2 eggs, 2 egg yolks, 1—1 1/3 oz. yeast, salt, lemon rind, sugar for top, egg for top, fat for baking sheet

Make leaven from 1 2/3 oz. flour, 2/3 oz. sugar, yeast and part of the warm milk. Set aside for it to rise. Blend eggs and egg yolks with sugar. Combine with leaven, salt, grated lemon rind, the remaining milk and sifted flour. Make a dough and knead well, adding melted fat towards the end. Cover with a cloth and set aside for it to rise. Make round buns and arrange on a greased baking sheet at equal intervals. Set aside to let them rise again. Brush with beaten egg, sprinkle with sugar and bake in a moderate oven.

ALMOND TORTE I

5 oz. butter or margarine, 5 oz. confectioners' sugar, 3 1/2 oz. almonds, 5 oz. chocolate, 2 2/3 oz. flour, 3 eggs, lemon extract, fat and bread-crumbs for baking pan

Blanch the almonds, dry in an oven and grind them. Wash the eggs, break them and separate the yolks from the whites. Blend butter with sugar, adding egg yolks one by one. Combine with lemon extract, almonds and stiffly beaten egg whites, alternately adding sifted flour. Transfer to a greased baking pan sprinkled with breadcrumbs. Smooth out the surface and bake in a moderate oven. When done, fill with any cream filling and pour chocolate icing over the cake.

ALMOND TORTE II

5 oz. almonds, 3 1/2 oz. chocolate, 3 1/2 oz. confectioners' sugar, 6 egg yolks, 4 egg whites, lemon rind, fat and breadcrumbs for baking pan

Blanch and grind the almonds. Blend egg yolks with sugar. Combine with melted chocolate, almonds, grated lemon rind and stiffly beaten egg whites. Transfer to a greased baking pan sprinkled with breadcrumbs. Smooth out the surface and bake in a moderate oven. When done, allow to cool. Slice into two parts horizontally and fill with any cream filling. Pour icing over cake and garnish with fruit preserves.

ALMOND TORTE III

9 1/2 oz. almonds, 9 1/2 oz. confectioners' sugar, 3 1/2 oz. butter or margarine, 5—6 hard-boiled egg yolks, 2 eggs, 1 2/3 oz. flour, 1 tablespoon lemon juice, lemon rind and cinnamon to taste, fat and breadcrumbs for cake pans, icing

Blanch the almonds and grind them. Wash the eggs, break them and blend with sugar. Combine with egg yolks forced through a strainer, lemon juice, melted butter, almonds and sifted flour. Mix well. Transfer to two greased cake pans sprinkled with breadcrumbs. Smooth out the surface and bake in a hot oven. When done, allow to cool. Fill with any cake filling. Spread filling over sides and top as well, pour icing over cake and garnish.

TORTE À LA MADAME WALEWSKA

7 oz. butter or margarine, 7 oz. confectioners' sugar, 7 oz. almonds, 5 oz. chocolate, 1 2/3 oz. grated ladyfingers, 10 eggs, 1 tablespoon Maraschino liqueur, fat and breadcrumbs for cake pans, butter cream filling, chocolate icing

Blanch and grind the almonds. Wash the eggs, break them and separate the yolks from the whites. Blend butter with sugar, adding egg yolks one by one. Combine with almonds, melted chocolate, Maraschino and stiffly beaten egg whites, alternately adding grated ladyfingers. Transfer to two or three greased cake pans sprinkled with bread-crumbs. Smooth out the surface and bake in a moderate oven. When done, allow to cool. Fill with butter cream filling, pour icing over cake and garnish.

SPICY TORTE

7 oz. confectioners' sugar, 3 1/2 oz. almonds, 3 1/2 oz. walnut meats, 3 1/2 oz. chocolate, 1 2/3 oz. grated whole-wheat bread, 4 egg yolks, 5 eggs, 1 teaspoon ground cinnamon and cloves, lemon and orange rind, fat and breadcrumbs for cake pan, butter cream filling, chocolate icing

Blanch and grind almonds and walnuts. Wash the eggs and separate the yolks from the whites. Blend egg yolks with sugar. Combine with almonds, walnuts, spices, grated rinds, melted chocolate and stiffly beaten egg whites, alternately adding bread. Transfer to two or three greased cake pans sprinkled with breadcrumbs. Smooth out the surface and bake in a moderate oven. When done, allow to cool. Fill with butter cream filling and pour chocolate icing over cake.

COFFEE TORTE

Cake: 9 1/2 oz. confectioners' sugar, 9 1/2 oz. almonds, 7—8 egg whites, lemon juice

Filling: 1/2 lb. butter or margarine, 2 2/3 oz. confectioners' sugar, 3 tablespoons strong coffee, 2 egg yolks, white icing

Blanch and grind the almonds. Beat egg whites until stiff, adding sugar towards the end. Combine with almonds and lemon juice. Transfer to two cake pans lined with greased waxed paper. Smooth out the surface and bake in a moderate oven. Blend butter with sugar, adding eggs one by one. Combine with coffee. Fill cake and allow to set. Pour icing over cake and garnish.

NUT TORTE

1/2 lb. walnut meats, 7 oz. confectioners' sugar, 8 eggs, 3 tablespoons strong coffee, 1 2/3 oz. grated whole-wheat bread, lemon and orange rind, fat and breadcrumbs for cake pan, white icing

Wash the eggs, break them and separate the yolks from the whites. Blend egg yolks with sugar and grated rinds. Combine with stiffly beaten egg whites, alternately adding blanched and ground walnuts, along with bread soaked in coffee. Transfer to two greased cake pans sprinkled with breadcrumbs. Smooth out the surface and bake in a moderate oven. When done, allow to cool. Fill with nut filling (q.v.), pour icing over cake and garnish.

FIG TORTE

Cake: 1/2 lb. confectioners' sugar, 1/2 lb. figs, 2 2/3 oz. breadcrumbs, 8 eggs, lemon rind, fat and breadcrumbs for cake pans
Filling: 12 1/2 oz. apples, 2/3 cup whipping cream, 3 1/2 oz. sugar, 2—2 2/3 oz. confectioners' sugar, 1 2/3 oz. raisins, lemon juice, lemon icing

Wash the eggs, break them and separate the yolks from the whites. Blend egg yolks with sugar and grated lemon rind. Combine with stiffly beaten egg whites, alternately adding breadcrumbs and finely chopped figs. Transfer to two greased cake pans sprinkled with breadcrumbs. Smooth out the surface and bake in a moderate oven. Wash,

peel and cut the apples in halves, removing the cores. Grate coarsely and combine with sugar. Fry lightly until translucent, stirring frequently. Remove from heat. Add rinsed raisins and lemon juice. Allow to cool, then combine with whipped cream and confectioners' sugar. Spread between cake layers. Pour lemon icing (q.v.) over cake and garnish.

POPPYSEED TORTE

7 oz. poppyseed, 1/2 lb. confectioners' sugar, 3 1/2 oz. almonds, 1 2/3 oz. raisins, 10 egg yolks, 5 egg whites, 1 tablespoon rum, cinnamon, cloves, vanilla bean, fat and breadcrumbs for cake pans, almond filling, lemon icing

Blanch and grind the almonds. Rinse and scald the poppyseed with boiling water. Heat it until tender. Strain and mince finely 2—3 times. Blend egg yolks with sugar. Combine with rum, ground spices, rinsed raisins and stiffly beaten egg whites, alternately adding poppyseed and almonds. Transfer to two greased cake pans sprinkled with breadcrumbs. Smooth out the surface and bake in a moderate oven. When done, allow to cool. Spread almond filling (q.v.) between the layers. Pour lemon icing (q.v.) over cake and garnish.

PLUM TORTE

7 oz. confectioners' sugar, 7 oz. almonds, 7 oz. butter or margarine, 7 oz. ladyfingers, 9 1/2 oz. plums, 1 1/3 oz. candied orange rind, 10 eggs, vanilla-flavoured sugar, fat and breadcrumbs for cake pans, lemon icing

Wash, scald and peel the plums. Cut them in halves, remove pits and cut into strips. Blanch and grind the almonds. Wash the eggs, break them and separate the yolks from the whites. Blend butter with sugar and grated orange rind, adding the egg yolks one by one. Combine with stiffly beaten egg whites, alternately adding grated ladyfingers and plums. Transfer to a greased cake pan sprinkled with breadcrumbs. Smooth out the surface and bake in a hot oven. When done, allow to cool. Pour lemon icing (q.v.) over cake and garnish.

WHITE ICING

7 oz. confectioners' sugar, 2 egg whites, lemon juice to taste

Pour egg whites into a bowl, add sugar and beat until smooth. Add lemon juice. Use on tortes and mazurkas, smoothing out with a knife.

LEMON ICING

1/2 lb. confectioners' sugar, 1 tablespoon cognac, 1 1/3 tablespoons lemon juice

Sift sugar and blend with cognac and lemon juice until smooth. Spread with a brush or a knife.

MILK ICING

1/2 lb. sugar, 1/3 cup milk, 1 1/3 tablespoons rum

Add sugar to milk and cook over low heat until thick. While cooking, stir from time to time to prevent burning. Mix until thick. Add rum before spreading on cake.

CHOCOLATE ICING

3 1/2 oz. chocolate, 1 2/3 oz. confectioners' sugar, 1 2/3 oz. butter, 3 tablespoons milk

Bring milk to a boil, add sugar and dissolve it. Allow to cool. Blend butter with grated chocolate and milk. When the mixture begins to thicken, pour over cake. Spread on sides with a knife.

GINGERBREAD ICING

1/2 lb. sugar, 1/2 cup water, 2 egg whites, 1/2 teaspoon vinegar

Bring water to a boil. Add sugar and vinegar and cook for 30 minutes. Sprinkle cooked syrup with cold water and cool to around 140°F. Mix with a wooden spoon for 6—8 minutes. Beat egg whites until stiff, adding hot syrup in a thin drizzle. Place dish with mixture into a larger saucepan with hot water and beat until thick. Add spices.

CHOCOLATE ICING WITH BUTTER I

2—3 egg yolks, 1 2/3 oz. confectioners' sugar, 1 2/3 oz. butter, 2 tablespoons water, 1 oz. cocoa

Combine cocoa with water. Bring to a boil and allow to cool. Blend butter with sugar, adding egg yolks one by one and cocoa.

CHOCOLATE ICING WITH BUTTER II

3 1/2 oz. chocolate, 1 2/3 oz. butter

Sprinkle water over chocolate and butter. Heat in the top of a double boiler. Pour over cake, smoothing out with a knife.

ALMOND FILLING

1/2 lb. almonds, 1/2 lb. confectioners' sugar, 1/3 cup whipping cream, vanilla extract

Blanch and grind the almonds. Blend with sugar, cream and vanilla extract.

NUT FILLING

1/2 lb. walnut meats, 1/2 lb. confectioners' sugar, 2—3 egg yolks, 7 oz. butter, 3 tablespoons liqueur

Blanch and grind the walnuts. Blend butter with sugar, adding egg yolks one by one. Combine with walnuts and liqueur.

Desserts

APPLE AND RASPBERRY SALAD

10 oz. apples, 5 oz. raspberries, 1 1/2 tablespoons cognac, 1/3 cup whipping cream, 2/3 oz. confectioners' sugar, 2/3 oz. confectioners' sugar for cream, lemon juice to taste

Wash, peel and halve the apples, removing the cores. Grate them coarsely. Rinse raspberries and remove stems. Combine with apples, cognac, sugar and lemon juice. Fold into a glass bowl and allow to cool. Just before serving garnish with whipped cream.

STRAWBERRY OR RASPBERRY SALAD

1 2/3 oz. strawberries or raspberries, 3 1/2 oz. apricots, 1 2/3 oz. confectioners' sugar, 2/3 cup whipping cream, 2/3 oz. confectioners' sugar for cream

Sort the fruit and rinse it on a strainer under a small stream of running water. Remove stems, arrange the fruit in compote dishes or glasses and chill. Wash the apricots, scald with boiling water and peel. Force through a strainer and combine with sugar and whipped cream. Decorate the fruit with cream and serve at once.

BLUEBERRY SALAD

1 lb. fruit, 2 oz. confectioners' sugar, 2/3 cup sour cream

Sort the blueberries and rinse on a strainer under a small stream of running water. Arrange the fruit in a glass bowl, adding sugar. Pour cream over the fruit and serve at once.

FRUIT SALAD

5 oz. apples, 5 oz. pears, 3 1/2 oz. grapes, 3 1/2 oz. plums, 3 tablespoons sweet white wine; 1 oz. confectioners' sugar, 1 2/3 oz. walnut meats, lemon juice to taste

Blanch and grind the walnuts. Wash the fruit and peel the apples and pears. Halve them, removing the cores, then dice them. Remove pits from plums and cut them into strips. Cut grapes in half and combine with apples, pears, plums, sugar, wine and lemon juice. Place in a glass bowl and chill. Sprinkle with walnuts and serve at once.

CURRANT AND RASPBERRY SALAD

1/2 lb. currants, 1/2 lb. raspberries, 2/3 cup sour cream, 1 2/3 oz. confectioners' sugar

Sort and clean the currants. Rinse them together with the raspberries under a small stream of running water. Arrange in a bowl. Blend sour cream with sugar and pour over fruit. Chill before serving.

GENERAL'S PINEAPPLE

4 slices canned pineapple, 1 oz. almonds, 7 oz. farmer's cheese, 1 1/3 oz. raisins, caramel syrup threads

Blanch and grind the almonds. Mince the farmer's cheese and mix with a small amount of pineapple juice. Combine with rinsed raisins. Arrange pineapple on glass plates. Cover decoratively with the cheese. Sprinkle with almonds and pour caramel syrup threads over.

PEACHES IN CHOCOLATE SAUCE

1 can peaches, 1 oz. cocoa, 2 egg yolks, 3/4 cup milk, 2/3 oz. butter, 1/2 oz. potato starch

Bring the milk to a boil. Combine cocoa with a small amount of water and potato starch. Pour in a thin drizzle into the hot milk, stirring with an egg-whisk. Bring to a boil and remove from heat. Combine egg yolks with peach juice. Gradually add to the hot milk, stirring with an egg-whisk. Place dish with egg yolks into a dish with cold water,

beating until cool and adding butter piece by piece. Arrange the peaches in compote dishes or glasses. Pour sauce over fruit and allow to set. Just before serving decorate with waffle cones.

PEARS IN CREAM

4 pears, 1 2/3 oz. confectioners' sugar, 5 oz. apricot jam, 1/2 cup whipping cream, 2/3 oz. confectioners' sugar for cream, 2 cups water, lemon juice to taste

Bring water with sugar to a boil. Wash, peel and cut the pears in half, removing the cores. Place them in the syrup. Add lemon juice and cook the pears. Cool them in the syrup. Take them out and fill with jam. Join two halves together and arrange horizontally on glass plates. Decorate with cream whipped with sugar. Use the remaining syrup for a jelly dessert or serve as a compote.

CASTELLAN'S PEARS

4 pears, 3 1/2 oz. sugar, 2 cups water, 1/2 cup whipping cream, 2/3 oz. confectioners' sugar for cream, 5 oz. cranberry preserves, 2/3 tablespoon cherry liqueur, 1 1/3 oz. raisins

Bring water with sugar to a boil. Wash and peel the pears, then remove the cores. Place them in the syrup and cook. Cool in the syrup. Take them out and fill with cranberries. Arrange vertically on glass plates. Decorate with cream whipped with sugar. Sprinkle with rinsed raisins soaked in liqueur.

Note: Dry white wine may be used for cooking the pears instead of water. This improves the flavour.

PEARS WITH FARMER'S CHEESE

4 stewed or bottled pears, 5 oz. farmer's cheese, 1/3 cup sour cream, 1 oz. confectioners' sugar, sour cherry jelly, 2/3 oz. raisins

Mince the farmer's cheese and combine with sour cream, sugar and rinsed raisins. Fill peach halves with farmer's cheese and arrange in compote dishes or glasses. Cover with nearly firm sour cherry jelly made according to package directions. Allow to set.

APPLES IN CREAM

4 apples, 1 2/3 oz. walnut meats, 2 tablespoons dry white wine, 1/2 lb. Bavarian Cream, 1 2/3 oz. raisins, lemon rind to taste

Wash the apples and remove the cores. Bake in an oven, sprinkling with wine, then cool. Blanch and grind the walnuts. Combine with rinsed raisins. Fill the apples and arrange them in compote dishes or glasses. Cover with Vanilla Bavarian Cream (q.v.). Allow to set.

CHEF'S APPLES

4 apples, 3 1/2 oz. strawberries, 2 2/3 oz. canned pineapple, 2/3 oz. confectioners' sugar for strawberries, 1 2/3 oz. sugar, 2 cups water, 1/2 cup whipping cream, 2/3 oz. confectioners' sugar for cream, 1 2/3 tablespoons cherry liqueur, lemon rind to taste

Bring water with sugar and lemon rind to a boil. Wash and peel the apples, removing the cores. Place them in the syrup and cook. Leave in the syrup until cool. Rinse the strawberries, remove stems and force them through a strainer. Combine with diced pineapple, cherry liqueur and confectioners' sugar. Fill apples and arrange them in compote dishes or glasses or on glass plates. Decorate with cream whipped with sugar. Use the remaining syrup for compote.

APPLES WITH ICE CREAM

4 apples, 4 small portions vanilla ice cream, 1 2/3 oz. red. currants, 1/2 cup whipping cream, 2/3 oz. sugar for cream, 2 cups water, 2—2 2/3 oz. sugar

Wash and peel the apples, removing the cores. Cook in the syrup and cool. Fill the apples with ice cream and arrange on glass plates. Decorate with cream whipped with sugar. Sprinkle with rinsed and cleaned currants. Serve at once.

BAKED APPLES

4 apples, 3 tablespoons dry white wine, 5 oz. jam

Wash the apples and remove the cores with a special spoon. Fill with the jam and bake in a hot oven, sprinkling with wine.

APPLE FRITTERS

4 apples, 9 1/2 oz. flour, 3 1/2 oz. jam, 5 oz. butter or margarine, 1 1/3 oz. confectioners' sugar, 3 tablespoons sour cream, 2 egg yolks, 1 1/3 oz. vanilla-flavoured confectioners' sugar, butter or margarine for greasing baking sheet, salt to taste

Sift flour onto pastry board. Cut in butter with a knife. Add egg yolks, sugar and salt. Knead quickly into a dough and set aside in a cool place for 30 minutes. Peel the apples and remove the cores with a special spoon. Fill with some jam. Roll the dough to 1/8 in. thickness and cut into squares. Place an apple in the centre of each square. Press down the edges and arrange on a greased baking sheet. Bake in a hot oven until golden. Sprinkle with vanilla-flavoured confectioners' sugar.

APPLES IN PASTRY

1 lb. apples, 5 oz. flour, 1 oz. confectioners' sugar, 3 eggs, ca. 2/3 cup sour cream or dry white wine, 1 1/3 tablespoons rum, 1 1/3 oz. vanilla flavoured confectioners' sugar, salt to taste, fat for frying

Wash the eggs, break them and separate the yolks from the whites. Blend egg yolks with sugar and combine with rum, sour cream and stiffly beaten egg yolks, alternately adding sifted flour. Add a little salt.

Wash and peel the apples, removing cores. Cut them into 1/4 in. thick slices. Pick them up with a fork, dip in the batter and fry in very hot fat on both sides until golden. When done, sprinkle with vanilla-flavoured confectioners' sugar.

APPLES IN YEAST PASTRY

1 lb. apples, 3 1/2 oz. flour, 1/3 oz. yeast, 2 eggs, 2—2 2/3 oz. sugar, 3 tablespoons milk, 1 oz. butter or margarine, salt to taste, fat for frying, vanilla-flavoured confectioners' sugar for top

Blend milk with sugar, yeast and flour (1/3 oz.). Wash the eggs, break them and separate the yolks from the whites. Blend butter with egg yolks. Combine with the leaven, sifted flour and stiffly beaten egg whites. Set aside for it to rise. Wash and peel the apples, removing the cores. Cut into 1/4 in. thick slices. Pick them up with a fork, dip in the batter and fry in deep fat on both sides. When done, sprinkle with vanilla-flavoured confectioners' sugar.

SPICE BAKED APPLES

4 apples, 1 2/3 oz. honey, 2 2/3 oz. almonds, 2—2 2/3 oz. sugar, ca. 2 cups water, 2—3 egg whites, 1 oz. confectioners' sugar for egg whites, cinnamon and cloves to taste

Wash and peel the apples, removing the cores. Bring the water to a boil with sugar and spices. Put in the apples and cook them. Allow to cool in the syrup. Blanch and grind the almonds. Combine with honey. Fill the apples with this and arrange in an oven-proof dish. Surround with stiffly beaten egg whites with sugar and bake in a hot oven.

CHEF'S APRICOTS

13 1/2 oz. stewed or bottled apricots, 4 small portions vanilla ice cream, 1/2 cup whipping cream, 1 oz. cocoa, 2/3 oz. confectioners' sugar

Remove pits from apricots and arrange in compote dishes or glasses together with ice cream. Decorate with cream whipped with sugar and combined with cocoa.

CASTLE APRICOTS

13 1/2 oz. stewed or bottled apricots, 1/2 lb. Vanilla Bavarian Cream, 1/2 package orange jelly

Rinse compote dishes or glasses with cold water. Add Vanilla Bavarian Cream (q.v.) and allow to set. Arrange pitted apricots in them and cover with nearly firm orange jelly (made according to package directions). Allow to set again.

ROYAL STRAWBERRIES

1 lb. strawberries, 1 2/3 oz. raisins, 1 oz. confectioners' sugar, 1/2 cup whipping cream, 2/3 oz. confectioners' sugar for cream, 2/3 cup milk, 1 1/3 tablespoons rum, 2—3 egg yolks

Rinse raisins, cover with rum and set aside for 2 hours. Blend egg yolks with sugar. Gradually add hot milk, stirring with an egg-whisk. Place dish with egg yolks into a dish with hot water and beat until sauce thickens. Allow the mixture to cool and combine with cream whipped with sugar. Sort and rinse the strawberries, then remove stems. Arrange in compote dishes or glasses. Cover with cream and sprinkle with raisins.

STRAWBERRIES WITH FARMER'S CHEESE

14 oz. strawberries, 7 oz. farmer's cheese, 1 oz. raisins, 2/3 cup sour cream, 1 2/3 oz. confectioners' sugar, grated orange rind to taste

Rinse the strawberries and remove the stems. Cut them in half and place in glass dishes. Force farmer's cheese through a strainer or mince

it. Combine with cream and arrange on top of strawberries with this. Sprinkle with sugar, rinsed raisins and grated orange rind.

STRAWBERRIES WITH RICE

3 1/2 oz. rice, 9 1/2 oz. strawberries, 2 oz. confectioners' sugar, 1/2 cup whipping cream, 2/3 oz. confectioners' sugar for cream, 3/4 cup milk, ca. 2/3 cup water, 1/2 oz. butter, salt, vanilla bean to taste

Rinse rice in warm water and drain it. Cover with milk combined with water, butter and ground vanilla bean. Add salt and cook for around 15 minutes on an asbestos plate. When done allow to cool and arrange on a round platter. Arrange on top rinsed and hulled strawberries. Sprinkle with confectioners' sugar and decorate with whipped cream.

PLUM SURPRISE I

1 lb. Damsons, 2 2/3 oz. almonds, 1/2 lb. chocolate Bavarian cream, caramel syrup threads, waffle cones for decoration

Wash the plums, remove pits without slicing to the end and place in refrigerator for 1 hour. Blanch the almonds and place in the plums in place of the pits. Arrange in compote dishes or glasses, cover with Chocolate Bavarian Cream (q.v.) and allow to set. Just before serving decorate with waffle cones and pour caramel syrup threads over.

PLUM SURPRISE II

1 lb. Damsons, 5 oz. walnut meats, 1 oz. butter, 2/3 cup cream, 2—3 egg yolks, 2/3 oz. confectioners' sugar for filling, 1 1/3 oz. vanilla-fla-voured confectioners' sugar

Blanch the walnuts, dry and grind them. Blend with butter and sugar. Wash the plums and remove pits without slicing to the end. Fill with

walnut filling and arrange in an oven-proof dish. Blend egg yolks with vanilla-flavoured confectioners' sugar and combine with cream. Cover plums with this sauce and bake in a hot oven.

PLUMS WITH MERINGUE

1 lb. plums, 1 2/3 oz. almonds, 5 egg whites, 7 oz. confectioners' sugar, 1 1/3 tablespoons rum, 1—1 1/3 oz. fat

Wash plums and remove pits. Blanch and grind the almonds. Beat egg whites until stiff, adding confectioners' sugar and almonds towards the end. Grease baking sheet, dip plums in beaten egg whites and arrange at regular intervals on baking sheet. Sprinkle with rum and bake in a moderate oven.

PLUM FRITTERS

1 lb. plums, 5 oz. flour, 2 eggs, 1 1/3 oz. confectioners' sugar, 3/4 cup dry white wine or beer, fat, 1 2/3 oz. vanilla-flavoured confectioners' sugar salt

Wash the eggs, break them and separate the yolks from the whites. Blend egg yolks with sugar and combine with wine and beaten egg whites, alternately adding sifted flour. Add salt. Wash the plums, remove pits and cut in half. Pick them up with a fork, dip in the batter and fry in very hot fat on both sides. When done, sprinkle with vanilla-flavoured confectioners' sugar.

RASPBERRY JELLY

9 1/2 oz. raspberries, 3 1/2 oz. confectioners' sugar, 2/3 cup whipping cream, 2 cups water, 2/3 oz. gelatin, 1 oz. confectioners' sugar

Sort, clean and rinse the raspberries. Beat them in a blender. Combine with boiled hot water and sugar. Add gelatin that has been soaked in

cold water. Bring to a boil, stirring with an egg-whisk. Rinse compote dishes or glasses with cold water. Pour in jelly and allow to set. Just before serving decorate with cream whipped with sugar.

GOOSEBERRY JELLY

9 1/2 oz. gooseberries, 3 1/2 oz. sugar, 2/3 cup whipping cream, 2 cups water, 2/3 oz. gelatin, 1 oz. confectioners' sugar

Sort, clean and rinse the gooseberries. Cover with boiling water, cook and drain. Combine with sugar and gelatin that has been soaked in cold water. Bring to a boil, stirring. Proceed as in Raspberry Jelly.

RHUBARB JELLY

9 1/2 oz. rhubarb, 3 1/2 oz. sugar, 2/3 cup whipping cream, 2 cups water, 2/3 oz. gelatin, 1 oz. confectioners' sugar

Clean, rinse and cut the rhubarb into pieces. Cover with boiling water, cook and drain. Combine with sugar and gelatin that has been soaked in cold water. Proceed as in Raspberry Jelly.

LEMON JELLY

5 oz. lemons, 3 1/2 oz. sugar, 2/3 cup whipping cream, 2 cups water, 2/3 oz. gelatin, 1 oz. confectioners' sugar

Wash and scald the lemons with boiling water. Dry them and grate the rind skin finely. Cover with boiling water blended with sugar. Add gelatin that has been soaked in cold water and bring to a boil, stirring. Pour in lemon juice. Proceed as in Raspberry Jelly.

FRUIT-JUICE JELLY

2/3 cup fruit juice, 1 1/4 cups water, 2/3 cup whipping cream, 2/3 oz. gelatin, lemon juice, 1 oz. confectioners' sugar

Bring water to a boil. Add gelatin that has been soaked in cold water and cook for a while, stirring. Combine with fruit juice and lemon juice. Proceed as in Raspberry Jelly.

WINE JELLY

1 1/4 cups dry white wine, 1/3 cup water, 3 1/2 oz. sugar, 2/3 oz. gelatin, lemon juice, 2/3 cup whipping cream, 1 oz. sugar

Bring water and sugar to a boil. Add gelatin that has been soaked in cold water and bring to a boil, stirring. Pour in wine and lemon juice. Proceed as in Raspberry Jelly.

APPLES IN JELLY

1 lb. apples, 1 2/3 cups water, 3 1/2 oz. sugar, 2/3 oz. gelatin, 1/3 cup dry white wine, lemon juice

Bring water and sugar to a boil. Wash, peel and halve the apples, removing the cores. Place them in the syrup and cook. Take out apples and place them in a bowl or in compote glasses. Blend syrup with gelatin that has been soaked in cold water. Bring to a boil, stirring. Pour in wine and lemon juice. Cover fruit and allow to set.

PEARS IN JELLY

1 lb. pears, 3 1/2 oz. sugar, 1/2 lb. Vanilla Bavarian Cream (q.v.), 2 cups water, 2/3 oz. gelatin, lemon juice to taste

Bring water and sugar to a boil. Wash, peel and cut the pears in halves, removing the cores. Place them in syrup and cook. Take them out of the syrup, cool and fill with cream. Join two halves together and place in compote glasses. Blend syrup with lemon juice and gelatin that has been soaked in cold water. Bring to a boil, stirring. Cover pears and allow to set.

PEACHES IN JELLY

13 1/2 oz. peaches, 3 1/2 oz. sugar, 2/3 cup whipping cream, 2 cups water, 2/3 oz. gelatin, 2/3 oz. confectioners' sugar

Bring water and sugar to a boil. Wash the peaches, cut them in halves and remove the pits. Place them in syrup and cook. Take them out of the syrup and arrange in compote glasses. Blend syrup with gelatin that has been soaked in cold water and bring to a boil, stirring. Cover the peaches and allow to set. Just before serving decorate with cream whipped with sugar.

APPLE MOUSSE

1 lb. apples, 3 1/2 oz. confectioners' sugar, 1/3 oz. gelatin, , 3 table-spoons dry white wine, 4 egg whites, lemon juice to taste

Wash the apples and bake them in a moderate oven, sprinkling with wine. Strain them and allow to cool. Beat the egg whites until stiff, towards the end adding sugar, dissolved gelatin, apple paste and lemon juice. Divide the thickened mousse into portions, chill and garnish. Serve no later than an hour after preparation.

ORANGE MOUSSE

13 1/2 oz. oranges, 3 1/2 oz. confectioners' sugar, 4 egg whites, 2/3 cup whipping cream, 1/3 oz. gelatin, 1 1/3 oz. stewed or bottled sour cherries, orange rind, 2/3 oz. confectioners' sugar

Wash the oranges and scald them with boiling water. Cut them in half and squeeze out the juice. Pour through a strainer and blend with part of the sugar. Proceed as in Apple Mousse. Decorate with whipped cream, pieces of orange and sour cherries.

PLUM MOUSSE

1 lb. plums, 1 oz. almonds, 4 egg whites, 3 1/2 oz. confectioners' sugar, 1/2 oz. gelatin, lemon juice to taste

Rinse the plums and remove pits. Sprinkle with water and simmer until tender. Blanch and grind the almonds. Combine with plum paste and lemon juice. Proceed as in Apple Mousse.

APRICOT MOUSSE

13 1/2 oz. apricots, 2—2 2/3 oz. confectioners' sugar, 2/3 cup whipping cream, 1 1/3 tablespoons cherry liqueur, 1/2 oz. gelatin

Wash the apricots and remove pits. Mix in a blender and combine with liqueur and dissolved gelatin. Chill the cream and whip it, adding sugar towards the end. Combine with apricot paste. Divide into portions and garnish.

FARINA MOUSSE WITH STRAWBERRIES

3 1/2 oz. farina, 7 oz. strawberries, 2 cups milk or water, 3 1/2 oz. sugar

Set aside farina in a cup of water or milk for 30 minutes. Cover with the remaining boiling liquid (milk or water) and bring to a boil, stirring. Stir until smooth over low heat for 15 minutes. Place in a moderate oven for 30 minutes. Rinse the strawberries, remove stems and mix to a paste. Combine with farina and sugar. Beat with an egg-whisk until stiff. Pour mousse into compote glasses and chill.

CHOCOLATE MOUSSE

7 oz. chocolate, 3 tablespoons milk, 5—6 egg whites, 1 2/3 oz. confectioners' sugar, 1/6 oz. gelatin, 1 1/3 oz. raisins

Dissolve chocolate in milk. Beat egg whites until stiff, towards the end adding sugar, chocolate and dissolved gelatin. Pour into compote glasses and sprinkle with rinsed raisins.

APPLE PUDDING

13 1/2 oz. apples, 3 1/2 oz. sugar, 1 1/3 cups water, 1/3 cup dry white wine, 1 oz. potato starch, lemon rind to taste

Wash the apples and remove the cores. Bake in an oven, but do not brown. Force them through a strainer and combine with water, wine and grated lemon rind. Place over high heat. Pour in potato starch and water mixture, stirring. Bring to a boil. Rinse compote glasses with cold water. Pour in pudding and allow to set.

STRAWBERRY PUDDING

13 1/2 oz. strawberries, 3 1/2 oz. sugar, 1 2/3 cups water, 1 oz. potato starch, lemon juice to taste

Rinse strawberries under running water. Remove stems. Cover with part of the boiling water and bring to a boil. Force through a strainer and combine with sugar and lemon juice. Pour in potato starch and water mixture, stirring, then bring to a boil. Proceed as in Apple Pudding.

LEMON PUDDING

9 1/2 oz. lemons, 2 cups water, 5 oz. sugar, 1 oz. potato starch

Wash the lemons and scald them with boiling water. Dry them and grate the rind finely. Add to 1 1/4 cups water. Add sugar and bring to a boil. Blend remaining water with potato starch. Pour slowly into the syrup, stirring briskly with an egg-whisk. Bring to a boil and season. Proceed as in Apple Pudding.

VANILLA PUDDING

2 cups milk, 2 oz. sugar, 1 oz. potato starch, 1/2 vanilla bean

Bring part of the milk (1 2/3 cups) to a boil together with chopped vanilla and strain. Blend remaining milk with potato starch. Gradually add to hot milk, stirring briskly with an egg-whisk. Bring to a boil. Proceed as in Apple Pudding.

EDITOR'S PUDDING I

2 cups milk, 1/2 vanilla bean, 2 egg yolks, 2—2 2/3 oz. confectioners' sugar, 2/3 cup whipping cream, 2/3 oz. confectioners' sugar for cream, 2—2 2/3 oz. stewed or bottled fruit

Bring part of the milk (1 2/3 cups) to a boil together with finely chopped vanilla bean and strain. Blend remaining milk with potato starch. Gradually pour into hot milk, stirring briskly with an egg-whisk. Bring to a boil. Blend egg yolks with sugar. Gradually add hot pudding, stirring constantly with an egg-whisk. Rinse compote glasses with cold water. Pour in warm pudding and allow to set. Just before serving decorate with whipped cream with sugar and fruit.

EDITOR'S PUDDING II

1 cup milk, 1 cup cream, 1 1/3 oz. butter, 2/3 oz. cocoa, 1/2 vanilla bean, 2 egg yolks, 1 2/3 oz. confectioners' sugar, 1/3 cup whipping cream, 2/3 oz. confectioners' sugar for cream, 1 oz. raisins, 1 tablespoon cognac

Bring milk to a boil together with finely chopped vanilla bean and strain. Blend cream with potato starch. Gradually pour into hot milk, stirring briskly with an egg-whisk. Bring to a boil. Blend egg yolks with sugar. Gradually pour in hot pudding, stirring constantly, at the same time adding butter piece by piece. Rinse compote glasses with cold water. Pour in warm pudding and allow to set. Decorate with cream whipped with cocoa and confectioners' sugar. Sprinkle with rinsed raisins soaked in cognac.

COFFEE PUDDING

2/3 oz. coffee, 1 2/3 oz. confectioners' sugar, 2 cups milk, 1/3 cup water, 1 oz. potato starch

Grind coffee, cover with boiling water and brew. Pour through a strainer. Bring part of the milk (1 2/3 cups) to a boil together with finely chopped vanilla bean, then strain. Blend remaining milk with potato starch. Gradually pour into hot milk, stirring briskly with an egg-whisk. Bring to a boil and combine with coffee and sugar. Rinse compote glasses with cold water. Pour in warm pudding and allow to set.

LEMON BAVARIAN CREAM

5 oz. lemons, 3 1/2 oz. confectioners' sugar, 5 eggs, 1 1/3 tablespoons rum, 2/3 oz. gelatin, 1/2 vanilla bean

Soak gelatin in a small amount of cold boiled water. Dissolve in the top of a double boiler over heat and strain. Wash the lemons and scald them with boiling water. Dry them and grate the rind finely. Beat egg whites until stiff, towards the end adding sugar, lemon juice, grated vanilla bean, lemon rind, rum and egg yolks one by one. Add gelatin, stirring constantly with an egg-whisk. Rinse mould with cold water. Sprinkle with sugar and pour in the cream. Allow to set. Before removing cream from mould, dip it in warm water for a moment. Transfer to a platter and garnish.

CHOCOLATE BAVARIAN CREAM

1 cup milk, 3 1/2 oz. hard chocolate, 1 1/3 oz. confectioners' sugar, 1/3 cup whipping cream, 2/3 oz. gelatin, 1/2 vanilla bean

Soak gelatin in a small amount of cold boiled water. Dissolve in the top of a double boiler over heat, then bring to a boil and allow to cool. Combine milk with finely chopped vanilla bean. Bring to a boil and strain. Add chocolate and dissolve it. Combine with gelatin. When mixture begins to thicken, combine with cream whipped with sugar, stirring lightly. Proceed as in Lemon Bavarian Cream.

ORANGE BAVARIAN CREAM

9 1/2 oz. oranges, 1 2/3 oz. butter, 3 eggs, 1 2/3 oz. confectioners' sugar, 1 2/3 tablespoons orange liqueur, 1 2/3 oz. almonds, 2/3—1 oz. sugar for egg whites, 2/3 oz. gelatin

Soak gelatin in a small amount of cold boiled water. Dissolve in the top of a double boiler over heat and allow to cool. Blanch and grind the almonds. Wash and scald the oranges with boiling water. Dry them and grate the rind finely. Peel oranges. Blend butter with sugar, adding egg yolks one by one. Combine with liqueur and stiffly beaten egg whites, alternately adding almonds and diced oranges. Gradually add gelatin, stirring constantly. Proceed as in Lemon Bavarian Cream.

COFFEE BAVARIAN CREAM

2/3 oz. coffee, 2/3 oz. confectioners' sugar for egg yolks, 2/3 oz. con-fectioners' sugar for cream, 2/3 oz. confectioners' sugar for egg whites, 2/3 cup whipping cream, 2/3 cup water, 4 eggs, 2/3 oz. gelatin

Soak gelatin in a small amount of cold boiled water. Dissolve in the top of a double boiler over heat and allow to cool. Brew coffee and strain it. Wash the eggs, break them and separate the yolks from the whites. Blend egg yolks with sugar. Gradually add hot coffee, stirring with an egg-whisk. Beat egg yolks in the top of a double boiler over heat until thick. Combine with gelatin, stiffly beaten egg whites with sugar and cream whipped with sugar. Proceed as in Lemon Bavarian Cream.

VANILLA BAVARIAN CREAM

2/3 cup whipping cream, 1 cup cream, 1 oz. confectioners' sugar for cream, 1 1/3 oz. confectioners' sugar for egg yolks, 4 egg yolks, 2/3 oz. gelatin, 1/2 vanilla bean

Soak gelatin in a small amount of cold boiled water. Dissolve in the top of a double boiler over heat and allow to cool. Bring cream to a boil together with finely chopped vanilla bean and strain. Blend egg yolks with sugar. Gradually pour in hot cream, stirring with an egg-whisk. Beat mixture in the top of a double boiler over heat until thick. Allow to cool and blend with gelatin and cream whipped with sugar. Proceed as in Lemon Bavarian Cream.

NUT OR ALMOND BAVARIAN CREAM

3/4 cup milk, 5 oz. confectioners' sugar, 5 eggs, 5 oz. vanilla-flavoured sugar, 3 1/2 oz. walnut meats or almonds, 2/3 oz. gelatin, orange rind to taste

Scald walnuts or almonds with boiling water. Peel and chop them, then brown in an oven, stirring frequently. Soak gelatin in a small amount of cold boiled water. Dissolve in the top of a double boiler over heat and allow to cool. Bring milk to a boil, blend with gelatin and allow to cool. Beat egg whites until stiff, towards the end adding sugar, grated orange rind and vanilla-flavoured sugar. Blend egg whites with the gelatin mixture, nuts and egg yolks, stirring lightly with an egg-whisk. Proceed as in Lemon Bavarian Cream.

STRAWBERRY BAVARIAN CREAM

1 cup dry white wine, 7 oz. strawberries, 5 oz. confectioners' sugar, 2/3 cup whipping cream, 2/3 oz. gelatin

Soak gelatin in a small amount of cold boiled water. Dissolve in the top of a double boiler over heat and allow to cool. Wash the fruit, remove stems and force through a strainer or beat in a blender. Bring

wine to a boil and combine with gelatin. Chill cream and whip it, adding sugar towards the end. When nearly firm, combine with cream and fruit paste. Proceed as in Lemon Bavarian Cream.

GRAPE BAVARIAN CREAM

1 cup dry white wine, 1/2 lb. grapes, 4 egg yolks, 2/3 oz. gelatin, 2/3 cup whipping cream, 3 1/2 oz. confectioners' sugar for fruit, 1 1/3 oz. confectioners' sugar for cream

Soak gelatin in a small amount of cold boiled water. Dissolve in the top of a double boiler over heat and allow to cool. Sort and rinse the fruit. Place in a blender and combine with sugar. Bring wine to a boil and allow to cool. Combine with fruit, gelatin and egg yolks, stirring with an egg-whisk. Chill and whip the cream, adding sugar towards the end. Combine with nearly firm mixture. Proceed as in Lemon Bavarian Cream.

APRICOT BAVARIAN CREAM

1 cup whipping cream, 3/4 lb. apricots, 2/3 oz. gelatin, 1/3 cup milk, 3 1/2 oz. confectioners' sugar for fruit, 1 2/3 oz. confectioners' sugar for cream

Bring milk to a boil and allow to cool. Soak gelatin in a small amount of cold boiled water. Dissolve in the top of a double boiler over heat and allow to cool. Wash the fruit and remove pits. Beat in a blender together with sugar, milk and gelatin. Chill and whip the cream, adding sugar towards the end. Combine with nearly firm mixture, stirring lightly with an egg-whisk. Proceed as in Lemon Bavarian Cream.

CHERRY BAVARIAN CREAM

1/2 lb. sour cherries, 3 1/2 oz. confectioners' sugar for fruit, 1 2/3 oz. confectioners' sugar for cream, 2/3 cup whipping cream, 1/4—1/3 cup dry white wine, 3 egg yolks, 2/3 oz. gelatin

Soak gelatin in a small amount of cold boiled water. Dissolve in the top of a double boiler over heat and allow to cool. Rinse cherries and remove pits. Beat in a blender together with the wine, sugar, egg yolks and gelatin. Chill and whip the cream, adding sugar towards the end. Combine with the nearly firm mixture. Proceed as in Lemon Bavarian Cream.

APPLE BAVARIAN CREAM

2 lb. apples, 4 egg whites, 1 oz. confectioners' sugar for egg whites, 2/3 cup whipping cream, 1 2/3 oz. confectioners' sugar for cream, 3 tablespoons dry white wine, 2/3 oz. gelatin, orange rind to taste

Wash the apples and bake in an oven, sprinkling with wine. Force them through a strainer. Soak gelatin in a small amount of cold boiled water. Dissolve in the top of a double boiler over heat. Pour into a blender together with the fruit paste and sugar. Turn on blender for 30 seconds. Divide into two parts. When it begins to set combine one part with stiffly beaten egg whites, the other with cream whipped with sugar and combined with grated orange rind. Rinse mould with cold water, sprinkle with sugar and fill with layers of cream. Allow to set.

WINE BAVARIAN CREAM

1 cup dry white wine, 3 1/2 oz. confectioners' sugar for egg yolks, 1 oz. confectioners' sugar for cream, 1/3 cup whipping cream, 5 egg yolks

Heat wine to 170° C. Blend egg yolks with sugar. Gradually pour in hot wine, stirring with an egg-whisk. Beat egg yolks in the top of a double boiler over heat until thick. Pour cream into individual cups and decorate with cream whipped with sugar.

CHEESE BAVARIAN CREAM

1 2/3 cups milk, 2 oz. confectioners' sugar for egg yolks, 1 oz. confectioners' sugar for pudding, 2/3 oz. powdered chocolate, 7 oz. farmer's cheese, 1 package vanilla pudding, 1 2/3 oz. butter, 3 eggs

Make pudding with milk according to package directions. Blend butter with sugar and egg yolks. Gradually pour in the pudding, stirring constantly. Combine with chocolate, minced cheese and stiffly beaten egg whites. Rinse compote dishes or glasses with cold water. Pour in cream and allow to set.

WHOLE-WHEAT BREAD BAVARIAN CREAM

1 lb. apples, 2 oz. sugar, 3 1/2 oz. grated whole-wheat bread, 1 cup whipping cream, 1 oz. confectioners' sugar for cream, 1 2/3 oz. raisins, 1/2 vanilla bean

Wash, peel and halve the apples, removing the cores. Grate them coarsely and combine with sugar and ground vanilla bean. Simmer over low heat for 5—8 minutes, stirring frequently. Combine with rinsed raisins and cream whipped with sugar, alternately adding grated bread. Place in compote dishes or glasses.

CARDINAL'S BAVARIAN CREAM

1 cup whipping cream, 1 oz. confectioners' sugar for cream, 1 1/3 oz. almonds, 9 1/2 oz. grapes, 1 oz. confectioners' sugar for fruit, lemon juice to taste

Blanch the almonds. Sort and rinse grapes. Set aside some for decoration. Place the rest in a blender together with sugar and lemon juice. Chill and whip the cream, adding sugar towards the end. Combine lightly with the grape pulp. Place in compote dishes or glasses. Decorate with grapes and almonds. Serve at once.

EDITOR'S BAVARIAN CREAM

1 cup whipping cream, 1 1/3 oz. confectioners' sugar for cream, 1 oz. puffs, 7 oz. wild strawberries, 1 oz. confectioners' sugar for fruit, 2/3 oz. chocolate

Sort and rinse the strawberries. Set aside some for decoration. Beat the rest in a blender together with sugar. Chill and whip the cream, adding sugar towards the end. Combine with fruit pulp. Place in round glasses. Decorate with strawberries and puffs. Sprinkle with grated chocolate.

HUSSAR'S BAVARIAN CREAM

7 oz. dried apricots, 1 1/3 oz. sugar, 1 1/3 oz. confectioners' sugar, 3 tablespoons rum, 4 egg yolks, 3 1/2 oz. butter

Rinse and soak the apricots. Cover with a small amount of water. Add sugar and cook. Force through a strainer and place in a blender together with egg yolks, confectioners' sugar, rum and butter. Turn on blender for 30 seconds. Use as filling for cakes, waffles etc.

VANILLA ICE CREAM

2 cups milk or cream, 3 1/2 oz. sugar, 5 egg yolks, vanilla bean

Bring milk or cream to a boil together with finely chopped vanilla bean, then strain. Blend egg yolks with sugar until smooth. Pour in hot milk, stirring with an egg-whisk. Heat over low heat until thick, without boiling. Chill quickly and half fill an ice-cream churn, as during churning the volume of ice cream increases. Place in freezer, turn on ice cream machine and churn until thick. Leave in freezer for 2—3 hours.

CHOCOLATE ICE CREAM

2 cups cream, 3 1/2 oz. sugar, 1 2/3 oz. chocolate, 5 egg yolks, 1/4 vanilla bean

Bring milk or cream to a boil together with finely chopped vanilla bean, then strain. Add chocolate and dissolve. Proceed as in Vanilla Ice Cream. Serve with whipped cream.

RAISIN, NUT AND FIG ICE CREAM

*2 cups milk or cream, 3 1/2 oz. confectioners' sugar, 5 egg yolks,
1 2/3 oz. raisins, 1 2/3 oz. walnut meats, 1 2/3 oz. figs*

Blanch and grind walnuts finely. Wash raisins and figs. Chop figs
finely. Make ice cream as in Vanilla Ice Cream. Just before placing
in churning machine combine with raisins, nuts and figs. Serve with
whipped cream or other cream topping.

LEMON OR ORANGE ICE CREAM

*3/4 cup milk, 2/3 cup whipping cream, 3 1/2 oz. sugar, 5 egg yolks,
9 1/2 oz. lemons or 13 1/2 oz. oranges*

Wash and scald the fruit with boiling water. Dry and grate the rind
finely. Squeeze out juice and remove pits. Bring milk to a boil together
with fruit rind. Proceed as in Vanilla Ice Cream. Towards the end
of freezing combine with lemon or orange juice. Serve with whipped
cream.

STRAWBERRY ICE CREAM

*Ca. 1 2/3 cups milk, 5 oz. sugar, 4 tablespoons whipping cream, 7 oz.
fruit, 4 egg yolks, 1/3 vanilla bean*

Sort and rinse the fruit. Remove stems and beat in a blender. Proceed
as in Vanilla Ice Cream. Towards the end of freezing combine with
strawberry pulp and cream.

MARASCHINO ICE CREAM

*Ca. 1 2/3 cups cream, 3 tablespoons Maraschino liqueur, 7 oz. sugar,
6 egg yolks*

Make ice cream as in Vanilla Ice Cream. Towards the end of freezing add Maraschino liqueur.

ICE CREAM BOMBE

2 cups whipping cream, 1 lb. fruit (strawberries, wild strawberries or raspberries), 9 1/2 oz. sugar

Sort and rinse the fruit. Remove stems, blend fruit and combine with sugar (7 oz.). Chill and whip the cream, towards the end adding the remaining sugar. Combine with fruit pulp. Proceed as in Vanilla Ice Cream. Place ice cream in mould and freeze. Place mould in hot water for several seconds and transfer ice cream onto a round glass platter.

ROYAL ICE CREAM BOMBE

1 1/4 lb. raisin, nut and fig ice cream, 1 1/4 lb. apricot ice cream, 3 1/2 oz. grated gingerbread, 1 lb. chocolate

Line mould with raisin, nut and fig ice cream (made as in Raisin, Nut and Fig Ice Cream, q.v.). Sprinkle with grated gingerbread. Fill to the top with apricot ice cream and close tightly. Place in freezer and freeze. Place mould in hot water for several seconds. Transfer ice cream onto a round platter and sprinkle with grated chocolate.

CARDINAL'S ICE CREAM BOMBE

1 3/4 lb. chocolate ice cream, 1 lb. Cardinal's Bavarian Cream

Line mould with Chocolate Ice Cream (q.v.). Fill to the top with Cardinal's Bavarian Cream (q.v.) and close tightly. Place in the freezer and freeze. Place the mould in hot water for several seconds. Transfer ice cream onto a round platter.

ICE CREAM WITH CARDINAL'S SAUCE

4 small portions raisin, nut and fig ice cream, 5 oz. oranges, 3 1/2 oz. Cardinal's Sauce

Wash and scald the oranges with boiling water. Peel and divide into pieces. Place ice cream in glasses. Pour Cardinal's Sauce (q.v.) oven them and decorate with orange pieces.

Beverages

TEA

1/3 oz. tea, 4 cups water, sugar

Rinse a porcelain, faience or stoneware teapot with boiling water several times. Put in the tea and add boiling water until tea is covered. Place on top of an uncovered kettle containing boiling water for 3—5 minutes. Fill the teapot to the top with boiling water and set aside for 2—3 minutes. Pour a small amount of this tea into warmed teacups. Add boiling water until full and serve at once. Serve sugar and lemon slices separately.

ARRACK TEA

1/3—2/3 oz. tea, 3 1/4 cups water, 2 2/3 tablespoons arrack, 2 2/3 oz. oranges, sugar

Make tea as above. Pour into warmed teacups together with arrack. Add a slice of scalded and peeled orange to each cup. Serve sugar separately.

ADVOCAAT TEA I

1/3 oz. tea, 3/4 cup Advocaat liqueur, 3 1/4 cups water, 2 tablespoons lemon juice, 1 2/3 oz. sugar

Brew the tea and blend with sugar. Allow to cool and combine with liqueur and lemon juice.

ADVOCAAT TEA II

1/3 oz. tea, 3 2/3 cups water, 3 egg yolks, 2 2/3 oz. confectioners' sugar, 1/3 cup rum

Brew the tea. Blend egg yolks with sugar. Gradually add the hot tea, stirring briskly with an egg-whisk. Allow to cool and combine with rum.

TEA WITH WINE

1/3 oz. tea, 3 1/4 cups water, 1 cup dry red wine, 2 oz. lemons, 1 2/3 oz. honey

Brew the tea and combine with honey and wine. Heat without boiling and pour into glasses. Add slices of scalded and peeled lemon.

TEA WITH VODKA

1/3 oz. tea, 2 3/4 cups water, 1 cup vodka, 3 1/3 tablespoons rum, sugar to taste

Brew the tea and pour into teacups. Pour in the vodka and rum. Serve sugar separately.

TEA WITH CREAM

1/3 oz. tea, 3 1/4 cups water, 1/2 cup whipping cream, 3 1/3 tablespoons rum liqueur, 1 2/3 oz. confectioners' sugar, lemon rind

Brew the tea and allow to cool. Pour in rum liqueur. Add grated lemon rind and cream whipped with sugar.

COFFEE I

1 2/3 oz. coffee, 3 1/4 cups water, 2 oz. sugar

Scald thermos with boiling water. Add finely ground coffee. Cover with measured out boiling water. Close thermos tightly for 10 minutes. Serve coffee in a jug. Serve sugar separately.

COFFEE II

1 2/3 oz. coffee, 3 1/4 cups water, 2 oz. sugar

Grind measured-out coffee to a powder. Combine with a part of the sugar. Place in a Turkish pot and cover with boiling water. Heat until coffee rises three times, but do not bring to a boil. Rinse jug with boiling water and pour in coffee. Serve remaining sugar separately.

SOPOT COFFEE

1 2/3 oz. coffee, 3 1/4 cups water, 2 oz. sugar, cinnamon and cloves to taste

Brew the coffee as in Coffee I together with the spices. Strain and pour into cups. Serve sugar separately.

ROYAL COFFEE

1 2/3 oz. coffee, 2 1/2 cups water, 1/2 cup coffee liqueur, 3 1/3 table-spoons cognac, 1/2 cup whipping cream, 2 oz. confectioners' sugar, 2/3 oz. powdered chocolate

Brew coffee as in Coffee I. Strain and combine with chocolate, sugar and spirits. Pour into cups and decorate with whipped cream.

ORANGE COFFEE

1 2/3 oz. coffee, 1 2/3 cups water, 1 1/4 cups orange juice, 3 1/3 table-spoons dry vodka, 4 egg yolks, 1 1/3 oz. sugar, vanilla bean to taste

Brew coffee as in Coffee I and strain. Blend egg yolks with sugar and grated vanilla bean. Gradually pour in coffee, stirring constantly with an egg-whisk. Chill and combine with orange juice and vodka.

PINEAPPLE COFFEE

1 2/3 oz. coffee, 1 1/4 cups water, 3 1/3 tablespoons pineapple juice, 2 2/3 oz. canned pineapple, 4 egg yolks, 1/2 cup whipping cream, 2/3 oz. sugar

Brew coffee as in Coffee I and strain. Blend egg yolks with sugar. Gradually pour in hot coffee, stirring constantly with an egg-whisk. Allow to cool and combine with pineapple juice. Pour into glasses. Decorate with whipped cream and chill well. Add diced pineapple just before serving.

COFFEE WITH CREAM

1 2/3 oz. coffee, 3 1/4 cups water, 3/4 cup whipping cream, 2 oz. sugar

Brew coffee as in Coffee I. Pour into warmed cups. Serve whipped cream and sugar separately.

CAPUCHIN COFFEE

1 2/3 oz. coffee, 3 1/4 cups water, 3/4 sweet cream, 2 oz. sugar

Brew coffee as in Coffee I. Pour into warmed cups. Serve cream and sugar separately.

ADVOCAAT COFFEE

1 2/3 oz. coffee, 3 1/4 cups water, 3 1/3 tablespoons liqueur, 3 egg yolks, 1 2/3 oz. sugar

Brew coffee as in Coffee I. Blend egg yolks with sugar. Gradually pour in hot coffee, stirring constantly with an egg-whisk. Pour in liqueur. Pour into cups and add ice cubes.

COFFEE WITH CHOCOLATE

1 2/3 oz. coffee, 2 3/4 cups water, 1 2/3 oz. powdered chocolate, 3 1/3 tablespoons cherry brandy

Brew coffee as in Coffee I. Pour into cups. Add chocolate and pour in cherry brandy.

COFFEE WITH ICE CREAM

1 2/3 oz. coffee, 2 1/3 cups water, 2 oz. sugar, 3 1/3 tablespoons rum, 1/2 cup whipping cream, 2/3 oz. chocolate, 4 scoops vanilla ice cream

Brew coffee as in Coffee I. Strain and combine with sugar. Chill and add rum. Place a scoop of ice cream in each glass. Pour in coffee. Place whipped cream on top and sprinkle with grated chocolate.

ICED COFFEE

1 2/3 oz. coffee, 2 cups water, 1 cup sweet cream, 2 2/3 oz. confectioners' sugar, 1/2 cup whipping cream

Brew coffee as in Coffee I. Strain and combine with sugar. Chill and combine with sweet cream. Place in an ice cream churning machine and turn on for 30 minutes. Pour into glasses and decorate with whipped cream.

AMATEUR'S COFFEE

1 2/3 oz. coffee, 1/3 cup water, 2/3—1 oz. sugar, nutmeg, ground paprika and white pepper to taste

Grind coffee to a powder and combine with sugar and ground spices. Place in a Turkish pot, cover with cold water and slowly heat to 190° F, then strain. Another way is to place all the ingredients in a thermos, cover with boiling water and set aside tightly covered for 6—8 minutes. Serve strained.

CHOCOLATE

4 cups milk, 3 1/2 oz. chocolate, 1/3 cup cream, 2 egg yolks, sugar to taste

Crumble chocolate into pieces. Combine with several tablespoons of milk and dissolve. Combine with boiling milk and allow to cool lightly. Combine with cream, then with egg yolks, stirring with an egg-whisk. Sweeten to taste and serve ot once.

APPLE OR PEAR COMPOTE

1 lb. apples, 2 cups water, 3—5 oz. sugar, lemon juice and lemon rind to taste

Bring water to a boil together with sugar and lemon rind. Wash, peel and halve the apples, removing the cores. Cut into pieces, place in syrup and cook for 3—4 minutes. Allow to cool, flavour to taste and pour into compote glasses.

PLUM COMPOTE

1 lb. plums, 2 cups water, 3 1/2 oz. sugar, orange rind to taste

Bring water to a boil together with sugar and orange rind. Wash the plums and remove pits. Place in syrup and cook slowly. Strain and pour into compote glasses.

STRAWBERRY COMPOTE

1 lb. strawberries, 1 2/3 cups water, 1/3 cup dry red wine, 2 2/3 oz. confectioners' sugar

Bring water to a boil together with sugar. Sort and rinse the strawberries. Remove the stems. Set aside the better ones and strain or beat the remaining in a blender. Place the strawberries in compote glasses, sprinkle with confectioners' sugar and cover with syrup blended with wine and strawberry pulp. Serve well chilled.

BLUEBERRY COMPOTE

14 oz. blueberries, 2 cups water, 5 oz. sugar

Bring water to a boil together with sugar. Sort and rinse the blueberries under a weak stream of running water. Place in syrup and bring to a boil. Allow to cool and pour into compote glasses.

SOUR CHERRY COMPOTE

14 oz. sour cherries, 2 cups water, 5 oz. sugar

Bring water to a boil together with sugar. Rinse the sour cherries and remove stems. Place in syrup and cook for 2—3 minutes. Allow to cool and pour into compote glasses.

CHERRY COMPOTE

1 lb. cherries, 2 cups water, 3 1/2 oz. sugar, lemon juice to taste

Bring water to a boil together with sugar. Rinse the cherries and remove the stems. Place in syrup and cook for 2—3 mintues. Allow to cool. Correct the flavour with lemon juice and pour into compote glasses.

CURRANT COMPOTE

7 oz. currants, 7 oz. apples or pears, 2 cups water, 5 oz. sugar

Bring water to a boil together with sugar. Sort and rinse the currants and remove the stems. Wash, peel, halve and core the apples or pears. Cut into pieces and place in the syrup together with the currants. Bring to a boil. Allow to cool and pour into compote glasses.

GOOSEBERRY COMPOTE

14 oz. gooseberries, 2 cups water, 5 oz. sugar

Bring water to a boil together with sugar. Sort and rinse the goose-berries, then remove the stems. Place in the syrup and cook for a while. Allow to cool and pour into compote glasses.

BLUEBERRY PUNCH

10 oz. blueberries, 3 1/2 oz. sugar, 2 cups water, 1/3 cup dry red wine, 1/3 vanilla bean

Bring water to a boil together with ground vanilla and sugar. Allow to cool. Sort and wash the blueberries. Force through a strainer and cook with syrup and wine. Allow to cool. Pour into glasses. Add ice cubes and serve at once.

STRAWBERRY OR WILD STRAWBERRY
ORANGE MILK SHAKE

1 lb. strawberries or wild strawberries, 1 2/3 cups milk, 1/3 cup cream, 1/3 cup orange juice, 3 1/2 oz. sugar

Bring milk to a boil together with sugar. Allow to cool. Sort and rinse the fruit. Remove the stems and force through a strainer. Place in a blender. Add milk, cream and orange juice. Turn on blender for 30 seconds. Pour drink into glasses and serve at once.

RASPBERRY AND HONEY DRINK

1 lb. raspberries, 2 cups milk, 1 2/3 oz. honey

Bring milk to a boil and allow to cool. Sort and rinse the raspberries. Force them through a strainer. Combine with milk and honey. Pour into glasses and serve at once.

BLACKBERRY JUICE

10 oz. blackberries, 7 oz. currants, 2 cups water, 5 oz. sugar

Bring water to a boil together with sugar. Allow to cool. Sort and rinse the fruit. Remove the stems and force through a strainer. Combine with syrup. Pour into glasses. Add ice cubes and serve at once.

PLUM MILK SHAKE

1 lb. plums, 2—3 oz. sugar, 2 cups milk, cinnamon to taste

Bring milk to a boil together with sugar and cinnamon. Force through a strainer and allow to cool. Wash and scald the plums with boiling water. Peel and remove pits. Place in a blender. Add milk and turn on blender for 30 seconds. Pour into glasses and serve at once.

SOUR CHERRY PUNCH

14 oz. sour chernès, 3—4 oz. sugar, 1 2/3 cups water, 1/3 cup dry red wine

Bring water to a boil together with sugar and allow to cool. Wash the sour cherries and remove pits. Force through a strainer and combine with syrup and wine. Pour into glasses. Add ice cubes and serve at once.

RHUBARB JUICE

14 oz. rhubarb, 2 cups water, 3—4 oz. sugar, lemon rind and cinnamon to taste

Wash the rhubarb and cut into pieces. Bring water to a boil together with lemon rind, cinnamon and sugar. Add rhubarb and bring to a boil again. Set aside for 10 minutes. Force through a strainer and chill. Pour into glasses. Add ice cubes and serve at once.

APPLE JUICE

1 lb. apples, 3—5 oz. sugar, 2 cups water, lemon juice and cloves to taste

Bring water to a boil together with sugar and cloves. Allow to cool. Wash and peel the apples. Cut into halves, removing the cores. Grate finely and sprinkle with lemon juice. Combine with syrup. Pour into glasses. Add ice cubes and serve at once.

LEMONADE OR ORANGEADE

1/2 lb. lemons or oranges, 2 cups water, 3—5 oz. sugar

Wash lemons or oranges. Scald with boiling water and dry. Grate surface rind finely and combine with water and sugar. Bring to a boil and allow to cool. Combine with juice squeezed from lemons or oranges, then chill. Pour into glasses. Add ice cubes and serve at once.

SOUR MILK BEVERAGE I

3 1/4 cups sour milk, 3/4 cups sour cream, fresh chives, fresh dill, salt to taste

Rinse the chives and dill, then chop them finely. Chill milk and combine with cream. Beat with an egg-whisk and combine with the herbs. Add salt to taste and pour into glasses.

SOUR MILK BEVERAGE II

3 1/4 cups sour milk, 5 oz. apples, 1/3 cup sour cream, 1 2/3 oz. tomato paste, parsley sprigs, salt, sugar and pepper to taste

Wash and peel the apples. Cut them in half, removing the cores. Grate them finely. Combine chilled milk with sour cream, tomato paste and apples. Beat with an egg-whisk and combine with rinsed and chopped parsley sprigs, then season. Pour into glasses.

SOUR MILK WITH RADISHES

3 1/4 cups sour milk, 3 1/2 oz. radishes, 1/2 cup sour cream, fresh dill or chives, salt to taste

Clean, rinse and grate the radishes coarsely. Wash chives or dill thoroughly and chop finely. Beat chilled milk with an egg-whisk together with sour cream. Combine with radishes and chives, then add salt. Pour into glasses and serve at once.

SOUR MILK WITH CUCUMBERS

3 1/4 cups sour milk, 7 oz. cucumbers, fresh dill, 1/3 cup sour cream, salt to taste

Wash and peel the cucumbers. Cut into thin strips, removing the seeds. Rinse and chop the dill. Chill the milk and beat with an egg-whisk together with sour cream. Combine with cucumbers and dill. Add salt to taste. Pour into glasses.

SOUR MILK WITH TOMATOES

3 1/4 cups sour milk, 1 2/3 oz. tomato paste, 1/3 cup cream, fresh dill, salt and sugar to taste

Combine chilled milk with cream and tomato paste. Beat with an egg-whisk. Combine with rinsed and finely chopped dill, then season. Pour into glasses and serve at once.

SOUR MILK WITH VEGETABLES

2 cups sour milk, 1/3 cup sour cream, 5 oz. apples, 1/2 lb. carrots, 5 oz. celeriac, fresh chives, salt to taste

Beat chilled milk and sour cream with an egg-whisk. Wash, peel and halve the apples, removing the cores. Wash, peel and rinse the vegetables. Put them through an electric blender together with the apples. Combine the juice with milk and chopped chives, then add salt. Pour into glasses.

SOUR MILK WITH SOURED BEET JUICE

2 cups sour milk, 1 2/3 cups soured beet juice (q.v.), 1/3 cup sour cream, parsley sprigs, salt, pepper and sugar to taste

Beat chilled milk and sour cream with an egg-whisk, gradually adding the beet juice. Combine with rinsed and chopped parsley sprigs. Season and pour into glasses.

YOGURT WITH SOUR MILK

1 2/3 cups yogurt, 1 2/3 cups sour milk, 3/4 cup buttermilk, salt to taste

Pour chilled milk, yogurt and buttermilk into a blender. Turn it on for 30 seconds. Add salt and pour into glasses.

YOGURT WITH TOMATOES

1 2/3 cups yogurt, 3/4 cup tomato juice, fresh dill, 1 2/3 cups mineral water, salt to taste

Pour chilled yogurt and tomato juice into a blender. Turn it on for 30 seconds. Combine with rinsed and finely chopped dill. Add salt and pour into glasses. Fill to the top with mineral water. Serve at once.

YOGURT WITH VEGETABLES

2 cups yogurt, 1 lb. soup vegetables (carrots, parsley root, celeriac, leek), 3/4 cup tomato juice, parsley sprigs and fresh dill, salt, pepper and sugar to taste

Wash, peel and rinse the vegetables. Dice them and cover with water, then cook. Strain and chill the stock. Pour yogurt into a blender together with tomato juice and stock. Turn on blender for 30 seconds. Combine with rinsed and finely chopped herbs, then season. Pour into glasses.

WHEY BEVERAGE

2 1/3 cups whey, 3/4 cup sour cream, 3/4 cup tomato juice, parsley sprigs, salt and sugar to taste

Combine chilled whey, sour cream and tomato juice. Beat with an egg-whisk. Add rinsed and chopped parsley sprigs. Season to taste. Pour into glasses. Add ice cubes and serve at once.

MINT DRINK

1/6 oz. tea, 2 mint teabags, 4 cups water, 1 2/3 oz. lemon, 1 2/3 oz. honey, salt and sugar to taste

Brew the tea (as in Tea). Use remaining water for brewing mint tea. Discard teabags. Combine mint with honey, tea brew, a little salt and sugar. When cooled pour into glasses. Add a slice of lemon to each glass and serve at once.

BUTTERMILK BEVERAGE

3 1/4 cups buttermilk, 1/3 cup sour cream, 1 bunch radishes, fresh dill, fresh chives, salt to taste

Clean, rinse and grate the radishes finely. Add to buttermilk together with finely chopped herbs. Add cream and salt. Beat with an egg-whisk. Pour into glasses and serve at once.

TOMATO JUICE BEVERAGE I

2 cups tomato juice, 2 cups kefir, parsley sprigs, salt and sugar to taste

Combine chilled kefir with tomato juice. Beat with an egg-whisk. Combine with finely chopped parsley sprigs and season. Pour into glasses and serve at once.

TOMATO JUICE BEVERAGE II

2 cups tomato juice, 1 cup sour milk, 1 cup vegetable juice, parsley sprigs, salt, sugar and garlic to taste

Combine milk with tomato and vegetable juices. Beat with an egg-whisk. Add rinsed and finely chopped parsley sprigs and season. Pour into glasses and serve at once.

CARROT JUICE WITH MILK

2 lb. carrots, 1 2/3 cups milk

Wash, peel and rinse the carrots. Cut them up and put them through an electric juice-maker. Combine with milk. Pour into glasses and serve at once.

CARROT AND APPLE JUICE

2 lb. carrots, 1 lb. apples, lemon juice to taste

Wash and peel the carrots. Rinse them and cut them up. Wash and halve the apples, removing the cores. Cut them up and put through an electric juice-maker together with the carrots. Season with lemon juice. Pour into glasses and serve at once.

SPRING DRINK

1 lb. carrots, 3 1/2 oz. radishes, 13 1/2 oz. kohlrabi, 1 2/3 cups water, fresh chives, sugar to taste

Bring water to a boil and allow to cool. Clean, rinse and grate the radishes finely. Wash, peel and rinse the kohlrabi and carrots. Cut them up and put through an electric juice-maker. Combine with water, radishes and rinsed, finely chopped chives. Season to taste. Pour into glasses and serve at once.

CELERIAC DRINK

1 cup water, 1 1/4 lb. celeriac, 1 lb. apples, 3/4 cup tomato juice, parsley sprigs, salt and sugar to taste

Bring water to a boil and allow to cool. Wash and peel the celeriac. Rinse it and cut it up. Wash the apples and halve them, removing the cores. Put them through an electric juice-maker together with the celeriac. Combine with water, tomato juice and rinsed, finely chopped parsley sprigs. Season to taste. Pour into glasses and add ice cubes. Serve at once.

CITEROS I

2 1/3 cups water, 1 2/3 oz. sugar, 1/4 oz. yeast, 3 1/2 oz. honey, 2 2/3 oz. lemons, 1 2/3 oz. raisins

Bring water to a boil together with sugar. Allow to cool. Combine with crumbled yeast, lemon juice, honey and rinsed raisins. Set aside at room temperature for 12 hours. Serve chilled.

CITEROS II

2 1/3 cups water, 2 2/3 oz. sugar, 1/3 oz. yeast, 1 1/3 oz. raisins, 1 2/3 tablespoons lemon juice, 1 1/3 oz. lemon

Bring water to a boil together with sugar and allow to cool. Combine 1/3 cup water with yeast and set aside to let it ferment. Add rinsed raisins, the remaining water and lemon juice. Set aside for 30 minutes. Chill and pour into glasses. Add a slice of peeled lemon to each glass.

OLD POLISH DRINK

2 1/3 cups water, 3 1/2 oz. honey, 2 2/3 oz. lemon

Bring water to a boil and combine with honey. Allow to cool. Combine with lemon juice.

LEMON-HONEY BEVERAGE

2 1/3 cups buttermilk, 2 egg yolks, 1 2/3 oz. honey, 2 2/3 oz. lemon

Blend egg yolks with honey, adding lemon juice towards the end. Pour into a blender and add buttermilk. Turn on blender for 30 seconds. Pour into glasses and serve at once.

POLISH DRINK

1 cup mead, 2/3 cup rowan-berry vodka, 1 2/3 tablespoons lemon juice, 1 2/3 oz. lemon

Combine mead with vodka and lemon juice. Pour into glasses. Add a slice of lemon and ice cubes into each glass. Serve at once.

CASTELLAN'S DRINK

1 1/3 cups beer, 2/3 oz. grated whole-wheat bread, 1/3 cup dry red wine, 2 1/3 oz. sugar, 1 2/3 oz. raisins, 1 2/3 tablespoons lemon juice, 1 2/3 oz. lemon

Heat 3/4 cup beer to 120° F. Pour over grated whole-wheat bread and set aside for 30 minutes. Bring remaining beer to a boil together with sugar. Combine with wine, rinsed raisins, lemon juice and strained beer, then chill. Serve in glasses with slices of peeled lemon.

CARAWAY DRINK

2 3/4 cups water, 5 oz. caraway seed, 5 oz. sugar, 1/6 oz. yeast, 1 2/3 tablespoons lemon juice, 3 tablespoons rowan-berry vodka

Cover caraway with boiling water and set aside for 25 minutes. Strain and combine with sugar. Allow to cool. Add crushed yeast and lemon juice. Set aside at room temperature for 12 hours. Strain and add vodka. Season with lemon juice.

CRANBERRY DRINK

16 cups water, 2 lb. cranberries, 13 1/2 oz. sugar, 1/3 oz. yeast, 2/3 oz. raisins

Sort and rinse the cranberries. Force them through a strainer and cover with boiling water. Allow to cool. Combine with sugar and yeast dissolved in lukewarm boiled water. Set aside for 8—10 hours. Pour into bottles that have been rinsed with boiling water. Add rinsed raisins. Close tightly with corks that have been boiled in water. Keep in a dark cool place for 3 days, in a horizontal position.

SOURED FRUIT JUICE

16 cups water, 2 lb. currants, 1/3 oz. yeast, 13 1/2 oz. sugar, 2/3 oz. raisins, cloves and cinnamon to taste

Sort and rinse the currants. Remove stems, cover with water and bring to a boil. Add crushed spices and allow to cool. Combine with sugar and yeast dissolved in lukewarm boiled water. Set aside for 8—10 hours. Proceed as above.

SOURED LEMON JUICE

16 cups water, 15 oz. lemons, 13 1/2 oz. sugar, 1/3 oz. yeast, 1 2/3 oz. raisins

Wash and scald the lemons with boiling water. Dry them and grate the rind finely. Place the rind in water, bring to a boil and allow to cool. Squeeze out the juice and remove pits. Combine with water, yeast dissolved in lukewarm water and with sugar. Set aside for 8—10 hours. Proceed as in Cranberry Drink.

SOURED BREAD JUICE

16 cups water, 7 oz. whole-wheat bread, 1/2 lb. sugar, 1/6 oz. yeast, 1 2/3 oz. raisins

Bring water to a boil. Cut bread into cubes and brown in the oven. Cover with boiling water and allow to cool. Combine with sugar and yeast dissolved in lukewarm boiled water. Set aside for 24 hours, then strain. Proceed as in Cranberry Drink.

MILK SHAKE I

2 cups milk, 1 2/3 oz. chocolate, 1 2/3 oz. confectioners' sugar, 4 eggs

Bring milk to a boil. Add crumbled chocolate and dissolve it. Wash the eggs and break them into the top of a double boiler. Combine with sugar and beat until stiff. Gradually add hot milk, stirring briskly with an egg-whisk. Beat for 3—5 minutes over hot water. Pour cocktail into a blender and turn it on for 30 seconds. Pour into glasses and serve at once.

MILK SHAKE II

1 2/3 cups milk, 3 1/2 oz. chocolate, 1/3 cup orange juice, 3 tablespoons Maraschino liqueur

Bring milk to a boil together with crumbled chocolate and allow to cool. Pour into a blender. Add orange juice and liqueur. Turn on blender for 30 seconds. Pour into glasses and serve at once.

STRAWBERRY MILK SHAKE I

2 cups milk, 1 lb. strawberries, 2 oz. confectioners' sugar, lemon juice to taste

Bring milk to a boil and allow to cool. Sort and rinse the strawberries. Remove stems. Place in a blender together with sugar. Add milk and lemon juice. Turn on blender for 30 seconds. Pour cocktail into glasses. Add ice cubes and serve at once.

STRAWBERRY MILK SHAKE II

1 lb. strawberries, 1 1/4 cups cream, 2 egg yolks, 1 2/3 oz. confectioners' sugar, 2/3 cup currant juice

Bring cream to a boil. Sort and rinse strawberries. Remove stems and beat in a blender. Blend egg yolks with sugar. Combine with hot cream, stirring briskly with an egg-whisk. Allow to cool. Pour into

strawberries together with currant juice. Turn on blender for 30 seconds. Pour cocktail into glasses and chill well.

STRAWBERRY SHAKE

1 lb. strawberries, 2 cups dry red wine, 2—3 oz. confectioners' sugar

Sort and rinse strawberries. Remove stems and place in a blender together with sugar. Add wine and turn on blender for 30 seconds. Pour cocktail into glasses. Add ice cubes and serve at once.

WILD STRAWBERRY MILK SHAKE I

13 1/2 oz. wild strawberries, 1/2 lb. vanilla ice cream, 1/3 cup whipping cream, 2/3 oz. confectioners' sugar, 2/3 oz. cocoa

Sort strawberries, rinse them and remove stems. Place in a blender together with ice cream. Turn it on for 20—30 seconds. Pour cocktail into glasses. Decorate with cream whipped with sugar and cocoa. Serve at once.

WILD STRAWBERRY MILK SHAKE II

13 1/2 oz. wild strawberries, 2—3 oz. confectioners' sugar, 1 cup cream, 2/3 cup dry red wine

Sort and rinse the strawberries. Remove stems and place in a blender together with sugar. Add cream and wine. Turn on blender for 30 seconds. Pour cocktail into glasses. Add ice cubes and serve at once.

GRAPE COCKTAIL

9 1/2 oz. grapes, 2 egg yolks, 2—3 oz. confectioners' sugar, 1 1/4 cups dry white wine, 3 tablespoons liqueur, lemon juice to taste

Sort and rinse grapes. Blend egg yolks with sugar. Place in a blender together with grapes. Add wine, liqueur and lemon juice. Turn on blender for seconds. Pour cocktail into glasses. Add ice cubes and serve at once.

APRICOT MILK SHAKE

13 1/2 oz. stewed or bottled apricots, 2 cups milk, lemon juice to taste

Bring milk to a boil and allow to cool. Remove pits from apricots. Place in a blender. Add milk and lemon juice. Turn on blender for 30 seconds. Pour into glasses and serve at once.

CURRANT MILK SHAKE

2 cups currant juice, 3/4 cup milk, 5 oz. vanilla ice cream

Place currant juice, milk and ice cream in a blender and turn in on for 30 seconds. Pour into glasses and serve at once.

CHEF'S COCKTAIL

2 cups dry red wine, 1 cup strong coffee, 2—3 egg yolks, 2 oz. confectioners' sugar

Place wine, coffee and sugar in a blender and turn it on for 30 seconds. Pour into glasses. Add ice cubes and serve at once.

BLUEBERRY MILK SHAKE

13 1/2 oz. blueberries, 1 1/3 oz. confectioners' sugar, 7 oz. vanilla ice cream, 1 cup cream, 1 2/3 oz. raisins

Sort and rinse blueberries. Place them in a blender together with sugar, ice cream and rinsed raisins. Add cream and turn on blender for 30 seconds. Pour into glasses and serve at once.

ORANGE COCKTAIL

3/4 cup orange juice, 2 egg yolks, 1 2/3 oz. confectioners' sugar, 1 1/4 cups dry white wine, lemon juice to taste

Blend egg yolks with sugar and place in a blender. Add orange juice, wine and lemon juice. Turn on blender for 30 seconds. Pour cocktail into glasses. Add ice cubes and serve at once.

LEMON COCKTAIL

5 oz. lemons, 2 oz. confectioners' sugar, 2 egg yolks, 1 cup cream, 3 tablespoons rum

Wash the lemons and scald them with boiling water. Dry them and grate the rind finely. Blend egg yolks with sugar and juice squeezed from lemons. Place in a blender. Add cream, rum and grated lemon rind. Turn on blender for 30 seconds. Pour into glasses and serve at once.

ALI BABA COCKTAIL I

3 tablespoons cherry brandy, 3 tablespoons vodka, 3 tablespoons vermouth

Mix cherry brandy, .vodka and vermouth in a shaker together with ice cubes. Pour into champagne glasses. Add a cherry to each.

ALI BABA COCKTAIL II

1/3 cup vermouth, 5 oz. juniper vodka, 3 tablespoons orange juice, 1 2/3 oz. lemon

Make cocktail as above. Pour into champagne glasses. Add slices of peeled lemon and ice cubes. Serve at once.

ALI BABA COCKTAIL III

1/3 cup vermouth, 3 tablespoons vodka, 1/3 cup grapefruit juice, 1 1/3 oz. lemon

Make cocktail as in Ali Baba Cocktail I. Combine with lemon juice. Pour into glasses and serve at once.

GDAŃSK COCKTAIL

3 tablespoons rum, 1/3 cup juniper vodka, 1 2/3 tablespoons lemon liqueur, 1 2/3 tablespoons orange juice, 3 tablespoons lemon juice, 1/6 oz. raisins

Make the cocktail as in Ali Baba Cocktail I. Pour into champagne glasses. Add rinsed raisins and ice cubes. Serve at once.

TICK-TACK COCKTAIL

1/2 bottle semi-dry wine, 2 tablespoons liqueur, 1/2 lb. apriocts, 1 oz. sugar, 2/3 oz. raisins, sparkling water

Wash the apricots and remove pits. Cut into slices, sprinkle with sugar and set aside for 12 hours. Cover with wine and set aside again for 4 hours. Pour wine into a glass cup. Add rinsed raisins soaked in liqueur, several slices of apricots and sparkling water to taste. Add ice cubes and serve at once.

PERSIAN WIND COCKTAIL

3/4 cup water, 1/3 cup rum, 2 2/3 oz. lemon, 2/3 oz. sugar, 4 stewed or bottled sour cherries, cloves and cinnamon to taste

Bring water to a boil together with cloves and cinnamon. Allow to cool. Strain and combine with rum, lemon juice and sugar. Pour into champagne glasses. Add sour cherries and ice cubes. Serve at once.

CONSUL COCKTAIL I

1/3 cup orange juice, 3 tablespoons cognac, 3 tablespoons cherry brandy, 4 stewed or bottled sour cherries

Make cocktail as in Ali Baba Cocktail I. Pour into champagne glasses. Add sour cherries and serve at once.

CONSUL COCKTAIL II

1/3 cup cherry brandy, 1/3 cup rye vodka, 3 tablespoons Maraschino liqueur, 4 stewed or bottled sour cherries

Make cocktail as in Ali Baba Cocktail I. Pour into champagne glasses. Add sour cherries and serve at once.

CAPTAIN'S COCKTAIL

2/3 cup dry white wine, 3 tablespoons cognac, 3 tablespoons orange liqueur, 1 2/3 oz. oranges

Make cocktail as in Ali Baba I. Pour into champagne glasses. Add a slice of peeled orange to each glass.

POLAR LIGHT COCKTAIL

2/3 cup cherry brandy, 3 tablespoons vermouth, 1 1/3 tablespoons rum, 3 tablespoons black currant juice

Make cocktail as in Ali Baba Cocktail I.

PINEAPPLE MILK SHAKE

2/3 cup whipping cream, 1 1/3 oz. confectioners' sugar, 4 slices canned pineapple, 7 oz. vanilla ice cream, 1/3 cup pineapple juice

Chill and whip the cream, adding sugar towards the end. Place ice cream, finely diced pineapple, the cream and pineapple juice in a blender and turn it on for 30 seconds. Pour into glasses and serve at once.

OLD GDAŃSK COCKTAIL

1 2/3 cups champagne, 1/3 cup winiak brandy, 1/3 cup banana liqueur, 3 tablespoons lemon juice

Blend all ingredients and chill well. Pour into glasses. Add ice cubes and serve at once.

GDAŃSK TOWNSWOMAN COCKTAIL

3/4 cup mead, 3 tablespoons Goldwasser, 1/3 cup orange juice

Blend all ingredients and pour into glasses. Add ice cubes and serve at once.

BIRD OF PARADISE COCKTAIL

3/4 cup champagne, 3 tablespoons orange juice, 4 raisins soaked in cognac

Make cocktail as in Ali Baba Cocktail I. Pour into champagne glasses. Add raisins and serve at once.

SURPRISE COCKTAIL

3 tablespoons cognac, 3 tablespoons dry white wine, 1 tablespoon pineapple juice, 1 2/3 oz. canned pineapple

Make cocktail as in Ali Baba Cocktail I. Pour into champagne glasses. Add finely diced pineapple and serve at once.

HOT WINE

1 1/4 cups dry white wine, 2 egg yolks, 1 2/3 oz. confectioners' sugar, 1 2/3 oz. lemon, 1/4 vanilla bean

Bring wine to a boil together with finely chopped vanilla bean and strain. Blend egg yolks with sugar. Gradually add hot wine, stirring briskly with an egg-whisk. Heat to 170° F. Pour into glasses. Add a slice of peeled lemon to each glass.

NEW YEAR'S EVE PUNCH

3 tablespoons dry white wine, 3 1/2 oz. sugar, 1/3 cup arrack, lemon and orange rind, lemon and orange juice to taste

Bring wine to a boil together with sugar, arrack and grated rinds. Add lemon and orange juices. Serve the hot punch in a special punch-bowl.

ORANGE PUNCH

2 cups water, 1 cup rum, 1/2 lb. sugar, 1 lb. oranges, 3 1/2 oz. lemon, cinnamon, cloves and vanilla bean to taste

Wash the lemons and oranges and scald them with boiling water. Dry them and grate the rind finely. Add to water together with sugar and spices. Bring to a boil, strain and allow to cool. Combine with rum and juice from squeezed lemons and oranges. Serve wih ice in tall glasses.

EGG YOLK PUNCH

1 cup arrack, 1 cup water, 1/2 lb. confectioners' sugar, 5 egg yolks, lemon and orange rinds to taste

Blend egg yolks with sugar. Bring water to a boil together with rum and grated rinds. Gradually add to the egg yolks, stirring briskly with an egg-whisk. Beat in the top of a double boiler until thick. Serve hot.

ICED PUNCH

1 bottle dry white wine, 1 cup water, 1/2 lb. lemons, 1/2 lb. sugar, 1 cup arrack, 3 tablespoons Maraschino liqueur, 1/3 cup orange juice

Wash the lemons and scald them with boiling water. Dry and grate the rind finely. Combine the rind with water and sugar. Bring to a boil, strain and allow to cool. Combine with wine, arrack, liqueur and juice squeezed from lemons and orange juice. Set aside for 2 hours. Serve with ice in champagne glasses.

MASCARADE PUNCH

3/4 cup cherry brandy, 1/2 lb. oranges, 1/3 cup Maraschino liqueur, 3 tablespoons raspberry juice, 1 bottle champagne

Wash the oranges and scald them with boiling water. Peel and dice them, removing the pits. Place in a glass punch bowl. Pour in liqueur, raspberry juice, cherry brandy and champagne. Add an ice cube and stir. Serve at once.

BAPTISM OF FIRE PUNCH

1 2/3 cups currant juice, 1 bottle dry red wine, 1/3 cup currant liqueur, 1/3 cup cherry brandy, cloves and lemon rind to taste

Combine currant juice with wine. Cook for a while together with the spices. Strain and allow to cool. Combine with liqueur and vodka. Pour into a glass punch bowl. Add ice cubes and serve at once.

CARDINAL

13 1/2 oz. oranges, 3 tablespoons dry white wine, 1 cup dry red wine, 2/3 oz. sugar, 3 tablespoons rum

Wash the oranges and scald them with boiling water. Dry them and grate the rind finely. Combine the rind with rum and set aside for 1 hour. Peel the oranges and remove the white fibres. Squeeze juice from one orange. Cut the remaining oranges into slices. Combine with strained rum, orange juice, wine and sugar. Stir and serve at once in tall glasses.

ORANGE LIQUEUR

1 2/3 cups water, 1 lb. sugar, 2 cups spirit, 1 lb. oranges, 3 1/2 oz. orange rind

Chop the rind finely. Cover with spirit in a bottle. Close tightly with a cork and set aside for 5 days. Wash the oranges and scald them with boiling water. Dry them and grate the rind finely. Bring water to a boil together with sugar and grated rind and allow to cool. Combine with strained spirit and orange juice. Cork the bottles tightly and set aside for 48 hours. Pour through a funnel with cotton into another bottle. Cork tightly and set aside for 2—3 months.

LEMON LIQUEUR

1 2/3 cups water, 2 cups spirit, 1 lb. sugar, 1/2 lb. lemons

Wash the lemons and scald them with boiling water. Dry them and grate the surface rind finely. Place in a bottle. Add spirit and juice squeezed from lemons. Cork tightly and set aside for 5 days. Bring water to a boil together with sugar and allow to cool. Combine with spirit. Pour through a funnel with cotton into another bottle. Cork tightly and set aside for 3—4 months.

PINEAPPLE LIQUEUR

2 cups spirit, 3/4 cup water, 2/3 cup pineapple juice, 9 1/2 oz. sugar, 3 dried apricots

Bring water to a boil together with sugar and allow to cool. Combine with spirit, pineapple juice and finely chopped apricots. Pour into a bottle, cork tightly and set aside for a week. Pour into another bottle through a funnel with cotton. Cork tightly and set aside for 3—4 months.

RASPBERRY LIQUEUR

4 cups spirit, 2 cups raspberry juice, 1 lb. sugar

Bring juice to a boil together with sugar and remove the surface foam. Combine with spirit and pour into bottles. Cork tightly and set aside for 5 days. Pour into other bottles through a funnel with cotton. Cork tightly and set aside for 3—4 months.

SOUR CHERRY LIQUEUR

4 cups spirit, 3 lb. sour cherries, 2 cups water, 2 lb. sugar

Rinse sour cherries (1 1/2 lb.) and place in a demijohn. Cover with spirit, cork tightly and set aside for 24 hours. Strain and pour over the remaining cherries, mashed together with the pits. Cork tightly and set aside again for 24 hours, then strain. Bring water to a boil together with sugar and pour over cherries. Stir, strain and combine with spirit. Pour into bottles through a funnel with cotton. Cork tightly and set aside for 6 months.

VANILLA LIQUEUR

4 cups spirit, 2 3/4 cups water, 1 1/2 lb. sugar, vanilla bean, 10 cloves

Cut up the vanilla bean and place in a bottle. Cover with spirit (2 cups) and add cloves. Cork tightly and set aside for a week. Bring water to a boil together with sugar and combine with spirit. Pour into bottles through a funnel with cotton. Cork tightly and set aside for 5 months.

COFFEE LIQUEUR

2 cups spirit, 1 cup water, 1 1/3 tablespoon cognac, 7 oz. sugar, 1 2/3 oz. coffee, 1/4 vanilla bean

Grind coffee to a powder and pour into a bottle. Add chopped vanilla bean and cover with spirit. Cork tightly and set aside for 10 days, shaking the bottle every day. Bring water to a boil together with sugar. Strain spirit through a funnel with cotton. Pour syrup into the coffee. Stir and strain like the spirit. Blend egg yolks with sugar. Thin down with syrup, stirring with an egg-whisk. Pour into a bottle together with the spirit and cognac. Cork tightly and mix well, shaking the bottle. Set aside for 5—7 days. Shake bottle just before pouring out the liqueur.

PORT LIQUEUR

2 cups spirit, 2 bottles port wine, 13 1/2 oz. sugar, 3 1/2 oz. honey, 1/4 vanilla bean, 1/3 oz. raisins, 2 cloves, piece of cinnamon

Place ground spices in a bottle and cover with spirit. Cork tightly and set aside for 10 days, shaking the bottle every day. Pour through a funnel with cotton. Blend a bottle of port with sugar and honey. Cook for a while, removing surface foam. Remove from heat and combine with the remaining beer. Pour spirit in slowly, stirring constantly. Pour into bottles and cork tightly. Set aside for several days.

EGG-NOG LIQUEUR

1 cup spirit, 3/4 cup water, 2/3 cup cognac, 2/3 cup milk, 13 1/2 oz. confectioners' sugar, 4 egg yolks

Bring milk to a boil and allow to cool. Blend egg yolks with sugar and combine with milk. Beat in the top of a double boiler over heat until thick. Bring water to a boil and allow to cool. Combine with spirit and cognac, then with the egg yolk mixture. Pour into a bottle and cork tightly. Set aside for 5 days.

NUT LIQUEUR

4 cups spirit, 2 cups water, 1 lb. sugar, 1 lb. green walnuts (picked in August), 1/3 oz. almonds, 10 cloves, piece of cinnamon

Wash the nuts and cut into four parts. Place in a small demijohn together with blanched almonds, cinnamon and cloves. Cover with spirit and cooled boiled water. Cork tightly and set aside for 2 weeks. Bring remaining water to a boil together with the sugar. Combine with strained spirit and pour into bottles through a funnel with cotton. Cork tightly and set aside for 10—12 months.

HONEY VODKA LITHUANIAN STYLE

4 cups spirit, 2 cups water, 1 lb. honey, 1/2 vanilla bean, 5 cloves, piece of cinnamon, nutmeg, 5 grains allspice, orange rind to taste

Combine honey with spices and brown. Add water and bring to a boil. Remove from heat. Combine with spirit and finely chopped orange rind. Pour into bottles and set aside for 24 hours. Pour through a funnel with cotton. Serve hot or cold.

HONEY VODKA

4 cups spirit, 2 cups water, 1 lb. honey, 1 cup rum, 1 2/3 oz. coffee

Brown honey. Pour in 1 cup water. Bring to a boil, then remove from heat. Combine with coffee (made as in Coffee), rum and spirit.

Pour into bottles and cork tightly. Set aside for 5—6 weeks. Pour into bottles through a funnel with cotton and cork tightly.

CARAWAY VODKA

2 cups spirit, 1 2/3 cups water, 7 oz. sugar, 2 tablespoons fresh green caraway seed

Bring water to a boil together with sugar and allow to cool. Rinse caraway seed and drain on a strainer. Place in a small demijohn. Pour in syrup blended with spirit. Cork tightly and set aside for 5 days. Pour into bottles through a funnel with cotton and cork tightly.

JUNIPER VODKA

4 cups spirit, 2 cups water, 5 oz. sugar, 2—3 oz. juniper berries

Rinse and dry juniper berries. Grind them and place in a small demijohn. Cover with spirit blended with cooled boiled water (3/4 cup). Cork tightly and set aside for 7—8 days. Bring water to a boil together with sugar and allow to cool. Pour spirit through a funnel with cotton. Combine with syrup. Pour into bottles and cork tightly. Set aside for 5—6 months.

CARAMEL VODKA

2 cups spirit, 1 oz. sugar, 1 2/3 cups water, 1/6 oz. prunes, 1/3 oz. raisins, 1/6 oz. almonds, 1/2 vanilla bean, 1 2/3 cups nut vodka

Blanch and chop the almonds. Wash the prunes and raisins. Chop them finely together with the vanilla bean. Place in a bottle together with almonds. Cover with spirit and cork tightly. Set aside for 2 weeks. Brown sugar to caramel. Combine with cooled boiled water and spirit.

Pour through a funnel with cotton. Add nut vodka and pour into bottles. Cork tightly and set aside for 5 days.

PEPPER VODKA

2 cups spirit, 2 cups water, 3 1/2 oz. sugar, 25 grains black pepper, 10 drops caramel syrup

Place pepper in a bottle and cover with spirit. Cork tightly and set aside for 12 days. Bring water to a boil together with sugar and allow to cool. Combine with caramel syrup and spirit poured through a funnel with cotton. Pour into bottles and cork tightly. Set aside for 3—4 days.

GINGER VODKA

2 cups spirit, 2 cups water, 3 1/2 oz. sugar, 1/6 oz. ginger, saffron

Bring water to a boil together with sugar. Add ground ginger and set aside for 24 hours. Pour through a funnel with cotton. Combine with spirit and food colouring. Pour into a bottle and cork tightly. Set aside for 3—4 days.

SLOE VODKA

2 cups spirit, 1 2/3 cups water, 1 2/3 oz. sugar, 3 1/2 oz. frozen sloe berries, 2/3 oz. pitted prunes, 2/3 oz. raisins, 2/3 oz. figs, 2/3 oz. dates

Wash and crumble sloes, prunes, raisins, figs and dates. Place them in a bottle and cover with spirit. Cork tightly and set aside for 4 weeks. Shake bottle from time to time. Bring water to a boil together with sugar and allow to cool. Combine with spirit strained through cotton. Pour into bottles and set aside for 4—5 months.

CHEF'S VODKA I

2 cups spirit, 1 cup water, 1 cup rum, 1 lb. sour cherries, 1 lb. red currants, 1/2 lb. sugar

Bring water to a boil together with sugar and allow to cool. Combine with spirit. Rinse the fruit and remove stems. Drain on a strainer. Place fruit in bottles and cover with spirit. Cork tightly and set aside for a month. Pour through a funnel with cotton. Combine with rum and pour into bottles. Cork tightly and set aside for 2 months.

CHEF'S VODKA II

2 cups spirit, 1 cup water, 4 oz. sugar, 5 cloves, 1/4 vanilla bean, piece of cinnamon, 1 2/3 oz. raisins

Bring water to a boil together with sugar and rinsed raisins. Add ground spices and set aside for 24 hours. Pour through a funnel with cotton and combine with spirit. Pour into a bottle, cork tightly and set aside for 2 weeks.

DEVIL'S TAIL

2 cups spirit, 3/4 cup water, 3 1/2 oz. sugar, 5 oz. ketchup, 1 2/3 oz. walnut meats, nutmeg to taste

Bring water to a boil together with sugar. Combine with ketchup, ground nutmeg and spirit. Pour into a bottle and add blanched ground walnuts. Cork tightly and set aside for 5 days. Pour into other bottles through a funnel with cotton. Cork tightly and set aside for 2—3 months.

INDEX